SUSTAINABILITY ACCOUNTING AND REPORTING

A CSRD PERSPECTIVE

Caroline Aggestam Pontoppidan

With contributions from Josef Baumüller

Cengage

Australia • Brazil • Canada • Mexico • Singapore • United Kingdom • United States

Cengage

Sustainability Accounting and Reporting: A CSRD Perspective
Caroline Aggestam Pontoppidan

Publisher: Annabel Ainscow

List Manager: Birgit Gruber

Marketing Manager: Louise Corless

Content Project Manager: Jyotsna Ojha

Manufacturing Buyer: Elaine Bevan

Manufacturing Manager: Eyvett Davis

Typesetter: Lumina Datamatics, Inc.

Text Design: Lumina Datamatics, Inc.

Cover Designer: Cyan Design

Cover Image(s): @Scott Graham

British Library Cataloguing-in-Publication Data

A catalogue record for this book is available from the British Library.

ISBN: 978-1-4737-9583-9

Cengage Learning, EMEA
Cheriton House, North Way
Andover, Hampshire, SP10 5BE
United Kingdom

Printed in the United Kingdom by CPI Antony Rowe
Print Number: 01 Print Year: 2025

MIX
Paper | Supporting responsible forestry
FSC www.fsc.org FSC® C013604

BRIEF CONTENTS

CONTENTS

PREFACE

The global pursuit of sustainable development has become a cornerstone of contemporary society. Sustainable development calls for organizations to reshape the way they operate, measure and ultimately disclose their impact on the world. The Corporate Sustainability Reporting Directive (CSRD) and the accompanying European Sustainability Reporting Standards (ESRS) represent a transformative framework for this journey. By setting companies up to act with transparency and accountability, the CSRD and ESRS call for organizations to play a pivotal role in achieving global sustainability goals.

This textbook is designed to serve as a comprehensive guide for students, equipping them with the knowledge and tools needed to navigate the complex landscape of sustainability accounting and reporting. Through an in-depth exploration of the CSRD and ESRS frameworks, students will gain a thorough understanding of how organizations report on their environmental, social and governance (ESG) performance and the implications of these disclosures for stakeholders. The rise of mandatory regulation of sustainability reporting has become increasingly prevalent across the globe as governments recognize the critical need for transparency in ESG practices. Although this book's focus is on CSRD and ESRS, each chapter, where relevant, explains how these regulations link to myriad international standards such as the Global Reporting Initiative (GRI), the Task Force on Climate-related Financial Disclosures (TCFD), IFRS Sustainability Disclosure Standards and many more.

Moving towards mandatory sustainability reporting is not an isolated European exercise. Beyond Europe, several countries are advancing mandatory sustainability reporting, reflecting a global trend towards enhanced corporate transparency and accountability in ESG matters. As an example, the US Securities and Exchange Commission (SEC) has adopted a significant set of rules known as the Climate Disclosure Act, officially titled 'The Enhancement and Standardization of Climate-Related Disclosures for Investors'. The advancement of sustainability reporting by organizations globally calls for new competencies in most functions within organizations. Accountants and auditors need to swiftly acquire new knowledge and skills.

The material in this textbook is structured to provide theoretical foundations as well as practical applications. Key features include:

- **Foundations of sustainability accounting:** A primer on the evolution of sustainability reporting, its role in modern business and the global context of the CSRD and ESRS.
- **Detailed analysis of CSRD and ESRS requirements:** Step-by-step guidance on the principles, metrics and disclosure requirements outlined in the Directive and standards.

- **Activities and real-world applications:** Insights into how leading organizations have adopted the CSRD and ESRS to improve transparency and drive meaningful change.
- **Tools for critical analysis:** Frameworks for evaluating sustainability reports, identifying best practices and recognizing opportunities for innovation.

As the field of sustainability accounting continues to evolve, the knowledge imparted by this textbook will enable students to approach the challenges of ESG reporting. Whether aspiring to careers in corporate sustainability, finance, consulting or public policy, students gain in-depth knowledge in the field of sustainability accounting and reporting, focusing on the CSRD and ESRS.

STRUCTURE AND PEDAGOGY

This book is structured around three key areas. Part One takes students through the historical, conceptual and theoretical basis of sustainability reporting. Part Two focuses on topic-specific standards for sustainability reporting. In this part readers gain technical insight into each of the topic-specific ESRSs. Part Three of the book engages with important themes in the area of sustainability reporting, including sustainability reporting in the financial sector, assurance and audit of sustainability reporting, data solutions and digital tagging, and sustainability reporting in the public sector.

The pedagogy of this textbook is designed to facilitate active and engaged learning. Each chapter begins with clear learning objectives that outline the key takeaways, enabling students to approach the material with a focused mindset. Concepts are presented in a structured and progressive manner, explaining fundamental theories before moving on to advanced applications. This layered approach ensures that students develop a comprehensive understanding of the subject matter, regardless of their prior exposure to sustainability accounting.

The textbook emphasizes interactive and experiential learning. Real-life examples and activities are integrated throughout, allowing students to connect theoretical knowledge with practical applications. At the end of each chapter, exercises challenge students to think critically, solve problems and apply what they have learned to realistic scenarios. Instructors can use the activities and exercises in multiple ways: as group projects, role-playing exercises and reflective discussions to further enhance the learning experience by encouraging collaboration and diverse perspectives.

ADDITIONAL MATERIALS

To enhance the learning experience, this textbook features a comprehensive case study on the accompanying website that spans across all chapters, serving as a continuous thread throughout the textbook. This cross-cutting case study allows students to build on their knowledge progressively, applying concepts and frameworks learned in each chapter to a single, evolving scenario. This approach not only reinforces understanding but also simulates real-world complexity and decision-making.

Instructors using this textbook will have access to an array of supplementary materials designed to facilitate teaching and deepen student engagement. These include PowerPoint presentations for each chapter, solutions to end-of-chapter exercises, additional examples and resources for further exploration. Together, these tools provide a robust foundation for creating a dynamic and effective learning environment.

IN CLOSING

In closing I would like to highlight that users of this textbook should remain attentive to the dynamic nature of sustainability regulations, as the landscape is constantly evolving. To give one example, the recent EU Regulation on Deforestation-free Products introduces stringent requirements for companies to mitigate their contribution to global deforestation. Additionally, forthcoming ESRS sector-specific standards will bring tailored reporting requirements for various industries, demanding heightened precision in sustainability disclosures. Staying informed about these and multiple other developments will be critical for effectively applying the concepts and practices covered in this textbook.

ACKNOWLEDGEMENTS

The development of this textbook is a collaborative effort between the authors, industry practitioners, regulatory authorities and academic texts to ensure its relevance and applicability. A passion for advancing the field of sustainability reporting, and more specifically enabling us to teach sustainability reporting, has been a key driver for this writing venture. This book is the culmination of extensive practice research and numerous collaborations in different forms.

First and foremost, I extend my deepest gratitude to the contributing author Dr Josef Baumüller. His subject matter expertise, insights and dedication have enriched the content of this book.

In addition, conversations with multiple organizations on their CSRD implementation journeys have served as an important input to this book. I also wish to thank my colleagues and peers in the field of sustainability and accounting for their constructive feedback and inspiration throughout this process.

A very special thank you to Birgit Gruber and Kim Dodgshon from Cengage EMEA for the most wonderful editorial support.

I am grateful to the growing community of sustainability advocates and professionals who continue to push boundaries and inspire change. It is my hope that this book contributes to a shared vision of a more sustainable and equitable future.

To my family, Jens and Björn, Sofia and Thea, thank you for your patience during the writing process.

While this book has been a collaborative effort in many ways, I am solely responsible for any errors or inaccuracies within the text.

The author and Publisher would like to thank the following academics for reviewing draft materials:

Josef Baumüller, TU Wien, Austria
Zhifeng Chen, University of Southampton, UK
Caroline Dale Ditlev-Simonsen, BI Norwegian Business School, Norway
Samaneh Elmi, Oxford Brookes University, UK
Akbulut Destan Halit, Galatasaray University, Türkiye
Yu-Lin Hsu, Glasgow University, UK
Joanna Krasodomska, Krakow University of Economics, Poland
Giovanna Michelon, University of Padua, Italy

ABOUT THE AUTHOR

Caroline Aggestam Pontoppidan is Associate Professor of Accounting at Copenhagen Business School, teaching courses on Perspectives on Governing Sustainable Development and Environmental, Social and Governance (ESG): data, accounting and reporting. Having earned her PhD in accounting from CBS in 2005, Caroline has carried out research in the areas of public sector accounting, accounting education and, since the mid-2010s, sustainability accounting and reporting. Her research interests also include the institutional interplay and governance of global sustainability reporting practices.

Cengage

Teaching & Learning Support Resources

Cengage's peer-reviewed content for higher and further education courses is accompanied by a range of digital teaching and learning support resources. The resources are carefully tailored to the specific needs of the instructor, student and the course. Examples of the kind of resources provided include:

A password-protected area for instructors with, for example, PowerPoint slides and an instructor's manual.

Lecturers: to discover the dedicated teaching digital support resources accompanying this textbook please register here for access: **account.cengage.com/login**

Students: to discover the dedicated learning digital support resources accompanying this textbook, please contact your instructor or Cengage via our website.

Learn more at **cengage.uk**

PART ONE

Historical, conceptual and theoretical basis of sustainability reporting

The first part of this book will support you in developing a sound understanding of sustainability accounting and reporting in a global setting. These chapters guide you through the global frameworks of sustainability reporting through to regional regulations and standards.

This first part illustrates how global standards are being adapted to meet specific regional priorities and regulations. You will learn how different regulatory initiatives for sustainability accounting and reporting have evolved over time and how recent regulations, such as the Corporate Social Responsibility Directive (CSRD) of the European Union (EU) and the accompanying European Sustainability Standards (ESRS) and other national regulations such as the US Securities and Exchange Commission (SEC) climate disclosure regulation, have evolved and why. Part One also addresses what sustainability is and its importance. For business and accounting students, understanding sustainability is essential for multiple reasons, for example sustainability accounting offers a framework that integrates environmental and social considerations into financial reporting and decision-making processes. By mastering sustainability accounting, students can contribute to the strategic planning and risk management processes within organizations, fostering long-term value creation across environmental, social and governance (ESG) parameters as well as resilience in an evolving economic landscape.

Globally, numerous countries are moving towards enforcing such regulations, signalling a widespread shift towards increased corporate transparency and accountability in ESG practices. This trend underscores a global commitment to integrating sustainability into the corporate sector, driving enhanced disclosure and performance across diverse economic landscapes. Notably, the SEC has recently adopted the Climate Disclosure Act. Other examples include China that has also introduced mandatory sustainability reporting requirements for larger listed entities on its stock exchanges, effective from May 2024, emphasizing both financial and impact materiality.

Part One walks you through the landscape of international standards and considers, for example, the Global Reporting Initiative (GRI), the Taskforce on Nature-related Financial Disclosures (TNFD), the IFRS® Sustainability Disclosure Standards and the Task Force on Climate-related Financial Disclosures (TCFD).

Adding to this, a theoretical element will stimulate you to develop the ability to think critically not only about the theories but also the existing approaches to sustainability accounting and reporting that you will encounter throughout the book.

Part One provides the foundational technical aspects of preparing sustainability reports, and Part Two puts these into practice. Part Three looks at the assurance and audit of sustainability reports and sustainability accounting in the public sector.

CHAPTER 1
Introduction to sustainability accounting and reporting

Learning objectives

After studying this chapter you will be able to:

- LO 1. Describe the key historical phases in the evolution of sustainability reporting.
- LO 2. Identify the key driving forces behind sustainability disclosures.
- LO 3. Discuss the sources of regulation of sustainability reporting.
- LO 4. Explain the main terminology used in sustainability reporting.
- LO 5. Describe the difference between mandatory and voluntary sustainability reporting.

> The development of mandatory common sustainability reporting standards is necessary to progress to a situation in which sustainability information has a status comparable to that of financial information. (CSRD, 2021, para. 32)

INTRODUCTION

Numerous regulations and standards targeted at sharpening the requirements for organizations to provide sustainability disclosures on various topics within the themes of environment, social and governance (ESG) are emerging. Within the **European Union** (**EU**) the introduction of the **Corporate Sustainability Reporting Directive** (**CSRD**) and the **European Sustainability Reporting Standards** (**ESRS**) vastly broaden the scope of mandatory sustainability disclosures.

It is not only within the EU that new regulatory interventions that expand **sustainability reporting** have been released. For example, in March 2024 in the United States, the **Securities and Exchange Commission** (SEC) adopted rules to enhance and standardize climate-related disclosures by public companies and in public offerings. Similar developments can be detected across capital markets globally. Countries like New Zealand and the UK require mandatory climate-related disclosures for large entities. At the international level the **International Sustainability Standards Board** (**ISSB**) was formed in November 2021 at COP26 in Glasgow, which has subsequently released two **IFRS® Sustainability Disclosure Standards**: **IFRS S1** ***General Requirements for Disclosure of Sustainability-related Financial Information*** and **IFRS S2** ***Climate-related Disclosures***.

In the past, sustainability reporting has been conceptualized as a tool for holding organizations to account to a wide range of **stakeholders**, by requiring them to report on the social and environmental impacts (e.g. externalities) of their businesses on their communities and society (refer to, for example, Cooper & Michelon, 2022). The movement towards tightening mandatory requirements for sustainability disclosures, and the assurance and audit of these reports, is indicative of a shift in the institutional environment shaping accounting and reporting standards. A review of research literature confirms that the majority of studies show that government-imposed regulations are the most effective means society has to influence corporate environmental strategies and performance (Aragòn-Correa *et al.*, 2020). Developments are also influenced by the indication of a shift in focus, driven by the increasing attention that financial markets and investors are placing on ESG issues (Starks, 2023).

Changing the regulatory landscape of sustainability reporting is driving the growing need for businesses to 'internalize the externalities' within their corporate decision-making processes, that is, businesses need to provide more information on the costs or benefits that affect third parties but which may not be reflected in their market prices,. Externalities, particularly negative environmental impacts like pollution and greenhouse gas emissions, have traditionally been overlooked in financial reporting. As these externalities become more apparent and their consequences more severe, regulatory interventions aim to ensure that companies account for the broader societal and environmental costs of their operations. For instance, mandatory **disclosure requirements** require companies to reveal information about their environmental footprint, social practices and governance structures, effectively internalizing some of these externalities by making them visible to stakeholders.

The rapid increase in regulatory interventions, such as the **US Climate Disclosure Act** and the CSRD in the EU, reflects a broader attempt to mitigate the adverse impacts of these externalities. By mandating comprehensive disclosures, these regulations seek to enhance corporate transparency and **accountability,** compelling companies to integrate ESG considerations into their core strategies and operations.

However, this regulatory push also raises challenges. The increased scope of disclosures necessitates significant adjustments to corporate reporting practices, including the development of new competencies among accountants and auditors. Ensuring the accuracy and reliability of these disclosures through rigorous assurance and audit processes is crucial, yet it poses additional burdens on firms, particularly smaller ones that may lack the resources to comply fully with these new standards.

Furthermore, there is a risk that the proliferation of mandatory reporting requirements could lead to a compliance-centric approach, where companies focus more on meeting regulatory demands rather than genuinely improving their sustainability performance. This regulatory emphasis on disclosure and assurance must be balanced with incentives for proactive sustainability initiatives that go beyond mere compliance, fostering a culture of genuine corporate responsibility and innovation in addressing externalities.

While the tightening of mandatory sustainability reporting and assurance requirements represents a positive step towards addressing the externalities of corporate activities, it also introduces complexities that necessitate careful consideration and management. One such complexity is that of differing approaches to materiality in sustainability reporting (for example, the CSRD uses the concept of **double materiality**, while the SEC's Climate Disclosure Act uses **financial materiality**). It has been suggested in research that focusing solely on material information for investors may overlook the broader societal and environmental costs, undermining the original intent of sustainability reporting as a comprehensive accountability tool (Cooper & Michelon, 2022). Balancing regulatory compliance with genuine sustainability improvements remains a critical challenge for the evolving field of corporate reporting.

WHAT IS SUSTAINABILITY?

The word 'sustainability' can be traced back to the term 'sustained yield', used in the 19th century. This was, however, a translation of the German word '*nachhaltig*', which dates back to the early 18th century. In his handbook on forestry, *Sylvicultura oeconomica*, Hanns Carl von Carlowitz (1645–1714) coined the use of this term in its modern sense. Being the head of the Royal mining office in Saxony, Germany, von Carlowitz addressed questions of conservation and cultivation of timber. He formulated the idea of the 'sustainable use' of forests stating that only so much wood should be cut from the forest as could be regrown through planned reforestation projects. This remains an important guiding principle of forestry to this day (Grober, 2007).

Now in the 21st century, 'sustainability' has been introduced to a much wider audience, both societal and political. This is attributed to the publication of the report *Limits to Growth*, which was the first major work by the Club of Rome (Meadows *et al.*, 1972). The Club of Rome was founded in 1968. It evolved into an international thinktank addressing heightened global concerns over issues such as population growth, industrialization and environmental degradation. In 1972, a group of researchers led by Dennis and Donella Meadows of the Massachusetts Institute of Technology (MIT) used computer models to evaluate the factors that determine and limit economic and population growth on Earth. They predicted that if humankind does not restrain these growth trends in order to establish a condition of ecological and economic stability, a collapse in the planet's ecosystem within the next century would be the likely outcome (Meadows *et al.*, 1972).

This call for action was taken up by global politics. In 1987, the United Nations Brundtland Commission defined sustainability (more specifically, 'sustainable development') as 'meeting the needs of the present without compromising the ability of future generations to meet their own needs' (Brundtland, 1987). This definition of sustainability from the Brundtland Report emphasizes the balance required between fulfilling human needs and preserving environmental resources to ensure that these needs can be met for future generations. What was seen as the breakthrough moment with the Brundtland Report was its ability to highlight the interconnectedness of economic development, social equity and environmental protection, establishing the three pillars of sustainability – economic, social and environmental – and bringing this to the policy arena.

Following the Brundtland Report, the global focus on sustainable development was furthered through the establishment of the United Nations Millennium Development Goals (MDGs) in 2000, which provided a deeper definition of sustainability. The MDGs consisted of eight goals aimed at addressing a range of global issues, including poverty, hunger, disease, illiteracy, environmental degradation and discrimination against women. Although not explicitly framed as sustainability goals, the MDGs contributed to the discourse by emphasizing the importance of integrating environmental sustainability with economic and social development (United Nations, 2000).

In 2015, the United Nations General Assembly adopted the 2030 Agenda for Sustainable Development, which introduced the **Sustainable Development Goals (SDGs)**. The SDGs consist of 17 goals and 169 **targets** designed to address the broad spectrum of global challenges identified by the MDGs and more. These include poverty, inequality, health, education, climate change, environmental degradation, peace and justice. The SDGs represent an evolution in the definition and scope of sustainability by incorporating a more comprehensive and integrated approach. Activity 1.1 looks at the evolution of the definition of sustainability in international policy documents and/or agreements.

ACTIVITY 1.1

Evolution of definition of sustainability in international policy

In 1987, the United Nations Brundtland Commission defined sustainability as 'meeting the needs of the present without compromising the ability of future generations to meet their own needs'.

In 2015 The United Nations Agenda 2030 agreed on a plan of action for people, planet and prosperity through the implementation of 17 Sustainable Development Goals.

Discuss how the definition of sustainability, or sustainable development, has developed from the Brundtland definition to that of Agenda 2030.

This broader scope of the definition of sustainability reflects an understanding that sustainability must encompass multiple dimensions and that progress in one area should not compromise another. There is a vast academic literature on sustainability and, in alignment with the work of the United Nations on the MDGs and the SDGs, it emphasizes the importance of an integrated approach. For example, Hopwood *et al.* (2005) argue that sustainable development requires addressing the complex interconnections between economic growth, social equity and environmental protection. The integration of these dimensions is seen as essential for achieving long-term sustainability. Example 1.1 looks at the critical work of Rockström *et al.* (2009), who undertook research to advance our understanding of the environmental aspect of sustainability.

Example 1.1

Furthering the definition of the environmental dimension of sustainability

Important research into the specific dimension of environment refers to the maintenance of Earth's systems within safe boundaries to ensure the planet remains a viable habitat for humanity. Rockström *et al.* (2009) introduce the concept of 'planetary boundaries', identifying nine critical processes that regulate the stability and resilience of Earth's systems. These boundaries are: climate change, ocean acidification, ozone depletion, biogeochemical flows, rate of biodiversity loss, freshwater use, land-system change, atmospheric aerosol loading and chemical pollution. Staying within these boundaries is essential to avoid catastrophic environmental changes that could undermine human civilization (Rockström *et al.*, 2009).

For business students and accounting students, understanding sustainability is crucial for several reasons. First, sustainability accounting provides a framework for integrating environmental and social considerations into financial reporting and decision-making processes. As businesses face increasing pressure from stakeholders, including investors, regulators and consumers, to disclose their sustainability practices, accountants play a pivotal role in ensuring that these disclosures are accurate and meaningful (Gray, 2010).

Second, sustainability accounting helps organizations to identify and manage risks related to environmental and social issues. For instance, climate change poses significant financial risks to businesses through regulatory changes, physical impacts and shifts in consumer preferences. Accountants equipped with knowledge of sustainability can help organizations develop strategies to mitigate these risks and seize opportunities associated with the transition to a low-carbon economy (Gibassier & Schaltegger, 2015). Recent studies explore questions on the role of financialization to save nature (Arjaliès & Gibassier, 2022).

Understanding sustainability principles allows accounting professionals to contribute to the broader goal of sustainable development. This involves not only ensuring the long-term viability of individual organizations but also promoting practices that support the well-being of society and the environment. Accountants with a strong grasp of sustainability can advocate for and implement practices that reduce negative externalities, such as pollution and resource depletion, thereby contributing to the global effort to achieve the UN SDGs (Bebbington & Unerman, 2020).

Activities 1.2 and 1.3 extend Activity 1.1 on the definition of sustainability from Brundtland to the SDGs to allow you to think critically about the potential impact of initiatives such as the SDGs. Activity 1.3 asks you to consider the challenges that can arise when considering sustainability.

ACTIVITY 1.2

How does the definition of sustainability, as progressed in global policy agreements, have a positive impact in a local and or global context?

A study by McArthur and Rasmussen (2018) asks the question 'did the Millennium Development Goals (MDGs) make any difference?' They argue that potentially no question is more important for assessing the results of global policy cooperation since the start of the 21st century. This is a difficult question to answer as pathways of cause and effect are difficult to discern. We need to ask the same question today with the SDGs in mind.

Drawing on the definition of sustainability as seen in the SDGs, discuss the impact of sustainability as well as its challenges in your local context.

ACTIVITY 1.3

ESG as a luxury phenomenon?

Researchers have asked the question as to whether ESG initiatives function as a luxury good, that is, 'a product whose demand increases with its high price tag'. During times of economic prosperity, shareholders have shown a willingness to forgo personal financial gain to support environmental and social objectives. However, in periods of economic hardship, their readiness to incur personal financial losses for the sake of ESG significantly diminishes. This trend suggests that the prioritization of ESG factors may be contingent on favourable economic conditions, reflecting a shift in investor priorities based on their immediate financial security (Larcker *et al.*, 2024).

Questions

- Is ESG a luxury good or a basic necessity? Discuss in the light of the text provided on the definition of sustainability.
- Is the current change in investor sentiment permanent, or will it rebound when economic conditions improve? (Tip: read Starks (2023) to assist you in discussing this question.)

Source: These questions were inspired by Larcker *et al.* (2024)

TERMINOLOGY OF SUSTAINABILITY REPORTING

This book uses the overarching terms sustainability reporting and sustainability disclosures interchangeably. In addition, the book engages with explicit ESG disclosures that include both narrative information and metrics.

Corporate social responsibility (CSR) refers to an organization's broader sustainability initiatives to assess and take responsibility for its impact on social, environmental and economic well-being. It encompasses a wide range of activities and practices aimed at contributing positively to society, beyond legal compliance and financial obligations. Coined by the book *Social Responsibilities of the Businessman* published in 1953 by Howard R. Bowen, CSR is rooted in the discussion on **corporate governance** of modern corporations. In the wake of the increased importance of sustainability since the 1970s, it was also taken up and further developed. Example 1.2 illustrates how the European Commission brings forward the definition of CSR and mandating it for business. An important shift.

Example 1.2

In its 'renewed EU strategy 2011–14 for Corporate Social Responsibility', the European Commission provided a definition of CSR that makes clear that CSR is mandatory for businesses – and requires the adaptation of processes and strategies accordingly:

> *The Commission puts forward a new definition of CSR as 'the responsibility of enterprises for their impacts on society'. Respect for applicable legislation, and for collective agreements between social partners, is a prerequisite for meeting that responsibility. To fully meet their corporate social responsibility, enterprises should have in place a process to integrate social, environmental, ethical, human rights and consumer concerns into their business operations and core strategy in close collaboration with their stakeholders, with the aim of:*
>
> - *maximising the creation of shared value for their owners/shareholders and for their other stakeholders and society at large;*
> - *identifying, preventing and mitigating their possible adverse impacts.*
>
> *The complexity of that process will depend on factors such as the size of the enterprise and the nature of its operations. For most small and medium-sized enterprises, especially micro-enterprises, the CSR process is likely to remain informal and intuitive.*
>
> *To maximise the creation of shared value, enterprises are encouraged to adopt a long-term, strategic approach to CSR, and to explore the opportunities for developing innovative products, services and business models that contribute to societal wellbeing and lead to higher quality and more productive jobs.*
>
> *To identify, prevent and mitigate their possible adverse impacts, large enterprises, and enterprises at particular risk of having such impacts, are encouraged to carry out risk-based due diligence, including through their supply chains. […].*

Source: European Commission (2011, p. 6)

Activity 1.4 requires you to discuss the similarities and differences inherent in the concept of sustainability and CSR.

ACTIVITY 1.4

Discuss the similarities and differences between the concepts of 'sustainability' and 'CSR' as defined by the Brundtland Report and the EU Commission, respectively.

ESG reporting is often described as the measured assessment of sustainability using benchmarks and **performance metrics** in the three given categories of environment, social and governance. ESG factors are a set of criteria used to evaluate a company's performance in key areas related to environmental sustainability, social responsibility and corporate governance. *Environmental factors* include issues such as climate change, energy efficiency, pollution and resource management. *Social factors* encompass topics like human rights, labour practices, diversity and inclusion, community relations and product safety. *Governance factors* involve aspects such as board diversity, executive compensation, anti-corruption policies, **risk management** and shareholder rights.

Sometimes, the term non-financial reporting is used. Non-financial reporting refers to the disclosure of information about a company's ESG performance, in addition to its financial results. What is more, this non-financial information is typically regarded as the driver of financial results. Sustainability reporting more broadly often includes quantitative and qualitative data, key performance indicators (KPIs), narrative descriptions and future-orientated information. These **sustainability performance indicators** can be integrated into organizations' annual reports or published as standalone sustainability reports, depending on regulatory requirements and reporting practices. Example 1.3 discusses the history of the term non-financial information.

Example 1.3

The term 'non-financial information' can be traced back to the 'Jenkins Report' of the AICPA in 1994

The report made the distinction between financial and non-financial data that is potentially of relevance for users of business reports. While the first category of information comprises data from financial statements, the second is described as 'high-level operating data and performance measurements that management uses to manage the business' (AICPA, 1994, p. 22f):

> *Operating data are statistics about a company's business activities, excluding data reported in financial statements and related disclosures, which the Committee considers to be financial data. Operating data may be denominated in terms of a currency or in terms of units of product or service, number of employees, units of time, and others. Performance measurements are data about a company's key business processes. For example, they relate to the quality of products or services, the relative cost of activities, and the time required to perform key activities, such as new product development. The distinction between operating data and performance measurements is unimportant and some measures may fall in both categories.*

This understanding of non-financial data was later adopted for the realm of environmental and social information – and thus tied to the discussions on sustainability reporting. This, however, also blurred the original focus of the term 'non-financial information' as a driver of financial performance (Baumüller & Sopp, 2022).

While nowadays, terms such as CSR, ESG, non-financial and sustainability reporting may be used in distinct ways in different regulations, standards and frameworks, they are interconnected and reflect the broader trend towards integrating sustainability considerations into business decision-making and reporting.

HISTORY OF SUSTAINABILITY REPORTING

The Brundtland Report (1987) played a pivotal role in raising global awareness about the importance of sustainability and the interconnectedness of ESG issues. It emphasized the need for a holistic approach to development that considers environmental protection, social equity and economic growth. Following the Brundtland Report, there was increasing recognition of the importance of integrating sustainability considerations into business operations and reporting. This led to the emergence of sustainability reporting frameworks and standards aimed at helping organizations measure, manage and communicate their ESG performance.

Social reporting practices can be traced back to European countries such as France and Germany in the early 1970s (Bebbington & Larrinaga, 2000). Subsequently, the first separate environmental reports started to emerge in the late 1980s (Kolk, 2004). Since then, the number of organizations publishing information on their corporate sustainability policies and impacts has increased exponentially. Organizations are moving towards practices of 'measuring, managing and communicating their corporate sustainability performance' (Grewal & Serafeim, 2020). Strengthening the quantitative and qualitative data provided by organizations regarding the **sustainability risks** they are exposed to as well as their own impact on people and the environment, is essential in order to achieve the targets set out in wide spanning agreements such as **Agenda 2030** and the **Paris Agreement**.

Examples of different forms of sustainability reporting initiatives that have evolved over time are shown in Table 1.1. Typically, the publication of the first edition of the **Global Reporting Initiative (GRI)** guidelines on sustainability reporting in 2000 is considered to be the start of our modern understanding of sustainability reporting.

Table 1.1 Examples of sustainability reporting initiatives that have evolved over time

Year	Initiative	Country/ region	Mandatory/ voluntary
1997	The Global Reporting Initiative (GRI) was established as a multi-stakeholder initiative to develop and disseminate globally applicable sustainability reporting guidelines.	International	Voluntary
2000	CDP (formerly known as the Carbon Disclosure Project) was launched as a platform for companies to disclose their environmental impacts, including carbon emissions.	International	Voluntary
2000	The United Nations Global Compact was launched, encouraging businesses to adopt sustainable and socially responsible policies and to report on their progress annually.	International	Voluntary
2007	The Climate Disclosure Standards Board (CDSB) came into being at the World Economic Forum (WEF) meeting in Davos in 2007 with a focus on establishing a generally accepted framework for climate risk reporting by corporations. Note that in 2022, the CDSB was consolidated into the IFRS® Foundation to support the work of International Sustainability Standards Board (ISSB).	International	Voluntary
2010	The International Integrated Reporting Council (IIRC) was founded to promote integrated reporting, which combines financial and sustainability information to provide a comprehensive view of an organization's performance. The IIRC has since merged with the Value Reporting Foundation (VRF).	International	Voluntary
2011	The Sustainability Accounting Standards Board (SASB) was founded to develop industry-specific standards for disclosing financially material sustainability information to investors.	US	Voluntary
2014	The EU introduced a Directive on non-financial reporting requiring certain large companies to disclose non-financial and diversity information in their annual reports (revised in 2018). This was the predecessor to the current CSRD.	European Union	Mandatory

Table 1.1 Examples of sustainability reporting initiatives that have evolved over time (Continued)

2015	The Financial Stability Board established the **Task Force on Climate-related Financial Disclosures (TCFD)** to develop recommendations for voluntary **climate-related financial disclosures.**	International	Voluntary at the time of development. Some countries have made it mandatory or included it in national regulation
2020	The initiative to establish a **Taskforce on Nature-related Financial Disclosures (TNFD)** was announced.	International	Voluntary
2021	The Value Reporting Foundation was established as a merger between the IIRC and the SASB. Note that in 2022 the IFRS Foundation announced the completion of the consolidation of the Value Reporting Foundation (VRF) into the IFRS Foundation.	International	Voluntary
2021	The International Sustainability Standards Board (ISSB) was formed in November 2021 at COP26. They issue Sustainability Disclosure Standards.	International	National jurisdiction will need to decide if these become mandatory or not
2022	European Union CSRD was approved. On 5 January 2023, the Corporate Sustainability Reporting Directive (CSRD) entered into force. The first companies will have to apply the new rules for the first time in the 2024 financial year, for reports published in 2025.	European Union	Mandatory
2023	The European Commission adopted the Delegated Act on the first set of European Sustainability Reporting Standards (ESRS). Adoption of ESRS by Delegated Act is mandated by the co-legislators in the CSRD – Directive (EU) 2022/2464) adopted in December 2022. Under the proposed CSRD, EFRAG was appointed technical adviser to the European Commission to develop draft ESRS.	European Union	Mandatory
2024	US SEC adopted the Enhancement and Standardization of Climate-Related Disclosures for Investors.	US	Mandatory

It is important to note that these frameworks often complement each other, and many organizations may choose to use multiple standards depending on their specific needs and stakeholders' expectations. The practice of using multiple standards in preparing an organization's sustainability report is likely to continue as a supplement to mandatory disclosure requirements.

In addition to disclosure standards, initiatives such as the International Organization for Standardization (ISO) standard number 14001 (an international standard for environmental management systems) was revised in 2004 to emphasize the importance of organizations considering environmental aspects in their operations.

The need for regulation of sustainability reporting

Regulating sustainability reporting serves several important purposes, driven by the growing recognition of sustainability as a critical aspect of business operations and the broader societal and environmental impact of corporate activities.

Key reasons for the regulation of sustainability reporting include:

- **Ensuring transparency and accountability:** Regulation helps to ensure that organizations provide accurate, relevant and consistent information about their ESG performance.
- **Promoting standardization and comparability:** Regulations can establish standardized frameworks and reporting requirements, making it easier for stakeholders to compare sustainability performance across organizations.

- **Encouraging long-term value creation:** By mandating the disclosure of **sustainability information**, regulations encourage organizations to consider the long-term impacts of their decisions on stakeholders, society and the environment. This focus on long-term value creation helps mitigate risks, enhance resilience and promote sustainable business practices.
- **Supporting investor decision-making:** Increasingly, investors are integrating ESG factors into their investment decisions to assess the resilience and sustainability of organizations. Regulatory requirements for sustainability reporting provide investors with essential information to evaluate the materiality of ESG risks and opportunities and make informed investment choices.
- **Driving innovation and improvement:** Regulatory frameworks can incentivize organizations to innovate and improve their sustainability performance by setting clear expectations, defining reporting metrics and establishing compliance mechanisms. This regulatory pressure encourages organizations to adopt more sustainable practices, invest in renewable energy, improve resource efficiency and address social and environmental challenges.
- **Addressing market failures:** In some cases, market forces alone may not adequately address sustainability issues due to externalities, information asymmetry or short-term incentives. Regulation can help correct market failures by internalizing environmental and social costs, reducing information asymmetry and aligning corporate incentives with broader societal goals.
- **Stakeholder expectations:** Stakeholders, including governments, civil society organizations and the public, increasingly expect organizations to demonstrate their commitment to sustainability through transparent reporting and accountability mechanisms. Regulatory requirements can help to ensure that organizations meet these expectations and fulfil their social and environmental responsibilities.

Overall, regulating sustainability reporting plays a crucial role in advancing corporate transparency, accountability and sustainability performance, contributing to more resilient, responsible and equitable business practices and outcomes. Scholars have provided in-depth accounts of the historical evolution of the institutionalization of sustainability reporting addressing the role of **governance** in the process (Larrinaga & Bebbington, 2021).

There is a vast amount of empirical work on the effects of reporting regulation (for example, Leuz & Wysocki, 2016), but as highlighted by Christensen *et al.* (2021) in their review of this literature, this work also has important limitations.

Example 1.4 expands on the link between CSRD and the concept of accountability of organizations. Some of the concepts and terms raised in this section on the need for regulation of sustainability reporting will be further addressed and discussed in Chapter 2, which focuses on theoretical perspectives of sustainability reporting. Example 1.5 introduces you to the ISSB and its role in, among other matters, addressing the need for globally standardized sustainability information.

Example 1.4

CSRD and accountability

The CSRD explicitly echoes an accountability deficit. It states that:

> *[n]on-governmental organisations, social partners, communities affected by undertakings' activities, and other stakeholders are less able to hold organisations (undertakings) accountable for their impacts on people and the environment. This creates an* accountability deficit *and could lead to lower levels of citizen trust in businesses, which in turn could have negative impacts on the efficient functioning of the social market economy. The lack of generally accepted metrics and methods for measuring, valuing and managing sustainability-related risks is also an obstacle to the efforts of undertakings to ensure that their business models and activities are sustainable. The lack of sustainability information provided by undertakings also limits the ability of stakeholders, including civil society actors, trade unions and workers' representatives, to enter into dialogue with undertakings on sustainability matters.* (para. 14; emphasis added)

The CSRD is a response to such lack of sustainability information and corresponding accountability deficit.

Source: EU (2022), paragraph 14

Example 1.5

The establishment of the International Sustainability Standards Board (ISSB)

The ISSB was established to address the growing demand for a globally recognized set of sustainability reporting standards. Several factors contributed to the establishment of the ISSB.

One factor was that of fragmentation of reporting frameworks. There was a proliferation of sustainability reporting frameworks and standards, each with its own set of principles, metrics and reporting requirements, as shown earlier in Table 1.1. This fragmentation made it challenging for organizations to navigate and comply with multiple frameworks and for stakeholders to compare sustainability performance across organizations. In addition, calls for standardization and international harmonization of sustainability reporting have increased since the mid-2010s. Stakeholders, including investors, regulators and businesses, have increasingly called for such standardization and harmonization. Standardization is widely seen to facilitate consistency, comparability and reliability of sustainability information, enabling more effective decision-making and risk assessment.

Integration of ESG data into financial reporting was also a driver for the establishment of the ISSB. There was a growing recognition of the materiality of ESG factors to financial performance and long-term value creation. Integrating ESG considerations into financial reporting was seen as essential for providing investors with a more comprehensive understanding of an organization's risk profile and growth prospects. Agenda 2030 and other important framework agreements raised the need for global leadership and coordination. As sustainability challenges transcended national borders, there was a need for global leadership and coordination in developing common sustainability reporting standards. The establishment of the ISSB aimed to fill this gap by bringing together stakeholders from around the world to develop globally applicable standards that reflect best practices and stakeholder expectations.

Overall, the establishment of the ISSB represents a step towards advancing global sustainability reporting practices and addressing the need for globally standardized sustainability information.

SOURCES OF REGULATION

Sustainability accounting and corresponding disclosures are regulated through a combination of voluntary frameworks and standards, as well as mandatory regulations imposed by governments and regulatory bodies. Research has highlighted that aspects that influence variation in the engagement of organizations with sustainability reporting include national parameters and elements such as existing regulatory frameworks that govern sustainability reporting practices (De Villiers & Marques, 2016).

We now look briefly at some of the regulatory mechanisms that have been put in place.

Mandatory disclosure requirements

Some countries have implemented mandatory reporting requirements for sustainability-related information. For example, the EU's CSRD mandates organizations (by size thresholds) to disclose non-financial information, including ESG matters, in their annual reports. The SEC has adopted rules to enhance and standardize climate-related disclosures by public organizations and in public offerings. The final version of the rules reflect the SEC's efforts to respond to investors' demands for more consistent, comparable and reliable information about the financial effects of climate-related risks on organizations' operations. In addition, the disclosure rules have introduced disclosures on how organizations manage climate risks. However, shortly after its introduction, the SEC had put its climate rule on hold pending legal review. At the time of writing, it is not clear when and how it will actually come into effect.

Stock exchange requirements

Stock exchanges in various countries impose listing requirements related to sustainability reporting. For instance, exchanges like the London Stock Exchange and the Nasdaq require listed organizations to disclose

ESG information as part of their listing obligations. The Johannesburg Stock Exchange (JSE) in South Africa is developing Sustainability Disclosure Guidance, along with a Climate Change Disclosure Guidance specifically tailored to the South African context.

Voluntary reporting standards and frameworks

Many organizations choose to report on their sustainability performance voluntarily using frameworks such as the GRI, the SASB and the TCFD. Another important initiative is that of the TNFD. The TNFD has developed a set of disclosure recommendations and guidance that encourage and enable businesses to assess, report and act on their nature-related dependencies, impacts, risks and opportunities.

These frameworks provide guidance on the disclosure of ESG information, helping organizations improve transparency and accountability.

In addition to the above, certain industry-specific regulations and/or standards exist. For example, organizations operating in the extractive industries need to comply with regulations such as the Extractive Industries Transparency Initiative (EITI), targeted at promoting transparency and accountability in the extractive sector through the disclosure of payments to governments. Another example is in the banking sector. More specifically, the Principles for Responsible Banking (PRB) were developed by the United Nations Environment Programme Finance Initiative (UNEP FI) in collaboration with banks and stakeholders worldwide. It aims to align the banking industry with global sustainability objectives and promote a more sustainable banking system.

Activity 1.5 asks you to reflect on the strengths and/or weaknesses of mandatory versus voluntary initiatives for sustainability reporting. A hint is to recall the work you did on the overall definition of sustainability and thus reflect on which form of governance of sustainability reporting may benefit sustainable development.

ACTIVITY 1.5

ESG as a luxury good

Discuss the strengths and/or weaknesses of mandatory versus voluntary sustainability reporting when considering whether 'ESG is a luxury good or a basic necessity' (Larcker *et al.*, 2024).

Other international initiatives

There are several other international initiatives that play a role in shaping sustainability reporting regulations. For instance, the International Organization of Securities Commissions (IOSCO) provides guidance to securities regulators on ESG disclosure practices. Investor demand for ESG integration has led to initiatives like the Principles for Responsible Investment (PRI), which encourage signatories to consider ESG factors in investment decision-making. Another example is the work of the International Organization for Standardization (ISO) that develops technical standards. Specifically, it has a standard devoted to providing a framework to be used by organizations to protect the environment and respond to changing environmental conditions in balance with socio-economic needs.

In conclusion, the regulation of sustainability reporting and disclosures involves a mix of voluntary frameworks, mandatory requirements, industry standards and stakeholder pressures, reflecting a growing recognition of the importance of ESG considerations in corporate decision-making and reporting. This mix of regulation is likely to call for strengthened 'regulatory cooperation' between a range of actors and regulatory mechanisms (Abbott, 2012).

Activity 1.6 explores the mandatory and voluntary frameworks as used by an organization for the preparation of their sustainability report. You are asked to choose an organization in your local context (or another context of your choice).

ACTIVITY 1.6

Locate the applicable mandatory and voluntary standards or frameworks for sustainability disclosures for organizations in your country. Note that you may find a blend of mandatory and voluntary sources. You may also find that there are no mandatory requirements yet and thus voluntary standards may be the dominating source for sustainability reporting.

Discuss your findings. An example is provided by Example 1.6.

Example 1.6 provides some insights into the country context of Malaysia. It allows you to gain a sense of the local governance mechanisms (in this case the requirements of the local stock exchange) and international standards, such as in this case IFRS S1 and S2.

Example 1.6

Malaysia

Stock exchange requirement: Since 2015, listed organizations on Bursa Malaysia (Bursa) have been required to provide sustainability disclosures through the inclusion of a Sustainability Statement in their annual report. Bursa enhanced its sustainability reporting requirements in September 2022 to better align with global reporting expectations, including recommendations of the TCFD.

The sustainability reporting requirements are being implemented in a phased manner for listed organizations. These include disclosures of common sustainability matters and indicators, at least three years' financial data for each reported indicator and corresponding performance targets and a statement of assurance on the Sustainability Statement.

Role of international standards: The Advisory Committee on Sustainability Reporting (ACSR) in Malaysia ran a consultation paper (February 2024) to seek public feedback on the proposed use of the sustainability disclosure standards issued by the ISSB Standards. They note that the IFRS® Sustainability Disclosure Standards will serve as a baseline standard which will constitute the National Sustainability Reporting Framework (NSRF) in Malaysia.

The ACSR aimed, through the consultation, to identify enablers that will facilitate the implementation of the Sustainability Disclosure Standards, specifically IFRS S1 *(General Requirements for Disclosure of Sustainability-related Financial Information)* and IFRS S2 *(Climate-related Disclosures)*. The consultation paper provides feedback on key issues including the scope and timing for implementation, the transition reliefs required and issues related to assurance for sustainability disclosures.

The ACSR stated that while the primary focus is on listed issuers and large non-listed companies, the ACSR strongly encourages participation from mid-tier organizations and SMEs to ensure a comprehensive understanding of industry needs and challenges.

Regulatory structure: The ACSR was established to support the implementation of the Sustainability Disclosure Standards in Malaysia. The ACSR comprises representatives from SC (as Chair), Bank Negara Malaysia, Bursa Malaysia, the Companies Commission of Malaysia, the Audit Oversight Board and the Financial Reporting Foundation.

Source: Malaysian Institute of Accountants (2023); Securities Commission Malaysia (2024)

COMPETENCIES OF THE FUTURE ACCOUNTANT

The CSRD and other emerging governance initiatives advancing sustainability reporting is raising issues regarding the required future competencies of accountants. The evolution of standards and regulations for sustainability reporting will require accountants to encompass a deeper understanding of sustainability issues and their integration into financial reporting. Research has explicitly argued that one hurdle to organizations contributing to a more sustainable future is the 'ecological illiteracy' of both managers and employees in organizations (Russel *et al.*, 2017; refer also to Ball and Milne, 2005). Rockström *et al.* (2009) importantly estimate that humanity has already transgressed three of their 'planetary boundaries'. These boundaries are climate change, rate of biodiversity loss and changes to the global nitrogen cycle. This means that it is vitally important that no profession, including the accounting profession, should be ecologically illiterate. The role of educators, specifically business schools, to support the requirements of Agenda 2030 is critical.

Accounting education has been criticized over the years for showing limited evidence of any significant change in regard to the content and overall orientation of education on sustainability issues. The mounting normative and coercive pressures for a change in the field of accounting education have increased over time to the point where we may be at a tipping point and change can no longer be resisted. This topic is covered in Chapter 16.

CONCLUSION

The Paris Agreement and Agenda 2030 (with its 17 SDGs) have become drivers for nation states to sharpen their requirements on sustainability disclosures by organizations.

Overall, this chapter has emphasized that we can observe a move towards tightening the mandatory requirements for the scope of disclosures as well as assurance and audit of sustainability disclosures. One prominent example is the adoption of the CSRD in the EU. Undertakings subject to the CSRD will have to report in accordance with the ESRS. In short, the institutional environment shaping the field of accounting and reporting has witnessed an increase in such regulatory interventions over a relatively short period of time.

The motivating factor for sustainability reporting is to contribute to more sustainable and resilient economies and societies. In closing this chapter we can echo the important point made by Dechow (2023, p. 481) who in her article about sustainability reporting wrote that:

> *[f]or accountants, this means that we can broaden our perspective of what we measure when evaluating firm performance. If we think in terms of monetary units and judge the actions of the company as positive or negative based on outcome variables such as sales, profits, or stock returns, then we are not considering the full impact of the firm on society and the planet.*

SUMMARY

The following items relate to the learning objectives listed at the beginning of the chapter.

- **LO 1. Describe the key historical phases in the evolution of sustainability reporting.**

  The initial phase of sustainability reporting emerged in the 1970s and 1980s, driven by growing environmental awareness and social activism. Companies began to recognize the importance of disclosing information about their environmental impact and social responsibilities. However, reporting was largely voluntary and lacked standardized frameworks. Since the mid-2010s sustainability reporting has become increasingly mainstream and global. The adoption of the SDGs in 2015 provided a universal framework for addressing global challenges. Recent developments include the EU's CSRD and the formation of the ISSB in 2021, which aim to harmonize global reporting standards.

- **LO 2. Identify the key driving forces behind sustainability disclosures.**
  These include increasing regulatory requirements arising from, for example, global policy agreements such as Agenda 2030 and the SDGs, in addition to investor demand and stakeholder pressure. Stakeholders, including consumers and NGOs, advocate for greater transparency and corporate accountability in addressing environmental and social impacts.
- **LO 3. Discuss the sources of regulation of sustainability reporting.**
  These include mandatory sustainability requirements pursued on a jurisdictional basis, stock exchange requirements and international standards.
- **LO 4. Explain the main terminology used in sustainability reporting.**
  Sustainability reporting is often described as the practice of measuring, disclosing and being accountable for organizational performance towards the goal of sustainable development. Corporate social responsibility reporting and ESG reporting are also used.
- **LO 5. Describe the difference between mandatory and voluntary sustainability reporting.**
  Mandatory sustainability reporting is required by law or regulation, asking organizations to disclose specific sustainability information. Voluntary sustainability reporting includes the optional disclosures that organizations choose to provide beyond legal requirements.

EXERCISES

1 Why did the Brundtland Report not lead to strengthening requirements in sustainability reporting of organizations? Discuss. (LO 1)

2 Explain the key driving forces behind sustainability disclosures. (LO 2)

3 Is the governance of sustainability reporting in your local context aligned with the targets of the Paris Agreement? Discuss. (LO 2)

4 Using the CSRD (or other regulation for sustainability reporting of your choice) locate what the regulation/standard says about the following (LO 3):

- Sustainability information to support investor decision-making
- Sustainability information to drive innovation and improvement
- Sustainability information to meet stakeholder expectations.

5 Is mandatory sustainability reporting a necessity for achieving true corporate accountability and sustainability? Discuss. (LO 5)

CHAPTER 2
Theoretical perspectives on sustainability reporting

Learning objectives

After studying this chapter you should be able to:

- LO 1. Discuss theories of standardization and regulation for sustainability reporting.
- LO 2. Explain why stakeholder perspectives are relevant in regard to sustainability reporting.
- LO 3. Discuss the main functions of sustainability reporting from various theoretical perspectives.

Buyback and Re-shop: IKEA's journey to zero waste

IKEA, the Scandinavian affordable furniture producer, puts forth many ambitions in its Sustainability Strategy. Falling under its commitments to 'climate, nature & circularity', IKEA's Buyback & Resell Service allows customers to return select IKEA furniture pieces for in-store credit. After receiving an online estimate, customers can return their fully assembled furniture to stores, where it will undergo a final assessment. Good quality returns are sent to the store's Re-shop and Re-use section while products that are not in a sellable condition are disposed of or recycled in line with IKEA's 'zero waste to landfill policy'. The customer can receive store credit up to 45% of the original selling price of the product (+15% if they are a part of the IKEA Family scheme). In 2021 in Eskilstuna, Sweden, IKEA took the further step of opening a dedicated store which exclusively sells second-hand IKEA furniture.

Customer-facing initiatives like this allow customers to understand a company's stance on key sustainability issues. Standardized, comparable, reliable and relevant sustainability information from companies can be viewed as a cornerstone of the sustainable finance ecosystem.

Incorporating an understanding of diverse theoretical perspectives relevant to sustainability reporting enriches our understanding of corporate accountability beyond traditional financial accountability.

Sources: www.ikea.com/gb/en/circular/buy-back/

www.ikea.com/se/sv/stores/vaerldens-foersta-ikea-second-hand-butik-pub8d553060/?msockid=3aaeba95af1f66111984afe1ae19674b

www.ikea.com/global/en/newsroom/sustainability/the-worlds-first-secondhand-ikea-popup-store-opens-in-sweden-201104/?msockid=3aaeba95af1f66111984afe1ae19674b

INTRODUCTION

A number of theoretical perspectives underpin sustainability reporting and thus provide insights into its development, motivations and implications. Different theoretical frameworks are used to serve as lenses through which scholars and practitioners can analyse the intricate dynamics shaping sustainability disclosures. The most common theories applied to study sustainability disclosures are: stakeholder, legitimacy, institutional, agency and signalling theories. These theoretical perspectives are frequently applied in combination with each other. In particular, legitimacy, stakeholder and institutional theories are seen to be combined in research on sustainability reporting (Del Gesso & Lodhi, 2024).

Each theory offers distinct insights into the motivations behind sustainability reporting practices and the broader implications for organizational behaviour and societal impact. For example, legitimacy theory, stakeholder theory, institutional theory and agency theory have been used in research to explain voluntary disclosure (Miles & Ringham, 2019). While this chapter does not cover all theoretical perspectives, it walks you through a selection of theories. Examples of different perspectives and foundational principles, applications and implications within the realm of sustainability reporting are introduced. By synthesizing selected theories, this chapter provides an overview of the interplay between organizational strategies, stakeholder expectations, regulatory environments and broader societal demands that shape the landscape of sustainability reporting. The chapter seeks to pave the way for deeper insights into the role of sustainability disclosures in fostering sustainable development and corporate accountability.

GOVERNING SUSTAINABILITY REPORTING

Theories that address regulation and governance of corporate practices provide valuable insights into the institutional, organizational and societal factors that influence sustainability reporting practices. By understanding the interplay between regulatory frameworks, governance mechanisms, stakeholder dynamics and market forces, policymakers, regulators, companies and investors can work together to promote responsible reporting practices and thus advance sustainable development.

Whereas financial reporting is required by law, non-financial disclosure or sustainability disclosures have until recently been predominantly voluntary (Kinderman, 2020). Making sustainability disclosures mandatory may help to address organizations' disregard for their social and environmental footprint (Kinderman, 2020). Knudsen and Moon (2022, p. 27) highlight that while 'societal expectations and embedding of values are clearly core to CSR, government provides the medium by which societal preferences are institutionalized'.

Theories concerned with regulation and governance mechanisms offer insights into the role of regulatory frameworks, standards, governance structures and institutional mechanisms that shape sustainability reporting practices.

Mandating sustainability disclosures

Chapter 1 of this book introduced the difference between mandatory and voluntary sustainability disclosures. Table 1.1 in Chapter 1 provided a high-level timeline that illustrates when selected mandatory requirements for sustainability reporting were approved and the introduction of voluntary international sustainability reporting standards.

This section dives into this topic a bit further by considering the research literature on the topic. At the global level we can observe that governments and policymakers are increasingly mandating organizations to publish sustainability information. Christensen *et al.* (2021) define mandatory sustainability reporting as the adoption of formal sustainability reporting standards that prescribe (i) what organizations have to report regarding their sustainability activities, risks and **policies**, (ii) which sustainability topics are relevant for certain industries and firms, (iii) which metrics are important and how they are computed, and (iv) where and how the information is to be presented. Regulations mandating sustainability disclosures thus provide structure and guidance for organizations' sustainability reporting and important definitions such as materiality.

The standardization of sustainability reporting through mandatory standards could generate considerable benefits. The exercise of mandating sustainability reporting comes with significant challenges for measurement, **comparability** and standardization of sustainability information on its own but is also relative to financial reporting (Christensen *et al.*, 2021).

Mandatory regulatory interventions aimed at enhancing sustainability reporting are a theme in research literature. Research has examined the impact of mandatory sustainability disclosure requirements on corporate behaviour and performance. Studies have found that regulatory mandates can lead to improvements in disclosure quality and enhanced corporate governance practices. Organizations subject to mandatory sustainability disclosures show a significant increase in sustainability disclosures, while at the same time extending the increased disclosures with initiatives aimed at increasing the comparability and credibility of the disclosed information (Ioannou & Serafeim, 2017).

Subsequent to mandating sustainability reporting in selected countries globally, researchers have been able to explore the costs and burdens associated with complying with mandatory sustainability disclosure requirements. Researchers have also studied whether mandating sustainability information influences organizations to change their processes, for example in their investment decisions and other decision-making in regard to sustainability outcomes (refer to, for example, Grewal & Serafeim, 2020). Studies have identified challenges related to data collection, verification, reporting formats and administrative burdens, particularly for **small and medium-sized enterprises (SMEs)** and non-listed companies.

Scholars have investigated how investors and financial markets respond to mandatory sustainability disclosures. Research suggests that transparent and reliable sustainability information can influence investment decisions, affect stock prices and mitigate information asymmetry between investors and companies. Other studies have highlighted the importance of comparability and standardization in sustainability reporting mandated by regulations. Scholars have explored the challenges of achieving consistency and comparability across companies, sectors and jurisdictions and have proposed strategies to enhance the reliability and comparability of sustainability disclosures.

Researchers have analysed the design features of regulatory frameworks for mandating sustainability disclosures, including scope, materiality thresholds, reporting formats, enforcement mechanisms and **stakeholder engagement** processes. They emphasize that it is important to align regulatory design with institutional contexts, market dynamics and stakeholder preferences. They suggest that the influence of mandatory regulation on sustainability information has become the dominant approach of regulators to promote sustainability practices. 'Mandatory' has even been described as the gradual end of the 'self-regulation' era (Khan *et al.*, 2020).

It is critical that researchers continue to study the short-term and long-term effects and outcomes of mandatory sustainability disclosure requirements on corporate behaviour, stakeholder relationships and environmental and societal impacts. Understanding how regulatory interventions contribute to the transition to a more sustainable economy, address systemic risks and advance sustainable development will continue to be of importance for decades to come. Example 2.1 provides some examples of jurisdictions that either have mandated sustainability reporting already or, like Australia, are moving towards mandating climate reporting. The example illustrates that although some harmonization is taking place, in particular in the area of climate reporting, the TCFD has played an important role as a basis for many jurisdictions and different approaches to mandatory sustainability reporting are evolving. Example 2.1 provides high-level examples of jurisdictions that have opted to adopt mandatory governance mechanisms for sustainability reporting, or are in the process of doing so.

Example 2.1

Mandatory governance mechanisms for sustainability reporting

1 **European Union**

The EU CSRD requires all large companies and all listed companies (except listed micro-enterprises) to disclose information on what they see as the risks and opportunities arising from social and environmental issues, and on the impact of their activities on people and the environment.

2 **United States**

In March 2024 the US SEC adopted rules to enhance and standardize climate-related disclosures.

In addition, the state of California enacted two senate bills (SB) in October 2023: **SB 253, Climate Corporate Data Accountability Act** and **SB 261, Greenhouse gases: Climate-related financial risk,** that mandate both climate risk and greenhouse gas disclosures for certain public and private organizations 'doing business' in California.

3 **Australia**

The Australian Government is moving towards implementing mandatory climate-related financial disclosures based on the IFRS Sustainability Disclosure Standards, IFRS S1 and IFRS S2.

The proposed Australian framework involves a phased rollout, starting with large entities from the 2024/25 reporting period. (AAASB, 2023)

4 **China**

In April 2024, three stock exchanges in China issued their respective guidelines on sustainability reporting disclosure requirements. Two of them require the first mandatory disclosures to be made in 2026 based on information for the financial year 2025, while the other just encourages voluntary disclosure. The guidelines cover 21 ESG topics, reporting on which are subject to double materiality assessment.

In May 2024, the Chinese Ministry of Finance published a consultation paper: 'Corporate Sustainability Disclosure Standard – Basic Standard'. The disclosures in the standard will apply to specific entities established within the territory of the People's Republic of China irrespective of whether they are listed or not. It is likely that a first climate standard will be published by 2027, with other standards to follow by 2030.

Sources: PwC (2024); Deloitte (2024)

An important topic in studies concerned with mandatory sustainability reporting is that of compliance and enforcement. Governance theory focuses on the mechanisms, processes and structures through which organizations are governed and controlled. In the context of sustainability reporting, governance mechanisms play a critical role in ensuring compliance with regulatory requirements and promoting responsible reporting practices. Governance mechanisms may include board oversight, management accountability, internal controls, risk management systems and stakeholder engagement processes related to sustainability reporting. Example 2.2 illustrates how, through the issuance of a Directive (namely the CSRD), the EU mandates that member states adopt sustainability reporting into their respective national laws and regulations. Mandating sustainability reporting brings new questions to the fore regarding enforcement and compliance mechanisms. Through Example 2.2 we learn that the **European Securities and Markets Authority (ESMA)** coordinates such enforcement activities by issuing guidelines.

Example 2.2

Enforcement of CSRD

CSRD Article 5(1) notes that 'Member States shall bring into force the laws, regulations and administrative provisions necessary to comply with Articles 1 to 3 of this directive by 6 July 2024'. This requires the harmonized enforcement and compliance mechanisms to be set up in each EU member state. The ESMA coordinates those national activities by issuing guidelines.

The enforcement procedure examines whether mandatory reports published by listed companies have been prepared in a legally correct manner. This examination is typically performed after the mandatory auditor of a company has performed their duties and has issued their statement. So, enforcement is considered to be an additional level of control for listed companies.

In every member state of the EU, different institutions are tasked with performing this procedure. It is either set up as a one-stage or two-stage process, depending on whether it is a public institution or a private institution that is tasked with the enforcement procedures. The ESMA is in charge of setting priorities for enforcement activities and further coordinating these activities throughout the entire EU.

Prior to the CSRD, enforcement activities were conducted in a very heterogenous way in each EU member state. Typically, little attention was given to sustainability-related information. However, this has changed over the last few years, also in the light of the upcoming legislation on sustainability reporting. As the following excerpt from the ESMA report on 2023 Corporate reporting enforcement and regulatory activities shows, currently more errors are found in sustainability reports than in financial reports.

Focus on Priorities: 2022 ECEP Assessment

Annual European Common Enforcement Priorities (ECEP) are an essential way to foster the prevention of misstatements and to enhance the quality and consistency of corporate reporting across the EEA. The following statistics illustrate the priorities for the 2022 ECEP, together with a breakdown of the examination sample and actions taken in relation to the 2022 ECEP.

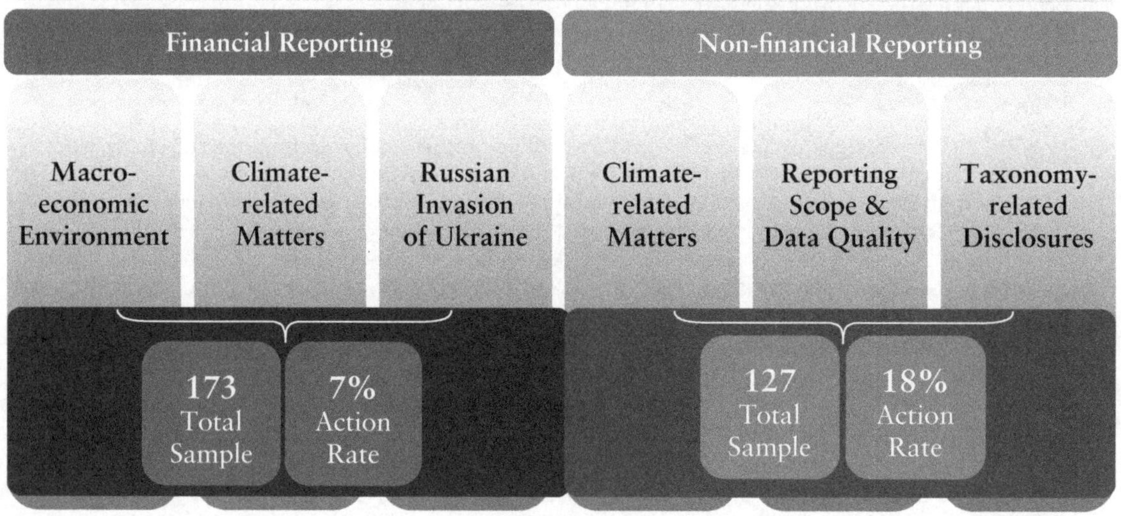

Source: ESMA (2023)

Example 2.3 provides a deeper view on, among other things, the challenges of mandating sustainability reporting, using the concept of upward regulatory harmonization.

Example 2.3

Upward regulatory harmonization

With the work of Kinderman (2020) on the EU's CSRD, and using the concept of upward regulatory harmonization, we can learn about both the role and the challenges of mandatory requirements for sustainability reporting.

Upward regulatory harmonization refers to the process of aligning regulations and standards across different jurisdictions to achieve greater consistency, coherence and effectiveness. In the context of sustainability reporting in the EU, there are several challenges associated with upward regulatory harmonization.

Upward regulatory harmonization entails the 'creation of new international rules to harmonize existing divergent domestic rules and then decrease the negative externalities that these engender', or the 'tighten[ing of] already existing international rules (De Bièvre *et al.*, 2014, p. 273)' (Kinderman, 2020, p. 675).

The challenges include:

Diverse national frameworks

The existence of diverse national frameworks for sustainability reporting across EU member states means each country can have its own reporting requirements, standards and guidelines, leading to fragmentation and inconsistency in reporting practices.

Complexity and burden

Harmonizing sustainability reporting regulations across EU member states involves navigating complex legal, political and institutional dynamics. Reconciling different national interests, regulatory traditions and stakeholder preferences can be challenging and time-consuming.

Scope and materiality

Determining the scope and materiality of sustainability reporting requirements poses challenges. Balancing the need for comprehensive disclosure with the practicality of reporting on material issues requires careful consideration and stakeholder engagement.

Data quality and verification

Ensuring the accuracy, reliability and comparability of sustainability data reported by companies is a significant challenge. Establishing robust verification mechanisms and ensuring data quality standards are met are essential for enhancing the credibility and usefulness of sustainability reporting.

Enforcement and compliance

Achieving consistent enforcement and compliance with sustainability reporting regulations across EU member states is challenging. Differences in regulatory capacity, enforcement mechanisms and corporate culture may affect compliance levels and undermine the effectiveness of harmonization efforts.

International alignment

Harmonizing EU sustainability reporting regulations with international standards and frameworks adds another layer of complexity. Ensuring compatibility with global reporting initiatives, such as the Global Reporting Initiative (GRI) and standards such as the IFRS Sustainability Disclosure Standards S1 and S2, requires ongoing coordination and alignment efforts.

Stakeholder engagement and transparency

Engaging stakeholders in the harmonization process and ensuring transparency in decision-making are essential for building trust and legitimacy. However, balancing competing stakeholder interests and ensuring meaningful participation can be challenging.

(Continued)

Adaptability and flexibility

Regulatory harmonization should be adaptable and flexible to accommodate evolving sustainability challenges, technological developments and market dynamics. Building resilience into the regulatory framework requires continuous monitoring, evaluation and adjustment.

Addressing these challenges requires a collaborative and iterative approach involving policymakers, regulators, companies, investors, civil society organizations and other stakeholders. By promoting dialogue, cooperation and shared learning, upward regulatory harmonization in sustainability reporting can contribute to more transparent, accountable and sustainable business practices in the EU and beyond.

VOLUNTARY SUSTAINABILITY DISCLOSURES

Voluntary sustainability disclosures are either the basis for sustainability reporting in a given national setting or are used by organizations to go beyond what is legally required. Voluntary disclosures can thus include additional information beyond what is mandated, providing stakeholders with a more comprehensive understanding of a company's sustainability practices, performance and impacts. Voluntary disclosures are often driven by the outcome of an organization's materiality assessment (refer to Chapter 5) and/or its broader commitment to specific sustainability issues.

Numerous globally applicable frameworks and standards exist that enable organizations to voluntarily disclose the environmental, social and economic dimensions of their activities. GRI, IFRS Sustainability Disclosure Standards and TNFD are examples of such international standards.

Researchers have pointed towards the failure of voluntary sustainability disclosures to deliver the expected results (Hess, 2007). More explicitly, it has been argued that the 'so-called business case', which stresses voluntarism and corporate self-interest as drivers for disclosure, 'simply leads to selective and strategic disclosure designed to protect the corporation's legitimacy' (Hess, 2014, p. 12 as quoted in Kinderman, 2020, p. 677).

GOVERNANCE INTERPLAY: MANDATORY AND VOLUNTARY SUSTAINABILITY DISCLOSURES

The interplay between mandatory and voluntary sustainability disclosures is an important aspect of corporate governance and sustainability reporting. Mandatory requirements for sustainability reporting are essential for companies to meet legal obligations and avoid regulatory sanctions. Mandatory disclosures enhance transparency and accountability by providing standardized information on ESG performance that can be easily compared across organizations and industries. This helps stakeholders, including investors, customers, employees and communities, to make informed decisions and hold organizations accountable for their social and environmental impacts.

Voluntary sustainability disclosures, on the other hand, allow organizations to go beyond minimum regulatory requirements and address a broader range of sustainability issues that are relevant to their stakeholders. Organizations may choose to disclose additional information to align with market expectations, industry norms or best practices, demonstrating their commitment to sustainability leadership and long-term value creation.

The interplay between mandatory and voluntary disclosures is facilitated by, for example, IFRS Sustainability Disclosure Standards, GRI, TNFD and a number of other international standards. These standards and frameworks encourage organizations to integrate financial and non-financial information into a single, comprehensive report, providing stakeholders with a holistic view of the organization's value creation process and performance. The interplay between mandatory and voluntary sustainability disclosures is a dynamic process that shapes corporate governance practices, influences stakeholder perceptions and drives organizational change towards more sustainable and responsible business practices.

Scholars are highlighting that the shift from voluntary to mandatory requirements for sustainability reporting can produce an effective change in non-financial disclosure by making effective integration between financial and non-financial disclosure possible (Doni *et al.*, 2020). Example 2.4 provides an illustration from the company Ørsted that shows the company makes reference to mandated regulations in the form of EU legislations as well as voluntary standards such as TNFD. The example serves to simply showcase that even though European companies are moving towards CSRD and ESRS and associated mandatory requirements, they continue using voluntary standards to supplement their reporting.

Example 2.4

The interplay between mandatory and voluntary disclosures

In addition to its mandatory reporting based on EU legislation, Ørsted lists several frameworks which it also applies on a voluntary basis.

Ørsted 2023 Integrated Annual Report

Source: Ørsted Annual Report 2023

Activity 2.1 builds on Example 2.4 by asking you to research a company of your choice and identify which, if any, mandatory sustainability standards it uses and which voluntary standards.

ACTIVITY 2.1

Locate an organization in your local context and identify its mandatory and voluntary disclosure requirements.

THEORETICAL PERSPECTIVES ON VOLUNTARY SUSTAINABILITY DISCLOSURES

This section provides an overview of legitimacy, stakeholder and agency theory perspectives as applied to voluntary sustainability reporting.

Legitimacy theory

Legitimacy theory suggests that organizations seek to maintain their legitimacy and social acceptance by conforming to societal norms, values and expectations. From this perspective, organizations engage in sustainability reporting to demonstrate their commitment to social and environmental responsibility, thereby enhancing their legitimacy in the eyes of stakeholders. Sustainability reporting serves as a mechanism for organizations to communicate their efforts to address societal concerns and maintain their social licence to operate.

Sustainability reporting and legitimacy theory are closely intertwined, as legitimacy theory provides valuable insights into why organizations engage in sustainability reporting and how it contributes to their legitimacy. Sustainability reporting helps organizations legitimize their actions and behaviours by providing evidence of their efforts to address societal concerns, reduce negative externalities and contribute to the well-being of stakeholders and the environment (Suchman, 1995).

Organizations can use sustainability reporting as a mechanism to maintain legitimacy over time by providing stakeholders with information about the organization's values, priorities and performance on sustainability-related issues. Through sustainability reporting, organizations continuously seek to align their activities with stakeholder expectations, address emerging sustainability challenges and respond to societal demands for transparency, accountability and responsibility (Yusoff *et al.*, 2006).

In summary, sustainability reporting is closely linked to legitimacy theory, as it serves as a strategic tool for organizations to maintain their legitimacy and social acceptance by demonstrating their commitment to sustainable practices and responsible business conduct. By engaging in sustainability reporting, organizations can enhance their credibility, trustworthiness and resilience in an increasingly complex and interconnected world.

It should be highlighted that scholars have been vastly critical of the reliability of firms' sustainability information on the basis that it does not represent actual practices, with this reporting viewed as being symbolic in form, and thus gained the term **greenwashing** (Khan *et al.*, 2020; Michelon *et al.*, 2015, 2020).

Example 2.5 (and discussion point) looks at the notion of greenwashing (we continue our discussion of greenwashing in Chapter 12). It exemplifies different forms of greenwashing. In Activity 2.2 we will then reflect upon the important question of mandatory versus voluntary sustainability reporting in regard to greenwashing.

Example 2.5

Greenwashing

A common definition of greenwashing can be found in the Springer *Encyclopedia of Corporate Social Responsibility*:

> *Greenwashing refers to the practice of falsely promoting an organization's environmental efforts or spending more resources to promote the organization as green than are spent to actually engage in environmentally sound practices. Thus greenwashing is the dissemination of false or deceptive information regarding an organization's environmental strategies, goals, motivations, and actions. (Becker-Olsen & Potucek, 2013)*

In addition, other terms such as 'bluewashing' (for social claims), 'bee washing' (for biodiversity-related claims) or just 'ESG washing' are commonly used.

Greenwashing can materialize in many different forms. In its 2023 report, the NGO planet tracker identified six different approaches to greenwashing (Planet Tracker, 2023):

- Greencrowding: Hiding in a crowd of similar companies in order to avoid detection of unsustainable practices.
- Greenlighting: Companies emphasize a particularly environmentally friendly feature of their activities or products in their communication (including advertising), however small, in order to divert attention from activities in other areas.
- Greenshifting: Companies blame their consumers in order to make them responsible for unsustainable practices.
- Greenlabelling: Marketers label something as green or sustainable, but on closer inspection this proves to be misleading.
- Greenrinsing: A company regularly changes its ESG targets before they are achieved.
- Greenhushing: Management conceals its sustainability data to avoid scrutiny from investors.

Greenwashing is problematic as it undermines any credible efforts to improve on negative environmental (or other) impacts. Stakeholders such as consumers, investors or the general public are misled. As a consequence, trust erodes and thus it becomes more and more difficult to motivate people for action that is needed in order to establish sustainable development.

ACTIVITY 2.2

Discuss the role of mandatory versus voluntary sustainability reporting in the light of greenwashing.

Stakeholder theory

Based on the work of Freeman (1984), the stakeholder theory perspective on ESG suggests that firms committed to social responsibility – those engaging in environmental protection, promoting social equality and enhancing community relations – often adhere to corporate governance practices that maximize value. Consequently, firms with effective governance are more likely to pursue socially responsible activities. Essentially, CSR activities can align with both the maximization of shareholder wealth and the fulfilment of wider societal objectives. Advocates of this perspective also contend that maximizing the value of a firm can encompass the value provided to all stakeholders, not solely to shareholders (Edmans, 2011; Deng *et al.*, 2013).

Organizations strategically employ sustainability reporting as a powerful tool to engage stakeholders, directly respond to their concerns and cultivate a foundation of trust. This practice not only demonstrates a commitment to transparency and accountability but also signals an organization's dedication to ethical business practices and long-term value creation. Through comprehensive sustainability reports, organizations can effectively showcase their efforts in environmental preservation, social responsibility and economic performance, thereby strengthening stakeholder relationships and fostering a culture of trust.

In the context of sustainability reporting, stakeholder theory provides a framework for identifying and understanding the various groups and individuals who have a stake in or are affected by the sustainability practices and reporting of an organization. Stakeholder theory, developed by Freeman and others, suggests that organizations should consider the interests and well-being of all their stakeholders, not just shareholders, in their decision-making processes. Stakeholders have varying degrees of influence and interest in sustainability reporting. Organizations must engage with these groups to understand their concerns and incorporate their perspectives into their sustainability strategies and reporting practices. (The importance of the stakeholder concept will visited again in Chapter 4 that looks at the double materiality process).

Activities 2.3 and 2.4 challenge you to consider potential connections between the two theories that this chapter has thus far addressed in the context of voluntary sustainability reporting.

ACTIVITY 2.3

Discuss the potential connections between stakeholder theory and legitimacy theory.

Agency theory

Agency theory examines the dynamics between principals (such as shareholders) and agents (such as management), focusing on how to align their often divergent interests. Fama and Jensen (1983) propose a solution to mitigate managerial agency problems by clearly separating 'decision management' (the initiation and execution of decisions) from 'decision control' (the ratification and monitoring of decisions).

Milton Friedman (1970) posited in *New York Times Magazine* that the primary duty of corporations is to generate profits, implying that CSR may stem from managerial agency issues. This viewpoint holds that CSR activities might serve managers' interests at the expense of shareholders, potentially leading to agency conflicts (Bénabou & Tirole, 2010; Cheng *et al.*, 2014; Masulis & Reza, 2015). The concern is that managers overly engaged in CSR could neglect their core responsibilities, adversely affecting shareholder value (Krueger, 2015; Jensen, 2001). Friedman further warned that deviating from the goal of profit maximization could compromise the integrity of a free society.

ACTIVITY 2.4

Compare stakeholder theory with the agency theory in the light of sustainability reporting. Discuss your findings.

ANOTHER PERSPECTIVE ON SUSTAINABILITY REPORTING

This section highlights research that considers sustainability reporting from an organizational purpose perspective as well as from a critical angle.

Organizational purpose

Recent advancements in governance literature suggest a paradigm shift towards the belief that the primary objective of organizations extends beyond profit generation to encompass societal value creation (Edmans, 2020; Mayer, 2019, 2020). Firms with a clear sense of purpose understand that solving societal problems can concurrently yield profits, positioning profit-making as a secondary outcome of fulfilling their core purpose (Mayer, 2019, 2020). However, for a purpose to be meaningful and effectively guide an organization's actions, it must be deeply embedded within the organization's governance structures, including its ownership model, incentive schemes and the role played by its board of directors. This integration ensures that the organization's purpose aligns with its strategic objectives and operational activities, thereby maximizing its potential to contribute positively to society (Edmans, 2020; Mayer, 2019, 2020).

Critical studies of sustainability reporting

Critical theory provides a lens through which sustainability reporting can be analysed, critiqued and improved (Fuchs, 2017). Critical theory studies of sustainability reporting typically focus on:

- **Power dynamics:** These include how power structures within organizations influence sustainability reporting practices and involve examining who controls the narrative of sustainability reporting, whose interests are prioritized and how marginalized voices are represented or excluded.
- **Social justice:** This scrutinizes whether reporting practices address or perpetuate social inequalities, such as disparities in access to resources, opportunities and decision-making processes. It also explores how sustainability reporting can contribute to more equitable outcomes for diverse stakeholders.
- **Language and discourse:** This analyses the language and discourse used in sustainability reporting, questioning, for example, how terms such as sustainability, responsibility and transparency are defined and deployed. It investigates how language constructs reality, shapes perceptions and influences behaviours, and how reporting narratives can be manipulated to serve certain interests. **Critical discourse analysis** has been applied to study how sustainability reports can drive change (Higgins & Coffey, 2016).
- **Colonialism and sustainability reporting:** This examines the colonial roots and global implications of sustainability reporting. It considers how colonial legacies continue to shape patterns of resource extraction, environmental degradation and social injustice, and how globalization processes influence sustainability reporting practices across borders and cultures (Alawattage & Azure, 2021; Alawattage & Fernando, 2017).
- **Corporate hegemony:** This scrutinizes the role of organizations in sustainability reporting and their influence over global sustainability agendas. It questions whether corporate-led reporting initiatives genuinely address systemic issues or merely serve as 'greenwashing' exercises to maintain corporate legitimacy and market dominance.

- **Accountability and transparency:** This emphasizes the importance of accountability and transparency in sustainability reporting. It interrogates whether reporting mechanisms adequately hold organizations accountable for their social and environmental impacts, or whether they merely create an illusion of accountability while allowing harmful practices to persist.
- **Alternative narratives:** This encourages the exploration of alternative narratives and counter-discourses in sustainability reporting. It seeks to amplify marginalized voices, challenge dominant paradigms and promote more inclusive, democratic and transformative approaches to reporting that address systemic issues and foster positive social and environmental change.

Overall, critical theory studies of sustainability reporting offer multidimensional perspectives that go beyond technical compliance and surface-level assessments. They illuminate the underlying power dynamics, social injustices and ideological struggles inherent in sustainability reporting practices, with the aim of promoting more ethical, equitable and sustainable outcomes for all stakeholders.

CONCLUSION

In the context of sustainability reporting, regulatory requirements, governance structures, market pressures, stakeholder engagement and investor behaviour interact to influence organizations' reporting practices and disclosure behaviours. Regulatory interventions may shape market expectations, investor preferences and corporate strategies related to sustainability reporting. 'Crises can generate pressure for change – and the crises of the past decade are indispensable for understanding what led the European Union (EU) to mandate non-financial or sustainability reporting for large firms' (Kinderman, 2020).

Theories that are concerned with the regulation of sustainability draw on various forms of regulatory, governance and regime theories (refer to, for example, Sulkowski & Jebe, 2022).

In order to explain voluntary disclosure practices, three important theories are discussed (legitimacy, stakeholder and agency theory); in the context of mandatory reporting regimes, organizations still have room for additional voluntary disclosure practices. Legitimacy theory suggests that organizations seek to maintain their legitimacy and social acceptance by conforming to societal norms, values and expectations. From this perspective, companies engage in sustainability reporting to demonstrate their commitment to social and environmental responsibility, thereby enhancing their legitimacy in the eyes of stakeholders. The concept of greenwashing emerged through the lens of legitimacy theory. Stakeholder governance expands the focus of corporate governance beyond the interests of shareholders to include a broader array of stakeholders such as employees, customers, suppliers and the community. This approach recognizes that long-term value creation depends on the well-being and support of all stakeholders. Firms adopting stakeholder governance aim to balance profit-making with social responsibility, such as environmental protection, social equality and community relations, thereby aligning corporate activities with broader societal goals. Agency theory delves into the relationship between principals (shareholders) and agents (management), examining the challenges in aligning their often divergent interests. It posits that due to information asymmetry and conflicting objectives, agents may not always act in the best interests of the principals. To mitigate these agency problems, the theory suggests mechanisms such as high-powered incentives (e.g. executive pay), monitoring (e.g. independent board of directors) and an active market for corporate control.

More recently, the concept of organizational purpose represents a shift in corporate focus towards defining and pursuing a core mission that transcends mere profit generation to include societal value creation. Purpose-driven companies identify and address social and environmental issues through their business operations, viewing profits as a byproduct of their commitment to their core mission. This paradigm asserts that a meaningful company purpose should be deeply integrated into the governance framework of the firm, influencing decisions and strategies to ensure alignment with both strategic objectives and societal contributions.

Critical studies of sustainability reporting illuminate underlying power dynamics, social injustices and ideological struggles inherent in sustainability reporting practices, with the aim of promoting more ethical, equitable and sustainable outcomes for all stakeholders.

SUMMARY

The following items relate to the learning objectives listed at the beginning of the chapter.

- **LO 1. Discuss theories of standardization and regulation for sustainability reporting.**

  To further our understanding of governance, harmonization and regulation of sustainability reporting this chapter has focused on two angles: 1) voluntary standardization of sustainability reporting and 2) mandatory governance of sustainability reporting. The work of Kinderman (2020) on upward regulatory harmonization was brought forward to explain the process of aligning regulations and standards across different jurisdictions to achieve greater consistency, coherence and effectiveness. In the context of sustainability reporting in the EU, there are several challenges associated with upward regulatory harmonization. Upward regulatory harmonization involves creating new international standards to align differing domestic regulations, thereby reducing the negative externalities they may cause. It can also mean strengthening existing international rules to achieve similar harmonization (Kinderman, 2020).

- **LO 2. Explain why stakeholder perspectives are relevant in regard to sustainability reporting.**

  In the realm of sustainability reporting, stakeholder theory serves as a crucial framework for identifying and comprehending the diverse groups and individuals with a vested interest in, or impacted by, an organization's sustainability practices and disclosures. This theory, pioneered Freeman and others, emphasizes that organizations should account for the interests and well-being of all stakeholders, rather than focusing solely on shareholders, in their decision-making processes. Stakeholders exhibit varying levels of influence and interest in sustainability reporting. Thus, organizations must actively engage with these groups to understand their concerns and integrate their perspectives into sustainability strategies and reporting efforts. The significance of the stakeholder concept will be further explored in Chapter 4, which will delve into the double materiality process.

- **LO 3. Discuss the main functions of sustainability reporting from various theoretical perspectives.**

  This chapter has provided a high-level overview of selected theories that are frequently used in studies that engage with sustainability reporting. The theoretical landscape is likely to evolve, as an increasing amount of research is being conducted in this area. Table 2.1 provides a summary of three of the key theoretical perspectives addressed in this chapter.

Table 2.1 Overview of legitimacy, stakeholder and agency theory in the context of ESG reporting

Theoretical perspective	Summarized description
Legitimacy theory	Legitimacy theory suggests that organizations seek to maintain their legitimacy and social acceptance by conforming to societal norms, values and expectations. From this perspective, companies engage in sustainability reporting to demonstrate their commitment to social and environmental responsibility, thereby enhancing their legitimacy in the eyes of stakeholders. The concept of greenwashing emerged through the lens of legitimacy theory.
Stakeholder theory	Stakeholder governance expands the focus of corporate governance beyond the interests of shareholders to include a broader array of stakeholders such as employees, customers, suppliers and the community. This approach recognizes that long-term value creation depends on the well-being and support of all stakeholders. Firms adopting stakeholder governance aim to balance profit-making with social responsibility, such as environmental protection, social equality and community relations, thereby aligning corporate activities with broader societal goals.
Agency theory	Agency theory delves into the relationship between principals (shareholders) and agents (management), examining the challenges in aligning their often divergent interests. It posits that due to information asymmetry and conflicting objectives, agents may not always act in the best interests of the principals. To mitigate these agency problems, the theory suggests mechanisms be used such as high-powered incentives (e.g. executive pay), monitoring (e.g. independent board of directors) and an active market for corporate control.

EXERCISES

1. Select an organization of your choice and identify the interplay between mandatory reporting requirements and voluntary reporting standards applied by the organization. (LO 1)
2. Use selected theoretical perspectives to discuss how mandatory requirements for sustainability reporting can combat greenwashing. (LO 2, LO 3)
3. Whose voices are represented in sustainability reporting, and whose perspectives are marginalized or excluded? (LO 2)
4. To what extent do sustainability reports effectively engage stakeholders and address their concerns and expectations? (LO 2)
5. What are the motivations for organizations to go beyond mandatory reporting requirements and disclose additional sustainability information voluntarily? (LO 3)
6. How do regulatory frameworks influence the content, format and frequency of sustainability reporting, and what are the implications for comparability and standardization? (LO 3)

CHAPTER 3
A global overview of emerging requirements for sustainability reporting

Learning objectives

After studying this chapter you should be able to:

- LO 1. Understand and discuss the global political agreements behind the evolution of sustainability reporting (for example, the Paris Agreement and Agenda 2030).
- LO 2. Understand and explain the role of the EU, the US SEC and other regional or national regulators in mandating sustainability disclosures.
- LO 3. Understand the structure of sustainability reporting regulations in the EU.
- LO 4. Describe extant international voluntary standards (for example, GRI, IFRS Sustainability Disclosure Standards, TNFD, etc.) for sustainability accounting and reporting.
- LO 5. Discuss the interplay between international standards, such as GRI, TNFD and IFRS Sustainability Disclosure Standards, with emerging national regulations.
- LO 6. Discuss efforts aimed at international harmonization of sustainability reporting standards.

Big shifts, small steps...

As policymakers and companies adopt mandatory and regulated sustainability reporting, KPMG's 2022 'Big shifts, small steps: Survey of sustainability reporting' investigates the current state of sustainability reporting and business strategies of 5,800 companies in 58 countries. By analysing websites, financial and ESG reports, the 2022 survey identifies new topics that reflect the evolving nature of sustainability disclosures.
New sections include the use of materiality assessments, along with reporting on social and governance risks. The findings summarize five major emerging trends in sustainability reporting:

- *Sustainability reporting is growing incrementally with movement towards the use of standards framed by stakeholder materiality assessments.*
- *There is increased reporting on climate-related risks and carbon reduction targets, in line with TCFD.*
- *There is a growing awareness of biodiversity risk.*
- *Reporting on the UN SDGs prioritizes quantity over quality.*
- *Climate risk reporting leads, followed by social and governance risks.*

Source: Adapted from KPMG (2022)

INTRODUCTION

The emerging requirements for sustainability reporting reflect a paradigm shift in corporate governance and accountability. Organizations are increasingly expected to transparently disclose their ESG performance to address regulatory mandates, meet investor demands, fulfil stakeholder expectations and drive long-term value creation.

Two international landmark agreements have stimulated global action towards sustainability: 1) the 2030 Agenda for Sustainable Development and 2) the Paris Agreement. The 2030 Agenda, adopted by United Nations member states in 2015, encompasses 17 Sustainable Development Goals (SDGs) and 169 targets aimed at addressing pressing global challenges and fostering a more sustainable future for all. Meanwhile, the Paris Agreement, ratified in 2015, commits signatory countries to combat climate change by limiting global warming to well below 2 degrees Celsius above pre-industrial levels, with efforts to limit it to 1.5 degrees Celsius. It should be highlighted that the **Intergovernmental Panel on Climate Change (IPCC)** plays a pivotal role in informing and guiding the implementation of the Paris Agreement.

These transformative agreements serve as guiding frameworks for policymakers, businesses and civil society alike, shaping the trajectory of sustainability reporting requirements worldwide. This chapter seeks to illuminate the diverse approaches and emerging trends in sustainability reporting requirements across regions and jurisdictions. From the European Union's Corporate Sustainability Reporting Directive (CSRD) to the Enhancement and Standardization of Climate-Related Disclosures for Investors in the United States, and beyond, the global landscape of sustainability reporting is evolving rapidly. Moreover, as stakeholders demand greater transparency, accountability and comparability in sustainability reporting, the integration of the SDGs and climate-related considerations into reporting frameworks becomes increasingly essential.

Through this exploration, we aim to provide insights into the drivers, challenges and opportunities associated with the evolving requirements for sustainability reporting on a global scale. By understanding the intersections between international agreements, regulatory initiatives and corporate practices, stakeholders can navigate the complexities of sustainability reporting with clarity and purpose, ultimately contributing to the collective pursuit of a more sustainable and resilient world.

THE ROLE OF GLOBAL POLITICAL AGREEMENTS

This section provides an overview of the political agreements at the global level that have had important implications for the evolution of standards and regulations for sustainability reporting.

Agenda 2030

Agenda 2030, also known as the Sustainable Development Goals (SDGs), is a comprehensive framework adopted by United Nations member states in 2015 to address global challenges and promote sustainable development across economic, social and environmental dimensions (United Nations, 2015). The SDGs encompass 17 interconnected goals and 169 targets aimed at eradicating poverty, protecting the planet and ensuring prosperity for all by the year 2030. Organizational sustainability reporting is seen as an important data source for the SDGs' monitoring framework (also refer to, for example, UNCTAD, 2022). Example 3.1 provides a visual illustration of how organizations can choose to show their engagement with the SDGs as an integral part of their sustainability report.

Example 3.1

Michelin and SDG alignment

By assessing its actions and accomplishments in light of the United Nations' SDGs, Michelin seeks to respond more effectively to increasing expectations from stakeholders (partners, customers, regulators and so forth) in relation to environmental and social topics (Figure 3.1).

Figure 3.1 Michelin's circular alignment between ESG and the SDGs

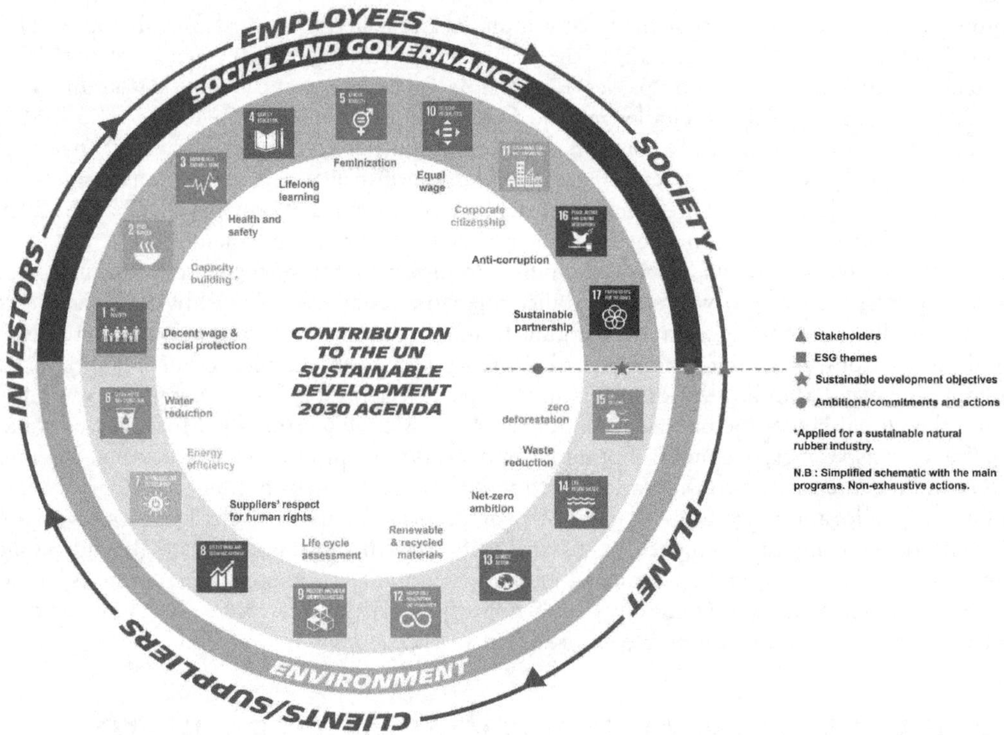

Source: Michelin (2022)

Activity 3.1 asks you to choose an organization that includes SDGs in their sustainability reporting so you can see how organizations report on SDGs in different ways.

ACTIVITY 3.1

UN Trade and Development (**UNCTAD**) prepared 36 case studies on the practical application of the core SDG indicators in different types of entities from various countries and industries, including listed organizations, SMEs and family businesses.

Locate an organization that uses SDGs or **SDG indicators** in their sustainability reporting. Discuss how the organization is using these SDGs or SDG indicators.

Source: UNCTAD (2021)

In research, studies are exploring multiple questions in regard to SDG reporting and the broader role of sustainability reporting to advance Agenda 2030. Some studies investigate organizations' level of engagement in reporting and monitoring their contributions to SDGs (Bebbington & Unerman, 2020; Calabrese *et al.*, 2021; Rosati & Faria, 2019).

The Paris Agreement

In December 2015, amid rising concerns over the escalating threats of climate change, representatives from nearly 200 countries gathered in Paris for the **United Nations Climate Change Conference** (**COP21**). Against a backdrop of urgency and global collaboration, these nations reached a critical decision: the adoption of the Paris Agreement, an international accord aimed at combatting climate change and fostering a sustainable future for our planet.

The Paris Agreement represents a moment in the global response to climate change, signalling a collective commitment to ambitious and concerted action to mitigate greenhouse gas emissions and adapt to the impacts of climate change. Central to the Paris Agreement's effectiveness is its inclusive and flexible approach which recognizes the diverse circumstances and capabilities of different countries while emphasizing the shared responsibility to address the climate crisis. Under the agreement, each participating country (known as a party) is required to set and regularly update nationally determined contributions (NDCs) outlining their targets for reducing emissions and enhancing resilience to climate impacts. These NDCs represent a critical mechanism for driving progress towards the collective goals of the agreement, fostering transparency and facilitating international cooperation. The success of the Paris Agreement ultimately hinges on the commitment, ambition and action of all nations and stakeholders. Activity 3.2 provides an opportunity to go a little deeper into how organizations, in this case the **European Bank for Reconstruction and Development** (**EBRD**), make reference to Paris Agreement alignment.

ACTIVITY 3.2

European Bank for Reconstruction and Development (EBRD): Paris Agreement alignment

The EBRD has now aligned all its new activities with the goals of the Paris Agreement. Referred to as 'Paris alignment', this means making finance flows consistent with a pathway towards low greenhouse gas emissions and climate-resilient development.

Article 2.1(c) of the Paris Agreement commits signatories to making 'finance flows consistent with a pathway towards low GHG emissions and climate-resilient development'. This relates to both mitigation and adaptation goals and, in putting its commitment into practice, the EBRD is guided by the 1.5°C goal (keeping global

(Continued)

warming within 1.5°C of pre-industrial levels). The Bank has worked with other multilateral development banks to develop an operational framework for alignment. The EBRD's commitment is reflected in the transactions financed and its interactions with clients.

Identify the methodology used by EBRD to determine the alignment to the Paris Agreement of EBRD investments.

Source: EBRD (2022)

INTRODUCTION TO REGULATORY INITIATIVES FOR SUSTAINABILITY REPORTING

Organizations face increasing demands to address sustainability challenges and demonstrate their contributions to a more sustainable future. In response, regulatory initiatives for sustainability reporting have emerged as a critical mechanism to drive sustainability disclosures and actions. These regulatory frameworks, established by governments, regulatory bodies and standard-setting organizations, aim to standardize and enhance the quality, comparability and reliability of sustainability disclosures across industries and jurisdictions. By imposing reporting requirements and guidelines on organizations, these initiatives seek to promote transparency, facilitate informed decision-making by stakeholders and incentivize responsible business practices.

In this section, we will explore some of the key regulatory initiatives for sustainability reporting, their objectives, scope and impact on corporate governance, accountability and sustainability performance. This overview of regulatory frameworks will support better navigation in the landscape of sustainability reporting.

European Union

The **EU Sustainable Finance Package** (refer to Figure 3.2) is a comprehensive set of legislative measures and initiatives designed to promote **sustainable finance** and integrate **environmental, social and governance (ESG) factors** into the financial system. The package aims to mobilize private capital towards sustainable investments, enhance transparency and disclosure of ESG-related risks and opportunities, and support the transition to a low-carbon, more resilient economy.

Figure 3.2 Key regulatory mechanisms of the EU Sustainable Finance Package

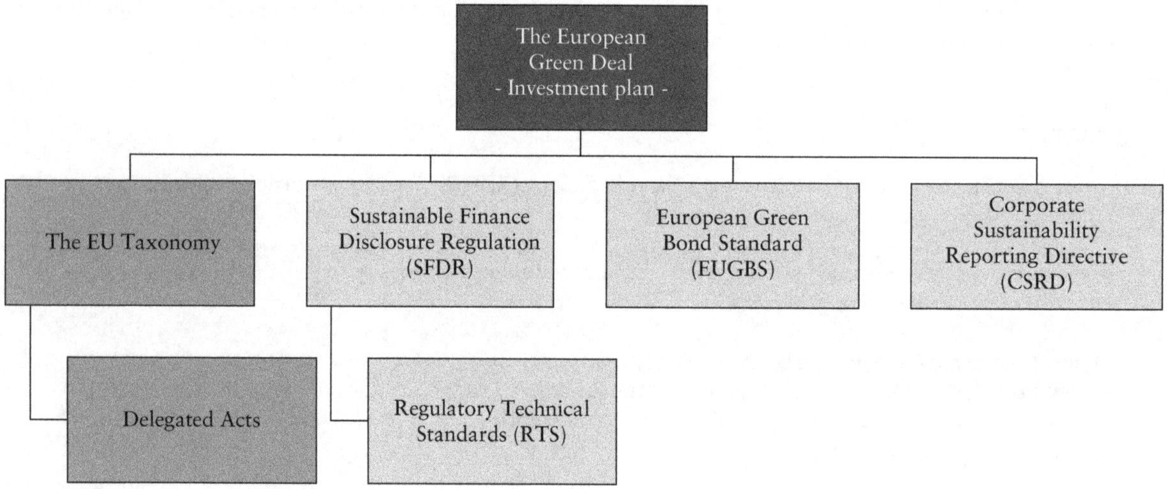

Example 3.2 provides a brief insight into the **European Green Deal**, which is the link between Agenda 2030 and the EU Sustainable Finance Package.

Example 3.2

The link between Agenda 2030 and the EU Sustainable Finance Package

Launched in December 2019, the European Green Deal is in response to the EU adopting Agenda 2030 and the Paris Agreement. The Green Deal is an initiative for transforming Europe into a climate-neutral continent by 2050. It encompasses a wide range of policy measures and actions across various sectors, including energy, transport, industry, agriculture and buildings. The EU Sustainable Finance Package is an integral part of the EU Green Deal.

Overall, the EU Sustainable Finance Package represents a significant step towards mainstreaming sustainable finance and integrating ESG considerations into the European financial system. By establishing frameworks, standards and disclosure requirements, the package aims to drive capital towards sustainable investments, foster transparency and accountability, and support the transition to a more sustainable and resilient economy.

The EU Sustainable Finance Package builds on an **action plan**: the Action Plan on Financing Sustainable Growth (EU, 2018a). In total, it set forth ten legislative measures to move European capital markets towards sustainability. Following the approaches formulated at COP21, the idea of sustainable finance – that is, promoting sustainability via financial (capital market) incentives – was considered to be a most promising way to establish this transformation.

EU Taxonomy Regulation

The **EU Taxonomy** Regulation establishes a classification system – or Taxonomy – for environmentally sustainable economic activities. It provides criteria for determining whether an economic activity is environmentally sustainable, with a focus on six environmental objectives: climate change mitigation, climate change adaptation, sustainable use and protection of water and marine resources, transition to a **circular economy**, pollution prevention and control, and protection and restoration of biodiversity and ecosystems. The taxonomy aims to provide clarity and transparency for investors, businesses and policymakers, enabling them to identify and support sustainable investments.

The specific elements of this classification system are laid out via delegated act – separate legislation that contains technical screening criteria that specify when an economic activity is performed in accordance with the requirements of an environmental objective. Also, reporting requirements that have to be included in sustainability reports based on EU legislation are laid out via such delegated act.

Sustainable Finance Disclosure Regulation (SFDR)

The SFDR sets out disclosure requirements for financial market participants and financial advisers regarding the integration of ESG factors into their investment decision-making processes. It requires them to disclose information on how they consider sustainability risks, the adverse impacts of investment decisions on sustainability factors, and whether they promote environmental or social characteristics in their investment products. The SFDR aims to improve transparency and comparability of ESG-related disclosures, helping investors make informed decisions and fostering sustainable investment practices.

The SFDR Level 2 measures provide detailed technical standards and regulatory requirements for the implementation of the SFDR. They specify the content, presentation and timing of ESG-related disclosures by financial market participants, including the content of pre-contractual and periodic disclosures, as well as requirements for the publication of sustainability-related information on websites and in annual reports.

EU Green Bond Standard (EU GBS)

The EU GBS aims to create a common standard for green bonds issued within the EU, ensuring transparency, integrity and credibility of green bond markets. It sets out eligibility criteria for green projects and investments as well as requirements for reporting and verification to provide investors with confidence that green bonds finance environmentally sustainable activities.

The CSRD

The CSRD entered into force in 2023. The Directive expands the scope of its predecessor, the **Non-Financial Reporting Directive (NFRD)**, concerning the social and environmental information that organizations have to report. The CSRD is based on a phased implementation spanning from 2024 to 2029, with varying deadlines based on factors such as company size and listing status. Subsequent to the adoption of the CSRD a broader set of large organizations, as well as listed SMEs, will be required to report on sustainability.

The categorization of companies or groups as micro, small, medium or large hinges on fulfilling or exceeding at least two of the three size criteria stipulated in the 2013 Accounting Directive (refer to Table 3.1 for size thresholds set for CSRD compliance and corresponding timeline):

1. number of employees
2. balance sheet total
3. net turnover.

Table 3.1 The size criteria have been adopted by the EC through a Delegated Directive on 17 October 2023

Size category	Balance sheet (EUR)	Net turnover (EUR)	Employee count
Large	>25,000,000	>50,000,000	>250
Medium	5,000,000–25,000,000	10,000,000–50,000,000	Up to 250
Small (lower end)	450,000–5,000,000	900,000–10,000,000	Up to 50
Micro	Up to 450,000	Up to 900,000	Up to 10

The size thresholds were approved on 17 October 2023 by the European Commission. Before these thresholds were suggested, the EU Commission estimated a total of 49,000 organizations in the EU would fall within the scope of the CSRD.

Size thresholds are used for the phased adoption of the CSRD (refer to Table 3.2). Organizations will have to apply the new rules for the first time in the 2024 financial year, for reports published in 2025.

The CSRD applies only to corporations, that is public and private limited companies. The sole exception is for insurance companies and credit institutions which have to apply the CSRD irrespective of their legal form. This is important for countries such as Germany or Austria where a large part of these companies are organized as cooperatives, foundations or associations.

SMEs are only required to publish sustainability reports if they are listed on a regulated market in the EU. Furthermore, micro-sized entities are exempted in any case. Also, small and non-complex institutions (refer to the Appendix) and captive insurance and reinsurance undertakings may also benefit from most of the reliefs granted to SMEs. Technically, those financial institutions are large as defined by the thresholds of the **EU Accounting Directive**; however, because of sector-specific regulations, they are subject to reduced transparency rules.

The CSRD is applicable to any non-EU company which satisfies both of the following criteria: 1) generates a net turnover of more than €150 million in the EU for each of the last two consecutive financial years at the consolidated level (or, if not applicable, at the individual level), and 2) has at least one EU subsidiary in scope of the CSRD, *or* has at least one branch which generated a net turnover of more than €40 million in the preceding financial year.

Table 3.2 Size thresholds used for the phased adoption of the CSRD

Date for CSRD compliance	Report issued in	Company category	Reporting standards
1 January 2024	2025	Entities that were already subject to the UN Non-Financial Reporting Directive (NFRD) and listed entities with over 500 employees	ESRS for large companies: • Cross-cutting standards • Topical sector agnostic standards Second set of ESRS: • Relevant sector-specific standards
1 January 2025	2026	Large EU subsidiaries of non-EU entities Large and listed entities with fewer than 500 employees	
1 January 2026 (option to delay to 2028)	2027 (option to delay to 2029)	Listed SMEs Insurance companies and credit institutions that are SMEs	ESRS: Standards for SMEs
1 January 2028	2029	Additional non-EU entity consolidated reporting	ESRS: Third country standards

In addition, the CSRD must also be applied by non-EU companies that are listed on a regulated market in the EU. In contrast to the group on non-EU companies discussed in the previous paragraph, these companies have to apply the same timelines and reporting standards as EU companies; thus they are subjected to even stricter regulations.

Organizations subject to the CSRD will have to report according to European Sustainability Reporting Standards (ESRS). These standards were introduced to provide organizations with more extensive guidance on the required contents of their reports. Examples of established standards such as the GRI Standards for sustainability reporting or the IFRS Accounting Standards for financial reporting on how they can improve company reporting were an important reason for the EU to take this step.

European Sustainability Reporting Standards (ESRS)

On 31 July 2023, the European Commission adopted the Delegated Act on the first set of ESRS. Adoption of ESRS by Delegated Act is mandated by the co-legislators in the CSRD. The ESRS have thus become an integral part of the European legal framework for sustainability reporting. **European Financial Reporting Advisory Group (EFRAG)** has played a key role in the process since September 2020 and regards this as a milestone in the progress of quality sustainability reporting in the EU and globally.

EFRAG is a private association established in 2001 with the encouragement of the European Commission to serve the public interest. Initially, its main task was to advise the EU Commission during the endorsement of IFRS Accounting Standards into European law. However, EFRAG extended its mission in 2022 following the new role assigned to EFRAG in the CSRD, providing technical advice to the European Commission in the form of fully prepared draft EU Sustainability Reporting Standards and/or draft amendments to these Standards. This new role was given to EFRAG as it was considered to be the most experienced body in standard-setting at the EU-level, although this required EFRAG to considerably extend the scope of its activities and undergo a governance reform.

Its member organizations are European stakeholders, national organizations and civil society organizations. With EFRAG's new responsibilities, activities are now organized in two pillars:

- First, a Financial Reporting Pillar: influencing the development of IFRS Accounting Standards from a European perspective and how they contribute to the efficiency of capital markets and providing endorsement advice on (amendments to) IFRS Accounting Standards to the European Commission.
- Second, a Sustainability Reporting Pillar: developing EU Sustainability Reporting Standards, and related amendments for the European Commission.

As EFRAG is not a public institution, its work cannot become legally binding in the EU. As a consequence, it transmits the ESRS it has drafted to the EU Commission. The EU Commission then has to consult on these drafts and has the right to make further changes. Only when it published the final version as a Delegated Act does it become applicable throughout the entire EU. To gain some insight into what a Delegated Act is, read Example 3.3.

Example 3.3

What is a Delegated Act?

Typically, new laws are made in the EU based on the trilogue process: The EU Commission has the right to make proposals for new laws; then, the European Parliament and the Council of the European Union have the right to make counter-proposals. Finally, all three parties have to agree upon a final compromise which is then adopted.

As this process is time-consuming and not always suited to very technical questions, both the **European Parliament** and the **Council of the European Union** have the right to delegate their competencies to the **European Commission**; however, in any case, they retain their right to veto.

The ESRS offer organizations a structured framework for reporting on ESG issues. They delineate the required disclosures regarding an organization's material impacts, risks and opportunities concerning **sustainability matters.** They ensure transparent and comprehensive reporting, facilitating informed decision-making by stakeholders and fostering accountability in sustainability practices.

In December 2023, the first 12 ESRS were published by the official journal of the EU, thus becoming effective at the start of 2024. These **sector-agnostic standards** comprise reporting requirements, that is disclosures that have to be made irrespective of the sector in which an organization operates. They are often referred to as 'set 1' of the ESRS. Many more standards are expected to be published ('set 2' – 'set X') in forthcoming years. Figure 3.3 and Table 3.3 provide a visual overview of the structure of set 1.

Figure 3.3 ESRS structure

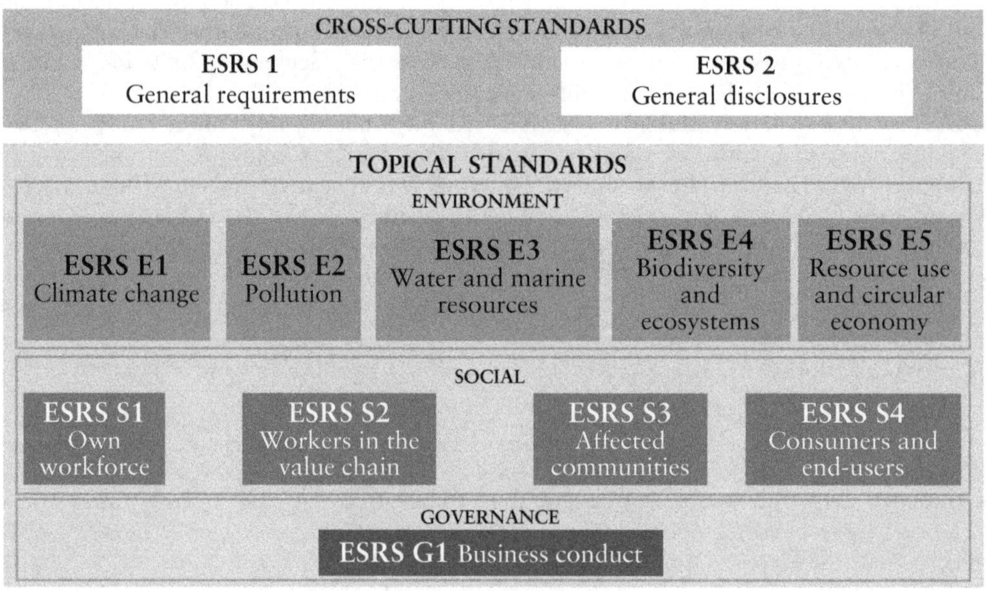

Table 3.3 Overview of ESRS

Environmental	
E1 Climate change	Disclosures on climate change mitigation, climate change adaptation and energy consumption. Disclosures on climate change mitigation relate to the company's efforts to limit global warming to 1.5°C in line with the Paris Agreement. Disclosures on Scopes 1, 2 and 3 greenhouse gas emissions and transition risks.
E2 Pollution	Disclosures on pollution of the air, water, soil, living organisms and food resources, as well as the use of substances of concern and microplastics. This standard covers pollutants generated or used during production processes and those that leave facilities as emissions, products, or as part of products or services.
E3 Water and marine resources	Disclosures on consumption, withdrawal and discharge from and into water (including ground and surface water) and marine resources. This standard also requires consideration of the extraction and use of marine resources.
E4 Biodiversity and ecosystems	Disclosures covering for example the drivers of biodiversity loss, impact on species, and impacts and dependencies on ecosystems.
E5 Circular economy	Disclosures on resource inflows, outflows, waste, resource optimization and the risks of the transition to a circular economy. A circular economy is one in which the value of products, materials and other resources in the economy are maintained for as long as possible, enhancing their efficient use in production and consumption, thereby reducing the environmental impact of their use, minimizing waste and the release of hazardous substances at all stages of the product life cycle.
Social	
S1 Own workforce	Disclosures on the organization's own workforce – including freedom of association, working conditions, access to equal opportunities and other work-related rights.
S2 Workers in the value chain	This standard is similar to ESRS S1 in content but requires consideration of the workers in the company's value chain(s).
S3 Affected communities	Disclosures on the impact of an organization's own operations and value chain. ESRS S3 thus includes consideration of, for example, product and service impacts on indigenous rights, civil rights, and social and economic rights and including water and sanitation.
S4 Consumers and end-users	Disclosures on the impacts of an organization's products and/or services on consumers and end-users, including access to quality information, privacy and the protection of children.
Governance	
G1 Business conduct	Disclosures on anti-corruption and anti-bribery practices, the protection of whistleblowers, political lobbying and the management of relationships with suppliers, including payment practices.

ESRS Sector-specific standards

The ESRS outlined earlier do not represent the entirety of potential disclosure obligations under the CSRD. As part of its mandate under the CSRD to provide technical advice to the European Commission on ESRS, EFRAG is tasked with developing sector-specific ESRS. This endeavour constitutes a multi-year exercise.

Sector-specific standards which will apply in addition to the current ESRS are expected to cover sectors such as textiles, information technology, electronics, pharmaceuticals and biotechnology. These standards would create additional disclosure requirements related to topics of particular materiality for specific industries. Research on sustainability reporting has echoed the need for sector-specific disclosure requirements (Eccles *et al.*, 2012), highlighting that such disclosures represent tailored language addressing specific risks or strategies related to given industries.

Table 3.4 gives an overview on sector-specific standards that EFRAG is currently working on. They comprise 35 sectors and 15 sector groups. Furthermore, more guidance will be issued on sector classification.

Table 3.4 Sector-specific ESRS

ESRS sector group	ESRS sector	Code
Agriculture	Agriculture, Farming and Fishing	AAF
	Forestry and wood products	AFO
Construction	Construction and Engineering	CCE
Utilities	Power Production and Energy Utilities	UPE
	Water and Waste Services	UWW
Entertainment	Recreation and Leisure	ERL
Financial Institutions	Capital Markets	FCM
	Credit Institutions	FCI
	Insurance	FIN
Health Care	Health Care and Services	HHC
Hospitality	Accommodations	HAC
	Food and Beverage Services	HFB
Durable goods	Household durables not elsewhere classified	DHD
Manufacturing	Aerospace, defence and services	MDE
	Bioenergy	MBE
	Chemicals and polymers	MCH
	Construction Materials	MMB
	Electronics and electrical equipment	MEL
	Food and Beverages	MFB
	Machinery and Equipment	MME
	Medical Instruments	MMI
	Metal Processing	MMP
	Motor Vehicles	MMV
	Pharma and Biotechnology	MPB
	Textiles, Accessories, Footwear and Jewelleries	MTA
Mining	Mining, Quarrying and Coal	MQC
	Oil and Gas	OG
Real Estate	Real Estate	RRE
Sales and Trade	Sales and Trade	SST
Services	Education	SED
	Professional Services	SPS
Technology	Information Technology	TIT
	Media and Communication	TMC
Transportation	Other Transportation	TTR
	Road Transport	TRO

Source: EFRAG SRB meeting, 4 June 2024

Example 3.4 provides further details on how sector classification will be applied in practice. It highlights that organizations will use one or more sector-specific ESRS.

Example 3.4

How is sector classification performed?

EFRAG plans to give companies the following guidance:

> *Undertakings shall use one or more sector-specific ESRS depending on the identification of NACE codes for their activities, as presented in the Appendix A and the sector description of each sector-specific [draft] ESRS. Undertakings shall use the NACE codes following the economic substance to define which sector-specific ESRS to use, looking at the substance of the economic activities they are operating – which sector they mostly operate in generating revenues and value added – rather than the form (the administrative use by registering under one or more particular NACE code).*

Source: EFRAG SRB meeting, 4 June 2024

Drafts of these standards initially were scheduled for 2023–24. Nevertheless, the Council and the European Parliament reached a provisional agreement in the first quarter of 2024 on a directive concerning the time limits for the adoption of sustainability reporting standards for certain sectors and third-country undertakings, amending the CSRD. This agreement provides additional time for companies to prepare for the sector-specific ESRS and for specific standards applicable to large non-EU organizations, which will now be adopted in June 2026, two years later than initially scheduled (European Council, 2024). Activity 3.3 allows you to discuss the sector-specific ESRS.

ACTIVITY 3.3

How do (or could) sector-specific standards improve the precision and applicability of sustainability metrics for different industries?

ESRS for SMEs

EFRAG has initiated a public consultation on the exposure drafts of the ESRS specifically tailored for listed SMEs, small and non-complex credit institutions, and captive insurance and reinsurance undertakings (collectively referred to as LSMEs). Additionally, a voluntary reporting standard has been proposed for non-listed SMEs.

The primary objective of the ESRS for LSMEs is to establish reporting requirements that are both proportionate and pertinent to the scale, complexity, capacities and characteristics of LSMEs. According to the CSRD, LSMEs are required to commence reporting for financial years starting on or after 1 January 2026, with reports being due in 2027. An additional two-year opt-out period is also available. Small and non-complex credit institutions as well as captive insurance and reinsurance undertakings can use the ESRS for LSMEs on a voluntary basis.

Even for large organizations, the ESRS for LSMEs is of relevance. The ESRS introduce a 'SME cap on value chain', that is when large organizations collect data in order to report on their value chains, they are not required to collect more information from their SME business partners than is set out by the ESRS for LSMEs. The cap mechanism shall protect these SMEs from burdensome data collection requirements and thus from an extensive factual reporting obligation that is extended to them.

For non-listed SMEs, the voluntary reporting standard aims to provide a simplified reporting tool. This tool is intended to help these entities that are not mandated to report under the CSRD to respond to requests for sustainability information, particularly when they are part of the value chain of entities that fall within the scope of CSRD reporting requirements. They are not formally adopted by the EU Commission and thus will be published by EFRAG itself as recommendation. In December 2024, the EFRAG published its 'Voluntary ESRS for non-listed small and medium-sized enterprises' (ESRS VSME). The first reports based on the ESRS VSME are expected to be published in 2025.

The organizations in the scope of the ESRS for SMEs were estimated by EFRAG (2023c) to be approximately:

- 700 listed SMEs
- 2,300 small and non-complex credit institutions
- 300 captive insurances and reinsurances.

Figure 3.4 provides a high-level overview of SMEs in scope of the ESRS, sorted by the nationality of the SME.

Figure 3.4 SMEs in the scope of the ESRS for SMEs by nationality

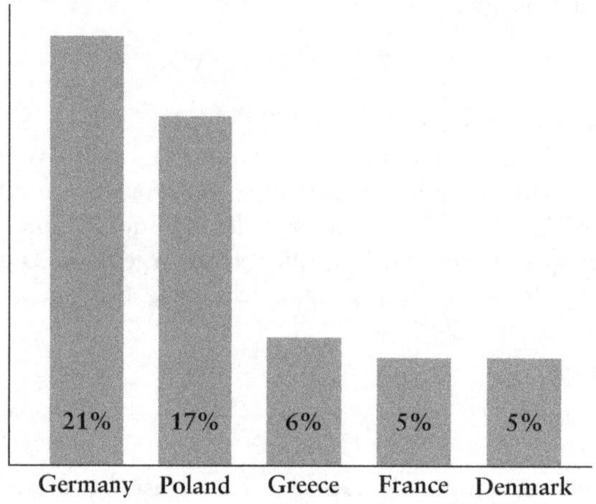

The number of European SMEs listed in EU-regulated markets was estimated to be **699 entities** before the size criteria update, with 523 medium-sized and 176 as small-scale enterprises.

Source: Greenomy (2023)

Almost 50% of non-complex credit institutions in the scope of the ESRS for LSMEs were estimated to be represented by Germany, 20 percent by Poland and 16% by Austria. In February 2025, the EU has issued a package of proposals called the **EU Omnibus** that suggests reconsidering the ESRS for LSMEs (refer to 'Outlook: EU Omnibus and its consequences for sustainability reporting').

ESRS for non-EU organizations

The extension of reporting requirements to non-EU organizations is one of the most important changes introduced to the sustainability reporting regime in the EU. However, as this poses specific challenges to organizations as well as legislators, for those non-EU organizations that have to report because of their economic activities in the EU, reduced reporting requirements are being put in place. This does not, however, apply to non-EU organizations which have to report because of their listing on an EU regulated market.

The CSRD sets forth the minimum contents that these standards have to cover. EFRAG started working on these ESRS at the end of 2024. Final standards should be published by 30 June 2026.

Instead of applying these ESRS, non-EU organizations will be granted the possibility to apply equivalent international or foreign reporting standards. A list of which standards will be considered equivalent will be provided to these organizations. Optionally, they can also apply the 'full version' of the ESRS for EU organizations.

Corporate Sustainability Due Diligence Directive (CSDDD)

The **Corporate Sustainability Due Diligence Directive (CSDDD)**, published in July 2024 in the official journal of the EU, aims to foster sustainable and responsible corporate behaviour across EU companies by imposing mandatory **due diligence** obligations regarding human rights and environmental impacts. The directive requires companies to identify, prevent, mitigate and account for adverse impacts of their activities on human rights and the environment throughout their value chains. This legislative framework signifies a shift towards legally binding sustainability practices, ensuring that businesses not only adopt but also integrate these principles into their core operations. By establishing clear due diligence requirements, the CSDDD is expected to enhance corporate accountability and transparency, contributing significantly to the EU's broader sustainability objectives.

The CSDDD refers to pronouncements such as the **UN Guiding Principles on Business and Human Rights** or the **OECD Guidelines for Multinational Enterprises**. They set forth the elements of due diligence processes that companies should employ to meet their obligations under the CSDDD and thus avoid liability. Organizations can find extended guidance on these processes in the OECD Due Diligence Guidance for Responsible Business Conduct. Figure 3.5 provides a visual illustration of the sustainability due diligence process as defined by the OECD.

Figure 3.5 Sustainability due diligence: Process definition as set forth by the OECD

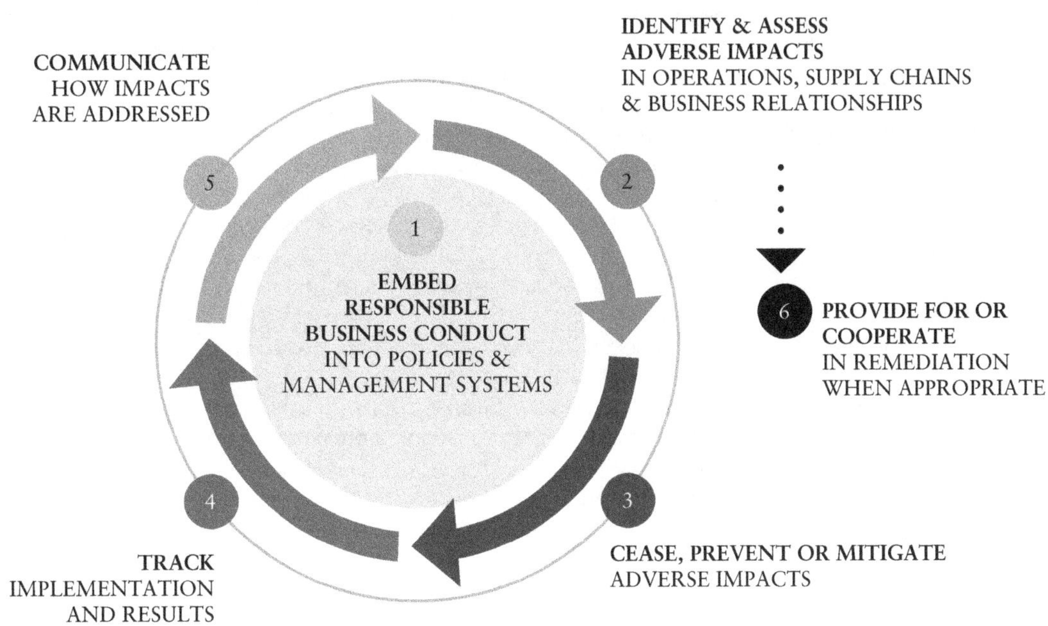

Source: OECD (2018). Reproduced under CC by 4.0

The CSDDD focuses on due diligence processes, while the CSRD mandates detailed sustainability reporting on these processes, and the ESRS provides the standards for such reporting. The CSDDD is covered in more detail in Chapter 5.

The United Kingdom

In 2023, the UK government confirmed that the incoming UK Sustainability Disclosure Standards would be based on the IFRS Sustainability Disclosure Standards. The UK government aims to consult on the first drafts of these standards in 2025. A similar proposal has been made in Singapore, where certain companies may be required to comply with the IFRS Sustainability Disclosure Standards incorporated into SGX Climate Reporting Rules as early as 2025. The publication of a summary comparing the ESRS to the Sustainability Disclosure Standards is expected in the future.

The United States

In March 2024 the SEC adopted rules to enhance and standardize climate-related disclosures by public organizations and in public offerings. The final rules reflect the SEC's efforts to respond to investors' demands for more consistent, comparable and reliable information about the financial effects of climate-related risks on a registrant's operations and how it manages those risks while balancing concerns about mitigating the associated costs of the rules.

The final rules will require an organization registered with the SEC to disclose the following:

- **Climate-related risks:** Climate-related risks that have had or are reasonably likely to have a material impact on the registrant's business strategy, results of operations or financial condition.
- **Material impacts:** The actual and potential material impacts of any identified climate-related risks on the registrant's strategy, business model and outlook.
- **Strategy and climate risk adaption and/or mitigation:** If, as part of its strategy, an organization has undertaken activities to mitigate or adapt to a material climate-related risk, a quantitative and qualitative description of material expenditures incurred and material impacts on financial estimates and assumptions that directly result from such mitigation or adaptation activities.
- **Disclosures on activities that mitigate or adapt material climate-related risks:** Specified disclosures regarding an organization's activities, if any, to mitigate or adapt to a material climate-related risk including the use, if any, of **transition plans**, scenario analysis or internal carbon prices.
- **Oversight:** Any oversight by the board of directors of climate-related risks and any role by management in assessing and managing the registrant's material climate-related risks.
- **Processes for identifying, assessing, and managing material climate-related risks:** Any processes the organization has for identifying, assessing and managing material climate-related risks and, if the organization is managing those risks, whether and how any such processes are integrated into the registrant's overall risk management system or processes.
- **Climate-related targets or goals:** Information about the organization's climate-related targets or goals, if any, that have materially affected or are reasonably likely to materially affect the registrant's business, results of operations or financial condition. Disclosures would include:
    - Material expenditures and material impacts on financial estimates and assumptions as a direct result of the target or goal or actions taken to make progress towards meeting such target or goal.
    - For **Large Accelerated Filers (LAFs)** and **Accelerated Filers (AFs)** that are not otherwise exempted, information about material **Scope 1 emissions** and/or **Scope 2 emissions**.
    - For those required to disclose Scope 1 and/or Scope 2 emissions, an assurance report at the limited assurance level, which, for an LAF, following an additional transition period, will be at the reasonable assurance level.
    - The capitalized costs, expenditures expensed, charges, and losses incurred as a result of severe weather events and other natural conditions, such as hurricanes, tornadoes, flooding, drought, wildfires, extreme temperatures, and sea level rise, subject to applicable 1% and de minimis disclosure thresholds, disclosed in a note to the financial statements.
    - The capitalized costs, expenditures expensed, and losses related to carbon offsets and renewable energy credits or certificates (RECs) if used as a material component of a registrant's plans to achieve its disclosed climate-related targets or goals, disclosed in a note to the financial statements.
    - If the estimates and assumptions a registrant uses to produce the financial statements were materially impacted by risks and uncertainties associated with severe weather events and other natural conditions or any disclosed climate-related targets or transition plans, a qualitative description of how the development of such estimates and assumptions was impacted, disclosed in a note to the financial statements.

Activity 3.4 allows us to investigate potential political, market economy and organizational reasons as to why **Scope 3 emissions** were eliminated from the final version of the US climate-related disclosures.

> **ACTIVITY 3.4**
>
> **US SEC climate-related disclosures – Scope 3 carbon emissions**
>
> Find out why Scope 3 was eliminated from the final version of the climate-related disclosures.

In addition to the SEC climate-related disclosures adopted in 2024, it is important to note that the state of California moved ahead and signed three groundbreaking climate disclosure bills in October 2023. This signalled a shift in climate reporting practices across the United States. These bills are estimated to impact over 10,000 organizations operating in the US, encompassing both publicly traded and privately held firms, as well as subsidiaries of non-US headquartered organizations.

The legislation mandates three key reporting requirements: 1) the disclosure of greenhouse gas (GHG) emissions following the guidelines outlined in the Greenhouse Gas Protocol (GHG Protocol), 2) reporting on climate-related financial risks in accordance with the recommendations put forth by the TCFD, and 3) the provision of information regarding specific emissions claims and the sale and utilization of carbon offsets. While the GHG Protocol and TCFD requirements are already recognized standards within the corporate reporting landscape, having been referenced in proposals such as those from the SEC, the European Sustainability Reporting Standards (ESRS) and the IFRS Sustainability Disclosure Standards, the California bills extend their reach significantly (Figure 3.6). Notably, these requirements apply to both public and private organizations conducting business activities within California, thus broadening the scope beyond that of the SEC's climate disclosure proposal.

Figure 3.6 Timeline of California's Climate Disclosure Bill

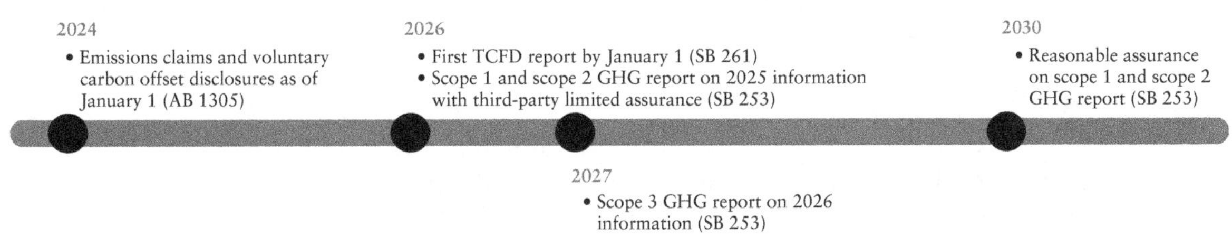

Australia

The Australian Accounting Standards Board (AASB) released draft Australian Sustainability Reporting Standards for consultation until 1 March 2024. The draft standards focus on climate-related disclosures and consider other Australian-specific modifications to the IFRS Sustainability Disclosure Standards IFRS S1 and IFRS S2. The Australian Government shared its proposed Sustainable Finance Strategy in late 2023. The objective of this strategy is to provide capital market stakeholders with more transparent, and comparable, insights into how sustainability and climate-related risks and opportunities affect a company's enterprise value.

In January 2024 the Australian Treasury released the Exposure Draft Treasury Laws Amendment Bill 2024: Climate-related Financial Disclosure (Exposure Draft legislation); it was passed in the second half of the year. The Australian Accounting Standards Board (AASB) met to approve the final Australian Sustainability Reporting Standards (ASRSs) on 20 September 2024. Reporting is mandatory for the first companies starting with 1 January 2025. On the audit and assurance side of sustainability reporting the Auditing and Assurance Standards Board (AUASB) approved on 28 January 2025 new assurance requirements for climate-related financial disclosure.

Asia

Selected examples from jurisdictions in Asia include Singapore and Japan:

- **Singapore:** Overall, while sustainability reporting in Singapore is currently voluntary, there is a growing momentum towards greater transparency and disclosure of ESG information among businesses. The Accounting and Corporate Regulatory Authority and Singapore Exchange Regulation launched a public consultation in July 2023 on recommendations that will require listed issuers to report ISSB-aligned, climate-related disclosures starting from financial year 2025, with large non-listed organizations to follow suit in financial year 2027.
- **Japan:** The Financial Services Agency publicized a press release issued by the IFRS Foundation Monitoring Board welcoming the finalization of the IFRS Sustainability Disclosure Standards. Japan has issued its draft sustainability disclosure standards, which are consistent with the ISSB's framework, on 31 March 2024, and plans to finalize these standards by 31 March 2025. These disclosure rules are expected to apply to all listed organizations in Japan.

Africa

The advancement of sustainability reporting in Africa is still in its early stages (Igwe *et al.*, 2023). Prior research has thus focused on developed countries, leaving the topic partly unexplored in relation to developing countries (Girón *et al.*, 2021). Some studies have, however, provided knowledge on sustainability reporting practices in Africa. One example is a study attending to sustainability reporting practices in Sub-Saharan African nations (Tilt *et al.*, 2021). These nations face major limitations despite the region‘s unique and substantial social and environmental challenges. The study showed that during the period 2014 to 2016, 483 organizations in Africa submitted reports to the GRI database, with 168 of these originating from Sub-Saharan African countries (Tilt *et al.*, 2021).

What is required and what is voluntary in sustainability reporting varies by country. Use Activity 3.5 and Activity 3.6 to develop your understanding of this fact.

ACTIVITY 3.5

Using a country of your choice, identify its requirements for sustainability reporting.

ACTIVITY 3.6

Identify the activities of the World Bank to support the advancement of sustainability reporting in developing economies.

INTERNATIONAL STANDARDS AND FRAMEWORKS

International standards on sustainability reporting play a crucial role in guiding organizations worldwide in disclosing their ESG performance. This section will provide a brief description of a few selected international reporting frameworks.

The ISSB

The ISSB, created under the auspices of the **IFRS Foundation** in 2021, represents a concerted effort to address the growing need for globally consistent and comparable sustainability-related financial disclosures.

It aims to meet the growing demand for consistent and comparable sustainability information that investors and other stakeholders need for decision-making. This initiative consolidates existing frameworks, notably those from the Climate Disclosure Standards Board (CDSB) and the Value Reporting Foundation (VRF), which includes the Integrated Reporting Framework and the Sustainability Accounting Standards Board (SASB) Standards. By harmonizing these various standards, the ISSB seeks to enhance the transparency, accountability and efficiency of global markets through improved sustainability reporting.

The ISSB was established in response to the fragmented voluntary sustainability reporting landscape. The proliferation of voluntary frameworks and standards was leading to inconsistencies and difficulties in comparing corporate performance. This lack of standardization was hampering investors' ability to assess the sustainability risks and opportunities embedded within companies' operations and value chains. Additionally, it created challenges for companies seeking to effectively communicate their sustainability efforts to a global audience (Baumüller and Leitner-Hanetseder, 2023).

The ISSB's primary objective is to develop a comprehensive set of globally accepted sustainability disclosure standards. These standards are intended to complement the existing IFRS Accounting Standards issued by the **International Accounting Standards Board (IASB)**, creating a unified reporting framework that addresses both financial and sustainability-related information. By promoting consistent disclosures, the ISSB aims to enhance transparency, comparability and, ultimately, investor confidence in sustainability information.

The introduction of ISSB Sustainability Disclosure Standards is expected to have far-reaching implications for companies and investors alike. For companies, it will likely necessitate a significant shift in reporting practices, requiring them to collect and disclose a broader range of sustainability-related data. This may entail investments in new systems, processes and expertise. However, it also presents an opportunity for companies to enhance their reputation, manage risks more effectively and attract capital from investors who prioritize sustainability considerations. The ISSB has to date released two standards: IFRS S1 and IFRS S2.

IFRS S1 *General Requirements for Disclosure of Sustainability-related Financial Information*

This standard sets out the overall requirements for an entity to disclose sustainability-related financial information. It aims to provide a comprehensive framework for consistent, comparable and reliable reporting across different sectors and regions, ensuring that investors receive pertinent information regarding the sustainability aspects that could impact financial performance and decision-making.

IFRS S2 *Climate-related Disclosures*

This standard focuses specifically on climate-related risks and opportunities. It incorporates recommendations from the TCFD and requires entities to disclose information about governance, strategy, risk management, and metrics and targets related to climate change. This standard aims to provide investors with detailed insights into how climate change affects an entity's financial position and performance as well as its strategy and resilience. Activity 3.7 requires you to analyse ways in which the ISSB can promote globally consistent sustainability reporting.

ACTIVITY 3.7

In what ways can the ISSB drive the adoption of consistent and comparable sustainability reporting standards globally?

The ISSB published its 2024–26 work plan in June 2024. Top priority was given to deepening strategic cooperations between itself and each of the Transition Plan Taskforce, GHG Protocol, CDP, TNFD and GRI. This could lead, among others, to improved interoperability guidelines. Also, the ISSB decided to initiate research projects on risks and opportunities associated with biodiversity, ecosystems and services, and human capital.

The ISSB aims to establish a 'global baseline' for sustainability reporting, that is it wants to provide a comprehensive set of standards that is based on a sound reporting methodology and enables jurisdictions to adopt the Sustainability Disclosure Standards as their own reporting requirements, or to build more extensive reporting requirements on their own provisions. To support those jurisdictions, the ISSB published a 'Jurisdictional Guide for the Adoption or Other Use of ISSB Standards'. Thus, the ISSB sees its standards as promoting global development for ever more comprehensive reporting requirements on sustainability matters. Example 3.5 provides some insights into the global adoption trend of the ISSB Sustainability Disclosure Standards.

Example 3.5

Global adoption of the IFRS Sustainability Disclosure Standards

A growing number of jurisdictions are moving ahead with or considering measures to ensure global comparability in companies' climate and other sustainability-related disclosures by relying on the global baseline established by the ISSB [Sustainability Disclosure] Standards.

More than 20 jurisdictions have already decided to use or are taking steps to introduce ISSB [Sustainability Disclosure] Standards in their legal or regulatory frameworks. Together, these jurisdictions account for:

- *nearly 55% of global GDP;*
- *more than 40% of global market capitalisation; and*
- *more than half of global greenhouse gas emissions.*

Source: IFRS (2024)

Mapping ISSB against ESRS

The CSRD requires the EFRAG to develop their draft standards as closely as possible in alignment with the pronouncement of international standards, most notably the IFRS Sustainability Disclosure Standards. Example 3.6 discusses how the CSRD emphasizes the quest for organizations to use, to the greatest extent possible, the main international sustainability reporting standards.

Example 3.6

The CSRD on interoperability

The development of mandatory common sustainability reporting standards is necessary to reach a situation in which sustainability information has a status comparable to that of financial information. The adoption of sustainability reporting standards by means of delegated acts would ensure harmonised sustainability reporting across the Union. Therefore, an undertaking would be compliant with the sustainability reporting requirements of Directive 2013/34/EU by reporting in accordance with the sustainability reporting standards. When defining such standards, it is essential to give due consideration, to the greatest extent possible, to the main sustainability reporting standards used worldwide, while not lowering the ambition of this amending Directive and delegated acts adopted pursuant thereto.

Source: EU (2022), recital 37

In May 2024, both the EFRAG and the ISSB published the results of their joint work: the 'ESRS–ISSB Standards Interoperability Guidance'. It contains a detailed comparison of IFRS S1 and IFRS S2 with the corresponding reporting requirements under ESRS. Most importantly, they lay out under what conditions an organization reporting under ESRS might also claim alignment with IFRS Sustainability Disclosure Standards, where options should be used to align harmonization and where remaining fields of divergence remain. Refer to Activity 3.8 to explore this publication further.

ACTIVITY 3.8

Review the **ESRS–ISSB Standards Interoperability Guidance**, especially the case of reporting on GHG emissions.

Source: IFRS (n.d.)

Global Reporting Initiative (GRI)

The GRI was founded in 1997 as a multi-stakeholder organization to develop sustainability reporting guidelines. As early as 2000 GRI released its first set of Sustainability Reporting Guidelines, later known as the GRI 2000 series. In 2013, GRI launched a comprehensive revision of its guidelines, resulting in the GRI Standards (currently in its latest iteration known as GRI Standards 2021) followed by recent revisions and the issuance of sector-specific standards. Figure 3.7 gives an insight into the structure of GRI Standards.

Today, GRI Standards serve as the foundation for sustainability reporting in numerous countries globally. More than 70% of the top 250 global companies either adhere to them or use them as a reference point (KPMG, 2022). Figure 3.7 explains the structure of the GRI Standards.

Figure 3.7 GRI Standards

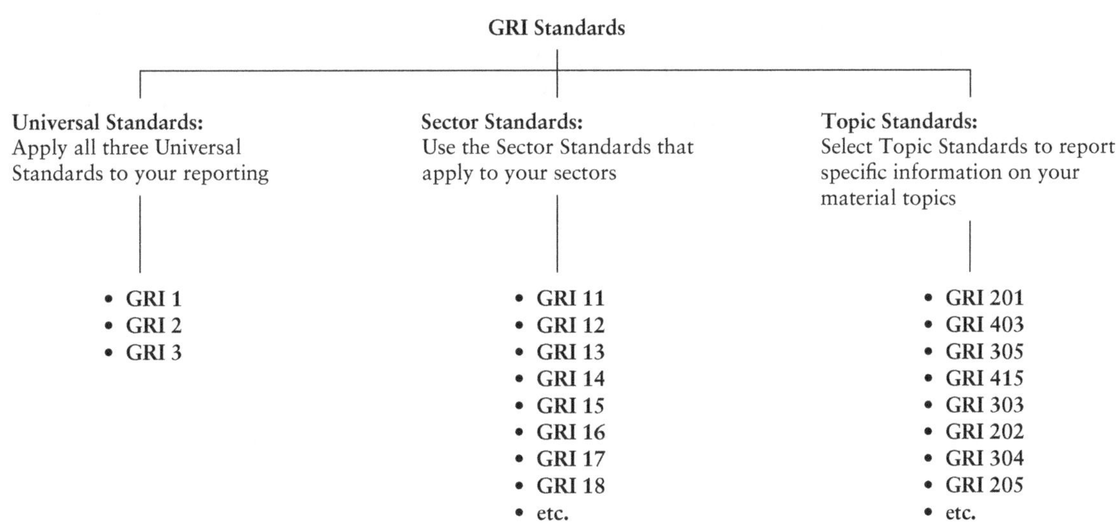

Source: GRI (2024a)

Mapping GRI against ESRS

EFRAG and GRI have acknowledged a high level of interoperability between the ESRS and GRI Standards in relation to impact reporting. In order to strengthen the transparency of such interoperability a [draft] index was prepared by EFRAG (refer to Table 3.5; EFRAG, 2023a).

Table 3.5 Interoperability index by EFRAG

	ESRS	GRI
Structure and topics	Consists of 12 topics categorized into four themes: general principles, environment, society and governance.	Consists of General Principles (GRI 1–3) and Environmental, Economic, and Social (200–400) themes (also refer to Figure 3.7).
Stakeholder engagement	Both standards require input or feedback on conclusions regarding significant impacts, risks and opportunities through dialogue with affected stakeholders (refer to Chapters 4 to 5 on materiality assessment for more in-depth coverage of stakeholder identification and engagement).	

GRI Standards often use 'should' or 'may' language, indicating recommendations. ESRS uses 'shall' language, indicating mandatory disclosure. Research studies are addressing the future role of GRI, in the light of sustainability reporting becoming mandatory in a number of jurisdictions (Pesci *et al.*, 2023). Examples of high-level differences between GRI and ESRS are highlighted in Table 3.6.

Table 3.6 Examples of high-level differences between GRI and ESRS

GRI	ESRS
GRI 1 Foundation	ESRS 1 General Requirements • ESRS sustainability reporting is more prescriptive than GRI Standards regarding the requirements for the reporting format. • ESRS require an organization to conduct a double materiality assessment, including the impact and financial perspectives, while GRI Standards are focused on impact materiality. • ESRS require the organization to use materiality on all levels, such as topics, sub-topics, sub-sub-topics, impacts and opportunities, while GRI Standards refer to materiality at a topic level.
GRI 302 Energy GRI 305 Emissions	ESRS E1 Climate Change • The differences between ESRS E1–5 and GRI 302–1, both dealing with data on energy consumption, lie in the way in which the energy consumption data is aggregated and disaggregated. • ESRS E1–5 requires the reporting of the intensity ratio for total Greenhouse Gas Emissions (GHG) involving Scopes 1, 2 and 3. • GRI 305–4 requires the reporting of the intensity ratio from Scope 1 and Scope 2 GHG emissions separately from Scope 3.
GRI 403 Occupational Health and Safety	ESRS S1 Own Workforce • GRI 403–1a requires the organization to report on the legal requirements and management system standards which its system relies on. • Such information is not required by the ESRS as this aspect is regulated by the EU.

Table 3.6 Examples of high-level differences between GRI and ESRS (Continued)

GRI 411 Rights of Indigenous Peoples	ESRS S3 Affected Communities • GRI 411–1 requires quantitative data on the number of incidents. • ESRS S3 requires narrative disclosures.
GRI 414 Supplier Social Assessment	ESRS G1 Business Conduct • While GRI 414–1 demands quantitative data on new supplier screening based on social criteria. • ESRS G1–2 demands a disclosure in narrative format.

Source: Sunhat (2023)

In closing it should be highlighted that EFRAG and GRI are working on a digital correspondence table to achieve digital interoperability for the ESRS and GRI Standards. Shared disclosures tagged under the **ESRS digital taxonomy** and the **GRI digital taxonomy** could be cross-referenced to allow for a streamlined digital reporting exercise on the preparer of sustainability reporting's side (EFRAG, 2023a).

Mapping GRI against IFRS Sustainability Disclosure Standards

Given the different strategic orientation of both sets of standards, interoperability is much harder to achieve between them. While the GRI Standards focus on impacts arising from the business activities of organizations, the ISSB develops standards that report on risks and opportunities that originate from sustainability matters on these organizations themselves.

However, outlining the possibilities and limits of interoperability between those two sets of standards are high priorities for both organizations behind the standards. Given their global importance, companies could decide to turn towards them for complementary guidance on more comprehensive business reporting. For that reason, the GRI and the ISSB published an interoperability guide focusing just on one core topic – reporting on GHG emissions – giving concrete guidance to companies that want to apply both. For the future, more work on other standards is expected.

Task Force on Climate-related Financial Disclosures (TCFD)

The TCFD was established in 2015 by the Financial Stability Board (FSB) to develop a set of voluntary, consistent, climate-related financial risk disclosures for use by companies, banks and investors in providing information to stakeholders. The TCFD's recommendations, published in 2017, aimed to improve and increase the reporting of climate-related financial information, thereby enhancing market transparency and stability. The framework focused on four key areas: governance, strategy, risk management, and metrics and targets. By providing a standardized approach to disclosing climate-related risks and opportunities, the TCFD sought to promote more informed investment, credit and insurance underwriting decisions, and to enable stakeholders to better understand the financial system‘s exposures to climate-related risks. Example 3.7 is an extract from practice to show how a TCFD statement by an organization might have been formulated.

Activity 3.9 allows you to consider how an organization can engage with investors in regard to climate strategy.

ACTIVITY 3.9

Unilever regularly engages with investors on its climate strategy. Is it apparent from its annual report how it engages with investors to shape the company‘s climate policies and actions? If yes, how does it achieve this?

What are the benefits and challenges of involving shareholders in climate strategy development?

Example 3.7

TCFD statement from Unilever's (2023) Annual Report

Task Force on Climate-related Financial Disclosures statement

The following statement, which Unilever believes is consistent with the Task Force on Climate-related Financial Disclosures (TCFD) Recommendations and Recommended Disclosures, details the risks and opportunities arising from climate change, the potential impact on our business and the actions we are taking to respond. We also integrate climate-related disclosures throughout this Annual Report and Accounts, including in our Climate Transition Action Plan (CTAP) Annual Progress Report on pages 43 to 47. A detailed breakdown of our emissions can be found on page 47. We have updated our CTAP, in advance of an advisory shareholder vote at our Annual General Meeting in May 2024. See our website for the latest CTAP.

Governance

The overall governance structure for managing Unilever's climate risks and opportunities is the same as for any of Unilever's other key risks and opportunities i.e. all of the following play a key role in governance: the Board, the Board subcommittees, ULE, ULE subcommittees, Business Group leadership teams, specialist management governance groups and specialist teams together with the support of relevant policies and procedures applied by everyone in the business (see page 88).

Whilst the Board takes overall accountability for the management of all risks and opportunities, including climate change (see page 70), our CEO is ultimately responsible for oversight of our climate change agenda. The Board delegates specific climate change matters to each of the Board subcommittees:

- The Corporate Responsibility Committee – oversees the development of Unilever's sustainability agenda (which includes climate matters), and the progress against that agenda, including performance against specific targets, whilst also reviewing sustainability-related risks, developments and opportunities (see page 114).
- The Audit Committee – oversees the non-financial disclosures in our Annual Report and Accounts, which includes climate-related disclosures. This includes reviewing the scope and results of any internal and external assurance activities obtained over the disclosures (see page 109).
- The Compensation Committee – supports the sustainability strategy which includes the climate strategy through alignment of Unilever's incentive plan to the sustainability agenda and ambitions (see page 128).
- The Nominating and Corporate Governance Committee – is responsible for ensuring that the composition of the Board provides sufficient skills and experience in sustainability matters including climate change to deliver on the sustainability agenda (see page 105).
- The Board is supported by the ULE and the Sustainability Advisory Council. The Council is made up of seven independent external specialists in social and environmental matters, and it convened in 2023 to guide and critique our strategy. The ULE discuss key strategic sustainability matters at least quarterly. During 2023, climate change matters were discussed at each meeting including progress against our climate-related Compass goals. The specific topics discussed included our GHG emissions measurement and setting a new baseline for our total emissions, GHG reduction plans for our Business Groups, and implications of the changes in the SBTi guidelines on setting new targets.

Additional ULE subcommittees are also in place to support our climate agenda and ULE decision-making, including:

- Business Operations Sustainability Steering Committee: Provides strategic guidance on implementation of our climate, nature and livelihoods goals within our extended supply chain. Chaired by our Chief Business Operations Officer, attended together with our Chief Sustainability Officer (CSO), Chief Procurement Officer and Head of Sustainable Business and Reporting.

- Climate and Nature Investment Committee: Evaluates and approves investment proposals and reviews progress against key milestones for the Climate & Nature Fund, our €1 billion commitment to fund disruptive transformations across our value chain. Chaired by our Chief Business Operations Officer together with our CSO, Chief R&D Officer, Head of Sustainable Business and Reporting, and our five Business Group Presidents.

Each Business Group has a sustainability lead to ensure that sustainability risks and opportunities are embedded into their strategies and performance is monitored.

We also have a specialist corporate team, the Global Sustainability Function, led by our CSO. This team supports the Business Group teams in developing their business strategies whilst also driving transformational change across markets through advocacy and partnerships.

In addition, included within the Supply Chain, R&D and Finance corporate functions, we have teams of experts who are focused on the sustainability agenda which includes climaterelated matters. Their activities include developing relevant policies and procedures, e.g. responsible sourcing and metric definitions (scope and calculation methodologies).

We regularly engage with our investors on a wide range of sustainability matters including our climate strategy. In 2021, we achieved shareholder support for our CTAP through an advisory vote at our AGM. During the fourth quarter of 2023, we commenced our engagement with investors on our updated CTAP. We engaged with more than 20 of our largest institutional investors and have used their feedback to help shape the updated CTAP.

Remuneration for management employees – up to and including the ULE – continues to be formally linked to performance against climate change goals. Their reward packages include fixed pay, a bonus as a percentage of fixed pay and eligibility to participate in a long-term Performance Share Plan (PSP).

The PSP is linked to financial and sustainability performance, guided by our Sustainability Progress Index (SPI), which accounts for 25% of the total PSP award. The SPI in 2023 was determined by considering performance against a number of sustainability goals – see page 136 for details.

See pages 136 to 137 for more on PSP including the role of the Board's Compensation Committee and Corporate Responsibility Committee in determining how the PSP operates, and the SPI outcome each year.

Source: Unilever (2023)

In 2024, the TCFD ceased operations and transferred its main tasks to the ISSB. The ISSB has fully integrated the TCFD recommendations into its framework.

Taskforce on Nature-related Financial Disclosures (TNFD)

The TNFD was established in 2021 to develop and deliver a risk management and disclosure framework for organizations to report and act on evolving nature-related risks. Drawing on similar principles to that of the TCFD, the TNFD aims to provide a standardized approach for assessing and disclosing nature-related risks and opportunities, which are increasingly recognized as critical to financial stability and business resilience.

The framework focuses on how organizations impact and depend on nature, encouraging the integration of nature-related considerations into corporate and financial decision-making processes. By enhancing transparency and accountability, the TNFD seeks to drive the allocation of capital towards more sustainable and **nature-positive outcomes**, ultimately contributing to the global efforts in **biodiversity conservation** and **ecosystem restoration**. Example 3.8 provides a practice illustration of how TNFD can be used by an organization.

Example 3.8

TNFD reporting. An extract from United Utilities' (2023) integrated report

In 2023, United Utilities, the UK's largest listed water company, published its Sustainability Report, emphasizing its dedication to addressing ESG concerns.

A noteworthy milestone in the report is United Utilities' pioneering adoption of the TNFD beta disclosure recommendations. This adoption positions United Utilities as one of the first UK public companies to report on nature-related financial risks and opportunities using the TNFD framework, complementing their existing TCFD reporting.

The report details how United Utilities integrates nature-related risks, opportunities, dependencies and impacts into its business strategy and planning. It outlines the company's progress and targets across four disclosure pillars: governance, strategy, risk and opportunity, and metrics and targets.

As the water sector comes under increasing scrutiny for its impacts on nature, United Utilities' adoption of the TNFD framework highlights its commitment to transparency and proactive management of nature-related risks and opportunities.

Nature-related metrics and targets

Managing nature-related risks and opportunities

Nature is fundamental to the sustainability of our business and so we monitor a wide variety of metrics and set targets to help monitor and assess nature-related risks and opportunities.

To measure our performance we demonstrate delivery against contributing targets from a number of statutory requirements, such as the condition of protected sites, biodiversity net gain, environmental performance, and supporting strategies. We were the only water company to set a natural capital outcome delivery incentive in our business plan for 2020–25. This is measured by demonstrating additional value created through ecosystem services for customers and the environment. We achieve this by implementing nature-based solutions where they offer best value compared against a hard-engineered solution.

We are a key contributor to the North West's first natural capital account developed in collaboration with many regional organisations. By considering this baseline value, we can benchmark the impact of future changes to our natural assets and quantify improvements. It is helping to understand how valuable the region's natural capital assets are. This year, we have updated our own natural capital account as part of a five-yearly review cycle.

Many of our targets in the short and medium term are regulatory performance commitments for 2020–25. We also have targets that go further, like our Better Rivers pledges and targets for monitoring and reducing storm overflow activations. We are in the process of preparing our business plan with targets for the 2025–30 period. Our long-term targets align with government expectations, such as achieving 75 per cent favourable condition for SSSI locations by 2042. We are committed to improving surface, groundwater and bathing water quality in the immediate term and beyond.

Progress this year

- Updated our corporate natural capital account so we can track and measure trends in our impact on nature.
- Developed our long-term environmental strategy.

Future focus

- Continue to engage with the Task Force to develop our nature-related disclosures, and work towards the global shared vision of 'living in harmony with nature by 2050'.
- Develop a strategy on how we will achieve the four 2030 biodiversity goals adopted by nations during COP15. By engaging in the TNFD process early we are already working towards achieving Target 15 to disclose on our interactions with nature.

Source: United Utilities (2023)

For aligning reporting requirements between ESRS and TNFD recommendations, an interoperability guidance document has been published. It shows a high degree of alignment and thus highlights ways forward for companies reporting under ESRS to also adopt the recommendations of the TNFD in their reports.

INTERPLAY BETWEEN INTERNATIONAL STANDARDS

The interplay between international standards and emerging national regulations highlights the evolving landscape of corporate sustainability reporting. Voluntary international standards have provided a framework that facilitates sustainability disclosures across borders. Bebbington and Larrinaga (2014) discuss the distinctions between harmonization and convergence in sustainability reporting. They define harmonization as the process of creating consistency and reducing differences between various reporting standards, while convergence refers to the gradual merging or alignment of different standards into a single, unified set of guidelines.

As national governments increasingly recognize the importance of sustainability, they are introducing their own regulations, which may align with, diverge from or build on these international standards. For instance, the CSRD integrates aspects of the GRI and TCFD, while also introducing specific regional requirements. This nationalization of sustainability reporting can create challenges for multinational corporations, as they must navigate both the global frameworks and the specific demands of the jurisdictions in which they operate.

The interaction between international standards and national regulations is thus a dynamic process, with potential synergies and conflicts. An example of a conflicting matter is that of the approach to materiality taken in the different frameworks (this is further discussed in Chapters 4 and 5). The concept of materiality is a fundamental, yet contentious aspect within the realm of sustainability standards, as its interpretation and application vary significantly across different frameworks. Materiality, in the context of sustainability reporting, refers to the threshold at which particular ESG issues are deemed sufficiently significant to warrant disclosure due to their potential impact on an organization's value, stakeholders or the broader environment.

However, the concept of materiality is not uniformly defined across all standards, leading to divergent practices and outcomes in sustainability reporting. For instance, the GRI adopts a broad, stakeholder-orientated approach to materiality. It encourages companies to consider a wide range of issues that could be significant from the perspective of any stakeholder group, not just those that have direct financial implications for the organization. This expansive view often results in the inclusion of a more comprehensive set of ESG issues in reports, which can enhance transparency but may also overwhelm users with information that is less directly relevant to financial performance.

In contrast, the IFRS Sustainability Disclosure Standards emphasize a narrower, investor-focused interpretation of materiality. These frameworks prioritize ESG issues that could affect an organization's financial performance or pose risks that investors would need to assess. This approach aligns more closely with traditional financial reporting practices but may exclude issues that while important to broader stakeholder groups, are not immediately linked to financial outcomes.

The differing interpretations of materiality across these voluntary standards create challenges for organizations attempting to navigate multiple frameworks. Companies may struggle to reconcile the broader stakeholder focus of frameworks like the GRI with the investor-centric approach that was embedded in the TCFD and then taken into the IFRS Sustainability Disclosure Standards, potentially leading to inconsistencies in disclosures. Furthermore, this divergence can complicate the comparability of sustainability reports across organizations, as the same issue might be considered material under one framework but immaterial under another.

This variability in the concept of materiality not only reflects the different objectives and audiences of each framework but also raises critical questions about the effectiveness of sustainability reporting in driving meaningful change. If materiality is interpreted too narrowly, there is a risk that significant ESG issues might be underreported or overlooked, thereby diminishing the value of sustainability disclosures for stakeholders beyond investors. Conversely, a broad interpretation might dilute the focus on financially significant ESG risks, potentially reducing the utility of reports for investors.

The varying definitions and applications of materiality across voluntary sustainability standards highlight the complex and sometimes conflicting goals of these frameworks. This inconsistency underscores the need for ongoing dialogue and convergence efforts to harmonize materiality criteria, ensuring that sustainability reporting serves the diverse needs of both investors and broader stakeholder groups.

In sum, while international standards aim to provide a universal baseline, national regulations can either reinforce these efforts by incorporating them into legal frameworks or introduce additional complexities through localized requirements. The ongoing convergence of these frameworks is crucial for reducing reporting burdens on companies, ensuring consistency in disclosures, and ultimately driving global progress towards sustainable development goals.

CONCLUSION

The global landscape for sustainability reporting is evolving rapidly as stakeholders increasingly recognize the importance of sustainability reporting and explicit ESG factors in business decision-making and risk assessment.

Efforts to harmonize and/or converge sustainability reporting standards at the international level have gained significant momentum in recent years, driven by the need for consistent, comparable and reliable ESG disclosures. The establishment of the ISSB by the IFRS Foundation in 2021 represents a pivotal step in this direction, aiming to develop a comprehensive global baseline for sustainability reporting (IFRS Foundation, 2021). This initiative seeks to unify disparate frameworks such as the GRI, the TCFD and others, by aligning their core principles and metrics. Such harmonization efforts are intended to address the fragmentation of standards that has previously led to inconsistencies in reporting practices and confusion among stakeholders (KPMG, 2022). Additionally, the EU's CSRD is integrating these global frameworks into its regulatory requirements, further reinforcing the move towards a common reporting language. However, achieving true harmonization remains challenging due to varying national priorities and the differing focuses of existing frameworks, which cater to diverse stakeholder needs (Eccles & Krzus, 2020). Despite these challenges, the ongoing dialogue and collaboration among standard-setting bodies, regulators and the private sector underscore the growing recognition of the importance of a unified approach to sustainability reporting. Table 3.7 provides an overview of important voluntary frameworks for sustainability reporting that exist around the world.

Table 3.7 Comparative overview of international voluntary frameworks for sustainability reporting

Organization/Standard	Short description	Area coverage and materiality principle
GRI	Established in 1997, the GRI Standards are among the most widely used frameworks for sustainability reporting worldwide. They provide comprehensive guidelines for reporting on a wide range of sustainability topics, including governance, environmental impacts, labour practices, human rights and community engagement.	E, S and G Impact materiality
TCFD	The TCFD Recommendations provide a framework for companies to disclose climate-related risks and opportunities in their financial filings. Recognizing the financial implications of climate change, the TCFD framework encourages companies to assess and disclose climate-related risks across four thematic areas: governance, strategy, risk management, and metrics and targets. By integrating climate-related disclosures into mainstream financial reporting, the TCFD framework helps investors and other stakeholders better understand the financial implications of climate change on companies' long-term value.	Climate Financial materiality
ISSB: IFRS S1 *General Requirements For Disclosure of Sustainability-related Financial Information* IFRS S2 *General Requirements For a Complete Set of Sustainability-related Financial Disclosures*	IFRS S1 is to be applied in conjunction with IFRS S2, which is a topic-based standard that specifies disclosures relating to climate.	Climate Financial materiality
TNFD	TNFD recommends that organizations use ISSB's definition of materiality.	Environmental reporting – biodiversity
GHG Protocol and materiality	Internationally accepted greenhouse gas (GHG) accounting and reporting standards for organizations. Materiality addressed from the perspective of verification. Materiality thresholds may also be outlined in the requirements of a specific GHG programme or determined by a national verification standard, depending on who is requiring the verification and for what reasons.	Climate – carbon reporting

It is important to highlight that CSRD has advanced documents that support the interoperability between sustainability reporting standards. You can glean insights into some of the collaborations that were in place in order to support such interoperability by looking at the GRI–ESRS Interoperability Index (EFRAG, 2023a).

Outlook: EU Omnibus and its consequences for sustainability reporting

As a result of the economic downturn in the European economy since 2020, political priorities have shifted. After her re-election as president of the European Commission in Summer 2024, Ursula von der Leyen announced a new political agenda: the **Clean Industrial Deal**. The agenda states that the competitiveness of European companies should be a core priority in the following years, without stepping back from the ambitions set forth by the Green Deal five years before. As part of this new agenda, a review and simplification of sustainability reporting rules in Europe was announced. On 26 February 2025, following the presentation of the EU Competitiveness Compass and finally the Clean Industrial Deal, the EU Commission's draft of a so-called Omnibus legislation was presented. As part of this draft regulation, the CSRD, the Taxonomy Regulation and the CSDDD shall be subjected to considerable changes.

1. The first-time application of the new reporting regime for companies required to report under the CSRD for the financial year 2025 or later is shifted back by two years (to 2027 or later). The first-time application of the CSDDD is also delayed by one year.
2. Major changes in the content of the CSRD, the Taxonomy Regulation and the CSDDD are proposed. Table 3.8 summarizes the most important of these proposals.

Table 3.8 Summary of the most important changes to the CSRD, the Taxonomy Regulation and the CSDDD following the draft EU Omnibus

CSRD	• Reporting obligation only for companies and groups with ≥1,000 employees • Limitation of data collection from business partners in the value chains – extended SME cap on value chain • Limited requirements with regard to digitization • Removal of intended step-up from limited assurance to reasonable assurance
Taxonomy Regulation	• Reporting obligation only for companies and groups with ≥1,000 employees and net turnover exceeding €450 million • Option to report on partial alignment of economic activities • Option to voluntarily report taxonomy alignment • (Also: separate delegated act to substantially cut the requirements of technical screening criteria)
CSDDD	• Specifications with regard to transition plans • Limitations with regard to stakeholders that have to be considered • Only 'tier 1' business partners in the value chain must be monitored • Continuous assessments required only every 5 years • Removal of the specific, EU-wide liability regime • Introduction of more flexible requirements with regard to fines

In a separate legislative act, substantial simplification of the Carbon Border Adjustment Mechanism (CBAM) is also proposed, especially with regard to the number of companies having to apply this mechanism. It must be noted that this Omnibus legislation is only a proposal at time of writing and has to undergo the trilogue process. Further changes are likely. The final version of the legislation will thus take a considerable amount of time to be finished. In addition, the EU Commissions will mandate EFRAG to rework the current version of the ESRS. The results of this work are to be expected by the end of 2025. The EU Commission plans to 'deliver swiftly on the simplification and streamlining of the ESRS' (within six months).

> *The revision of the delegated act will substantially reduce the number of mandatory ESRS datapoints by (i) removing those deemed least important for general purpose sustainability reporting, (ii) prioritising quantitative datapoints over narrative text and (iii) further distinguishing between mandatory and voluntary datapoints, without undermining interoperability with global reporting standards and without prejudice to the materiality assessment of each undertaking.* (European Commission, 2025, p. 6)

It is currently not clear to what extent this would change the ESRS in their current format. However, substantial changes could be possible. To further decrease the reporting burden, the EU Commission also announced that it will not adopt sector standards, and the development of ESRS for LSMEs shall be removed from the agenda. In turn, the ESRS VSME shall be modified and adopted in a separate legal act.

SUMMARY

The following items relate to the learning objectives listed at the beginning of the chapter.

- **LO 1. Understand and discuss the global political agreements behind the evolution of sustainability reporting (for example, the Paris Agreement and Agenda 2030).**

  The 2030 Agenda, known as the Sustainable Development Goals (SDGs), is a comprehensive framework established by United Nation member states in 2015 to tackle global challenges and foster sustainable progress across economic, social and environmental spheres. In the same year, with growing concerns over the intensifying impacts of climate change, representatives from nearly 200 countries convened in Paris for the United Nations Climate Change Conference (COP21). Amid a sense of urgency and international cooperation, these nations reached an agreement, the Paris Agreement, a global commitment to combat climate change and promote a sustainable future. This Agreement symbolizes a collective pledge to take ambitious, coordinated action to reduce greenhouse gas emissions and adapt to climate impacts. Together, the SDGs and the Paris Agreement have driven the push to enhance sustainability reporting among organizations worldwide.

- **LO 2. Understand and explain the role of the EU, the US SEC and other regional or national regulators in mandating sustainability disclosures.**

  The summary for LO2 focuses on the EU and the US, both of which have mandated sustainability disclosures. The EU Sustainable Finance Package is an extensive legislative initiative designed to promote sustainable finance by embedding ESG considerations into the financial system. Its goals include mobilizing private capital for sustainable investments, increasing transparency and disclosure of ESG risks and opportunities, and supporting the transition to a low-carbon, resilient economy. Key components of the package include the CSRD, Taxonomy Regulation, SFDR and the Green Bond Standard. In the US, in March 2024, the Securities and Exchange Commission (SEC) adopted new rules to enhance and standardize climate-related disclosures by public companies and in public offerings. These rules underscore the SEC's commitment to providing investors with consistent, comparable and reliable information on the financial impact of climate-related risks on companies' operations, while balancing the need to manage compliance costs effectively.

- **LO 3. Understand the structure of sustainability reporting regulations in the EU.**

  The EU Sustainable Finance Package represents a robust suite of legislative measures designed to foster sustainable finance by integrating ESG factors into the financial framework. This package mobilizes private capital towards sustainable investments, boosts transparency and strengthens ESG risk and opportunity disclosures. Key elements include the CSRD, Taxonomy Regulation, SFDR and the Green Bond Standard, which are all geared towards guiding the EU's transition to a resilient, low-carbon economy.
- **LO 4. Describe extant international voluntary standards (for example, GRI, TNFD, etc.) for sustainability accounting and reporting.**

  International standards for sustainability reporting are essential in guiding organizations globally to disclose their ESG performance. Key frameworks include the ISSB, GRI, GHG Protocol, TNFD and the SDGs. In 2023, the IFRS Foundation's ISSB released two standards, collectively known as the IFRS Sustainability Disclosure Standards (IFRS SDS). The GRI Standards are widely used as a foundation for voluntary sustainability reporting across numerous countries. Established in 2021, the TNFD aims to create a risk management and disclosure framework to help organizations report and address nature-related risks. The TCFD's recommendations focused on enhancing climate-related financial disclosures. As of 2024, the TCFD has ceased operations, transferring its primary responsibilities to the ISSB, which has fully integrated TCFD recommendations into its framework.
- **LO 5. Discuss the interplay between international standards, such as GRI, TNFD, IFRS Sustainability Disclosure Standards, with emerging national regulations.**

  The interplay between international standards with emerging national regulations, highlights the evolving landscape of corporate sustainability reporting. Voluntary international standards have provided a framework that facilitates sustainability disclosures across borders. International standards aim to provide a universal baseline, and national regulations can either reinforce these efforts by incorporating them into legal frameworks or introduce additional complexities through localized requirements. The ongoing convergence of these frameworks is crucial for reducing reporting burdens on companies, ensuring consistency in disclosures, and ultimately driving global progress towards sustainable development goals.
- **LO 6. Discuss efforts aimed at international harmonization of sustainability reporting standards.**

  The interaction between international standards, alongside new national regulations, underscores the dynamic nature of corporate sustainability reporting. Voluntary international standards have created a cross-border foundation for sustainability disclosures, aiming to set a universal baseline. National regulations may either support these standards by embedding them in legal requirements or add complexity with unique local mandates. The continued alignment of these frameworks is essential for easing reporting demands on companies, promoting consistency in disclosures and advancing global sustainable development goals.

EXERCISES

1. Explain the global political agreements behind the evolution of sustainability reporting. (LO 1)
2. Describe the requirements for mandatory sustainability reporting in selected countries of your choice. (LO 2)
3. Research the role of the EU Corporate Sustainability Reporting Directive (CSRD) within the EU Green Deal. (LO 3)
4. Compare and contrast two or more voluntary sustainability reporting standards. (LO 4 and 5)
5. Discuss the potential synergies and opportunities for harmonization among different sustainability reporting standards/frameworks to enhance consistency and comparability of sustainability disclosures. (LO 6)
6. What could be some challenges for the ISSB in harmonizing existing sustainability disclosure practices (such as GRI, ESRS and TNFD) across different regions with varying regulatory environments and stakeholder expectations? (LO 5 and 6)
7. Research the following:
   - What is the EU Sustainability Omnibus proposal (2025)? (Write 3–5 bullet points.)
   - What is the EU Clean Industrial Deal (Write 3–5 bullet points.) (LO 3)

Appendix 3.1 – What is a small and non-complex institution?

It is an institution that:

(i) is not a large institution as defined in Article 4(1)(146) Regulation (EU) No 575/2013;
(ii) the total value of its assets is on average equal to or less than €5 billion over the four-year period immediately preceding the current annual reporting period;
(iii) is not subject to any obligations in relation to recovery and resolution planning;
(iv) has a trading book business that is classified as small;
(v) the total value of derivative positions held with trading intent does not exceed 2% of its total on- and off-balance sheet assets and the total value of its overall derivative positions does not exceed 5%;
(vi) more than 75% of both the institution's consolidated total assets and liabilities relate to activities with counterparties located in the EU;
(vii) does not use internal models to meet the prudential requirements;
(viii) has not communicated to the competent authority an objection to being classified as a small and non-complex institution; and
(ix) the competent authority has not decided is not to be considered a small and non-complex institution (Article 4(1)(145) Regulation (EU) No 575/2013).

Source: EU (2024a)

PART TWO

Topic-specific standards for sustainability reporting

Part Two of this book delves into the topic-specific European Sustainability Reporting Standards (ESRS), offering an in-depth exploration of specific standards, from ESRS E1–E4 to S1–S4 and G1. The primary objective of this Part is to equip readers with a thorough understanding of the disclosure requirements associated with each topic-specific ESRS. These requirements are designed to ensure that organizations provide comprehensive and accurate information on their sustainability impacts, dependencies and performance across ESG dimensions. By the end of this Part, readers will not only grasp the technicalities of the reporting standards but also appreciate their practical implications for business strategy and decision-making.

Each chapter addresses the financial effects on organizations arising from sustainability-related risks and opportunities. The chapters will guide readers in analysing how these risks and opportunities influence an undertaking's operations and performance over the short, medium and long term. The discussion will emphasize the interconnected nature of sustainability impacts and dependencies, highlighting how they shape an organization's resilience, competitiveness and value creation in a rapidly evolving economic and regulatory landscape. By navigating through the disclosure requirements in each of the ESRSs the aim is to provide readers with the tools to critically evaluate and apply the ESRS in practice.

CHAPTER 4
Foundations of sustainability reporting: Cross-cutting standards

Learning objectives

After studying this chapter you should be able to:

- LO 1. Explain and discuss the general importance of cross-cutting general requirements for sustainability reporting.
- LO 2. Discuss the meaning of materiality and double materiality in CSRD and ESRS.
- LO 3. Discuss the role of the value chain in CSRD and ESRS.
- LO 4. Explain the importance of defining reporting boundaries for sustainability reporting.
- LO 5. Explain the relevant formal requirements for sustainability reports under ESRS.
- LO 6. Discuss the importance of transitional provisions under ESRS.
- LO 7. Discuss how the general disclosures under ESRS 2 relate to the concepts in ESRS 1 and the specific disclosure under topical standards.

Why is the Commission adopting European Sustainability Reporting Standards (ESRS)?

EU law requires all large companies and all listed companies (except listed micro-enterprises) to disclose information on what they see as the risks and opportunities arising from social and environmental issues, and on the impact of their activities on people and the environment. This helps investors, civil society organisations, consumers and other stakeholders to evaluate the sustainability performance of companies, as part of the European Green Deal. Nonetheless, there is ample evidence that the sustainability information that companies currently report is not sufficient. They often omit information that investors and other stakeholders think is important. Reported information can be hard to compare from company to company, and users of the information, such as investors, are often unsure whether they can trust it.

Problems in the quality of sustainability reporting have knock-on effects. It means that investors lack a reliable overview of sustainability-related risks to which companies are exposed. Investors increasingly should be made aware about the impact of companies on people and the environment and their plans to reduce such impacts in the future. This knowledge will help them to meet their own disclosure requirements under the Sustainable Finance Disclosure Regulation (SFDR). More generally, if the market for green investments is to be credible, investors need to know about the sustainability impact of the companies in which they invest. Without such information, money cannot be channelled towards environmentally friendly activities. [...] The European Sustainability Reporting Standards (ESRS) will be mandatory for use by companies that are obliged by the Accounting Directive to report certain sustainability information. By requiring the use of common standards, the Accounting Directive, as amended by the CSRD in 2022, aims to ensure that companies across the EU report comparable and reliable sustainability information.

Source: European Commission (2023a)

INTRODUCTION

ESRS 1 General requirements and ESRS 2 General disclosures play a foundational role within the suite of European Sustainability Reporting Standards (ESRS). Unlike the other ESRS which focus on specific topics (for example, climate, biodiversity, human rights), ESRS 1 and 2 are cross-cutting. This means they apply to all organizations subject to the Corporate Sustainability Reporting Directive (CSRD), regardless of their industry or the specific sustainability issues they face. Furthermore, the requirements of these standards are not subject to **materiality assessment**.

ESRS 1 does not contain any explicit reporting requirements. It gives definitions, explains concepts and elaborates on specific core procedures required for sustainability reporting under ESRS. Thus, it may be considered the 'theory standard' under ESRS.

ESRS 2, in contrast, contains reporting requirements. These are considered to be of a very fundamental nature: they address aspects that are important for understanding the context of the report and thus to interpret all subsequent information from the topical standards. Furthermore, ESRS 2 interacts with the reporting requirements of topical standards in several ways (for example, via 'minimum disclosure requirements') that are very important to understand.

ESRS 1 GENERAL REQUIREMENTS

The objective of ESRS 1 is to provide an understanding of the structure of ESRS, fundamental concepts and the overall requirements for compiling and presenting sustainability information in alignment with the CSRD. The concepts and principles defined in ESRS 1 underpin the entire reporting process and thus guides organizations in how to approach, structure and disclose their sustainability information.

The primary purpose of ESRS 1 is to establish a common language and set of expectations for sustainability reporting across all sectors and industries. The scope of ESRS 1 is far-reaching. It applies to all organizations subject to the CSRD, requiring them to consider and integrate these general requirements into their reporting practices. This standardization is crucial for fostering a level playing field and enabling stakeholders to make informed decisions based on reliable and comparable information.

ESRS 1 consists of ten chapters and several appendices. The core topics throughout all parts of the standard are:

- structure of ESRS
- qualitative characteristics of sustainability information
- materiality and sustainability due diligence
- reporting boundaries
- formal requirements for sustainability reports
- transitional provisions.

Structure of ESRS

The 'grammar' of each ESRS (with the exception of ESRS 1) are 'disclosure requirements' and 'data points'. Disclosure requirements are highlighted in each standard and numbered: 'ESRS S1–3' means the third disclosure requirement of the standard ESRS 1. Currently, the ESRS comprises 82 of these disclosure requirements:

- 12 general disclosure requirements from ESRS 2
- 32 disclosure requirements from environmental standards
- 32 disclosure requirements from social standards
- 5 governance-related disclosure requirements.

Every disclosure requirement consists of data points. These data points are not separately flagged in the ESRS; however, EFRAG IG 3 gives a list of all data points identified under ESRS. Example 4.1 provides insights and references to materials developed by EFRAG to support organizations with the implementation of the ESRS. Note that in December 2024, EFRAG published a corrigendum to this implementation guidance.

Example 4.1

Implementation guidance and FAQ

To support organizations with the implementation of the ESRS, the EU Commission tasked EFRAG with developing further supportive materials. As a consequence, two types of these materials are being developed:

- Implementation guidance, which covers specific questions of fundamental importance in depth. These are referred to as EFRAG IG. Currently, there are three IGs: IG 1 on materiality assessment, IG 2 on value chain and IG 3 on data points. More IGs are under development.
- FAQ: For questions addressed by organizations or a broader public directly to EFRAG; however, the scope of these questions is too narrow to merit the development of IGs. FAQs are published on a regular basis by EFRAG. Each question is numbered with an 'ID'.

You should note that these supportive materials are not laws and thus are not binding. They are just interpretations by EFRAG – and some of these materials are inconsistent with the ESRS themselves. However, in any case, they provide further reasonings and help with understanding some of the most complex concepts or application questions. Furthermore, regulators such as ESMA refer to these materials for their enforcement activities.

EFRAG IG 3 identifies more than 1,000 data points. However, there are optional and alternative disclosure requirements as well. Furthermore, some data points are tables, meaning that the actual amount of information that has to be collected by organizations may be much higher. Estimations go up to 4,000 different pieces of information. However, most data points are subject to materiality assessment, which means that not all will be applicable for all companies. Example 4.2 provides an excerpt from ESRS S1 to illustrate how disclosure requirements and data points are linked.

Example 4.2

Disclosure requirements and data points

The following excerpt from ESRS S1 illustrates how these two elements are linked.

Disclosure requirement

↓

Disclosure Requirement S1-8 – Collective bargaining coverage and social dialogue

58. **The undertaking shall disclose information on the extent to which the working conditions and terms of employment of its employees are determined or influenced by collective bargaining agreements and on the extent to which its employees are represented in social dialogue in the European Economic Area (EEA) at the establishment and European level.**
59. The objective of this Disclosure Requirement is to enable an understanding of the coverage of ***collective bargaining*** agreements and ***social dialogue*** for the undertaking's own ***employees***.

Data point

↓

60. The undertaking shall disclose:
    (a) the percentage of its total ***employees*** covered by ***collective bargaining*** agreements;
    (b) in the EEA, whether it has one or more collective ***bargaining agreements*** and, if so, the overall percentage of its ***employees*** covered by such agreement(s) for each country in which it has significant employment, defined as at least 50 employees by head count representing at least 10% of its total number of employees; and
    (c) outside the EEA, the percentage of its own employees covered by collective bargaining agreements by region.

Extending Example 4.2, Activity 4.1 allows you to gain hands-on experience with being able to locate specific ESRS data points.

ACTIVITY 4.1

Identifying reporting areas

Go to ESRS E1 and search for disclosure requirement E1–2. Then, open the Excel documentation for EFRA IG 3. How many data points does ESRS E1–2 comprise?

Information that has to be reported – if material – is indicated by the formulation 'shall disclose'. Mere recommendations, in contrast, use 'may disclose'. Also, formulations like 'shall consider' means that specific methodologies have to be employed in order to meet the requirements of a data point. Activity 4.2 asks you to identify mandatory and voluntary disclosure requirements in ESRS E1.

ACTIVITY 4.2

Mandatory and voluntary information

Go to ESRS E1 and identify two examples each for mandatory and voluntary disclosures.

ESRS 1 distinguishes four 'reporting areas' (refer to Table 4.1). They represent different sections of a standard which cluster disclosure requirements. The ESRS have adopted the structure initially developed by the TCFD; the IFRS Sustainability Disclosure Standards from the ISSB also share the same structure.

Table 4.1 ESRS 1 reporting areas

Reporting area	**Explanation** (adapted from ESRS 1.12)
Governance: 'GOV'	The governance processes, controls and procedures used to monitor, manage and oversee impacts, risks and opportunities.
Strategy (and Business Model): 'SBM'	How the organization's strategy and business model interact with its material impacts, risks and opportunities, including how the undertaking addresses those impacts, risks and opportunities.
Impacts, risks and opportunities management: 'IRO'	The process(es) by which the organization: • identifies impacts, risks and opportunities and assesses their materiality, • manages material sustainability matters through policies and actions.
Metrics and Targets: 'MT'	The organization's performance, including targets it has set and progress towards meeting them.

Furthermore, there is a second layer of classification for disclosure requirements. This one is not obviously flagged in the ESRS; nevertheless, typically it is quite obvious from the name of the disclosure requirement or from the explanations under which of the following categories it falls. In order to meet many of the requirements of ESRS, it is important to link disclosure requirements to this second layer as well (refer to Table 4.2).

Table 4.2 ESRS 1 secondary reporting areas

'Secondary reporting area'	**Explanation** (adapted from the glossary of terms)
Policies	A set or framework of general objectives and management principles that the organization uses for decision-making. A policy implements the organization's strategy or management decisions related to a material sustainability matter. Each policy is under the responsibility of defined person(s), specifies its perimeter of application and includes one or more objectives (linked when applicable to measurable targets). A policy is validated and reviewed following the organization's applicable governance rules. A policy is implemented through actions or action plans.
Actions	Actions refer to: • actions and action plans (including transition plans) that are undertaken to ensure that the organization delivers against targets set and through which the organization seeks to address material impacts, risks and opportunities • decisions to support these with financial, human or technological resources.
Metrics	Qualitative and quantitative indicators that the organization uses to measure and report on the effectiveness of the delivery of its sustainability-related policies and against its targets over time. Metrics also support the measurement of the organization's results in respect of affected people, the environment and the organization.
Targets	Measurable, outcome-oriented and time-bound goals that the organization aims to achieve in relation to material impacts, risks or opportunities. They may be set voluntarily by the organization or derive from legal requirements on the organization.

Activity 4.3 asks you to identify disclosure requirements in ESRS E1 to familiarize yourself with reading and working with the ESRS.

ACTIVITY 4.3

Identifying reporting areas

Go to ESRS E1 and look out for disclosure requirement E1–2. Under which reporting area does it fall? Furthermore, do you consider it a policy, an action, a metric or a target?

Each ESRS includes one or several appendices. The first appendix is always called 'application requirements' (AR); it is binding to the same extent as the main body of the standard. The ARs refer to specific sections of the main text and provide further elaboration. It is important to know that sometimes reporting or other requirements that must be considered are not found in the main body of an ESRS but in the appendix. Thus, it is necessary to read the related parts carefully together.

The other appendices can be binding or just illustrative. This information is always given at the beginning of the respective appendix. Example 4.3 shows an extract of the appendices to ESRS. These appendices are very helpful in providing illustrations to organizations that implement CSRD and ESRS.

Example 4.3

ESRS Appendices

ESRS 1 contains several appendices that are non-binding and should just act as illustrations. One such appendix is Appendix F:

Appendix F – Example of structure of ESRS sustainability statement

This appendix complements ESRS 1. It provides a non-binding illustration of the structure of the ***sustainability statement*** outlined in section 8.2 of this Standard. In this illustration, the undertaking has concluded that biodiversity and ecosystems, pollution, and affected communities, are not material.

The ESRS are accompanied by a glossary of terms. It contains definitions that are used in the standards and that are important for a proper understanding of a disclosure requirement. Whenever a word or phrase is written in bold and italic in an ESRS, it means that it can be found in this glossary.

Qualitative characteristics of sustainability information

Appendix B of ESRS 1 contains **qualitative characteristics of sustainability information**. These are abstract requirements that should guide organizations when preparing their sustainability reports.

These qualitative characteristics are built on the corresponding qualitative characteristics as defined by the International Financial Reporting Standards (IFRS Accounting Standards). Also, for sustainability reporting, the GRI Standards refer to similar characteristics. Organizations need to refer to these characteristics if they have to interpret how to apply a requirement of the ESRS in practice. Many of these characteristics are also directly referred to in various reporting requirements.

The ESRS set forth the main guiding principles for preparers of sustainability reports in terms of decision usefulness. Decision usefulness depends on the **relevance** of information given as well as whether the information is being faithfully represented (refer to Figure 4.1). These concepts are defined in Appendix B and augmented by further supportive principles.

Figure 4.1 Elements and hierarchy of qualitative characteristics of sustainability information according to ESRS

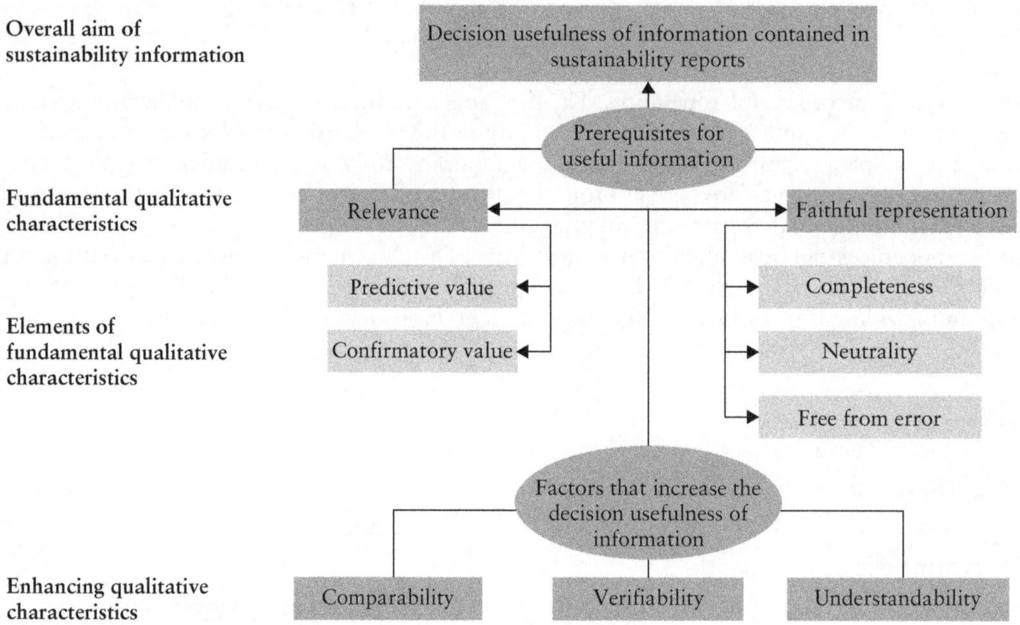

Source: Baumüller *et al.* (2024)

Materiality and sustainability due diligence

The principle of materiality is the cornerstone of sustainability reporting under ESRS. Most of the disclosure requirements set out in the ESRS are only mandatory if they relate to material sustainability matters. So, for the most part, the content of any sustainability report based on ESRS depends on the results of a so-called materiality analysis that has to be conducted before the report is prepared.

The CSRD defines materiality in European sustainability reporting as being based on the concept of 'double materiality'. The ESRS provide further explanations on how to interpret and utilize this concept. This concept has become a core feature of ESRS that distinguishes their reporting requirements from the corresponding provisions of such standards as the IFRS Sustainability Disclosure Standards or the GRI Standards that mandate different concepts of materiality.

The provisions in ESRS 1 on double materiality build on the following definition:

> *Double materiality has two dimensions: impact materiality and financial materiality. A sustainability matter meets the criterion of double materiality if it is material from the impact perspective or the financial perspective or both.*

Double materiality means that two analyses have to be performed: one on the materiality of impacts and one on the materiality of risks and opportunities:

- **Impact materiality** refers to the impact an organization has on people and the environment. This is often referred to as the 'inside-out' perspective of sustainability reporting.
- Financial materiality refers to the financial impacts that sustainability matters might have on the organization. From this perspective, sustainability matters are related to material risks and opportunities; it is also referred to as the 'outside-in' perspective.

Both perspectives are often linked to each other, for example risks and opportunities for an organization may appear as a consequence of material impacts.

Figures 4.2 and 4.3 visualize the scope of sustainability matters that fall under the definition of double materiality under ESRS.

Figure 4.2 Double materiality under ESRS: Information content

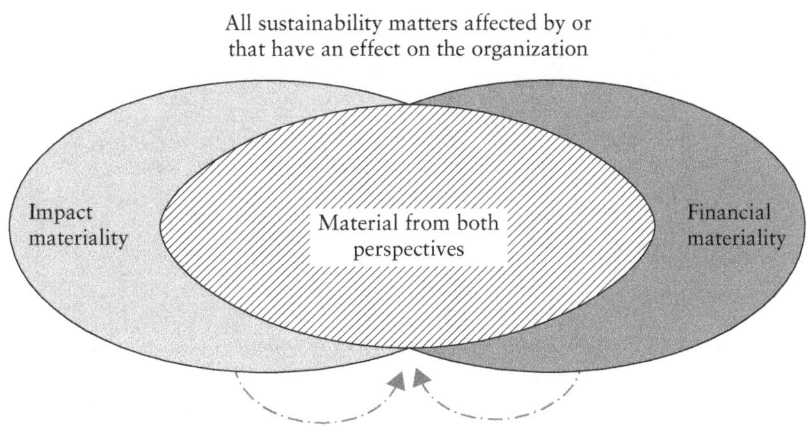

Source: EFRAG, IG (2024b), recital 35

Sustainability matters are defined as matters that are related to either environmental, social or governance matters. To further provide guidance to organizations, but also to ensure completeness and comparability of materiality analyses, Appendix A of ESRS 1 contains a list of minimum sustainability matters an organization has to assess. They are structured into topics, sub-topics and sub-sub-topics. Organizations reporting under ESRS have to consider matters on all three levels and arrive at a conclusion as to whether they are material. A sustainability matter is material if it is associated with at least one material impact, one material risk or one material opportunity. However, the list in Appendix A is non-exhaustive. So, other sustainability matters that might be material for the organization also have to be identified and considered.

Materiality analysis is deeply embedded into the process of sustainability due diligence. ESRS 1 discusses this in Chapter 5. It makes clear that ESRS cannot mandate organizations to establish such a process. However, sustainability due diligence informs organizations for their social and **environmental impact assessment**. Also, ESRS 2 requires them to report on their sustainability due diligence process. For that reason, there is high factual pressure on organizations to establish such processes to give further substance to their sustainability report; something that is important as well with regard to the external assurance requirements set forth by the CSRD.

Figure 4.3 Double materiality under ESRS: Inside-out and outside-in explained

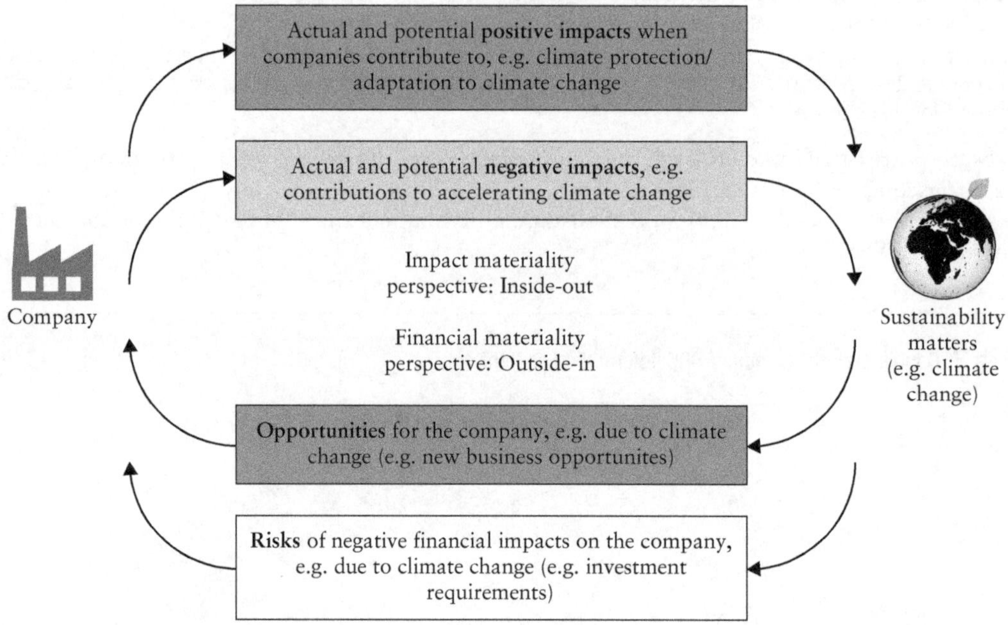

Source: Based on Baumüller *et al.* (2024)

Sustainability due diligence in the context of materiality analysis means that organizations should engage constantly with their stakeholders. They should use this information to assess their impacts and react accordingly. Most importantly, negative impact should be avoided, minimized or remediated. Materiality analysis should not be a one-off exercise in order to be able to prepare a sustainability report. It is just the snapshot of a set of activities organizations are engaged in during the entire year. The relevant assessments, and more importantly the necessary engagements, should be embedded in all relevant processes and systems of an organization.

Because of this, stakeholders are at the core of both materiality analysis and sustainability due diligence. Organizations have to identify their relevant stakeholders and engage with them actively. By understanding their interests and how these are affected, an organization gains a deeper understanding of the nature and severity of its impacts – but also on how it depends on these stakeholders.

The glossary of terms in ESRS 1 gives the following definition of 'stakeholder'. It also distinguishes two main groups of stakeholders that must be separated.

Those who can affect or be affected by the undertaking. There are two main groups of stakeholders:

i. Affected stakeholders: individuals or groups whose interests are affected or could be affected – positively or negatively – by the undertaking's activities and its direct and indirect business relationships across its value chain; and

ii. Users of sustainability statements: primary users of general purpose financial reporting (existing and potential investors, lenders and other creditors including asset managers, credit institutions, insurance undertakings), as well as other users, including the undertaking's business partners, trade unions and social partners, civil society and non-governmental organisations, governments, analysts and academics.

Some, but not all, stakeholders may belong to the two groups.

Engaging with those two groups of stakeholders through all steps of materiality analysis is mandatory under ESRS. But from the perspective of sustainability due diligence, this engagement should be conducted on an institutionalized basis throughout the entire year. Further explanation on how to apply the principle of double materiality under ESRS reporting is given in Chapter 5.

ESRS 1 distinguishes a second type of materiality that is equally important: information materiality. Once an organization has identified its material sustainability matters, it has to decide which information to include about these matters in its sustainability report. To assist, Appendix E of ESRS 1 contains a useful flow chart that sums up the related requirements of the standard.

If a sustainability matter is material, an organization has to refer to the respective ESRS that covers this matter. Then, in the next step, the distinction between policies, actions, metrics and targets becomes important:

- Organizations always have to report on policies, actions and targets related to a material sustainability matter. However, the ESRS do not oblige organizations to establish such policies, pursue actions or set targets. If this is not the case, they have to disclose the fact and meet the reporting requirement as well – which is called 'omissions'. Otherwise, they have to make their disclosures based on the requirements of the standards.
- Metrics, in turn, only have to be reported if their information is material to the users of sustainability reports. And even if this is the case, then data points of a metric might be omitted. This flexibility is necessary as many of the topical ESRS cover a wide range of sustainability matters and metrics – but not every metric is suitable to depict a given sustainability matter.

Information materiality is deeply linked to the concept of decision usefulness as set out by the qualitative characteristics of sustainability information (Appendix B of ESRS 1), and mostly concern the characteristic of 'relevance'. This requires companies to obtain an understanding of the information needs of their stakeholders who are 'users of sustainability reports'. ESRS 1.31(a) also mentions a second consideration: 'the significance of the information in relation to the matter it purports to depict or explain'; however, the ESRS do not give any further advice on how to interpret this perspective. So, most likely, there will be little distinction between this perspective, which might be referred to as 'accountability' and 'relevance' as elaborated more clearly in ESRS 1. As part of its FAQ, EFRAG published a mapping table that links the list of sustainability matters (ESRS 1. AR 16) to the relevant disclosure requirements in the topical ESRS (ID 177). This should give organizations reporting under ESRS more guidance on how to properly apply the principle of information materiality.

When an organization identifies a material matter which is not covered by an ESRS, it has to disclose entity-specific information. This requirement should prevent organizations from following a 'box-ticking approach' towards their sustainability reporting. Especially while only a limited number of ESRS are available to organizations, analysing and disclosing entity-specific information is considered to be very important. ESRS 1.AR 1–5 contain further guidance on how to identify and disclose such information. Activity 4.4 allows you to consider a practical example of an organization's **entity-specific disclosures**.

ACTIVITY 4.4

Look up the Annual Report 2023 of Ørsted. Did the organization make any entity-specific disclosures? If yes, what are these disclosures and where are they located?

Reporting boundaries

The definition of **reporting boundaries** deals with the question of which parts of an organization to cover in a report. For sustainability reporting, ESRS 1 sets forth a basic rule. Reporting boundaries for sustainability reports shall be the same as for corresponding financial reports. There are, however, some very important deviations from this basic rule.

For non-consolidated sustainability reports, the reporting boundaries follow the ones from the respective financial statement, that is, typically, the organization itself is reflected with all attributable impacts, risks and opportunities in the sustainability report.

For consolidated sustainability reports, the reporting boundaries comprise the scope of consolidation from the consolidated financial statements. However, joint ventures and associated companies are not included, that is only subsidiaries and joint arrangements (IFRS 11) shall be considered. Example 4.4 provides an extract of how an organization explains the boundaries of its reporting scope.

Example 4.4

SGL Group

SGL Group gave a statement about its reporting boundaries for the consolidated sustainability report for the year 2023.

> *Information in the sustainability statement includes SGL Group and all of its subsidiaries and has been prepared on the same consolidated basis as SGL Group's 2023 financial statements.*

Source: SGL (2023), p. 14

Financial accounting is based on the notion of 'financial control' – and consequently the ESRS build on this concept as well. For specific disclosures in environmental standards, however, organizations are required to extend their general reporting boundaries for entities, sites, operations or assets that they operationally control. This concept of operational control was developed by international standards and frameworks such as the GHG Protocol: Corporate Accounting and Reporting Standard, but it is only established in certain industries such as oil and gas, and it is difficult to apply in other industries.

The glossary of terms gives a definition of 'operational control' that has to be considered:

> *Operational control (over an entity, site, operation or asset) is the situation where the undertaking has the ability to direct the operational activities and relationships of the entity, site, operation or asset.*

Entities, sites, operations or assets included in the reporting boundaries are referred to as 'own operations'. Typically, they must be fully integrated into the reporting systems and processes. The sustainability report gives a comprehensive depiction of all sustainability matters and related impacts, risks and opportunities of these own operations.

However, there is an even more important extension for both consolidated and non-consolidated reports that go beyond the corresponding scopes for financial reporting: the organization also has to assess its value chains. When material impacts, risks or opportunities do materialize, information has to be included accordingly in the sustainability report. In contrast to its own operations, need only provide information on these material impacts, risks or opportunities – a more comprehensive report is not required. The glossary of terms gives the following definition of 'value chain':

> *The full range of activities, resources and relationships related to the undertaking's business model and the external environment in which it operates.*
>
> *A value chain encompasses the activities, resources and relationships the undertaking uses and relies on to create its products or services from conception to delivery, consumption and end-of-life. Relevant activities, resources and relationships include:*
>
> *i. those in the undertaking's own operations, such as human resources;*
>
> *ii. those along its supply, marketing and distribution channels, such as materials and service sourcing and product and service sale and delivery; and*

iii. the financing, geographical, geopolitical and regulatory environments in which the undertaking operates.

Value chain includes actors upstream and downstream from the undertaking. Actors upstream from the undertaking (e.g. suppliers) provide products or services that are used in the development of the undertaking's products or services. Entities downstream from the undertaking (e.g. distributors, customers) receive products or services from the undertaking.

More information on how to consider an organization's value chain for sustainability reporting purposes is given in Chapter 5. Example 4.5 is an illustration of how companies can visually present their value chain for the purposes of sustainability reporting.

Example 4.5

AGRANA

AGRANA presents a visualization of its value chains that include various actors on all levels as well as inputs, outputs and key metrics for impact assessment.

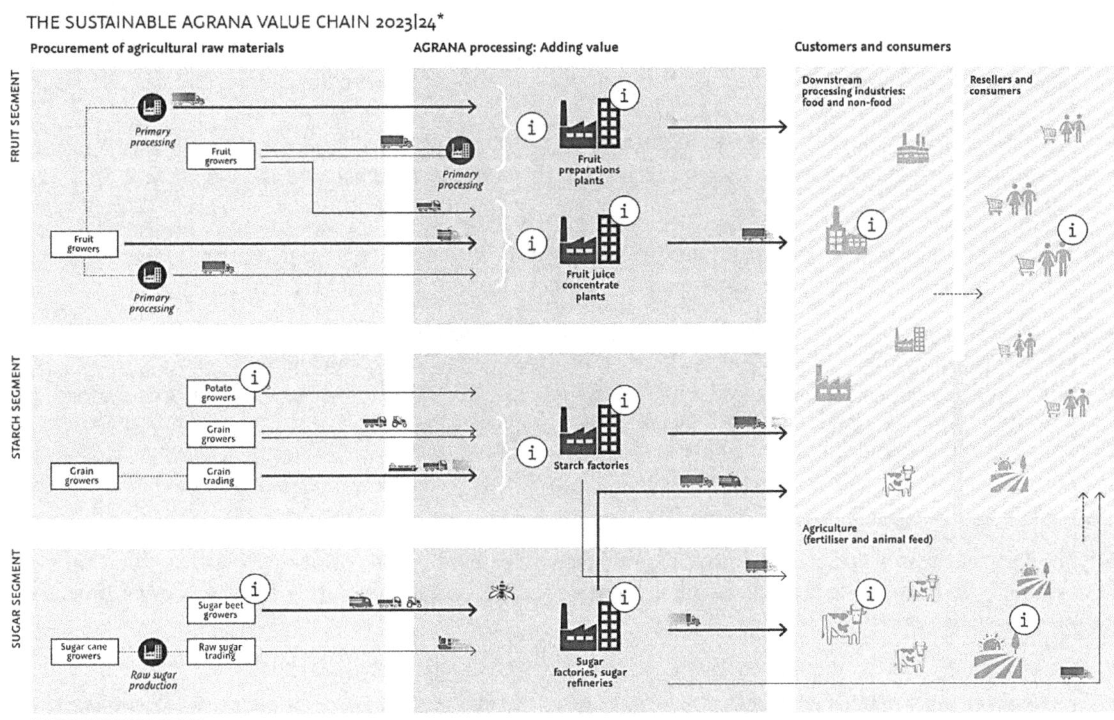

Source: AGRANA (2024)

Formal requirements for sustainability reports

ESRS 1 also outlines formal requirements for structuring sustainability reports in accordance with ESRS. First, it requires organizations to include the report in their management commentary. It has to be a separate section; an integration of financial and sustainability information is not possible. However, there are clear rules for references from one report to the other. Second, ESRS 1 also outlines how the sustainability report is structured. It must comprise four parts, reflecting the structure of disclosure requirements under ESRS as well:

- general information (i.e. ESRS 2)
- environmental information (i.e. ESRS E1–E5 and information required by the EU Taxonomy Regulation)
- social information (i.e. ESRS S1–S4)
- governance information (i.e. ESRS G1).

Furthermore, information within these four parts shall be structured by reporting area. These few requirements still give organizations a lot of flexibility with regard to their reports. Organizations structure their sustainability reports in various ways.

ESRS 1 sets forth that the reporting period for the sustainability report shall be the same as for the financial report, that is typically the last financial year. Also, it contains information on how to include comparative information, how to deal with estimates and how to report on errors made. Under certain circumstances, organizations are required to update their disclosures about events after the end of the reporting period.

Often, the ESRS require considerations of short-, medium- and long-term periods of time. ESRS 1 defines these periods, and exceptions are available and are based on the business model or the nature of a specific analysis, but they still have to be disclosed:

- Short-term: the same period as the reporting period in the financial statements of an organization, that is typically one calendar year.
- Medium-term: from the end of the short-term reporting period up to five years.
- Long-term: more than five years, at least theoretically for an infinite period of time into the future.

Connectivity is another important formal requirement of ESRS 1. It requires organizations to link various pieces of information within their sustainability report and with other types of report. This has to be done via an explicit reference. There are three types of connectivity that have to be considered:

- Information from different reporting areas shall be connected, for example narrative information on GOV, SBM or IRO needs to be linked to the related quantitative information from metrics and targets.
- Monetary amounts included in sustainability statements shall be linked to the respective figures presented in the financial statements if they are above a defined threshold, even if these monetary amounts are just an aggregation or form part of information presented in the financial statements.
- Also, any corresponding data, assumptions and qualitative information shall be cross-referenced between the sustainability report and the financial statements.

Finally, ESRS 1 addresses safeguard clauses. They allow organizations to omit disclosures which they would have to make based on the requirements of the respective ESRS. However, this right to omit information is restricted to specific cases:

- Classified and sensitive information, that is information related to the public interest.
- Information on intellectual property, know-how or results of innovation that might cause significant financial harm to the organization if it is published.

There are strict requirements for making use of these safeguard clauses. Beyond these two options, there is one other safeguard clause set out in the CSRD that organizations might apply (refer to Example 4.6). Otherwise, an organization always has to follow the disclosure requirements. Most notably, there is no general safeguard clause for omitting information because of an organization's financial or other interests.

Example 4.6

An additional safeguard clause

The CSRD contains one additional safeguard clause. However, it formulates requirements that have to be met, and these are very restrictive. As a consequence, there is little room for making use of this option for most organizations.

> *Member States may allow information relating to impending developments or matters in the course of negotiation to be omitted in exceptional cases where, in the duly justified opinion of the members of the administrative, management and supervisory bodies, acting within the competencies assigned to them by national law and having collective responsibility for that opinion, the disclosure of such information would be seriously prejudicial to the commercial position of the undertaking, provided that such omission does not prevent a fair and balanced understanding of the undertaking's development, performance and position, and the impact of its activity.*

Source: CSRD (2021) Article 19a (3)

Transitional provisions

ESRS lays out several provisions for organizations applying the ESRS for the first time. Considering the work load involved, several reliefs are granted:

- For the first reporting period, no comparative information has to be provided.
- With regard to required entity-specific disclosures, companies can refer to international standards or frameworks as well as to information included in former sustainability reports in order to satisfy this requirement.
- With regard to the reporting requirements addressing the value chain, companies are granted a transitional period of three years in order to get the information required from their business partners.
- Finally, certain disclosure requirements or at least specific data points are subject to 'phase-in regulations', that is they can be omitted for a defined number of reporting periods. For organizations that do not exceed the average number of 750 employees, even entire standards can be omitted from reporting.

ESRS 2 GENERAL DISCLOSURES

ESRS 2 complements ESRS 1 by specifying detailed disclosure obligations that facilitate transparency and comparability across organizations. Building upon ESRS 1, this standard specifies the essential information that organizations must disclose in their sustainability reports in order to give users of these reports an understanding of the organization's fundamental characteristics. This includes information about their business model and strategy, governance mechanism and the risks, opportunities and impacts that arise out of the activities of the organization.

Similar to ESRS 1, materiality plays an important role in ESRS 2. It sets the framework for understanding the organization's analyses and results. Most importantly, ESRS 2 requires organizations to report on their materiality analysis processes in order to make more transparent how companies make use of the flexibility granted to them by ESRS 1 in this regard.

As already mentioned, the disclosure requirements in ESRS 2 are not subject to materiality assessment themselves. Disclosures have to be made by every organization reporting under ESRS. This further underlines their fundamental importance.

Reporting area: Basis for preparation

ESRS 2 is the only standard that includes disclosure requirements classified under the reporting area 'Basis for preparation' (BP). These are addressing technical aspects relevant for understanding the scope and fundamental contents of the sustainability report (refer to Table 4.3).

Table 4.3 Basis for preparation disclosure requirements

Disclosure requirement	Brief description
BP-1 General basis for preparation of the sustainability statement	The organization shall make disclosures about the general basis of its sustainability report; examples include giving a statement on whether the sustainability statement has been prepared on a consolidated or individual basis; to what extent the organization's upstream and downstream value chain is covered; or if (and which) safeguard clauses have been used.
BP-2 Disclosures in relation to specific circumstances	The organization shall make disclosures about specific circumstances defined by the disclosure requirement: they include disclosures on definitions of time horizons; value chain estimations; changes in preparation or presentation of sustainability information; incorporations by reference; or use of phase-in provisions in accordance with ESRS 1.

Following the nature of the relevant disclosures, the data points falling under BP-1 always have to be disclosed. Disclosures in accordance with BP-2 only have to be made to the extent that the matters that are addressed by these disclosures actually exist (e.g. phase-in provisions were used or references were made). Example 4.7 describes the reporting boundaries for one organization's consolidated sustainability report.

Example 4.7

Ørsted

Ørsted describes the reporting boundaries for its consolidated sustainability report.

Consolidation

The data is consolidated according to the same principles as the financial statements. Thus, the consolidated quantitative ESG data comprises the parent company Ørsted A/S and subsidiaries controlled by Ørsted A/S. Joint operations are also included with Ørsted's proportionate share. Associates and joint ventures are not included in the consolidated ESG data points.

Source: Ørsted (2023), p. 69

Example 4.8 is an illustration of how an organization can make disclosures about reporting errors in previous periods.

Example 4.8

Lenzing's disclosure about reporting errors in previous periods

Reporting errors in prior periods

A recalculation of scope 3 emissions from 2017 to 2021 was necessary due to updated market pulp supplier data (tables 01 and 16).

Source: Lenzing (2023), p. 50

Reporting area: Governance (GOV)

Disclosure requirements that fall under reporting area GOV are distinct from the disclosure requirements set forth in ESRS G1 in so far as ESRS 2 relates to the integration of ESG matters into the governance mechanisms of an organization. This covers both the work and incentives of management and supervisory bodies of the organization as well as how risk management and internal control extend to the process of sustainability reporting (refer to Table 4.4).

Table 4.4 Governance disclosure requirements

Disclosure requirement	Brief description
GOV-1 The role of the administrative, management and supervisory bodies	The organization shall make disclosures about the composition of the administrative, management and supervisory bodies; about their roles and responsibilities; and about their access to expertise and skills with regard to sustainability matters. This also includes information about the diversity of the members of the organization's administrative, management and supervisory bodies.
GOV-2 Information provided to and sustainability matters addressed by the undertaking's administrative, management and supervisory bodies	The organization shall disclose how the administrative, management and supervisory bodies are informed about sustainability matters; and how these matters were addressed during the reporting period. Also, a list of the material impacts, risks and opportunities that were addressed during the reporting period by the administrative, management and supervisory bodies shall be included.
GOV-3 Integration of sustainability-related performance in incentive schemes	The organization shall disclose whether and how sustainability-related performance is integrated in incentive schemes. This includes the proportion of variable remuneration dependent on sustainability-related targets and/or impacts; as well as the level in the organization at which the terms of incentive schemes are approved and updated.
GOV-4 Statement on due diligence	The organization shall disclose a mapping of the information provided in its sustainability report about the due diligence process. This might be done based on a table presented in ESRS 1.AR 10.
GOV-5 Risk management and internal controls over sustainability reporting	The organization shall explain the main features of its risk management and internal control system in relation to the sustainability reporting process. This includes a description of how the findings of its risk assessment and internal controls in regard to the sustainability reporting process are integrated into relevant internal functions and processes and reported to the administrative, management and supervisory bodies.

Some of these disclosures are similar to disclosures required in other reports, such as corporate governance reports or remuneration reports. Here, providing cross-references might be a viable solution to avoid redundant information. Also, it enables the process of sustainability due diligence referencing to be prominent, underlining the importance of this process for the entire sustainability report. Example 4.9 is an extract of reporting practice on risk management and internal controls in relation to sustainability reporting. This is an area that is likely to undergo considerable development over the coming years, as organizations have to work to update risk management processes and internal control to align and embed sustainability.

Example 4.9

Hydro

Hydro provides a brief outline of its risk management and internal control over sustainability reporting. This information serves as an example for the requirements in ESRS 2 GOV-5.

Risk management and internal controls over sustainability reporting

Hydro regularly assesses risk and controls over its sustainability reporting process. The risks are discussed with the Board Audit Committee, and also discussed with Hydro's external auditors who provide limited assurance over the sustainability statement. The external assurance process is risk based, and the external auditors provide feedback on their assessment of risks to the Board Audit Committee and Hydro's management. The auditors also provide feedback to the Board of Directors in relation to the Board's review and approval of the annual report.

Hydro is exposed to risks associated with incomplete or inconsistent reporting on sustainability topics, including risks associated with greenwashing. There are also risks related to the accuracy of data inputs and manual errors in the reporting process from aggregating data from multiple systems into the corporate disclosure management system.

Source: Hydro (2023), p. 69

Reporting area: Strategy (SBM)

Disclosure requirements under the reporting area SBM aim at a fundamental description of the organization and those elements that are of special importance for sustainability reporting: its activities, its value chain and its stakeholders (refer to Table 4.5).

Table 4.5 Strategy disclosure requirements

Disclosure requirement	Brief description
SBM–1. Strategy, business model and value chain	The organization shall describe its sustainability strategy, its business model and its value chain. This includes various quantitative disclosures (such as headcounts or revenue breakdowns) and disclosures about relationships to stakeholders.
SBM–2. Interests and views of stakeholders	The organization shall describe how its strategy and business model reflects the interest and views of its stakeholders. This requires disclosures about the stakeholder engagement and how an organization reacts to the outcomes of this engagement.
SBM–3. Material impacts, risks and opportunities and their interaction with strategy and business model	The organization shall disclose its material impacts, risks and opportunities as well as how they interact with its strategy and business model. This includes extensive descriptions about the identified material impacts, risks and opportunities (e.g. their nature, origin and consequences); also information about the resilience of the undertaking's strategy and business model must be disclosed.

With regard to the concepts that are fundamental to sustainability reporting under ESRS, disclosure requirements falling under the reporting area SBM set the context for materiality analysis and the disclosures required under reporting area IRO. Thus, it is important to give a holistic understanding of the connections between the activities of an organization, its stakeholders and the resulting impacts, risks and opportunities. This should also make the results of sustainability assessment more plausible. Example 4.10 is an illustration of reporting that outlines stakeholder dialogue as well as material impacts, risks and opportunities.

Example 4.10

DFS

Stakeholder dialogue

Why we engage	How we engage	Key topics and concerns discussed
CUSTOMERS Strong engagement with our customers enables us to understand their needs and anticipate market trends Preference discovery platforms and consumer insight programmes allow us to understand and predict consumer preferences and adapt to cultural tastes. We protect our customers by ensuring product quality and safety and through our compliance with applicable laws, regulations, and policies.	• Customer sustainability requests • Audits • Customer innovation days • Customer and industry conferences and events • Key account manager relationships – ongoing dialogue • Use of consumer insight programmes for consumer understanding, cultural insights and sensorial decoding • Leveraging digital capabilities to enhance insights in consumer trends	• Climate change • Consumer health and wellbeing • Governance and business conduct, ethics, transparency • Human rights • Innovation capabilities • Product/ingredient environmental and social performance • Product quality and safety • Responsible sourcing and traceability
SUPPLIERS Our suppliers are genuine partners, and we work with them towards mutual value creation: open dialogue secures a pipeline of technological knowledge through supplier-enabled innovation, supplier engagement and collaboration ensure our suppliers have high standards in business ethics and respect for people and the environment. We protect them through active collaboration and by staying compliant with rapidly changing regulatory requirements. Our collaboration allows them to strengthen their innovation approach and contributes to the achievement of their own targets.	• Assessments • Supplier audits • Collaborations to improve performance • Multi-stakeholder groups • Supplier events: capacity building, discussing issues • Direct engagement with supplier relationship managers	• Climate change • Plastics • Human rights • Innovation capabilities • Raw material availability • Responsible sourcing and traceability

(Continued)

EMPLOYEES We engage with our people to foster an environment of open dialogue to mutually resolve conflicts, to identify development initiatives and innovative ideas that will help drive our business. We protect employees against reprisals and other negative impacts on their rights such as providing protection against intimidation, threats, or acts that could have a negative impact on their employment or work angagement, including termination, demotion, loss of compensation, discipline, and any other unfavourable treatment. We cannot achieve our goals without a true sense of unity and a workplace where we all love to be and grow.	• Provide policies and process to provide protection against a negative impact on their employment or work engagement • Works Council consultations • Employee engagement survey • Annual performance dialogue • Talent management processes • Learning and development opportunities • Ongoing dialogue with Givaudan Green Teams	• Climate change • Diversity, equity and inclusion • People development • Employee health, safety and wellness • Governance and business conduct, ethics, transparency • Human rights • Innovation capabilities

Source: Givaudan (2023), p. 197

Reporting area: Impact, risk and opportunity management (IRO)

Reporting area IRO addresses the process of materiality analysis and its outcomes. Given the fundamental importance of materiality analysis for the entire process of sustainability reporting under ESRS, this understanding is of relevance to stakeholders to better understand how and why an organization is reporting on specific sustainability matters – and subsequently addresses these matters with its policies, actions and targets (refer to Table 4.6).

Table 4.6 Impact, risk and opportunity management disclosure requirements

Disclosure requirement	Brief description
IRO–1. Description of the processes to identify and assess material impacts, risks and opportunities	The organization shall describe its process of materiality analysis, i.e. how it has applied the requirements in ESRS 1 for its analyses.
IRO–2. Disclosure requirements in ESRS covered by the undertaking's sustainability statement	The organization shall report on the disclosure requirements complied with in its sustainability report as a consequence of the results of materiality assessment. Two lists are required, one containing the disclosure requirements set forth by the ESRS – often referred to as 'content index' – and one table of all the data points that derive from other EU legislation as listed in Appendix B of ESRS 2.

IRO–2 covers one notable exception from the rule that no information about non-material sustainability matters is required. If a company assesses climate change to not be material, it does not have to apply the respective standard (ESRS E1). However, ESRS 2.57 requires it in this case to 'disclose a detailed explanation of the conclusions of its materiality assessment with regard to climate change [...], including a forward-looking analysis of the conditions that could lead the undertaking to conclude that climate change is material in the future'. A similar requirement for other sustainability matters/ESRS does not exist. So, this requirement exerts at least factual pressure on companies to give priority to climate-related disclosures.

Minimum disclosure requirements (MDR)

Another specific element that only ESRS 2 contains are MDR. They relate to the classification of disclosure requirements in ESRS as policies, actions, metrics and targets. Whenever an organization is making such disclosures, it not only has to adhere to the specific requirements in the topical standards but also the requirements set forth by MDR (refer to Table 4.7).

The introduction of these MDR should avoid redundancies in ESRS. Whenever applicable, the topical standards include concrete references to the applicable MDR.

Table 4.7 Minimum disclosure requirements

Disclosure requirement	Brief description
MDR-P Policies adopted to manage material sustainability matters	Organizations shall provide information such as key contents and scopes of policies; the most senior levels in an organization responsible for the implementation of policies; and how policies are made available to stakeholders.
MDR-A Actions and resources in relation to material sustainability matters	Organizations shall, e.g. provide a list of key actions taken in the reporting year and planned for the future; disclose the expected outcomes of actions; and time horizons.
MDR-M Metrics in relation to material sustainability matters	Organizations shall disclose the methodologies and significant assumptions behind their metrics and if they are validated by third parties. Furthermore, clear and precise names and descriptions have to be given to metrics.
MDR-T Tracking effectiveness of policies and actions through targets	Organizations shall provide information about the nature of their targets. This includes how their targets relate to policy objectives; the methodologies and significant assumptions used to define targets, and if targets related to environmental matters are based on conclusive scientific evidence.

A notable requirement is set out in MDR-M (ESRS 2.75): 'The undertaking shall disclose any metrics that it uses to evaluate performance and effectiveness, in relation to a material impact, risk or opportunity.' This is similar to the idea of a 'management approach' in financial reporting (most notably, IFRS 8). As a consequence, internal reports of an organization also have to be evaluated and can give rise to additional disclosures that have to be performed.

Disclosure requirement related to ESRS 2 in topical standards

All topical standards of the ESRS also include disclosure requirements that make reference to ESRS 2. Appendix C of ESRS 2 contains a list of disclosure requirements in topical standards that have to be taken into account when reporting on the respective disclosure requirements of ESRS 2. In these cases, when an organization discloses the respective information in accordance with ESRS 2, it also has to include the data points set forth by the topical standards, but only if the topical standard has to be applied. This is the case when at least one sustainability matter that can be linked to this standard is assessed as being material.

ESRS have chosen this splitting of related disclosure requirements arguably for convenience reasons: ESRS 2 just contains universal disclosure requirements, whereas topic-specific additional requirements are included in the standards for such sustainability matters. This makes the disclosure requirements more focused and coherent; however, for the users of these standards it also increases the technical complexity of identifying the relevant disclosures for their sustainability report (and placing them correctly in these reports).

Deviating from the general rule, disclosures that are referencing IRO–1 always have to be made, that is even if sustainability matters are not material and an entire standard does not have to be applied, an organization still has to describe how it performed its materiality analysis with regard to these specific matters. This makes the basis for the materiality assessments of the organization more transparent for stakeholders. However, with the sole exception of ESRS E1 on climate change, ESRS do not require organizations to justify why they did not assess sustainability matters to be material.

Location of disclosures

With regard to the location of the disclosures made in accordance with ESRS 2, the standard offers some flexibility to organizations. As a principle, these disclosures shall be made under the section 'general information'. However, sometimes individual disclosure requirements permit companies to include the information required in other sections of the sustainability report (e.g. BP-2 or SBM-3). Disclosures under SBM-3 can also be presented in the topical chapters; in this case, however, a reduced number of disclosures have to be made in the general information as well:

> *The undertaking may disclose the descriptive information required in paragraph 46 alongside the disclosures provided under the corresponding topical ESRS, in which case it shall still present a statement of its material impacts, risks and opportunities alongside its disclosures prepared under this chapter of ESRS 2.* (ESRS 2.49)

These requirements still allow organizations to make use of references. Most often, organizations might want to use this possibility with regard to the content indexes required by IRO–1 and IRO–2. In its FAQ, EFRAG was asked to outline how far references are possible for these tables. In turn, they highlighted how to apply the general rules for references to them (refer to Example 4.11).

Example 4.11

For question 'ID 906 – Structure of sustainability statement – annex / appendix possible?' was asked as follows: 'Is there the possibility to implement an "Appendix" as another part of the Sustainability Statement (mainly for the Content Index, EU Datapoint Table etc.)?'

> EFRAG answered: *'It is possible to have the content index and the EU datapoint table as another section of the management report.*
>
> *The sustainability statement shall consist of four parts (ESRS 1 paragraph 56). The first part is related to general information. As the content index and the datapoints that derive from other EU legislation are part of the ESRS 2 Disclosure Requirement IRO–2 – Disclosure Requirements in ESRS covered by the undertaking's sustainability statement, they need to be included in the part related to general information. However, information can, subject to the incorporation by reference requirements of ESRS 1 paragraph 120, also be placed in "another section of the management report" (ESRS 1 paragraph 119 (a)).'*

Source: EFRAG (2024d)

For disclosure requirements related to ESRS 2 in topical standards, the general rule is that this information is given alongside the disclosure requirements set out in ESRS 2, that is typically under 'general information'. Only disclosure requirements related to ESRS 2 SBM-3 grant the flexibility to include them under topical standards – as SBM-3, as regulated in ESRS 2 per se, offers this option. To consolidate your understanding of the various requirements, try Activity 4.5.

ACTIVITY 4.5

As mentioned, the FAQ issued by EFRAG are non-binding. Some of their interpretations have to be considered with great care as they can even be misleading. One important example refers to the location of disclosures for disclosure requirements related to ESRS 2.

Under question 'Question ID 38 – Structure of the sustainability statement', EFRAG states:

Regarding the overall sustainability reporting, ESRS 1 paragraph 115 clarifies that the sustainability statement must be structured in four parts: 'general information, environmental information, social information and governance information'. A particular treatment is anticipated for ESRS 2 SBM-3 related disclosures required by topical standards, which can be either presented alongside the other ESRS 2 General disclosures or alongside the respective topical disclosures (environmental, social and governance). In case the ESRS 2 General disclosures required by topical standards are presented alongside other topical disclosures, the undertaking still has to present a statement of its material impacts, risks and opportunities alongside its disclosures prepared under ESRS 2 SBM-3. Appendix F of ESRS 1 provides a non-binding structure for a sustainability statement.

Compare this statement with the explicit requirements of the ESRS, e.g. ESRS E1.12:

The requirements of this section should be read and applied in conjunction with the disclosures required by ESRS 2 on Chapter 2 Governance, Chapter 3 Strategy and Chapter 4 Impact, risk and opportunity management. The resulting disclosures shall be presented in the sustainability statement alongside the disclosures required by ESRS 2, except for ESRS 2 SBM-3 Material impacts, risks and opportunities and their interaction with strategy and business model, for which the undertaking may, in accordance with ESRS 2 paragraph 46, present the disclosures alongside the other disclosures required in this topical standard.

Can you outline possible contradictions?

ISSB

The IFRS Sustainability Disclosure Standards have many similarities with regard to the fundamental requirements of the required sustainability report. These are laid out in IFRS S1 *General Requirements for Disclosure of Sustainability-related Financial Information.*

Similar to ESRS, the IFRS Sustainability Disclosure Standards distinguish four reporting areas which are based on the TCFD's classification, albeit with slightly different wording. Organizations are required to perform materiality analysis that also covers their value chains. IFRS S1 also contains general disclosures which show many similarities to the disclosures required in ESRS 2, but in a more condensed way, for example there is no requirement to disclose lists about the disclosures made such as in ESRS 2 IRO–2.

Unlike ESRS, IFRS Sustainability Disclosure Standards follow a so-called 'single materiality' approach. Aligned with IFRS Accounting Standards for financial reporting, only those sustainability matters that are associated with financial risks or opportunities for the organization have to be reported. So, only one of the two perspectives covered by ESRS is mandatory for IFRS Sustainability Disclosure Standards reporting.

IFRS Sustainability Disclosure Standards require organizations to set their reporting boundaries in accordance with the scope of financial reporting. In contrast, considerable flexibility is granted regarding providing the location of the required disclosures. The sustainability report should be part of the general purpose financial statements and could be included in a management commentary or a similar report. Also, organizations might decide themselves how they define short-, medium- and long-term time horizons for reporting purposes. With regard to safeguard clauses, IFRS Sustainability Disclosure Standards more often stress 'undue cost and effort' as a possible justification for omitting disclosures.

Connectivity of information – called 'connected information' – is also a requirement of IFRS Sustainability Disclosure Standards. However, as the ISSB has also taken responsibility for the International Integrated Reporting Framework, different activities of the ISSB aim to promote this framework and thus provide closer links between financial and sustainability-related information in their company reporting. So, arguably, this concept is of even higher importance under IFRS Sustainability Disclosure Standards than under ESRS.

In contrast to ESRS, the IFRS Sustainability Disclosure Standards currently comprise only one topical standard: IFRS S2 on climate-related disclosures. In order to publish more comprehensive reports, organizations are encouraged to refer to standards by other organizations, such as the ESRS or the GRI Standards. In turn, however, the IFRS Sustainability Disclosure Standards include comprehensive guidelines for sector-specific disclosures. The sector-specific standards of the Sustainability Accounting Standards Board (SASB) were also integrated into the IFRS Foundation. So, these sector-specific disclosures already play an important role in reporting under IFRS Sustainability Disclosure Standards, while the ESRS recommend organizations to refer to other organizations' sector-specific standards (such as the ones now maintained by the ISSB). This goes to show how closely related these sets of standards already are.

To understand the specifics of the ISSB's reporting standards, it is important to remember their specific background. The work on the IFRS Sustainability Disclosure Standards started when the IFRS Foundation decided to complement its financial reporting standards with standards on sustainability-related information so as to offer a more comprehensive framework for corporate reporting. However, the target group of this information – providers of capital – remained undisputed. Following the global ambition of the IFRS Foundation and its work, the standards require flexibility in order to fit into each jurisdiction's specific requirements. Activity 4.6 invites you to investigate how organizations can comply with ESRS as well as IFRS Sustainability Disclosure Standards.

ACTIVITY 4.6

Look up the 'ESRS–ISSB Standards Interoperability Guidance' which was published by EFRAG and the ISSB. What is the main conclusion of these two organizations about the alignment of both their sets of standards? What do they consider as the most important differences? And what do organizations have to do in order to publish sustainability reports that are aligned with both sets of standards?

GRI

Even more than ESRS as well as IFRS Sustainability Disclosure Standards, the GRI Standards offer a lot of flexibility to their users. The GRI Standards recommend that organizations set reporting boundaries in accordance with the scopes of financial reporting. The report should cover the same period of time and should be published at the same time as the financial statements. A specific location for the sustainability report is not required; however, organizations have to disclose a 'GRI content index' that lists the relevant disclosures and includes references. There are also more possibilities for omissions under GRI Standards, that is for not having to make a disclosure that is required under other disclosure regimes, in particular in respect of disclosures about an organization's value chain.

Beyond that, there are considerable similarities between the concepts and disclosure requirements of GRI Standards and ESRS. Notably, sustainability due diligence is laid out as a fundamental requirement for both – the GRI's approach arguably influenced the corresponding statements in ESRS 1. In consequence, this also applies to the central role of stakeholder engagement that both standards mandate. There are also general disclosures in place, however, covering different data points and information on an organization's workforce that is covered mostly by ESRS S1.

Similar to IFRS Sustainability Disclosure Standards, but in contrast to ESRS, the GRI Standards follow a 'single materiality' approach. For these standards, impact materiality is at the core of all disclosure requirements.

This makes them complementary to the IFRS Sustainability Disclosure Standards while at the same time covering part of the double materiality approach of the ESRS. Both sets of standards' definition of impact materiality is aligned. An important difference to ESRS is that entity-specific disclosures are not required but are recommended.

The GRI is currently developing new sector standards. They are also referred to by the ESRS as a possible source for sector-specific guidance. However, it will still take several years until a considerable number of these standards are available. So far, only sector standards for Oil and Gas (GRI 11), Coal (GRI 12), Agriculture, Aquaculture and Fishing (GRI 13) as well as Mining (GRI 14) have been published.

Because of the close cooperation between the GRI and the EFRAG from the very beginning of the latter's work, the degree of alignment and interoperability is arguably higher between those standards. This is also reflected in the fact that every organization that reports under ESRS also might claim reporting 'in reference to' the GRI Standards without any further conditions. However, in order to claim 'alignment with' the GRI Standards, specific modifications have to be made by organizations reporting under ESRS. Now assess in Activity 4.7 how organizations can align with both GRI and EFRAG Standards.

ACTIVITY 4.7

Look up the corresponding interoperability guidance published by EFRAG and GRI. What is the main conclusion of these two organizations about the alignment of both their standards? What do they consider to be the most important differences? And what do organizations have to do if they want to publish sustainability reports that show stronger alignment with rather than just 'referencing' a standard?

CONCLUSION

ESRS 1 and 2 form the backbone of the ESRS, providing a solid foundation and guiding principles for all sustainability reporting under the CSRD. They are essential tools for organizations as they strive to meet the growing demands for transparency and accountability in the area of sustainability.

ESRS 1 is the 'theory standard' under ESRS. It defines the most important concepts on which the other extant ESRS is built. Notably, ESRS 1 provides the definition of double materiality as a core reporting principle. Also, important aspects such as reporting boundaries, formal requirements for sustainability reports (including the principle of connectivity) and **transitional provisions** are covered. ESRS 1 makes it clear that it is not enough to consider sustainability reporting as a one-off activity in the course of the ordinary reporting cycle within a year. It requires continuous activities, most of all stakeholder engagement, and more broadly, a process of sustainability due diligence.

ESRS 2, in contrast, contains general disclosures that outline the most important context factors of sustainability reports. It covers aspects such as sustainability governance, strategy and business model, and the value chain. Also, specific attention is given to the process of materiality analysis. Some disclosure requirements of ESRS 2 are linked to the disclosure requirements topical standards – MDR as set forth in ESRS 2 and disclosure requirements in the topical standards that reference to ESRS 2 and its respective disclosure requirements.

Implementing ESRS is more than just a reporting project. It requires deep organizational change. The requirements set forth in ESRS 1 and 2 address fundamental questions on how an organization is managed. Implicitly, many of these requirements also have expectations on how this management should be redesigned. ISS-Corporate, a global consultancy on business practices, illustrates stakeholder expectations in that respect and sets out immediate priorities (www.iss-corporate.com/library/esrs-a-new-chapter-in-sustainability-reporting/):

1. Strengthen sustainability governance
2. Determine materiality
3. Embed sustainability in business strategy.

SUMMARY

The following items relate to the learning objectives listed at the beginning of the chapter.

- **LO 1. Explain and discuss the general importance of cross-cutting general requirements for sustainability reporting.**

  ESRS 1 General requirements and ESRS 2 General disclosures play a foundational role within the suite of ESRS. While other ESRS focus on specific topics (for example climate, biodiversity, human rights), ESRS 1 and 2 are cross-cutting. This means they apply to all organizations subject to the CSRD, regardless of their industry or the specific sustainability issues they face. The requirements of these standards are not subject to materiality assessment.

- **LO 2. Discuss the meaning of materiality and double materiality in CSRD and ESRS.**

  The CSRD defines that materiality in European sustainability reporting shall be based on the concept of 'double materiality', and the ESRS provide explanations on how to interpret and operationalize this concept. ESRS define double materiality as having two dimensions: impact materiality and financial materiality. A sustainability matter meets the criterion of double materiality whether it is material from the impact perspective or the financial perspective or both. The double materiality concept has become a core feature of ESRS that distinguishes their reporting requirements from the corresponding provisions of such standards as the IFRS Sustainability Disclosure Standards or the GRI Standards that mandate different concepts of materiality.

- **LO 3. Discuss the role of the value chain in CSRD and ESRS.**

  Value chain is defined in the ESRS glossary as the full range of activities, resources and relationships related to the undertaking's business model and the external environment in which it operates. A value chain encompasses the activities, resources and relationships the undertaking uses and relies on to create its products or services from conception to delivery, consumption and end-of-life. Relevant activities, resources and relationships include:

  a those in the undertaking's own operations, such as human resources

  b those along its supply, marketing and distribution channels, such as materials and service sourcing and product and service sale and delivery

  c the financing, geographical, geopolitical and regulatory environments in which the undertaking operates.

  Value chain includes actors upstream and downstream from the undertaking. Actors upstream from the undertaking such as suppliers *provide* products or services that are used in the development of the undertaking's products or services. Entities downstream from the undertaking such as distributors and customers *receive* products or services from the undertaking.

- **LO 4. Explain the importance of defining reporting boundaries for sustainability reporting.**

  The definition of reporting boundaries deals with the question of what parts of an organization to cover in a report. For sustainability reporting, ESRS 1 sets forth a basic rule. Reporting boundaries for sustainability reports shall be the same as for corresponding financial reports. However, there are some very important deviations from this basic rule. For non-consolidated sustainability reports, the reporting boundaries follow the ones from the respective financial statement, that is typically, the organization itself is reflected with all attributable impacts, risks and opportunities in the sustainability report. For consolidated sustainability reports, the reporting boundaries comprise the scope of consolidation from the consolidated financial statements.

- **LO 5. Explain the relevant formal requirements for sustainability reports under ESRS.**

  ESRS 1 also outlines formal requirements for structuring sustainability reports in accordance with ESRS. First, it requires organizations to include the report in their management commentary. It has to be a separate section; an integration of financial and sustainability information is not possible. However, there are clear rules for cross-referencing from one report to the other. Second, ESRS 1 also outlines how the sustainability report is structured.

- **LO 6. Discuss the importance of transitional provisions under ESRS.**

  ESRS lays out several provisions for organizations that apply the ESRS for the first time. Considering the workload involved, several reliefs are granted:

  - For the first reporting period, no comparative information has to be provided.
  - With regard to required entity-specific disclosures, companies can refer to international standards or frameworks as well as to information included in former sustainability reports in order to satisfy this requirement.
  - With regard to the reporting requirements addressing the value chain, companies are granted a transitional period of three years in order to get the information required from their business partners.
  - Finally, certain disclosure requirements or at least specific data points are subject to 'phase-in regulations', that is they can be omitted for a defined number of reporting periods. For organizations that do not exceed the average number of 750 employees, even entire standards can be omitted from reporting.

- **LO 7. Discuss how the general disclosures under ESRS 2 relate to the concepts in ESRS 1 and the specific disclosure under topical standards.**

  ESRS 2 complements ESRS 1 by specifying detailed disclosure obligations that facilitate transparency and comparability across organizations. Building on ESRS 1, this standard specifies the essential information that organizations must disclose in their sustainability reports in order to give users of these reports an understanding of the organization's fundamental characteristics. This includes information about their business model and strategy, governance mechanism and the risks, opportunities and impacts that arise out of the activities of the organization.

EXERCISES

1. Identify an organization of your choice and identify its ESRS 2 disclosures on the strategy and business model. Evaluate and discuss your findings. (LO 1)
2. Think about three or four different business models of organizations, for example oil companies, logistics companies or social services providers. What are their characteristic impacts, risks and opportunities that you would expect distinguish them from one another? To what extent would these impacts, risks and opportunities be reflected differently in a sustainability report based on ESRS, IFRS Sustainability Disclosure Standards or GRI Standards? (LO 2)
3. Choose an organization in your local context and obtain its sustainability report. Identify their value chain. Evaluate and discuss your findings. (LO 3)
4. Discuss the advantages and disadvantages of the strict requirements under ESRS with regard to the formal presentation of sustainability reports. Why did EFRAG consider it necessary to formulate these requirements in such a way? What do we learn about perceived deficits in sustainability reports in the past? (LO 4)
5. Discuss the role of transitional provisions under ESRS for first-time preparers. Which one will be especially helpful? Do you think that there are also reasons for why an organization might refrain from making use of these transitional provisions? Explain your reasonings. (LO 5)
6. Link the most important concepts described under ESRS 1 with the disclosure requirements under ESRS 2. To what extent do the latter's requirements refer to the underlying concepts? Do you think that the disclosure requirements also imply specific ways in which an organization should apply these concepts, that is influence the behaviour of these organizations? (LO 6)
7. Discuss the real effects of ESRS 2 GOV disclosures on the job profiles of members of the administrative, management and supervisory bodies of organizations? Do you think that the new disclosure requirements will affect the work that has to be done at the board level? What could be new competencies needed in the future at that level? (LO 6)

CHAPTER 5
Materiality and the value chain

Learning objectives

After studying this chapter you should be able to:

- LO 1. Discuss the difference between financial materiality and impact materiality in the context of sustainability reporting.
- LO 2. Understand how materiality is defined for sustainability reporting in selected reporting standards and frameworks.
- LO 3. Discuss how a 'double materiality assessment' can be undertaken.
- LO 4. Define an organization's value chain.
- LO 5. Discuss the role of the value chain in the context of CSRD and ESRS.
- LO 6. Understand the link between the CSDDD and the CSRD.

Redefining the value chain via sustainability

Sustainability and the creation of ethical and sustainable value chain should go hand in hand for maximum business and ESG impact. Sustainability principles need to drive value chains from the beginning, but how can companies make this a reality?

Value chains need to be carefully scrutinized with regard to any sustainability risks and opportunities. To create lasting, meaningful impact, business organizations need to consolidate scattered sustainability initiatives and prioritize ESG efforts over mere compliance. Such a changed approach would facilitate corrective measures that equally contribute to sustainable development and their growth prospects.

Take for example a European chocolatier that has become a leading market player: its entire value chain – and the very heart of its business – is premised on slavery-free labour, where farmers and labourers they partner with are assured of fair and sustainable livelihoods. Another Europe-based tech company and social enterprise has developed modular smartphones that create a much smaller environmental footprint, and which are likewise produced under fair, ethical labour, low carbon and circular conditions.

The new premise should be that sustainability is what makes value chains successful, thereby preventing profits arising from harmful activities.

Source: Adapted from kpmg.com/xx/en/what-we-do/ESG/sustainable-supply-chain.html

INTRODUCTION

The concept of materiality is of fundamental importance for corporate reporting – often, it is referred to as 'one of the cornerstones of accountancy' (Frishkoff, 1970, p. 116). It plays a key role in most assessments aimed at enhancing the decision-making value of corporate reporting for its intended audience. In short, it concerns what information should be provided for which stakeholders of an organization.

Traditionally, for financial reporting purposes, these assessments focus primarily on financial performance and risks. However, the evolving dynamics of global challenges, such as climate change, social inequality and biodiversity loss, have underscored the need for a broader perspective that encompasses not only financial considerations but also environmental and social impacts. This has led to the establishment of sustainability reporting in corporate practice in the first instance and then in the regulatory landscape. This extended perspective on the business activities of organizations and how to report them also raises questions with regard to our understanding of materiality.

In the EU, the concept of double materiality has emerged as a pivotal framework over the last few years, shaping the landscape of contemporary reporting practices in its entirety (Baumüller & Sopp, 2022; Jørgensen *et al.*, 2022). Double materiality recognizes the interdependency between an organization's financial performance and its broader environmental and social footprint. Organizations have to take a more holistic approach towards their position and the way they report it, addressing a broader range of topics for stakeholders that go beyond just investors. This new understanding of corporate reporting requires organizations to look beyond the boundaries of their own operations. Organizations are part of a broader **value chain** – the way they manage their business relationships has an impact on both the financial and non-financial values they create. So, not only is information on the direct impact of activities by an organization important for any assessment but the indirect effects might also play a crucial role. Indeed, sometimes, they might even be more relevant than anything under the direct control of the organization.

This chapter explores the concept of double materiality under ESRS, delving into its definition, significance, implications and practical applications within the context of sustainability reporting. Double materiality transcends the traditional boundaries of financial reporting by acknowledging the materiality of ESG factors together with financial factors. These factors have to be analysed for the entire value chain of an organization where impacts, risks and opportunities might most often arise. Double materiality, consequently, can be viewed as a guiding principle for advancing sustainability, resilience and long-term value creation in an interconnected world. Its proper application not only benefits the users of sustainability reports but also the organizations themselves.

DOUBLE MATERIALITY EXPLAINED

Traditionally, information is deemed material – or 'relevant' – if it holds the potential to influence stakeholders' decision-making concerning the reporting entity. This is reflected in definitions of materiality that can be found in the EU's Accounting Directive (EU, 2013) or the **International Financial Reporting Standards (IFRS Accounting Standards)** for financial reporting.

According to IAS 1 *Presentation of Financial Statements* para. 7, information is considered material if omitting, misstating or obscuring it could influence the decisions of primary users of the financial statements, typically assumed to be investors.

The embedded emphasis in financial materiality is on the financial consequences of information. Investors use financial statements to assess an organization's financial health and future prospects. So, material information is anything that could significantly affect their understanding of the organization's financial position, performance and cash flows. Examples of material financial information under IFRS Accounting Standards include significant accounting estimates (e.g. depreciation methods), contingent liabilities (e.g. potential lawsuits), unusual or infrequent items impacting profits and changes in accounting policies. IFRS Accounting Standards provide guidance for organizations to make materiality judgements, but it doesn't prescribe a specific quantitative threshold. Also, organizations must consider qualitative factors such as the size and nature of the item, its pervasiveness across the financial statements and the potential to mislead users. So, there is also a considerable amount of subjectivity involved. The process on which organizations base their assessments is thus of special importance. Under IFRS Accounting Standards, IFRS Practice Statement 2 *Making Materiality Judgements* aims to provide a structure for this process.

Financial materiality has provided a strong foundation for ensuring transparency and investor protection. However, it doesn't encompass the full picture of an organization's impact (refer to Chapter 4 for a basic explanation of these two perspectives on an organization's activities), for example not every environmental impact by an organization's operations automatically triggers financial effects for the organization. These effects might just materialize in the future or cause risks and ultimately costs for others but not for the organization itself. In economics, this is called 'externalities'. Only by extending their perspective in their reports from financial materiality to impact materiality can companies create a more comprehensive understanding of their contribution to environmental and social matters and how they contribute to a more sustainable future.

The need to integrate the impact perspective in corporate reporting has emerged in response to demands for improved corporate accountability. Corporate accountability commonly refers to the explanations or justifications of performance and actions to stakeholders to whom organizations are deemed to be accountable (Boiral, 2016). Accountability pressures on organizations regarding the ESG implications of business have led to increasing demand for transparency about organizational behaviour on a whole range of issues (Kolk, 2004).

As a consequence, double materiality is a concept that aims to bridge this gap between impacts and financial effects. It is important to note that double materiality does not replace financial materiality, but rather extends it – to introduce a more holistic and also long-term orientated view. Financial information remains crucial for investor decision-making. However, double materiality emphasizes the need to integrate sustainability considerations alongside traditional financial metrics.

The CSRD explains double materiality as follows:

> *[The] EU requires reporting not only on information to the extent necessary for an understanding of the organization's development, performance and position, but also on information necessary for an understanding of the impact of the organization's activities on environmental, social and employee matters, respect for human rights, anti-corruption and bribery matters.*
>
> *The CSRD therefore require organizations to report both on the impacts of the activities of the undertaking on people and the environment, and on how sustainability matters affect the organization. That is referred to as the double materiality perspective, in which the risks to the organization and the impacts of the undertaking each represent one materiality perspective. The fitness check on corporate*

reporting shows that those two perspectives are often not well understood or applied. It is therefore necessary to clarify that undertakings should consider each materiality perspective in its own right, and should disclose information that is material from both perspectives as well as information that is material from only one perspective. (para. 29, p. 24)

The CSRD mandates the implementation of a 'double materiality' assessment for reporting entities falling under its scope. The term 'double' signifies that companies reporting on sustainability must evaluate the significance of a sustainability issue from two angles. First, organizations must assess their *impact* on people and the environment (the inside-out view or impact materiality). This includes considerations such as environmental damage or human rights violations. Second, they must analyse how sustainability-related developments and events pose (new) risks and opportunities for the organization (the outside-in view or financial materiality). Examples of these include reputation risks stemming from corruption incidents, the implementation of new carbon taxes, or opportunities for the development of new circular and sustainable products.

In the concept paper that formed the starting point for the ESRS, the European Lab 2021 (p. 17) stated that:

The purpose of publicly available sustainability reporting is to provide relevant, faithful, comparable and reliable information on:

- material sustainability impacts *of the reporting entity on affected stakeholders (including the environment) and* material sustainability risks *and opportunities for* its own value creation;
- *enabling users of information (i) to understand the reporting entity's sustainability objectives, position and performance and (ii) to inform their decisions relating to their engagement with the entity.*

The notion of value creation as a main point of reference for double materiality is a new element introduced into European accounting law by the CSRD (refer also to Baumüller & Sopp, 2022). Value is now extended to comprise not only financial value for organizations themselves, that is investors and other providers of capital, but also value to stakeholders other than investors. This is a fundamental change introduced to the debate on corporate governance by European organizations that transcends the realm of corporate reporting by far.

DIFFERENT UNDERSTANDINGS OF MATERIALITY FOR SUSTAINABILITY REPORTING

The concept of materiality, while crucial for sustainability reporting, is not universally defined. Two contrasting examples can be seen in the Global Reporting Initiative (GRI) versus the IFRS Sustainability Disclosure Standards. Both follow approaches that are called 'single materiality' to show their focus on just one aspect of double materiality. This is a consequence of the different understanding of which users of sustainability reports should be addressed by the information provided.

GRI emphasize a stakeholder-centric approach, focusing on issues that are both significant to an organization's operations and of concern to its stakeholders. This can encompass environmental and social impacts alongside financial considerations. The Sustainability Disclosure Standards, on the other hand, draw on financial materiality. These standards have a specific approach that focuses on investors as the main target group of sustainability reports. Consequently, the disclosures should emphasize information that could significantly influence the economic decisions of investors and other financial stakeholders.

However, there are also other important standards and frameworks on sustainability reporting. Table 5.1 gives an overview on some of these and the way they approach materiality, and thus the required content of sustainability reports drawn up in accordance with these standards and frameworks.

Table 5.1 Description of materiality in various standards/frameworks

Regulation/ Standard/ Framework	Description	Financial or double materiality
CSRD and ESRS	Requires organizations to report both on the impacts of the activities of the undertaking on people and the environment, and on how sustainability matters affect the organization.	Double
ISSB	An organization is asked to disclose material information about the sustainability-related risks and opportunities that could reasonably be expected to affect its prospects. The definition of material information is aligned with that used in IFRS Accounting Standards, that is information is material if omitting, obscuring or misstating it could be reasonably expected to influence investor decisions.	Financial
GRI	Material topics are topics that reflect the organization's most significant impacts on the economy, environment and people, including impacts on human rights.	Double
US SEC The Enhancement and Standardization of Climate-Related Disclosures for Investors	In those instances where the rules reference materiality, consistent with our existing disclosure rules and market practices, materiality refers to the importance of information to investment and voting decisions about a particular organization, not to the importance of the information to climate-related issues outside of those decisions.	Financial
TCFD	Similar to IFRS Sustainability Disclosure Standards, the TCFD recommendations emphasize a 'reasonable person' perspective. Information is considered material if a reasonable investor would consider it important to understand the organization's exposure to climate-related risks and opportunities. Even without a specific definition, the TCFD recommendations provide guidance for organizations assessing climate-related materiality. They encourage organizations to consider factors such as: • Severity of potential impacts from climate change (e.g. physical risks, transition risks) • Likelihood of those impacts occurring • Timeframes associated with the risks and opportunities • Financial implications for the organization.	Financial
TNFD	TNFD acknowledges that different organizations and investors may have varying definitions of materiality. They avoid prescribing a single definition and instead offer a flexible framework. TNFD focuses on dependencies and impacts encouraging companies to assess not only their impacts on nature but also their dependencies on natural resources and ecosystems.	Flexible

This divergence in materiality definitions also highlights the ongoing development of sustainability reporting and the need for companies to navigate these different approaches when crafting their sustainability disclosures. Let's look at a practical example of disclosure on impact and financial materiality from the 2023 financial statements of Barry Callebaut (Example 5.1), then you can try Activity 5.1.

Example 5.1

Disclosure on impact and financial materiality

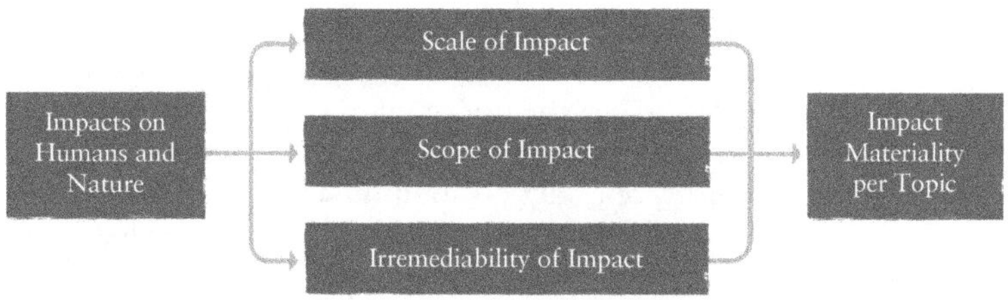

Key results

In our evaluation of impacts on humans and nature, three topics stood out with notable assessment results in scale, scope, and irremediability: Climate and Energy, Biodiversity and Ecosystems, and Supply Chain Traceability. Additionally, Affected Communities and Workers in the Value Chain were other topics that registered a high impact assessment.

Highest-rated topics assessing impact materiality from stakeholder's perspective:

- Climate and Energy
- Biodiversity and Ecosystems
- Workers in the Value Chain

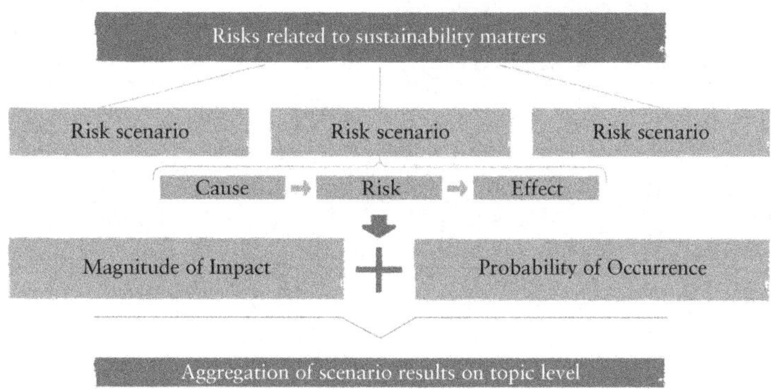

Key results

We've determined that Supply Chain Traceability holds the highest potential financial impact on out business. This is largely because many measures require traceable supply chains as a base to be successful. Other high-rated topics include Biodiversity and Ecosystems, Workers in the Value Chain, Climate and Energy, and Affected Communities.

Highest-rated topics assessing financial materiality from stakeholder's perspective:

- Supply Chain Traceability
- Biodiversity and Ecosystems
- Workers in the Value Chain

Source: Barry Callebaut (2023), pp. 9–10

ACTIVITY 5.1

Discuss the outcomes of Barry Callebaut's impact and financial materiality assessment or that of another organization of your choice.

Dynamic materiality

Other terms such as 'dynamic materiality' are also referred to in some documents. It is based on the primacy of 'financial materiality' but has been extended by the notion of 'pre-financial information' (GRI, 2022). The point of departure is that some sustainability issues have no direct monetary impact on the organization's financial value creation in the here and now, but may do so in the medium or long term.

Blurring the lines between financial and impact significance, by acknowledging that certain data is fluid rather than fixed, adds complexity to how sustainability disclosures should be approached. Dynamic materiality essentially defers the concept of double materiality, urging organizations to disclose both factors that impact financial value (financial materiality) and those that affect the broader economy, environment and society (impact materiality).

However, dynamic materiality also introduces flexibility into standard setting and shows the possible paths for aligning different standards and frameworks (Figure 5.1). The World Economic Forum (2020), for example, emphasizes that what should be disclosed in sustainability reports varies according to regional regulations and expectations, thus they engage with the term 'dynamic materiality'.

Figure 5.1 Dynamic materiality

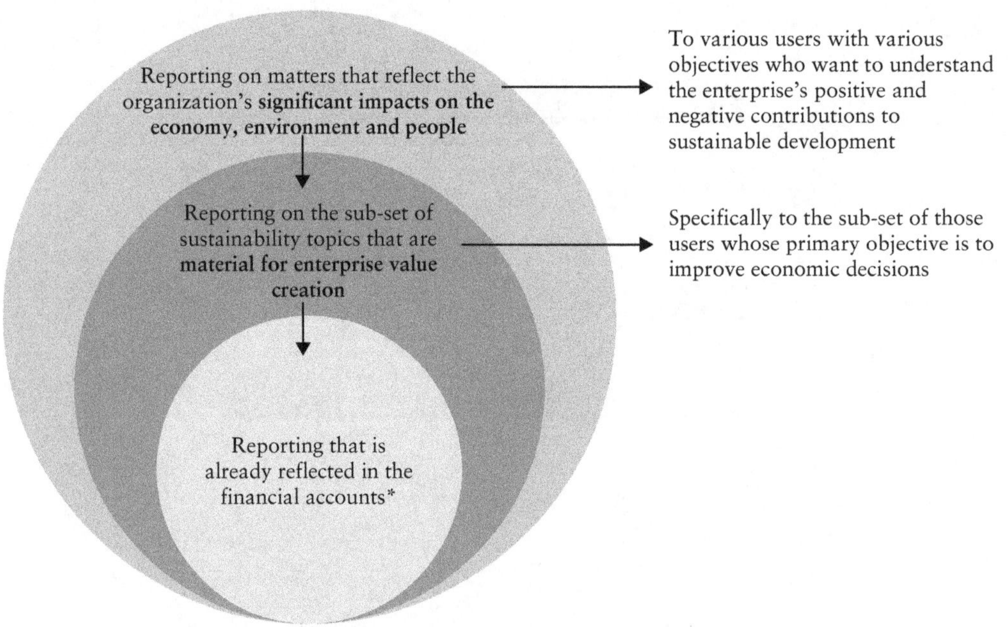

*Including assumptions and cash flow projections

Source: Adapted from Deloitte (2020)

In a position paper by the GRI, the **Sustainability Accounting Standards Board (SASB)**, the **CDP**, the **Climate Disclosure Standards Board (CDSB)** and the **International Integrated Reporting Council (IIRC)**, dynamic materiality was also presented as a concept that shows how the standards of the respective organizations can be aligned with certain layers of information that should be provided to different users. However, the matters depicted are the same; the more focus on financial matters, the more limited the information provided. The notion of value creation is the unifying principle of all relevant reporting standards – only how broad value is understood makes them differ from each other, for example the GRI focuses on the outer layer of the graph (matters reflecting significant impacts, that is value created for society) while the other standard-setters have a narrower understanding of relevant information for reporting (matters that are material for enterprise value creation). In that sense, understanding impacts as 'pre-financial information' is key to bringing structure to the global landscape of heterogenous standards and frameworks for sustainability reporting – and most importantly, aligning their underlying understandings of materiality as a core reporting principle.

Now move on to Activity 5.2 to consolidate your understanding of dynamic materiality.

ACTIVITY 5.2

Discuss the concept of dynamic materiality. Do you find dynamic materiality similar to double materiality in the ESRS? Prior to engaging in the discussion please read the beginning of a speech by IOSCO chair Ashley Alder in 2022, available at www.regulationasia.com/issb-climate-standard-wont-ignore-impact-iosco/.

CONDUCTING DOUBLE MATERIALITY ASSESSMENT UNDER ESRS

This section delves into the concept of double materiality assessments as a cornerstone for effective sustainability reporting under the CSRD framework. It thus focuses on the practical application through the ESRS with regard to double materiality.

Important guidance on how to conduct double materiality assessments can be found in ESRS 1. For further clarification, EFRAG issued the Implementation Guidance 1: Materiality Assessment (EFRAG IG 1) in May 2024. There, the relevant steps are described in detail and further details are given via FAQs.

The process of materiality assessment under ESRS

The process of how to conduct materiality assessments is described in ESRS 1, Application Requirement (ESRS 1 AR) 9. It comprises three different steps that are iterative, as often at the end of the third step, important information has been obtained that requires a company to challenge or extend its initial assumptions. EFRAG IG 1 gives an overview of these three steps and how they relate to each other and ultimately to the resulting sustainability report in Figure 5.2.

Figure 5.2 Double materiality assessment under ESRS

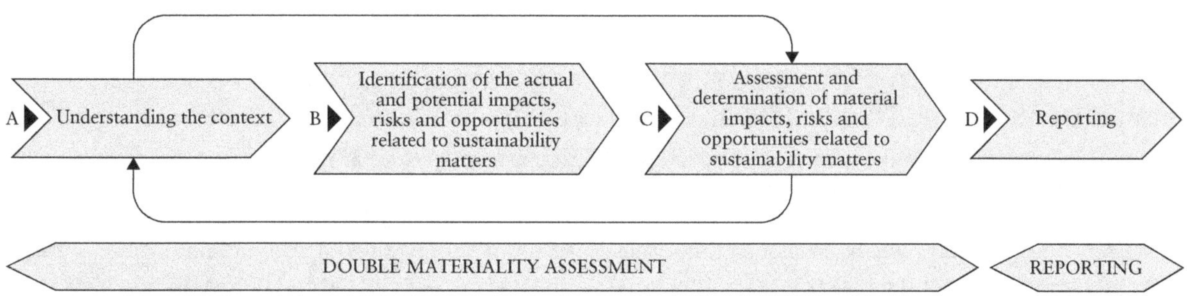

Source: Adapted from EFRAG IG 1 (2024b)

In addition to the overarching steps outlined in Figure 5.2, organizations need to consider the data collection process. Throughout the double materiality assessment process, reliable data collection is crucial to support the assessment and ensure the credibility of reported information. However, given the sheer quantity of information that is required, data management is also one of the main challenges that companies face in their implementation projects.

Maintaining transparency in the assessment process ensures consistent application of the double materiality concept throughout the organization.

Step A: Understanding the context

Gaining a holistic picture of an organization is the starting point for materiality analysis. This requires an understanding of the organization and its activities, its business relationships and its affected stakeholders. Also, it is important to work out how these elements interact with an organization's broader context such as legal environments or local communities. In line with the concept of double materiality, this interaction is bi-directional: how an organization impacts its context but also how its activities and position are affected by this context.

EFRAG IG 1 gives a detailed description of factors that should be considered in Step A, as shown in Table 5.2.

Table 5.2 Factors that should be considered in Step A

Activities and business relationships	Other contextual information	Understanding of affected stakeholders
Business plan, strategy, financial statements and other information provided to investors	Relevant legal and regulatory landscape	Existing stakeholder engagement initiatives (such as via communication, investor relations, business management, sales and procurement teams)
Activities, products/services and the geographic locations of these activities	Published documentation, such as media reports, analysis of peers, existing sector-specific benchmarks and other publications on general sustainability trends	Mapping of affected stakeholders across the undertaking's activities and business relationships. Separate groups of affected stakeholders may be identified per activity, product or service and are to be prioritized for a particular sustainability matter
Mapping of business relationships and upstream and/or downstream value chain, including type and nature of business relationships	Scientific articles	

Source: EFRAG IG 1.69–71 (2024b)

To consider the value chain in the analysis under Step A is vital, not only for materiality assessment but also for the entire reporting process. This is considered to be one of the most challenging requirements of reporting under ESRS.

Step B: Identification of the actual and potential impacts, risks and opportunities related to sustainability matters

As a next step, organizations are required to identify IROs that might be material and thus should be assessed under Step B. Often, this step is described as working out a 'short list' of IRO.

Starting point for this analysis are the sustainability matters covered by ESRS. However, it is not the matters themselves that have to be assessed but one or several IRO linked to a specific matter. These IROs have to be identified by the organization. EFRAG IG 1 presents a visualization that should illustrate how sustainability matters and IRO are linked (refer to Figure 5.3).

Figure 5.3 Linking sustainability and IRO

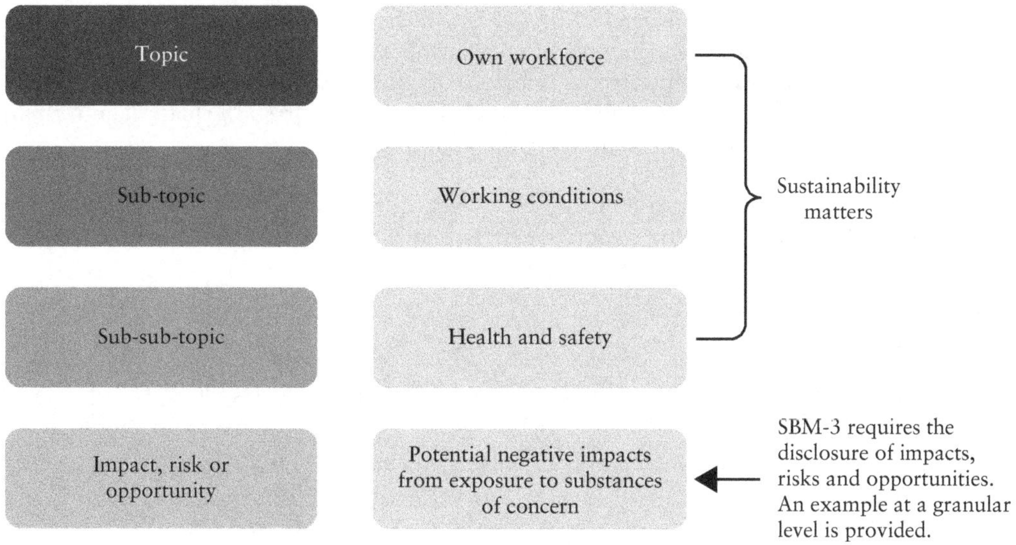

Source: EFRAG IG 1.45 (2024b)

The term 'sustainability matter' under ESRS comprises 'topics', 'sub-topics' and 'sub-sub-topics'. Each of these three levels has equal weight and is considered a sustainability matter for itself. The granularity of topical levels ultimately depends on the complexity of the underlying topic:

- 'Topics' are sustainability matters that are covered by an individual ESRS, for example 'climate change' (ESRS E1) or 'own workforce' (ESRS S1).
- 'Sub-topics' are the first level of granularity, for example climate change addresses such sustainability matters as 'climate change adaptation' and 'climate change mitigation'.
- 'Sub-sub-topics' give additional granularity for complex 'sub-topics'. Figure 5.2, for example, shows that 'health and safety' might be a specific sustainability matter falling under the broader sub-topic 'working conditions'.

To guide organizations in their assessments and to ensure ambition and thus the completeness of the relevant sustainability matters being considered, ESRS 1.AR 16 contains a list of sustainability matters. These matters have to be assessed by every organization subject to ESRS – they are the baseline with regards to possible contents of sustainability reports. However, it should be noted that the sustainability matters in that list should be seen as the bare minimum.

ESRS do not want to encourage a 'tick box mentality', as a comprehensive picture of each organization and its IROs should be at the core of sustainability reporting. Companies therefore have to assess whether there are additional matters that might be specifically relevant to organizations in their sector or to them individually – and include these in their assessments. Special attention should be paid to sustainability matters covered in other standards and frameworks, most notably in sector-specific disclosure requirements. If they are material, they shall lead to the inclusion of entity-specific disclosures in an organization's sustainability report.

Given the flexibility that organizations are granted for conducting their materiality analyses, this list of sustainability matters also contributes to ensuring a minimum level of comparability of sustainability reports published. The list provided in ESRS 1.AR 16 is also referred to as the 'long list'. At the end of Step B, organizations have added IROs to the relevant matters, excluded some of these matters and maybe added others. Then they move on to Step C where they assess whether their IROs are material or not.

When identifying IROs, organizations should track whether they relate to either their own operations and/or upstream or downstream value chain activities. Also the relevant time horizon for potential impacts and risks and opportunities must be tracked in order to make the required disclosures under ESRS 2 and topical ESRS.

Step C: Assessment and determination of material IROs related to sustainability matters

Finally, the IROs on the 'short list' are assessed. Only if they are assessed to be material should these IROs and the sustainability matter they relate to be included in the sustainability report. Otherwise, if they are found not to be material, ESRS mandates that immaterial information must not be included in a sustainability report in order not to confuse the users of sustainability reports or distract them from the material information. For that reason, special care is required when conducting the assessment.

ESRS 1 lists the relevant criteria for the assessments under Step C. They differentiate between assessment criteria for impact materiality and for financial materiality. Typically, however, a combined assessment of severity and probability of IROs are required. For impact materiality assessment, ESRS 1 requires organizations to classify its impacts from Step B in terms of their:

- positive or negative impact
- potential or actual impact.

The most extensive assessment is required for potential negative impacts. Here, the severity of such impacts must be assessed by analysing three factors explained in ESRS 1.AR10:

- Scale: how grave is the negative impact on people or the environment?
- Scope: how widespread are the impacts? For environmental impacts, this often refers to geographical perimeters; for social impacts, it might be considered as the number of people adversely affected.
- Irremediability: can negative impacts be remediated? This might be the case with restoring the environment or affected people to prior states.

ESRS 1.AR11 states that any of the three characteristics can make a negative impact severe. Consequently, it is not enough to calculate averages. However, there is no further guidance on how to measure these impacts, how to employ scales and how to set materiality thresholds, that is how to decide which degree of severity implies that an impact is material. The organization has to define the appropriate methodologies for each sustainability matter by itself.

Likelihood refers to the occurrence of a certain impact. ESRS 1 does not contain any further requirements with regard to this factor. EFRAG IG 1.122 gives at least some indication: 'The likelihood of an impact can be measured or determined qualitatively or quantitatively depending on the available information. It could be described by using general terms (e.g. 'unlikely', 'highly likely'), mathematically by using statistics terms (e.g. '10 in 100', '10 per cent') or by using frequency over a given time-period (e.g. 'once every 10 years').' In some cases, it might be appropriate to multiply likelihood by severity in order to calculate an expected value; however, in many cases, it is better to consider likelihood as a threshold (how probable is it that a certain impact will happen?). The importance of likelihood of course also depends on the severity of an impact; for that reason, EFRAG IG 1 also recommends a heatmap visualization in order to set thresholds for material impacts (refer to Figure 5.4).

Figure 5.4 EFRAG heatmap visualization for material impacts

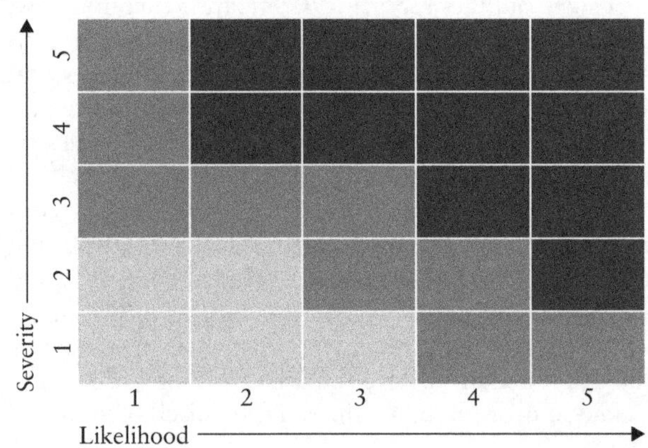

Source: EFRAG IG 1.123 (2024b)

ESRS 1.AR11 requires that in the case of a potential negative human rights impact, the severity of an impact is more important than its likelihood, that is that even lower thresholds for likelihood shall apply for assessing impacts with regard to human rights-related sustainability matters. In fact the majority of sustainability matters linked to social ESRS address such human rights matters; thus, the requirement in AR11 is of the utmost importance.

For actual impacts, organizations are not required to consider probability, as it would be 100%. In case of positive impacts, 'irremediability' does not have to be assessed.

The distinction between positive and negative impacts is at times difficult, however. For example, activities can either have a positive impact or reduce negative impact. Organizations should refer to benchmarks such as the SDGs or planetary boundaries to decide whether their activities are currently to be considered harmful to the environment or society or not (refer to Figure 5.5).

Figure 5.5 Assessment criteria for impact materiality

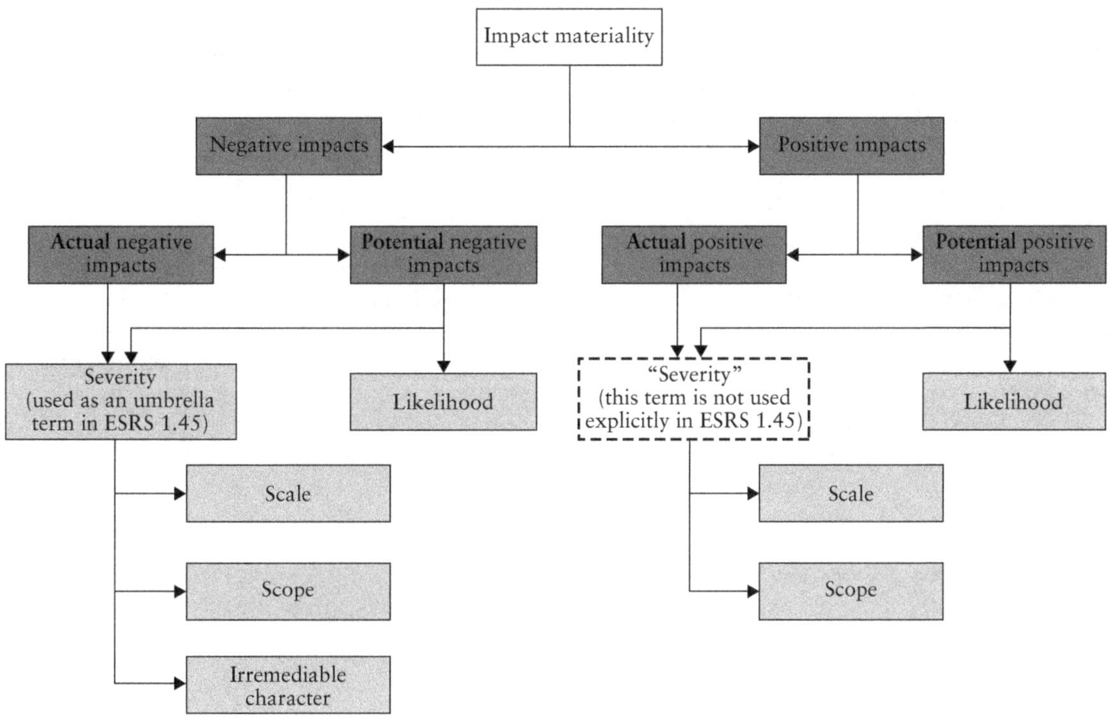

Source: Baumüller & Schönauer (2023)

For financial materiality, only risks and opportunities have to be assessed, in other words the potential financial effects. This is because actual financial effects are already reflected in the financial statements. For both risks and opportunities, the potential size of the effect and the likelihood of its occurrence have to be taken into consideration.

Organizations have to apply the assessment methodologies commonly used in their established financial risk management and apply it to risks and opportunities as well. Furthermore, there are two specific aspects that are stressed by ESRS 1.

First, special attention shall be given to dependencies as a source of risks and opportunities. The availability as well as quality and pricing of these resources have to be considered. Second, a link to an impact materiality assessment is also required. ESRS 1 assumes that in many cases, material impacts also give rise to risks and opportunities. For that reason, it is recommended that organizations start with the impact assessment before they continue with their impact materiality assessment (refer to Figure 5.6).

Figure 5.6 Assessment criteria for financial materiality

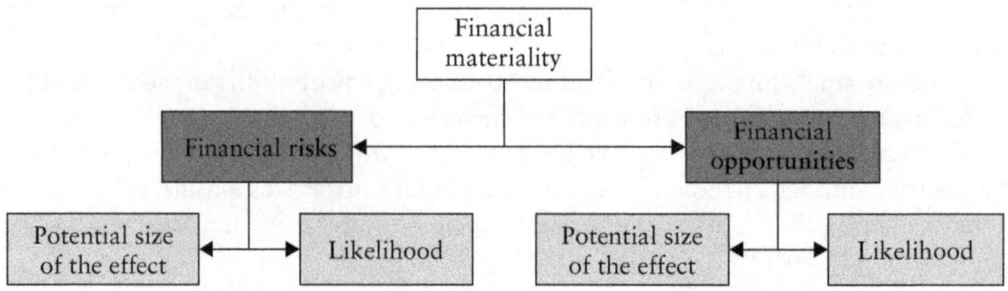

Source: Baumüller & Schönauer (2023)

For both impact materiality assessment and financial materiality assessment IROs must be assessed for the short, medium and long terms. Organizations also have to consider the cumulative effects in the given period of time.

Also, with the exception of actual impacts (which will have already materialized in the past), an assessment of gross impacts is required, that is the likelihood of occurrence before considering mitigation activities. The following formula is typically applied to risk management assessments:

$$\text{Gross impact} - \text{Mitigation activities} = \text{Net impacts}$$

In other words, even if an organization has relevant preventative measures in place to avoid the realization of a certain impact, it might nevertheless be required to report the substance of that impact. Users of sustainability reports should be informed about this threat and about how the organization has reacted to it, even if it is highly unlikely that the impact will materialize as a result of the organization having taken precautionary steps.

Very frequently, the results of Step C are visualized as a matrix. Financial materiality and impact materiality are the two axes; if a sustainability matter is material, that is related IROs exceed the defined materiality threshold, then it must be reported. If not, then they must not be included in the sustainability reporting. Thus, via a matrix, the nature of double materiality can be depicted in the best way. The example shown in Figure 5.7 outlines the basic structures of such a matrix; then, an example from corporate practice is given.

Figure 5.7 Structure of a materiality matrix adapted to the rationale of double materiality analysis

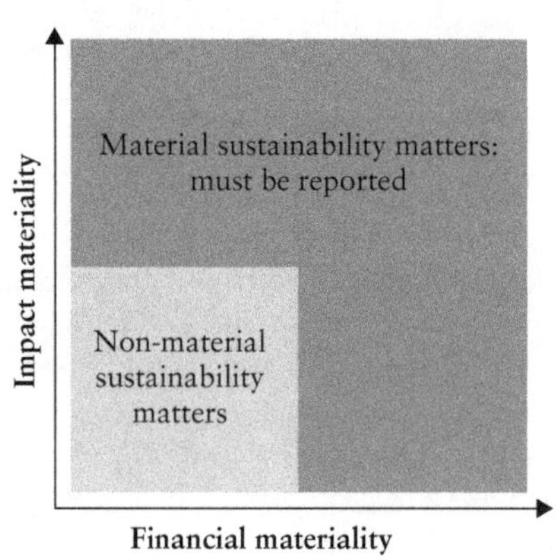

Source: Baumüller *et al.* (2024)

Example 5.2 uses an excerpt from the 2023 Ørsted Annual Integrated Report to illustrate a materiality matrix that is aligned with ESRS.

Example 5.2

Materiality matrix aligned with ESRS – Ørsted

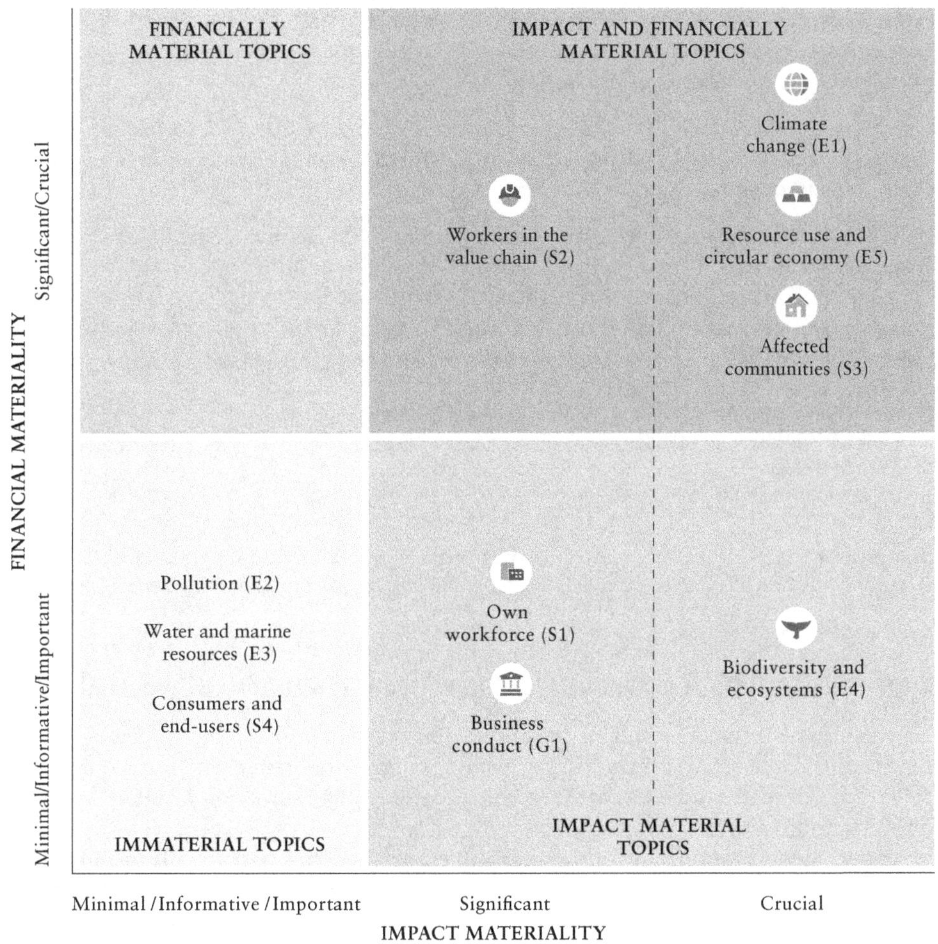

Source: Ørsted (2023), p. 71

Level of disaggregation

The reporting boundaries define on which organizational level materiality has to be assessed, that is how thresholds for materiality should be set. This can either be the individual organization or, in the case of consolidated sustainability reporting, at group level. For the latter, this means that although a matter might be material for a subsidiary that is part of a group, it might not be material from the entire group's perspective.

However, in such cases, chapter 3.7 of ESRS 1 sets forth additional requirements. Under certain circumstances, in addition to the sustainability matters that are material for the entire group, additional information shall be given for individual companies that are part of the group. However, the requirements in ESRS 1 go one step further than organizational levels and may also demand information be given on a country level, site level or even asset level – levels that might also be relevant for non-consolidated sustainability reports:

When needed for a proper understanding of its material impacts, risks and opportunities, the undertaking shall disaggregate the reported information:

a) by country, when there are significant variations of material impacts, risks and opportunities across countries and when presenting the information at a higher level of aggregation would obscure material information about impacts, risks or opportunities; or
b) by significant site or by significant asset, when material impacts, risks and opportunities are highly dependent on a specific location or asset.

When defining the appropriate level of disaggregation for reporting, the undertaking shall consider the disaggregation adopted in its materiality assessment. Depending on the undertaking's specific facts and circumstances, a disaggregation by subsidiary may be necessary. (ESRS 1.54–55)

ESRS 1 chapter 7.6 further expands on such heterogenous IROs within a group. It requires additional disclosures be made about the IROs of a subsidiary in the consolidated sustainability report if the IRO profile of the group differs significantly from the IRO profile of the subsidiary. These requirements also have implications for the process of materiality analysis. Three different approaches are possible, which are further described in EFRAG IG 1. In all instances, analyses and interactions between the group level and the subsidiary level are necessary, as follows:

- **Top-down approach:** materiality analysis is performed at the group level in co-operation with subsidiaries in order to obtain the necessary information.
- **Bottom-up approach:** materiality analysis is performed at the subsidiary level, then the results are consolidated at the group level.
- **Hybrid approach:** as a starting point, materiality analysis is performed at the group level to identify those IROs that are common across the group; then, IROs that are specific to one or more subsidiaries are assessed using the thresholds for the materiality assessment at group level.

The role of stakeholder engagement for materiality analysis

Stakeholder engagement is vital for each of the three steps of materiality analysis. Most importantly, the views and interests of their affected stakeholders are main points of reference when an organization identifies and assesses its material impacts (whereas for the identification and assessment of material risks and chances, different rationales apply).

Stakeholder engagement is defined as follows in the glossary of terms in Annex II of EFRAG (2024b): 'An ongoing process of interaction and dialogue between the undertaking and its stakeholders that enables the undertaking to hear, understand and respond to their interests and concerns.' This definition also allows the concrete requirements of the quality of this engagement to be determined. It is deeply rooted in the idea of sustainability due diligence and thus requires ongoing processes. Organizations should also deal with their stakeholders' interests throughout the entire year and at top management levels. And as interaction is two-way, they should also show how they actually consider the interests of their affected stakeholders in their business models and strategies.

It is therefore not enough to simply send out questionnaires to stakeholders and ask them about specific interests and engagements. Instead, more diverse and more qualitative approaches are required.

However, it is not always possible for organizations to gain direct access to their affected stakeholders and to engage with them. For that reason, ESRS 1 addresses specific proxies that organizations might refer to:

- Organizations might engage with representatives of their affected stakeholders. This might be workers' representatives for work-related sustainability matters or NGOs for environmental matters. Other ESRS also specify that organizations should refer to 'legitimate representatives' or 'credible proxies', thus outlining that choosing such representatives should be done with great care.

- With regard to environmental matters, ESRS 1 also introduces the idea of 'silent stakeholders'. This allows organizations to reduce complexity and cost by basing their assessment on available scientific evidence about the state of nature.

ESRS 1.AR7 defines the term 'silent stakeholders' as follows: 'Nature may be considered as a silent stakeholder. In this case, ecological data and data on the conservation of species may support the undertaking's materiality assessment.' To meet their requirements concerning silent stakeholders, organizations might refer to scientific journals or to available databases, some of which are also referred to in the ESRS, while others are provided by organizations such as the World Wildlife Fund for Nature. Most importantly, the data has to be based on sound scientific methodology and should be up-do-date with recent knowledge advances.

Activity 5.3 asks you to consider the sustainability of water and marine resources.

ACTIVITY 5.3

ESRS E3 covers the sustainability matter 'water and marine resources'. One important element of the standard refers to 'Area of high-water stress' that organizations have to assess. Such areas are defined as follows in the glossary of terms:

'Regions where the percentage of total water withdrawn is high (40–80%) or extremely high (greater than 80%) in the Aqueduct Water Risk Atlas tool of the World Resources Institute (WRI).'

Go to the webpage of the Aqueduct Water Risk Atlas (www.wri.org/applications/aqueduct/water-risk-atlas/). Then search for the address where you live, study or work. Analyse the 'baseline water stress indicator' for the 'business as usual' scenario for this location. What are your conclusions?

FINAL CONSIDERATIONS

While ESRS 1 sets the overall framework for double materiality assessments, ESRS 2 does not define materiality. However, it provides specific reporting requirements for various sustainability topics across different sectors, which can inform the development of the organization's materiality matrix. The focus of ESRS 2 comes after the material topics through the double materiality assessment have been identified. ESRS 2 may be used as a reference point to understand the specific disclosure requirements associated with the topics required for the sustainability report. Each ESRS standard outlines various sustainability topics and breaks them down into subtopics. For each subtopic, ESRS 2 provides specific disclosure requirements. This allows companies to understand the level of detail and type of information they need to include in their sustainability report for each material topic. This, in turn, also indirectly influences the granularity of how they conduct materiality analysis. By following these steps and considering the role of both ESRS 1 and ESRS 2, organizations can conduct a robust double materiality assessment that lays the foundation for effective sustainability reporting under the CSRD framework.

A final consideration is the dialogue between the organization conducting CSRD compliant double materiality assessment and the external auditor. Here are some guidelines for addressing auditors during a double materiality assessment for CSRD compliance:

- Maintain clear and comprehensive documentation of the double materiality assessment process. This includes:
    - stakeholder engagement efforts (e.g. meeting minutes, survey results)
    - list of potential sustainability matters considered
    - rationale for prioritizing specific material topics (double materiality matrix)
    - data sources used for impact and risk assessments.

- Demonstrate a sound understanding of ESRS 1 and ESRS 2. Be prepared to explain how their principles were applied to the double materiality assessment.
- Maintain transparent documentation of the double materiality assessment. Include a description of the stakeholder engagement process and how it informed the identification of potential sustainability matters.

Organizations need to be able to explain:

- How they arrived at the final list of material sustainability matters. Highlight the double materiality matrix and the rationale behind prioritizing certain topics based on both impact and financial considerations.
- How different data sources were used for impact and risk assessments. Discuss the limitations of any data and how this has been addressed.
- If there are data gaps, the organization needs to acknowledge them and explain its plan to address them in future assessments.

Example 5.3 provides insights into the narrative description of a company's anchoring of sustainability aspects in due diligence before Activity 5.4 explores the issue further.

Example 5.3

Double materiality analysis

The Example Group is a family-run industrial company with around 500 employees (sector: electrical engineering). These are spread across four production sites in Austria, Germany and the Czech Republic. A separate staff unit has been set up to coordinate sustainability agendas within the company; this team reports directly to the CFO.

How are social sustainability aspects anchored in due diligence with regard to the company's own workforce?
There is an ongoing exchange with the company's employees. Channels such as 'submission boxes' for anonymous feedback, for suggestions for improvement and for reporting grievances have been set up. An ESG Day is held once a year (at alternating times at the individual locations), where all employees can find out about current developments and contribute their views. Institutionalized exchange also takes place at the level of the Central Works Council. In regular business meetings, topics relevant from an employee perspective are discussed with the Management Board and the relevant division heads. The Sustainability Management department receives the minutes of these meetings.

KPIs on social issues are included in the company's quarterly reporting. This includes key figures such as hours worked, employee structure (including diversity) and staff turnover. The company formulates targets in this regard, which are also included in the remuneration of the Management Board and, in some cases, in the remuneration systems of the division heads. These targets are evaluated and adjusted at regular intervals. Last year, for example, the results of an internal satisfaction survey were incentivized with regard to working conditions.

Source: Modified and translated from www.researchgate.net/publication/376558463_WWF_CSRD_Quick-Guide_Wesentlichkeitsanalyse_gemass_CSRD_und_ESRS

ACTIVITY 5.4

Refer to Example 5.3: How does the Example Group identify material topics with regard to its own workforce as part of the materiality analysis? And how does the company report on this impact?

A PRACTICAL CASE: BORREGAARD

Borregaard, a manufacturer of bio-based chemicals and biomaterials headquartered in Norway, exemplifies the practical application of double materiality assessments within the European context. Example 5.4 delves into Borregaard's approach to identifying and prioritizing sustainability topics under the recently implemented CSRD. Extracts from their 2023 Double Materiality report illustrate how Borregaard leverages stakeholder engagement and a robust assessment process to define material topics that encompass both their environmental and social impacts alongside financial considerations.

Example 5.4

Double Materiality Assessment Report 2023: Borregaard

Borregaard has conducted a double materiality assessment according to the ESRS and follows the practices of a materiality assessment according to GRI Universal standards of 2021.

A double materiality assessment is the process by which we determine material matters and material information to be reported on in our sustainability statement. This assessment is not limited to Borregaard's own operations but includes the upstream and downstream value chain. Double materiality assessments require that we recognise how Borregaard can affect and be affected by sustainability matters. (p. 3)

Borregaard identifies and assesses our impacts on the environment and the society regularly while engaging with relevant stakeholders and experts. When assessing matters concerning environment, social and governance, our stakeholder's views and concerns are evaluated through regular dialogue, media analyses, meetings, as well as other relevant arenas. The stakeholder dialogue and impact assessment through research of output from our day-to-day process results in an overview of our negative and positive impacts. This provides us valuable input on the actual and potential positive and negative impacts on the environment and society including human rights for each of the stakeholder groups. The results are documented and reported to our internal Sustainability Board (SB) by those responsible for each stakeholder group. Throughout the year we have separate meetings for each material stakeholder group where the results from the impacts of relevant material topics are discussed. The results of the discussion are used as input to the annual update of the impact materiality assessment presented in the Board of Directors Report, published in the Annual Report and in a separate Double Materiality Assessment Report. Climate and nature-related impacts, risks and opportunities are disclosed in line with the International Financial Reporting Standards (IFRS) S2, which includes a scenario analysis, and Nature-Related Financial Disclosures (TNFD) framework and presented in the separate Climate and Nature Risk report. To understand our impacts, risks and opportunities, the assessment is based on a value chain mapping of our business relationships, our stakeholder dialogue, and additional relevant sources. This way we can identify impacts, risks and opportunities directly connected to Borregaard's own operations and indirect impacts through our business relationships. The results are included in our double materiality assessment (p. 4).

Borregaard's Sustainability Board (SB) is responsible for the due diligence process of materiality outcome. SB addresses and monitors the material topics and reports the results of the Sustainability Statements in the Annual Report (p. 5)

Source: Borregaard (2023), pp. 3–5

Borregaard makes detailed disclosures on how they conducted the impact as well as materiality assessment (refer to Figure 5.8).

Figure 5.8 ESRS double materiality assessment Borregaard: method

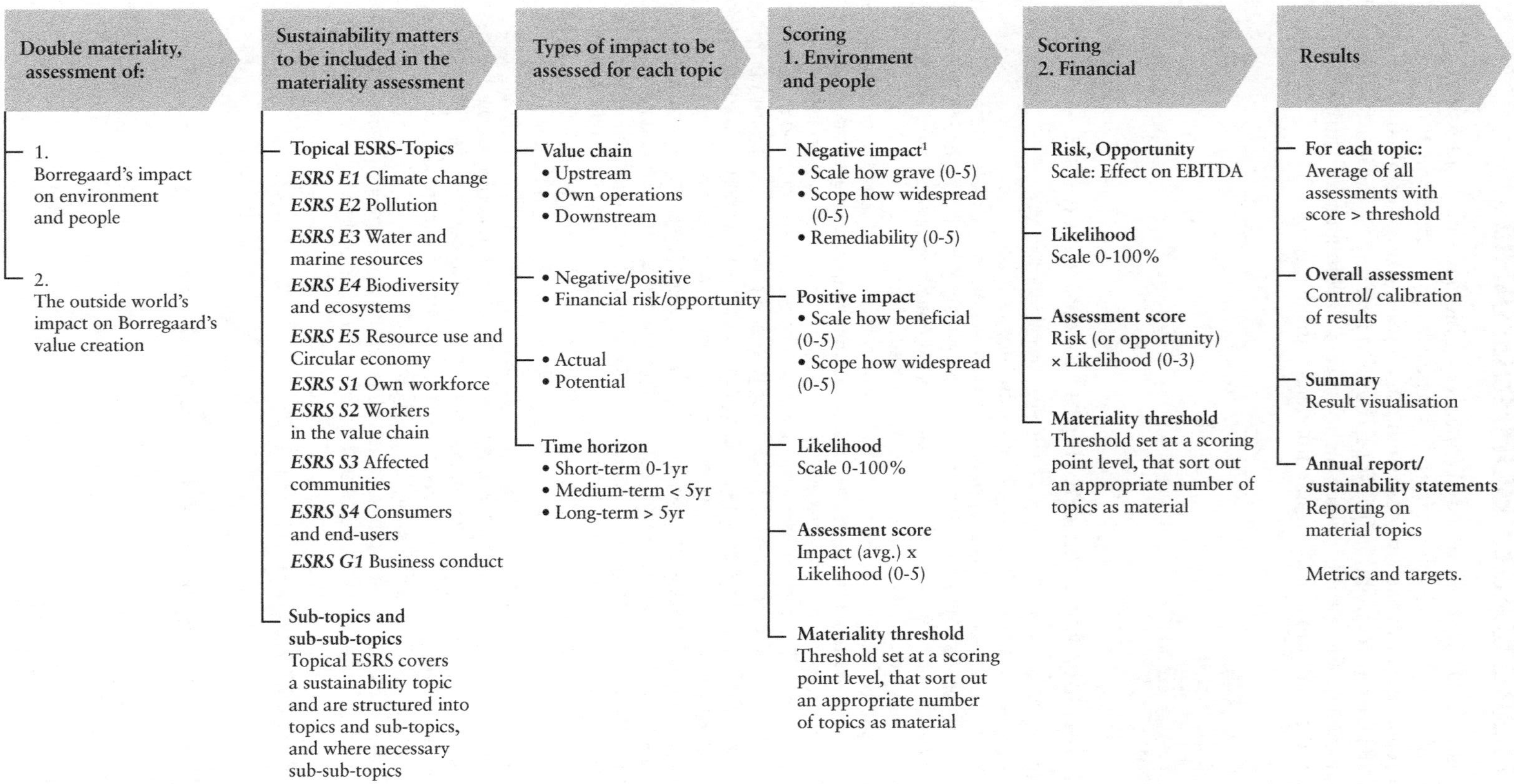

Source: Borregaard (2023), p. 5

The report also includes detailed sections on impact materiality scoring and financial materiality scoring that are worth reviewing. Another matrix in this report captures the link between double materiality and the value chain, which is illustrated in Table 5.3.

Table 5.3 Link between double materiality and the value chain

Topical ESRS	Topic	Sub-topic	Upstream				Own Operations				Downstream			
			I Neg	I Pos	R	O	I Neg	I Pos	R	O	I Neg	I Pos	R	O
ESRS E1	Climate change	Energy												
		Climate change mitigation												
ESRS E2	Pollution	Pollution of water												
		Pollution of soil												
		Pollution of air												
ESRS E3	Biodiversity and ecosystems	Direct impact drivers of biodiversity loss												
ESRS E5	Resource use and Circular economy	Waste												
		Resources inflows, including resource use												
ESRS S1	Own workforce	Working conditions												
		Equal treatment and opportunities for all												
ESRS G1	Business conduct	Management of relationships with suppliers including payment practices												

Note: I - impact on environment and people. R - financial risk. O - financial opportunity. Neg – negative. Pos – positive.

Source: Borregaard (2023), p. 11

MAPPING THE SDGS TO MATERIALITY

The important role of the private sector in contributing to the achievement of the SDGs is noted both in academic studies (Betti *et al.*, 2018; Thammaraksa *et al.*, 2024) and international organizations (refer to, for example, United Nations Conference on Trade and Development, 2023). The 17 SDGs address critical challenges such as poverty, inequality, climate change and environmental degradation. By mapping SDGs to an organization's double materiality assessment, organizations can identify priorities through the SDG lens.

The SDGs provide a comprehensive framework for sustainability issues. Aligning the organization's materiality assessment with relevant SDGs helps focus efforts on the most critical areas for both the organization and society. Based on the identified material issues, the organization selects the most relevant SDGs that their business activities can influence. The organization then maps its material issues to the specific targets and indicators of the chosen SDGs. This opens up the possibility to demonstrate how an organization's activities contribute to (or hinder) progress towards the SDGs. Mapping requires robust data collection and transparent reporting on the organization's impact on the SDGs. Organizations such as the GRI have provided helpful material on performing this task. Activity 5.5 invites you to consider the pros and cons of organizations undertaking assessments against the SDGs.

ACTIVITY 5.5

How do you perceive the risk of 'SDG washing' (greenwashing risk) where organizations simply align themselves with the goals for communication purposes without taking concrete action? Discuss the advantages and disadvantages of organizations making disclosures on their assessments against the SDGs.

There are various ways to visually approach this assessment against the SDGs. Figure 5.9 illustrates how Tryg has approached this task and Figure 5.10 demonstrates how Nestlé shares material issues across the value chain.

Figure 5.9 Overarching assessment against SDGs: Tryg

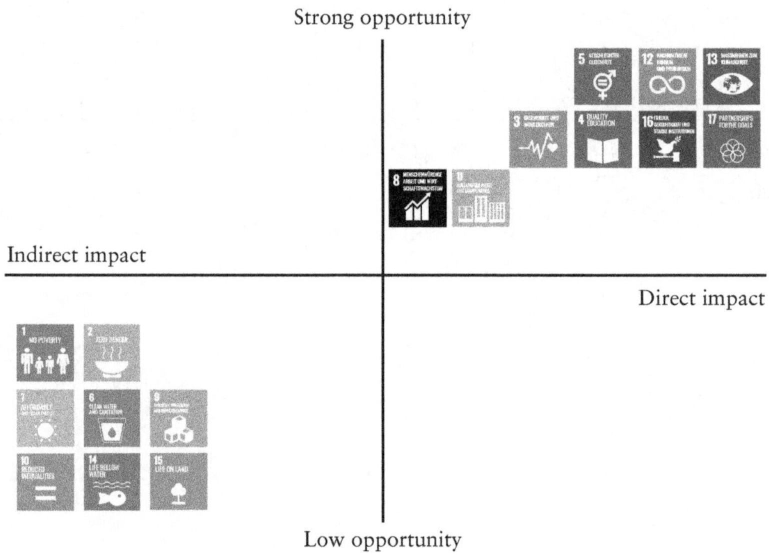

Source: Tryg (n.d.)

Figure 5.10 Nestlé material issues across the value chain (2023)

KEY: ○ Moderate ● Significant ● Major

Material issues and sub-issues	Agriculture	Tier 1 suppliers	Nestlé	Retail/business channels	Consumers
For the planet					
Water stewardship Implementing the actions, individually and/or collectively, needed for the sustainable management of shared water resources. Sub-issues: • Bottled water • Water quality • Water security • Water use	Major	Significant	Major	Significant	Significant
Water, sanitation and hygiene Improving access to safe water and sanitation, and appropriate facilities to ensure personal hygiene, across our value chain.	Major	Significant	Major	Significant	Major
Natural resource stewardship Identifying and preserving natural resources and ecosystem services. Sub-issues: • Biodiversity • Deforestation • Soil fertility	Major	Major	Significant	Moderate	Moderate
Climate change Reducing greenhouse gas emissions and contributing to the mitigation of and adaptation to the negative effects of climate change. Sub-issues: • Climate change adaptation • Climate change mitigation • Advocacy on climate policy	Major	Significant	Major	Major	Significant

Source: Nestle (2023), p. 3

IMPLICATIONS OF DOUBLE MATERIALITY FOR ORGANIZATIONS

Double materiality can introduce new complexities for organizations to attend to. As illustrated in this chapter, determining material sustainability issues necessitates a robust assessment process that considers not only an organization's direct impact but also the broader influence of its value chain. This can be resource-intensive, especially for organizations with intricate global operations. Furthermore, effectively integrating sustainability factors into strategic decision-making requires a cultural shift within organizations, potentially demanding adjustments to governance structures and employee training programmes.

Double materiality represents a significant step towards more sustainable business practices. By acknowledging the interconnectedness of financial, environmental and social spheres, it compels organizations to take a more comprehensive view of their impact. Nevertheless, navigating the complexities of double materiality assessment and implementation necessitates careful planning, **resource allocation** and a commitment to organizational transformation. Challenges can range from data collection, stakeholder engagement and integration with existing reporting frameworks, while the opportunities include improved risk management.

Activity 5.6 provides an opportunity for you to discuss the potential benefits and drawbacks of double materiality.

ACTIVITY 5.6

Discuss the potential benefits and drawbacks of double materiality for both organizations and financial statement users.

THE CORPORATE SUSTAINABILITY DUE DILIGENCE DIRECTIVE (CSDDD) AND DOUBLE MATERIALITY

EFRAG IG 1 on conducting double materiality assessments highlights that the ESRS specifically clarifies that the materiality assessment process is guided by the due diligence procedures outlined in international frameworks, namely the OECD Guidelines for Multinational Enterprises (MNE Guidelines) and the UN Guiding Principles on Business and Human Rights (UNGPs). Engaging with affected stakeholders is a crucial element of the undertaking's due diligence and impact assessment (ESRS 1.24). This engagement can provide valuable evidence or insights into actual or potential impacts on people and the environment associated with the undertaking. By identifying sustainability matters such as human rights violations and environmental harm in the value chain, companies gain insights into potential negative impacts they may not have considered before.

Figure 5.11 describes how sustainability due diligence and materiality assessment are inseparably linked.

Figure 5.11 How sustainability due diligence and materiality assessment are linked

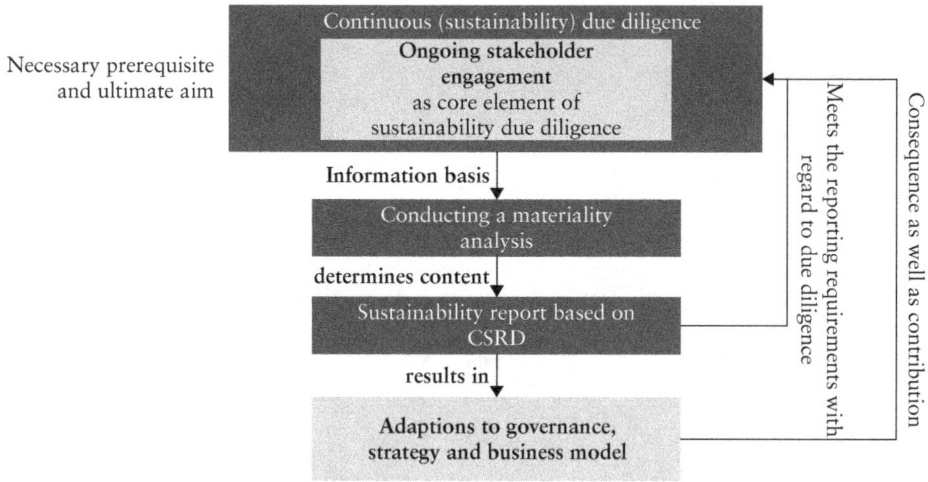

Source: Adapted from Baumüller & Schönauer (2023)

Thus, the Corporate Sustainability Due Diligence Directive (CSDDD) and the double materiality assessment under the CSRD are complementary regulations that work together to enhance corporate sustainability practices. The CSDDD focuses on requiring companies to conduct human rights and environmental due diligence throughout their value chain. This due diligence process essentially strengthens the impact materiality assessment under CSRD. This information feeds directly into the materiality assessment, helping companies prioritize the most significant sustainability issues across their entire operations and value chain. The CSRD's double materiality assessment makes companies report on these sustainability issues, while the CSDDD compels them to take action to address them. Also, the CSRD provides the platform for companies to report on how they have implemented the requirements of the CSDDD. Find out in Example 5.5 how double materiality is approached and presented in Barry Callebaut's Double Materiality Assessment Report 2022/2023, then tackle Activities 5.7 and 5.8.

Example 5.5

Barry Callebaut Double Materiality Assessment Report 2022/2023

Understanding one's own value chain in detail is the basis for conducting a high-quality materiality assessment and developing an appropriate list of ESG topics for further analysis. Our materiality analysis centers on a comprehensive examination of Barry Callebaut's value chain, encompassing both direct and indirect value chains. This analysis combined our knowledge of our processes with comprehensive research, systematically reviewing activities across our operations. Our goal was to identify both apparent and potential touchpoints related to ESG matters along the entire value chain. (p. 5)

(Continued)

An overview of Barry Callebaut's value chain

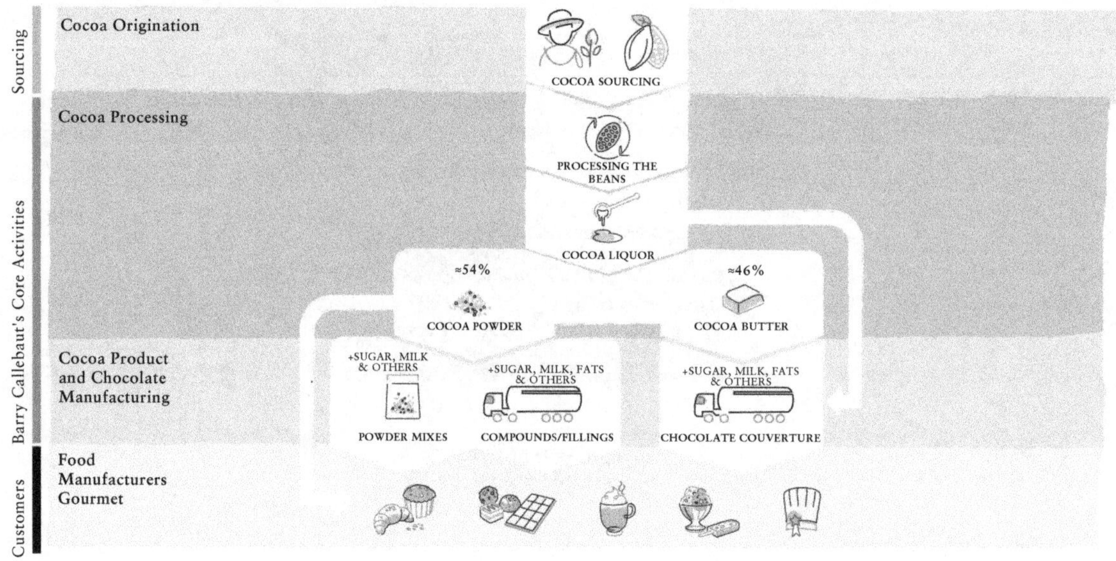

Source: Barry Callebaut (2023), p. 5

ACTIVITY 5.7

Identify and discuss what Borregaard says about its value chain in their double materiality report of 2022/23 (refer to Example 5.4).

ACTIVITY 5.8

An organization with a complex global supply chain struggles to define the boundaries of its 'value chain for due diligence purposes'. Investigating every single subcontractor seems impractical, yet leaving out crucial actors could lead to missed risks.

How can an organization establish clear materiality thresholds for their due diligence efforts, ensuring compliance with the CSDDD while avoiding overwhelming itself with information?

Discuss the role of industry best practices and stakeholder engagement in defining the scope of due diligence. Explore how the double materiality assessment under CSRD can inform this process by identifying the most impactful aspects of the value chain.

THE VALUE CHAIN UNDER ESRS

EFRAG's Implementation Guidance 2: Value chain (EFRAG IG 2) provides a comprehensive framework for understanding and reporting value chain IROs in the context of sustainability reporting. This guide is particularly relevant for organizations aiming to comply with the ESRS under the CSRD.

EFRAG IG 2 builds on the ESRS definition that the value chain is to be understood as the full range of activities involved in the creation, delivery and post-sale services of a product, encompassing all direct and indirect relationships, from suppliers to end consumers. The importance of including both upstream and downstream activities in sustainability reporting is emphasized and is aimed at capturing all significant IROs across the entire value chain. 'Entire' means that there is no restriction on starting and end points, an approach which is often called 'cradle to grave'.

However, it should be noted that ESRS do not properly distinguish between 'business relationships' and 'actors in the value chain'. The first one is the broader term, while the latter is an important part of business relationships. The main difference is that in general, organizations have to consider their business relationships, that is their direct contacts with suppliers, customers, etc. When such business relationships are part of the organization's value chain, indirect business relationships also have to be considered, for examples suppliers of suppliers. Example 5.6 shares ways in which these relationships can be presented in a real-world scenario. Activity 5.9 invites you to investigate due diligence processes for yourself.

Example 5.6

A deep dive into the raw material (rubber) value chain: Michelin

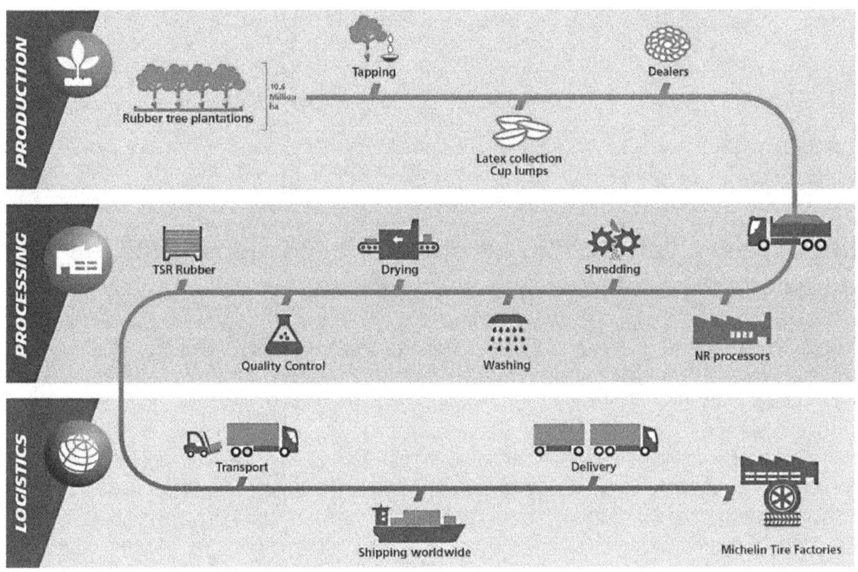

Source: Michelin website (n.d.)

Another good representation of a value chain can be found in 'Nokian Tyres as a part of society' in the company's Sustainability Report 2023 (nokiantyres.studio.crasman.cloud/pub/web/attachments/publications/Nokian_Tyres_Sustainability_report_2023.pdf, p. 19).

ACTIVITY 5.9

Pick an organization of your choosing that has to report in accordance with CSRD. Determine whether their disclosures reveal how they have established mechanisms for sustainability due diligence while considering the economic impact of responsible and ethical business processes. Discuss your findings.

Most often, an organization is part of several value chains. Accordingly, all these value chains have to be considered for sustainability reporting purposes, starting with materiality analysis. However, ESRS 1.39 allows organizations to 'focus on areas where impacts, risks and opportunities are deemed likely to arise, based on the nature of the activities, business relationships, geographies or other factors concerned'. Key to this is undertaking a value chain assessment prior to the materiality assessment.

Subsequently, EFRAG IG 2 outlines a process for identifying and prioritizing material sustainability issues within the value chain. This involves stakeholder engagement, impact assessments and the application of criteria to determine the significance of various sustainability aspects.

EFRAG highlights the challenges and best practices for data collection across the value chain. Accurate and reliable data is essential for effective sustainability reporting, and the guide provides strategies for improving data quality, such as leveraging digital technologies and enhancing supplier collaboration. The identification and management of sustainability-related risks and opportunities within the value chain are addressed and the need for robust risk management frameworks that integrate sustainability considerations into overall business strategies.

Effective stakeholder engagement is crucial for understanding value chain impacts and improving sustainability performance. EFRAG IG 2 advises on methods for engaging with stakeholders, including suppliers, customers and local communities, to gather insights and drive collaborative sustainability initiatives. Example 5.7 uses the case of Borregaard to describe how the value chain can be mapped in practice.

Example 5.7

Description of how a value chain mapping was carried out: Borregaard, 2023

VALUE CHAIN MAPPING AND STAKEHOLDER ENGAGEMENT

We have used value chain mapping to assess the impacts on and of Borregaard's operations, focusing on risks, opportunities and dependencies as described in the **Climate and Nature Risk Report**. This systematic analysis provides valuable insights into the direct and indirect activities in the supply chain and further the strategies to reduce risks related to the environment and people in our value chain. Additionally, this evaluation reveals opportunities for the integration of sustainable practices and innovative solutions.

The mapping of dependencies within the value chain allows for the identification of vulnerabilities and interconnections that may amplify risks. This enables us to implement strategic measures for resilience, ensuring a proactive approach to addressing potential challenges and enhancing the sustainability of our operations.

Our stakeholders' feedback is vital to assess the significance of impact by degree of severity of benefit or significance of risk and opportunities by financial effect and likelihood in the value chain mapping process. The stakeholders can be divided into two groups, affected stakeholders and users of sustainability statements. The first one mostly consists of suppliers, employees, local communities and the society in large, as well as nature. Users of sustainability statements are often customers, investors, lenders and authorities.

We have identified our stakeholders by surveying the groups, organisations and individuals that are either impacted by our operations or which, in a variety of ways, have an impact on our strategy and goal achievement. Our stakeholders include existing and potential customers, investors and lenders, current and potential employees, the authorities, suppliers, local communities and neighbours, business partners, organisations and the media.

The most important stakeholders are shown in the figure below.

The individual units in the Borregaard Group continuously assess issues that are relevant for the relationship between the company and society. We believe a good dialogue with our stakeholders is a valuable means of building trust and understanding of the role we play in local communities and society.

Complaints and other enquiries from external stakeholders are considered and dealt with appropriately, including through our grievance mechanisms. Borregaard has established guidelines on whistleblowing, how expressions of concerns are handled, and which channels can be used for addressing concern. In 2023, we will include public disclosure of grievances logged and actions taken in our reporting. The Transparency act, relating to transparency and work on fundamental human rights and decent working conditions entered into force in Norway on 1 July 2022, further expanding our focus on our value chain and external stakeholder engagement.

The most important subject in the stakeholder dialogue in 2023, was resilience towards uncertainty in the global economy and how this may impact Borregaard's markets, cost inflation and interest rates. This was especially important for our customers and investors. Several of our stakeholders pay increasing attention to sustainability issues such as climate impact from our products, scope 3 emissions, nature-related risks (in particular biodiversity) from the use of wood as a raw material as well as emerging changes in sustainability regulations from the EU Green Deal. Transparency in the value chain is important for our stakeholders to better understand impacts, risks, and opportunities from our business, including human rights.

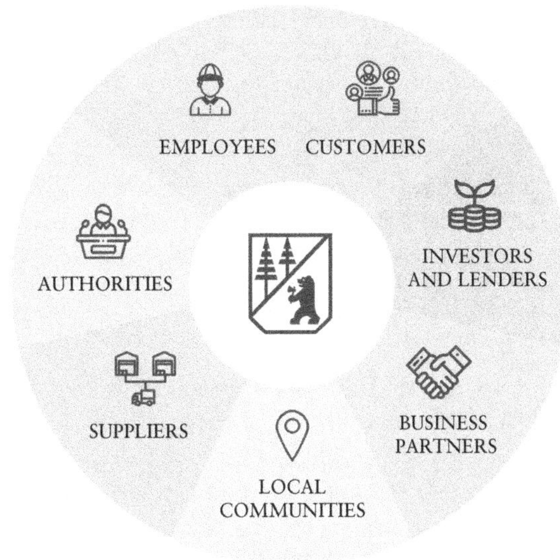

Source: Borregaard (2023), p. 6

The CSDDD and the value chain

Some, but not all, organizations that fall under the CSRD also have to adhere to the provisions of the CSDDD. The CSDDD lays down the rules on:

- obligations for organizations regarding actual and potential human rights adverse impacts and environmental adverse impacts, with respect to their own operations, the operations of their subsidiaries, and the operations carried out by their business partners in the chains of activities of those organizations;
- liability for violations of the sustainability due diligence obligations bestowed upon them; and
- the obligation for companies to adopt and put into effect a transition plan for climate change mitigation which aims to ensure, through best efforts, compatibility of the business model and of the strategy of the *organization* with the transition to a sustainable economy and with the limiting of global warming to 1.5°C in line with the Paris Agreement.

Organizations should take appropriate steps to set up and carry out due diligence measures with respect to their own operations, those of their subsidiaries, as well as those of their direct and indirect business partners throughout their chains of activities in accordance with this Directive.

The CSDDD emphasizes the term 'chain of activities' (rather than value chain). The chain of activities should cover activities of an organization's upstream business partners related to the production of goods or the provision of services by the organization, including the design, extraction, sourcing, manufacture, transport, storage and supply of raw materials, products or parts of the products and development of the product or the service, and activities of an organization's downstream business partners related to the distribution, transport and storage of the product, where the business partners carry out those activities for the organization or on behalf of the organization. This Directive should not cover the disposal of the product.

The term 'value chain' was used in the Commission's initial proposal for the CSDDD. However, it was replaced by a neutral term of 'chain of activities' in order to reflect divergent views of Member States on the issue of whether to cover the whole 'value chain' or limit the scope to the 'supply chain', and to avoid confusion with already existing definitions since the content of the term has been modified.

However, the CSDDD (rec. 25) makes clear that the value chain of an organization is a broader term than chain of activities: 'The term 'chain of activities' as defined in this Directive is without prejudice to the terms 'value chain' or 'supply chain' as defined in or within the meaning of other Union legislation.'

A 'chain of activities' (refer to Figure 5.12) then means:

- activities of an organization's upstream business partners related to the production of goods or the provision of services by that organization, including the design, extraction, sourcing, manufacture, transport, storage and supply of raw materials, products or parts of products and the development of the product or the service; and
- activities of a company's downstream business partners related to the distribution, transport and storage of a product of that company, where the business partners carry out those activities for the organization or on behalf of the organization, and excluding the distribution, transport and storage of a product that is subject to export controls under Regulation (EU) 2021/821 or to the export controls relating to weapons, munitions or war materials, once the export of the product is authorized. (CSDDD)

'Business partner' in turn, is a common term used by CSDDD and CSRD. According to the definition of the CSDDD, the term refers to an entity:

- with which the company has a commercial agreement related to the operations, products or services of the company or to which the organization provides services pursuant to point (g) ('direct business partner'); or
- which is not a direct business partner but which performs business operations related to the operations, products or services of the organization ('indirect business partner').

Figure 5.12 CSDDD chain of activities

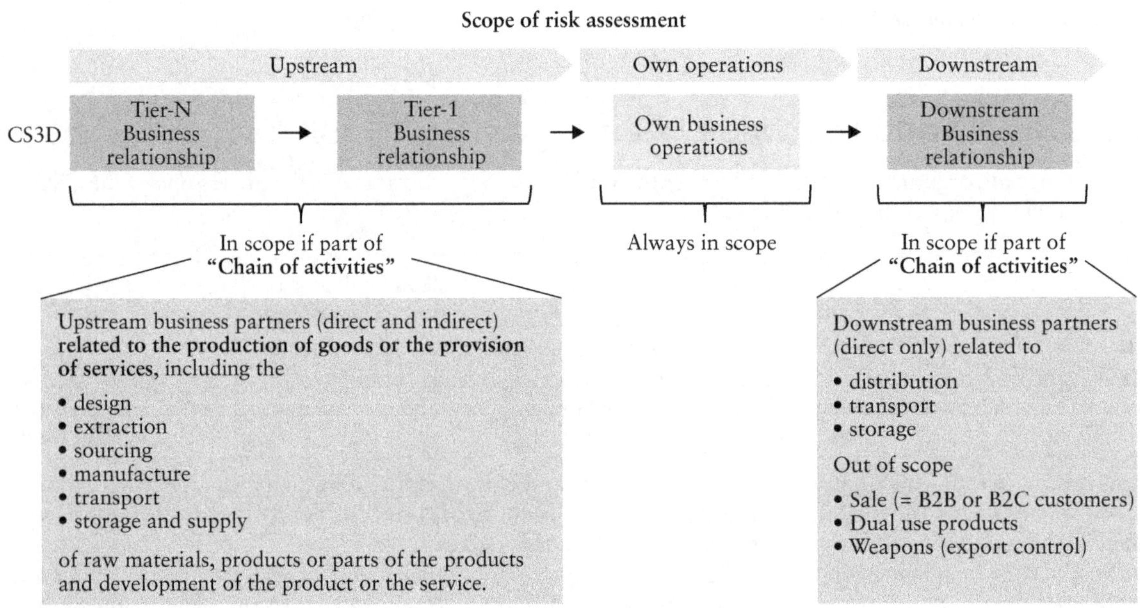

Source: Prewave on LinkedIn (n.d.)

Activity 5.10 asks you to identify the definitions for value chain and chain of activities in CSDDD and CSRD.

ACTIVITY 5.10

Use the glossary of terms for ESRS, EFRAG IG 2 on the value chain and the CSDDD in order to compare the CSRD definition and explanation of the value chain with that of the CSDDD description of chain of activities.

CONCLUSION

By elucidating the intricate relationship between financial and non-financial dimensions, this chapter has aimed to provide a comprehensive understanding of double materiality and the role of the value chain for analyses.

The concept of materiality has become a cornerstone of sustainability reporting. It transcends mere disclosure by requiring organizations to identify and prioritize the environmental and social issues that most significantly impact their business and stakeholders. This focus on materiality fosters a more strategic approach to sustainability, encouraging organizations to integrate these considerations into core decision-making processes.

The emergence of frameworks such as the EU's CSRD and initiatives like the IFRS Sustainability Disclosure Standards further solidify the importance of materiality. However, the concept is not without its challenges. Defining and assessing materiality can be complex, particularly in the context of intricate global supply chains. Furthermore, ensuring consistent and comparable reporting of material sustainability information across different companies and industries remains an ongoing challenge. Future advancements in data collection, standardization and assurance practices may support the strengthening of materiality-based reporting, ultimately leading to a more transparent business environment.

These challenges are of specific importance to the inclusion of value chains in materiality analysis. However, it has become commonly accepted that an organization's responsibility for its impacts also addresses its direct and indirect business relationships. So, organizations under the CSRD have to make all necessary efforts to identify material IROs with regard to their entire value chains and to include information about these IROs in their sustainability reports.

SUMMARY

The following items relate to the learning objectives listed at the beginning of the chapter.

- **LO 1. Discuss the difference between financial materiality and impact materiality in the context of sustainability reporting.**

  The two key dimensions of double materiality, as defined in the CSRD, are financial materiality and impact materiality, each addressing different stakeholder needs and perspectives. Financial materiality focuses on the implications of sustainability matters for the organization itself. It seeks to identify risks, opportunities and other sustainability-related factors that could significantly influence the organization's financial performance, value creation or position over the short, medium or long term. Impact materiality emphasizes the organization's effects on external stakeholders and the broader environment, including people, communities, ecosystems and societies. This perspective requires the disclosure of information about the organization's contributions – positive or negative – to ESG outcomes.

- **LO 2. Understand how materiality is defined for sustainability reporting in selected reporting standards and frameworks.**

  Materiality serves as a guiding principle in sustainability reporting, helping organizations determine what information should be disclosed to ensure relevance and decision-usefulness for stakeholders. Different reporting standards and frameworks define materiality in varying ways, often reflecting their underlying objectives, target audiences and regulatory contexts. Frameworks such as the GRI and ESRS emphasize impact materiality, considering broader societal and environmental concerns. In contrast, the ISSB (and former TCFD) focus on financial materiality, addressing the implications of sustainability on organizational value.

- **LO 3. Discuss how a 'double materiality assessment' can be undertaken.**
  A double materiality assessment is a structured process to evaluate and disclose sustainability matters that are material from two perspectives: financial materiality (how sustainability issues affect the organization's financial position) and impact materiality (how the organization impacts the environment, society and stakeholders). A shortened version of this process would typically involve the following steps: 1) define the purpose and establish a governance structure for the assessment; 2) identify relevant topics (using for example ESRS); 3) gather input from stakeholders through surveys, interviews or workshops to understand priorities; 4) assess impact materiality; 5) assess financial materiality; 6) prioritize issues and 7) integrate material topics with strategy and make corresponding disclosure findings transparently in sustainability disclosures.
- **LO 4. Define an organization's value chain.**
  ESRS define an organization's value chain as encompassing all activities, relationships and entities involved in the creation and delivery of products or services. These include upstream activities, operations and downstream activities.
- **LO 5. Discuss the role of the value chain in the context of CSRD and ESRS.**
  CSRD and ESRS emphasize the need for organizations to assess and report on sustainability impacts, risks and opportunities across their entire value chain, ensuring a comprehensive understanding of their role in broader ESG contexts.
- **LO 6. Understand the link between the CSDDD and the CSRD.**
  The CSDDD and the CSRD are two complementary Directives from the EU. Both aim to promote corporate accountability and transparency in ESG matters. While they address distinct aspects of sustainability governance, they are closely interconnected and work together to enhance corporate responsibility across the EU. The CSDDD focuses on organizational action and accountability, while the CSRD ensures transparency in how these actions and impacts are reported/disclosed.

EXERCISES

1. Explain the difference between materiality according to ESRS and other standards and frameworks for sustainability reporting. (LO 2)
2. Explain the difference between financial and impact materiality. (LO 3)
3. How can regulators and standard-setters ensure consistency and comparability in double materiality disclosures, while still allowing companies the flexibility to address their unique sustainability challenges? Why is this important? (LO 3)
4. Define an organization's value chain according to the ESRS. Include its key components and explain the relevance of value chain analysis in sustainability reporting. (LO 4)
5. Explain the importance of including an organization's value chain in materiality analysis and sustainability reporting. (LO 5)
6. Explain the role of the CSDDD in the light of CSRD compliant double materiality assessment. (LO 6)
7. Assume that an organization claims to use sustainable materials in their products based on their direct suppliers. However, an NGO investigation reveals unsustainable practices lower down the supply chain.
   - **a** How can the double materiality assessment under CSRD be used to address greenwashing concerns related to complex supply chains?
   - **b** How can regulators leverage the CSDDD to ensure companies actively investigate potential human rights and environmental violations across their entire value chain?
   - **c** Discuss the challenges of ensuring transparency throughout a multi-tiered supply chain. Explore the potential role of independent verification bodies in mitigating greenwashing risks.
   - **d** What role does the outcome of a double materiality assessment have for the organization's strategy and business model? (LO 1, LO 3, LO 5)

CHAPTER 6
Environmental reporting I: Climate reporting

Learning objectives

After studying this chapter you should be able to:

- LO 1. Explain the disclosure requirements for ESRS E1 Climate change.
- LO 2. Understand the reporting requirements for GHG emissions.
- LO 3. Explain the role of scenario analysis for climate disclosures.
- LO 4. Understand the different metrics and targets for climate reporting.
- LO 5. Discuss the financial effects on an organization over the short, medium and long term caused by the risks and opportunities arising from the organization's impacts and dependencies on climate change.
- LO 6. Understand the connections between key sustainability reporting frameworks for climate reporting.

The top three climate risks and what to do about them

The **World Economic Forum** publishes a Global Risks Report every year that addresses 'some of the most severe risks we may face over the next decade, against a backdrop of rapid technological change, economic uncertainty, a warming planet and conflict'.

In its 2024 report, besides geo-political competition, disinformation and inflation, climate-related risks were raised as critical challenges facing humanity, later highlighted in a separate article. The three most threatening climate risks they listed were extreme weather events, biodiversity loss and critical change to Earth systems, the latter of which is a new entrant this year. These three risks are interconnected; critical changes to Earth's systems will lead to more extreme weather events, for example, and the World Economic Forum exemplifies the increased risk of storm surges we may face if we see a 1.5°C increase in preindustrial temperatures (scientists reported temperatures 1.48°C above this average in 2023). This increase in temperature will kill 99% of coral reefs which at present act as a protective barrier against coastal storm surges. Loss of coral reefs will also impact the 25% of all marine life that is dependent on them, leading to a devastating loss of biodiversity as well.

Despite this, 'nearly all IPCC scenarios' expect us to pass the 1.5°C threshold in the early 2030s. The World Economic Forum outlines the preventative actions that humanity must take to remain on the current side of this critical tipping point:

'The priority solution is faster emissions reduction and credible steps by all actors in our economic system to accelerate the speed and scale of a clean transition. Human emissions is the swiftest lever to postpone or avoid critical changes to Earth systems.'

Source: Originally published on the World Economic Forum (2024)

INTRODUCTION

This chapter addresses ESRS E1 Climate change. This standard is considered to be the 'flagship standard' of the ESRS in their current form. This is underlined by the number of disclosure requirements within E1 (only exceeded by ESRS S1) and by the special treatment the standard requires in the course of an organization's materiality analysis (refer to ESRS 1.32).

Addressing climate change has been the key priority of European sustainability regulation since the mid-2010s. On a global level, standards and frameworks that provide organizations with guidance on how to deal with the challenges of climate change have been at the core of all developments regarding sustainability reporting for decades. In 1990, the UN's Intergovernmental Panel on Climate Change (IPCC)'s First Assessment Report stated it was certain that 'human activities are substantially increasing the atmospheric concentrations of greenhouse gases' (IPCC, 1992, p. 117).

ESRS E1 CLIMATE CHANGE

Following the ESRS's double materiality approach, ESRS E1 requires organizations to think about climate change in two ways:

- How is the organization contributing to climate change?
- How is the organization affected by climate change?

In both cases, the organization must consider adapting its strategy and business model to react to the challenges that climate change brings. Most importantly, organizations have to consider their alignment with the Paris Agreement, especially concerning how their strategies and business models can become compatible with limiting global warming to 1.5°C.

An organization's **greenhouse gas (GHG)** emissions play a crucial role in all relevant considerations. ESRS E1 builds on existing definitions, international convention and methodologies for measuring GHG emissions. Most importantly, the standard refers to the seven GHG covered by the Kyoto Protocol. These were taken over into various pieces of EU legislation:

> *Greenhouse Gases (GHG): The gases listed in Part 2 of Annex V of Regulation (EU) 2018/1999 of the European Parliament and of the Council. These include Carbon dioxide (CO_2), Methane (CH_4), Nitrous Oxide (N_2O), Sulphur hexafluoride (SF_6), Nitrogen trifluoride (NF_3), Hydrofluorocarbons (HFCs), Perfluorocarbons (PFCs).*
>
> (ESRS G1 Annex II)

GHG emissions are typically calculated as CO_2 equivalents. To make the effects of different types of GHG comparable, the IPCC has defined the so-called 'Global Warming Potential' (GWP). This factor compares the warming effect of a certain amount of a GHG over a set period of time (usually 100 years) with the warming effect of CO_2. Thus, CO_2 equivalents (or CO_2eq) provide a more comparable overview of a company's impact on climate via its emissions, as demonstrated in Example 6.1.

Example 6.1

IPCC Global Warming Potential (GWP) values relative to CO_2

Common chemical name or industrial designation	Chemical formula	GWP values for 100-year time horizon		
		Fourth Assessment Report (AR4)	Fifth Assessment Report (AR5)	Sixth Assessment Report (AR6)
Major Greenhouse Gases				
Carbon dioxide	CO_2	1	1	1
Methane – non-fossil	CH_4	25	28	27.0
Methane – fossil	CH_4	N/A	30	29.8
Nitrous oxide	N_2O	298	265	273
Nitrogen trifluoride	NF_3	17,200	16,100	17,400
Sulfur hexafluoride	SF_6	22,800	23,500	24,300

Source: IPCC (2024)

Use Activity 6.1 to develop your understanding of how GWP and CO_2eq can help standardize GHG outputs from various sources for easier comparison.

ACTIVITY 6.1

A single cow is estimated to produce 70–120kg of methane a year. Calculate the CO_2 equivalent amount of gases produced by a herd of 10 cows over one year.
Compare this with a car. A typical passenger vehicle emits about 4.6 metric tons of CO_2 per year.

Sustainability matters applicable for ESRS E1 (ESRS 1.AR 16)

Appendix A of ESRS 1 contains the list of minimum sustainability matters an organization has to assess during its materiality analysis. In ESRS E1, only a very limited number of sub-topics are distinguished, as outlined in Table 6.1. They both refer to the two perspectives of climate change (adaptation: outside-in perspective; mitigation: inside-out perspective) and one of the most important drivers of fighting climate change: energy sources and consumption.

Table 6.1 Discussion of ESRS E1 in ESRS 1 Appendix A

Topic	Sub-topic	Sub-sub-topic
Climate change	Climate change adaptation	
	Climate change mitigation	
	Energy	

In addition, the definition of climate change mitigation directly addresses the highest ambitions of the Paris Agreement: 'The process of reducing GHG emissions and holding the increase in the global average temperature to 1.5°C above pre-industrial levels'. As a consequence, organizations have to reflect on the extent to which their business models are aligned to these ambitions and how they must adapt their business models to reach that required level of alignment. The IPCC predicts that surpassing the temperature threshold of 1.5°C will result in severe consequences, with an increase in the frequency and severity of droughts, heatwaves and rainfall. For more information on the importance of the 1.5°C alignment readers may consult the Paris Agreement. As already discussed in Chapter 4, ESRS 1 puts a lot of emphasis on climate change as covered by ESRS E1. If an organization does not assess climate change and any of the sub-topics of ESRS E1 as material, ESRS 2.57 requires the organization to 'disclose a detailed explanation of the conclusions of its materiality assessment with regard to climate change [...], including a forward-looking analysis of the conditions that could lead the undertaking to conclude that climate change is material in the future'.

Reporting area: Governance (GOV)

Together with ESRS G1, ESRS E1 is the only topical ESRS that features a disclosure requirement under the reporting area GOV. According to ESRS E2 GOV-3, organizations are required to report on the 'Integration of sustainability-related performance in incentive schemes'.

If climate change is a material topic, then organizations shall disclose whether and how climate-related considerations are included in the remuneration systems of members of the administrative, management and supervisory bodies. Organizations shall explain these climate-related considerations and address:

- if performance has been assessed against the GHG emission reduction targets as reported under disclosure requirement ESRS E1–4
- the percentage of the remuneration that is linked to climate related considerations.

This disclosure requirement underlines the steering effect which the ESRS aim for. As reporting standards, they cannot mandate concrete behaviour. But with the content of their disclosure requirements, they require organizations to evaluate certain aspects of their behaviour and to be transparent about it towards their stakeholders. This, in turn, can serve as a 'nudge' to adopt certain payment and incentive practices that guide managerial behaviour, induce improved performance on sustainability matters and signal to stakeholders that the importance of sustainability matters is perceived accordingly by the owners and managers of an organization. BMW's report on GHG emission reduction targets and level of achievement is demonstrated in Example 6.2.

Example 6.2

GHG emission reduction targets as part of remuneration systems at BMW

Targets set and extent of achievement for the RoCE component for the 2023 financial year

RoCE in the Automotive segment for the 2023 financial year is defined as segment profit before the financial result, divided by the average capital employed in the segment. In December 2022, the Supervisory Board determined the following values for the RoCE component for the vesting year 2023, based on the long-term corporate planning: minimum value: 12% (target achievement 50%), target value: 16% (target achievement 100%), maximum value: 21% (target achievement 180%). The RoCE achieved in the Automotive Segment for the 2023 financial year is 20.2% and the RoCE factor for calculating the personal cash investment amount is therefore 1.67.

Targets set and extent of achievement for the strategic focus targets component for the 2023 financial year

In December 2023, the Supervisory Board set the following strategic focus targets for the vesting year 2022 in accordance with the remuneration system:

- Reduce fleet carbon emissions in the EU according to WLTP; weighting in relation to individual personal cash investment target: 25%.
- Sales of all-electric vehicles (battery electric vehicles, BEV); weighting in relation to individual personal cash investment target: 25%.

Targets set and extent of achievement – RoCE component

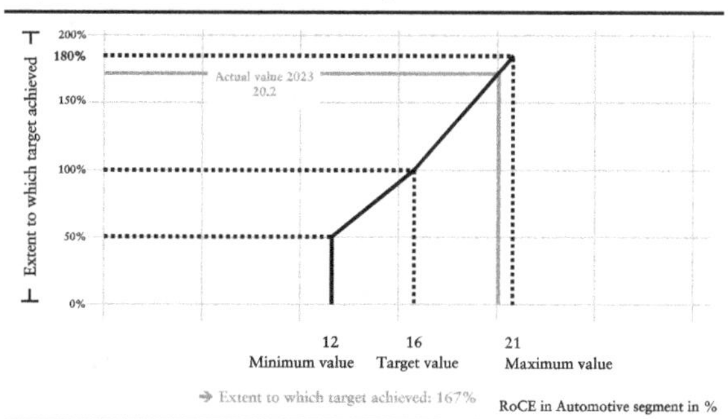

Targets set and extent of achievement – reduction of fleet carbon emissions (EU)

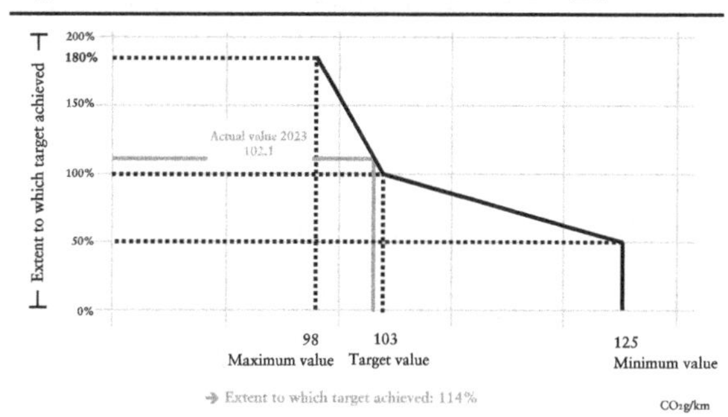

Source: BMW (2023), p. 275

Currently, ESRS E1 is the only standard that requires such a specific disclosure on their remuneration system. However, general disclosures for all sustainability matters are required by ESRS GOV-1 irrespective of the results of materiality analysis. From the perspective of sustainable performance management, it is important that organizations consider their most material sustainability matters as well in their remunerations systems in order to avoid misleading incentives for management. KPMG did an analysis of Dutch companies' remuneration systems, which is presented in Example 6.3.

Example 6.3

Insights into the elements of incentive systems from large European organizations

A 2024 report by KPMG Advisory N.V., a Dutch limited liability company, discusses the remuneration of management boards on the basis of sustainability performance that occurs in 80% of Dutch companies. KPMG argues that the 'remuneration structures do not yet reflect the breadth and complexity of the sustainable transformation challenge'.

Among its recommendations to bridge the gap between current practice and ideal procedure are the following points:

- Incentives should cover a wider range of sustainability matters.
- Companies must meet the increased stakes and urgency of the CSRD and ESRS.
- Leadership must be determined and focused for sustainable transformation to occur, and managing boards held accountable for their company's environmental impacts.

A good incentive plan must motivate management to fully understand their organization's sustainability goals and practices, act in the company's best interests with regard to the goals, take accountability for the present and future risks and opportunities relating to sustainability and win the support of external stakeholders.

Currently, incentive plans may fail to address sustainability matters that are difficult to measure (for example, 'circularity, biodiversity, human rights in the value chain and wider employee diversity metrics'). A more robust linkage of remuneration to these presently under-scrutinized aspects of ESRS is necessary in Dutch companies, as well as companies from other countries analysed by KPMG, namely the UK, Germany and Sweden.

Source: KPMG (2024c)

Reporting area: Strategy (SBM) for ESRS E1

Under the reporting area SBM, organizations have to report on their strategies and business models and how they affect or are affected by climate change. The information required focuses on the organization, as shown in Table 6.2.

Table 6.2 ESRS E1–1 disclosure requirements

Disclosure requirement	Brief description
E1–1. Transition plan for climate change mitigation	The organization must report on its climate change mitigation efforts to ensure that its strategy and business model are compatible with: • the transition to a sustainable economy • the limiting of global warming to 1.5°C • the transition to climate neutrality by 2050. Where relevant, the organization's exposure to coal, oil and gas-related activities must also be reported.

ESRS E1 defines transition plans as follows:

> *A transition plan relates to the undertaking's efforts in climate change mitigation. When disclosing its transition plan, the undertaking is expected to provide a high-level explanation of how it will adjust its strategy and business model to ensure compatibility with the transition to a sustainable economy and with the limiting of global warming to 1.5°C in line with the Paris Agreement (or an updated*

international agreement on climate change) and the objective of achieving climate neutrality by 2050 with no or limited overshoot as established in Regulation (EU) 2021/1119 (European Climate Law), and where applicable, how it will adjust its exposure to coal, and oil and gas-related activities.

(ESRS E1, Appendix A, AR 1)

If the organization has a transition plan, it must disclose this plan. The organization's GHG emission reduction targets (as required by ESRS E1–4) and climate change mitigation actions (as required by ESRS E1–3) are the foundations of this plan. Furthermore, ESRS E1–1 sets forth several elements of a transition plan that have to be addressed. Among others, these elements include:

- how an organization's targets are compatible with keeping below the 1.5°C threshold
- the decarbonization levers identified and key actions planned, including changes to product and service portfolios and the adoption of new technologies within an organization's operations or its value chain
- any investments or funding given to an organization to aid in the implementation of a transition plan
- the potential locked-in GHG emissions of key assets and products that the organization has (emissions are 'locked in' if they are likely to be caused by an organization within the operating lifetime of these assets and products)
- how an organization's transition plan is embedded in and aligned with its overall business strategy and financial planning
- whether or not the transition plan has been approved by relevant administrative, management and supervisory bodies
- the progress in implementing the transition plan.

Example 6.4 illustrates how a company may communicate its Climate Transition Plan to stakeholders.

Example 6.4

GEA's Climate Transition Plan

-> Net Zero by 2040

The race for a better world

Our climate strategy is deliberately ambitious. We aim to achieve climate neutrality along the full length of the value chain by 2040, outpacing both the European Union (Net Zero 2050) and the Germany (Net Zero 2045).

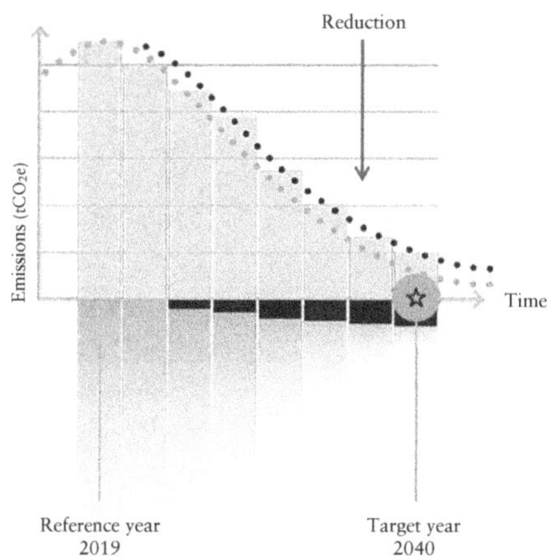

Net Zero
Net zero involves reducing all direct and indirect emissions by at least 90 % and then neutralizing the greenhouse gas emissions by permanently removing carbon from the atmosphere.

How will we achieve this?

Reduction
GEA will implement measures to avoid, reduce or eliminate greenhouse gas emissions at every stage of the value chain.

Neutralization (max. 10 %)
GEA will use permanent carbon removal and storage solutions to counterbalance the maximum of 10 % of residual emissions that cannot be eliminated.

Offsetting
Since 2021, GEA has been investing in climate protection projects that lead to a reduction in greenhouse gases and, at the same time, are good for the local environment and meet the population's social needs.

GEA pathway to Net Zero 2040 | Paris-compliant emissions reduction strategy | Total emissions

Source: GEA (2024), p. 13

Institutions are also developing further guidance on transition planning. For example, EFRAG has its Draft Implementation Guidance (IG) 4 on transition plans (under consultation in 2025). Internationally, the Transition Plan Taskforce aims at bundling and streamlining the various works of NGOs, regulators and standard-setters on climate transition plans. In October 2024, the Transition Plan Taskforce published the report 'Progress Achieved and the Path Ahead: The Final Report of the Transition Plan Taskforce', which gives an overview on current practices around the world as well as on resources available for transition planning (Transition Plan Taskforce 2024). If the company does not have such a transition plan, it shall disclose whether and when it will adopt one in the future.

There is one further disclosure requirement in ESRS 2 SBM–3 Material impacts, risks and opportunities and their interaction with strategy and business model. An organization is required to disclose further details on financial risks that it has identified under its materiality analysis.

For each material climate-related risk it has identified, the organization shall explain whether it considers the risk to be a climate-related physical risk or climate-related transition risk.

The ESRS distinguish these two different types of climate-related risks as follows:

> *Climate related physical risks: Risks resulting from climate change that can be event-driven (acute) or from longer-term shifts (chronic) in climate patterns:*
>
> - *Acute physical risks arise from particular hazards, especially weather-related events such as storms, floods, fires or heatwaves.*
> - *Chronic physical risks arise from longer-term changes in the climate, such as temperature changes, and their effects on rising sea levels, reduced water availability, biodiversity loss and changes in land and soil productivity.*
>
> *Climate-related transition risks: Risks that arise from the transition to a low-carbon and climate-resilient economy. They typically include policy risks, legal risks, technology risks, market risks and reputational risks.*
>
> (ESRS G1 Annex II)

These definitions follow the distinction made by the recommendations of the TCFD.

Furthermore, the organization has to give information on the resilience of its strategy and business model in relation to climate change, that is to disclose if and how it has conducted such a resilience analysis. This includes:

- the scope of its **resilience analysis**
- the time at which the analysis was conducted
- how it was conducted
- the results of the analysis.

These disclosures also require information on the use of climate scenario analyses for their resilience analysis. This refers to the corresponding disclosure requirement under reporting area IRO. This disclosure requirement requires organizations to describe the process of using climate scenario analyses for their materiality assessments. As with Climate Transition Plans, companies will present the results of their resilience and climate scenario analyses in different ways. Refer to CapitaLand Investment (2024; p. 13) for an example of clear communication in this area.

Reporting area: Impacts, risks and opportunities management (IRO) for ESRS E1

ESRS E1 requires organizations to report on both their policies and actions with regard to climate change mitigation and adaptation. The disclosure requirements for ESRS E1–2 and ESRS E1–3 are presented in Table 6.3.

Table 6.3 Disclosure requirements for ESRS E1–2 and ESRS E1–3

Disclosure requirement	Brief description
E1–2. Policies related to climate change mitigation and adaptation	The organization must disclose any of its policies that address the identification, assessment, management and/or remediation of its material climate change mitigation and adaptation impacts, risks and opportunities.
E1–3. Actions and resources in relation to climate change policies	The organization shall disclose any actions concerning climate change mitigation and adaptation. A description of which resources are allocated for the implementation of these actions is also required.

With regard to its policies, an organization has to disclose its approach towards climate change. To do so, ESRS E1.25 indicates that they must include information on whether and how their policies address:

- climate change mitigation
- climate change adaptation
- energy efficiency
- renewable energy deployment
- other.

ESRS E1–2 recommends that policies addressing climate change mitigation and climate change adaptation are disclosed separately, as they differ with regard to their objectives and the actions and resources needed to implement them. Any policy might directly address one of these aspects or just indirectly, for example via training policies, emergency or health and safety policies. An example of how this may be disclosed is presented in Example 6.5. Towards the end of the report, the Science-Based Targets Initiative (SBTi) is discussed – this is discussed towards the end of the chapter. The terms **carbon capture and storage (CCS)**, **biomass-fuelled CHP plants** and **Power-to-X (P2X)** are defined in the glossary at the end of this book.

Example 6.5

Reporting on policies addressing climate change

Our approach and policies

As a long-standing industry leader in sustainability, we recognise that, alongside our positive impact from scaling renewable energy deployment, we have a key role in reducing possible negative impacts, such as emissions from the extraction and manufacturing of materials and main components needed for the successful transition towards renewable energy sources.

We are committed to not only measuring and tracking greenhouse gas emissions, but also actively working towards their reduction. Our approach for our own operations includes phasing out coal in 2024. To address possible negative impacts in our value chain, we actively engage and partner with suppliers to mature low-emission solutions for our continued renewables build-out.

Renewable energy deployment

We invest in the development, construction, and operation of renewable energy assets, which include offshore and onshore wind farms, solar farms, battery storage, carbon capture and storage (CCS), bio-mass-fuelled CHP plants, and Power-to-X (P2X) for renewable hydrogen and e-fuels. While investments in wind and solar directly contribute to the increase in renewable energy generation capacity, bioenergy serves as an alternative to fossil fuels, P2X enables non-electric applications (e.g. transport and chemicals) and helps to reduce emissions from hard-to-abate sectors, and CCS enables permanent storage of carbon underground. Together, these technologies play a key role in building sustainable global energy systems.

(Continued)

Science-aligned climate action

To align our core business activities with our sustainability ambition, we have adopted a science-based target to reach net-zero emissions by 2040, which has been formally validated by the Science Based Targets initiative (SBTi). This overarching target is supported by a suite of near-term and long-term decarbonization targets across our full value chain. In addition to tracking and monitoring our company-wide emissions reduction progress, we utilise the climate targets internally to anchor our strategic initiatives. These include, for example, decarbonisation of our supply chains for materials and components.

Source: Ørsted (2023), pp. 87–88

ESRS E1–3 requires organizations to report on their key actions related to climate change policies. With regard to climate change mitigation, these disclosures shall present actions according to different decarbonization levers (including nature-based solutions). The GHG emission reductions that are achieved or expected must be presented. SGL Group reports on the required disclosures from ESRS E1–3 in Example 6.6.

Example 6.6

Reporting on actions addressing climate change

SGL Group's Scope 1 and 2 emissions represented under 1% of total emissions in 2023, but they are within our direct control to reduce. [...]

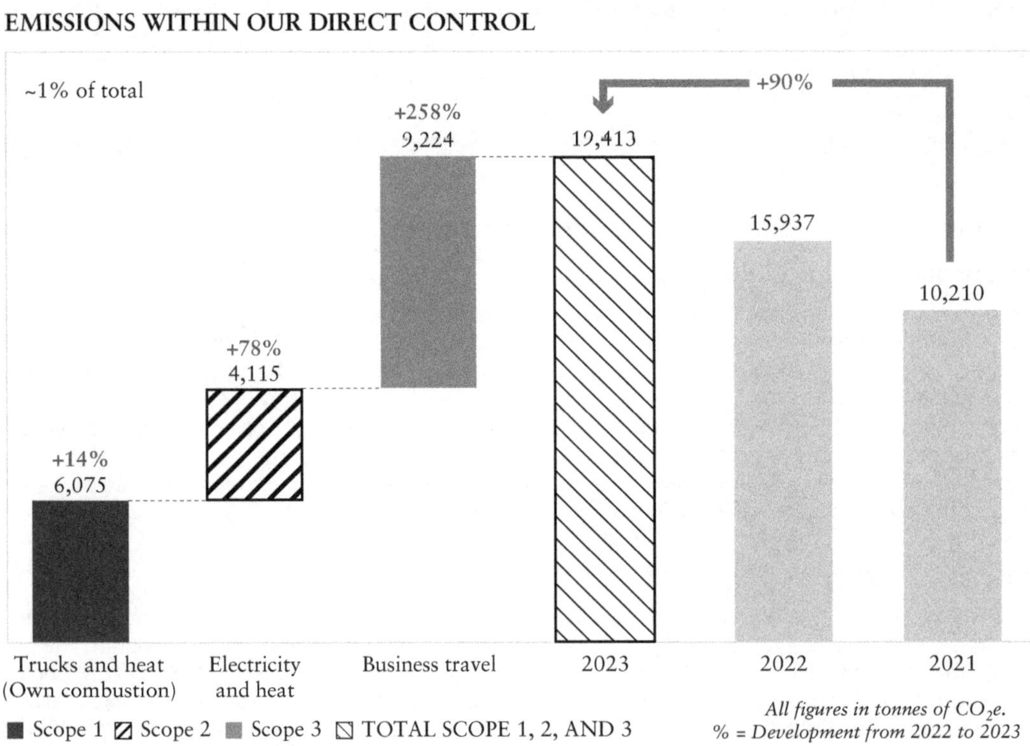

Source: SGL Group (2024), p. 47

One further disclosure requirement relates to ESRS 2: ESRS 2 IRO–1 Description of the processes to identify and assess material climate-related impacts, risks and opportunities. When disclosing how the organization has conducted its materiality analysis, information on the following aspects is required:

- how the organization's GHG emissions and energy use impact climate change
- climate-related physical risks in the organization's own operations and in the value chain
- climate-related transition risks and opportunities in the organization's own operations and in the value chain.

The organization shall also include information on how it has included climate-related scenario analyses for identification and assessment of physical risks and transition risks and opportunities over the short, medium and long term. ESRS E1.AR 14 contains a list of possible references for organizations with further guidance on how to conduct such scenario analysis.

ESRS E1 does not mandate that organizations must conduct such climate risk analysis for their materiality analyses. However, they have to be explicit about whether they conduct such analysis and to what extent the aspects addressed by ESRS E1 have been covered. In its application requirements, the standard sets forth a long list of such matters which are relevant. Among others, this includes a list of relevant climate-related hazards and transition events that must be addressed, as disclosed in Table 6.4.

Table 6.4 Examples of climate-related transition events, ESRS E1.AR 12

Policy and legal	Technology	Market	Reputation
Increased pricing of GHG emissions	Substitution of existing products and services with lower emissions options	Changing customer behaviour	Shifts in consumer preferences
Enhanced emissions-reporting obligations	Unsuccessful investment in new technologies	Uncertainty in market signals	Stigmatization of sector
Mandates on a deregulation of existing products and services	Costs of transition to lower emissions technology	Increased cost of raw materials	Increased stakeholder concern
Mandates on and regulation of existing production processes			Negative stakeholder feedback
Exposure to litigation			

Source: ESRS E1.AR 13

Now use Activity 6.2 to consolidate your knowledge of the different climate-related hazard and risk disclosure requirements.

ACTIVITY 6.2

ESRS E1 also includes a list of climate-related hazards. Look this list up under ESRS E1.AR 11.

Compare the requirements of this regulation with the climate risk analysis requirements of ESRS E1. What are the most important differences?

Example 6.7 demonstrates how the climate-related hazards list in ESRS E1.AR 11 may be applied within company reports to succinctly disclose key information to stakeholders.

Example 6.7

Climate-related risk analysis

Classification of climate-related hazards, cf. the TCFD classification and the EU taxonomy's Climate Delegated Act

CHRONIC	ACUTE
Temperature-related	
✓ Changing temperature (air, freshwater, marine water) ✓ Heat stress ✓ Temperature variability ✘ Permafrost thawing	✓ Heat wave ✓ Cold wave/frost ✓ Wildfire
Water-related	
✓ Changing precipitation patterns and types (rain, hail, snow/ice) ✓ Precipitation or hydrological variability ✓ Ocean acidification ✓ Saline intrusion ✓ Sea level rise ✓ Water stress	✓ Drought ✓ Heavy precipitation (rain, hail, snow/ice) ✓ Flood (coastal, fluvial, pluvial, groundwater) ✘ Glacial lake outburst
Wind-related	
✓ Changing wind patterns	✓ Cyclone, hurricane, typhoon ✓ Storm (including blizzards, dust, and sandstorms) ✓ Tornado
Solid mass-related	
✓ Coastal erosion ✓ Soil degradation ✓ Soil erosion ✓ Solifluction	✘ Avalanche ✓ Landslide ✓ Subsidence
✓ Hazard included in assessment ✘ Hazard not relevant to include due to geographical location of assets	

Source: Ørsted (2023), p. 86

Reporting area: Metrics and targets (MT) for ESRS E1

ESRS E1–4 to ESRS E1–9 cover metrics and targets – refer to Table 6.5.

Disclosures on GHG emissions reduction targets are of fundamental importance for reporting requirements in ESRS E1. If the organization has set such reduction targets, then a long list of disclosures is required, including:

- those targets in an absolute value (either in tonnes of CO_2eq or as a percentage of the emissions of a base year) and in intensity value where relevant
- targets for Scope 1, 2 and 3 GHG emissions, either separately or combined
- the current **base year** for those targets and its baseline value
- target values for the year 2030 and after every five-year period; if available, target values for the year 2050 shall be disclosed as well

- a statement whether the GHG emission reduction targets are science-based and compatible with limiting global warming to 1.5°C
- the expected decarbonization levers and their overall quantitative contributions to achieve the GHG emission reduction targets.

Table 6.5 Disclosure requirements for ESRS E1–4 to ESRS E1–9

Disclosure requirement	Brief description
E1–4. Targets related to climate change mitigation and adaptation	The organization must disclose any GHG emissions reduction targets it has set and/or any other set targets that aim to manage material climate-related impacts, risks and opportunities.
E1–5. Energy consumption and mix	The organization must disclose its total energy consumption in an absolute value. Any improvements in energy efficiency and exposure to coal, oil and gas-related activities also need disclosing. The organization will also report the proportion of renewable energy in its overall energy mix.
E1–6. Gross Scopes 1, 2, 3 and total GHG emissions	The organization must disclose in metric tonnes of CO_2 equivalents its total GHG emissions as well as individually within its Scope 1, 2 and 3 emissions.
E1–7. GHG removals and GHG mitigation projects financed through carbon credits	The organization must report on its GHG removals and storage in metric tonnes of CO_2 equivalents. Also, the amount of GHG emission reductions or removals through any purchase of carbon credits must be disclosed.
E1–8. Internal carbon pricing	The organization must disclose whether it applies internal carbon pricing schemes. If so, the organization must describe how these schemes support internal decision-making and incentivize the implementation of climate-related policies and targets.
E1–9. Anticipated financial effects from material physical and transition risks and potential climate-related opportunities	The organization must disclose quantitative and qualitative information on financial effects from climate-related risks and opportunities.

The prevailing understanding of science-based targets is influenced by the work of the **Science-Based Targets Initiative (SBTi)**. This initiative was developed by an alliance of environmental organizations (like the UN Global Compact and the WWF) to provide a framework that allows companies to reduce their GHG emissions based on the latest scientific evidence. The SBTi also offers checks and validation services to organizations. The SBTi states the following:

> *Science-based targets provide a clearly-defined pathway for companies to reduce greenhouse gas (GHG) emissions, helping prevent the worst impacts of climate change and future-proof business growth.*
>
> *Targets are considered 'science-based' if they are in line with what the latest climate science deems necessary to meet the goals of the Paris Agreement – limiting global warming to 1.5°C above pre-industrial levels.*
>
> (Science Based Targets, 2024)

ESRS E1.AR 31 recommends that organizations report on their emission reduction targets together with their climate change mitigation actions as a table or graphical pathway showing developments over time. Both methods are demonstrated in Example 6.8.

Example 6.8

Methods of representing emission reduction targets

Emission reduction targets and actions as a graphical pathway.

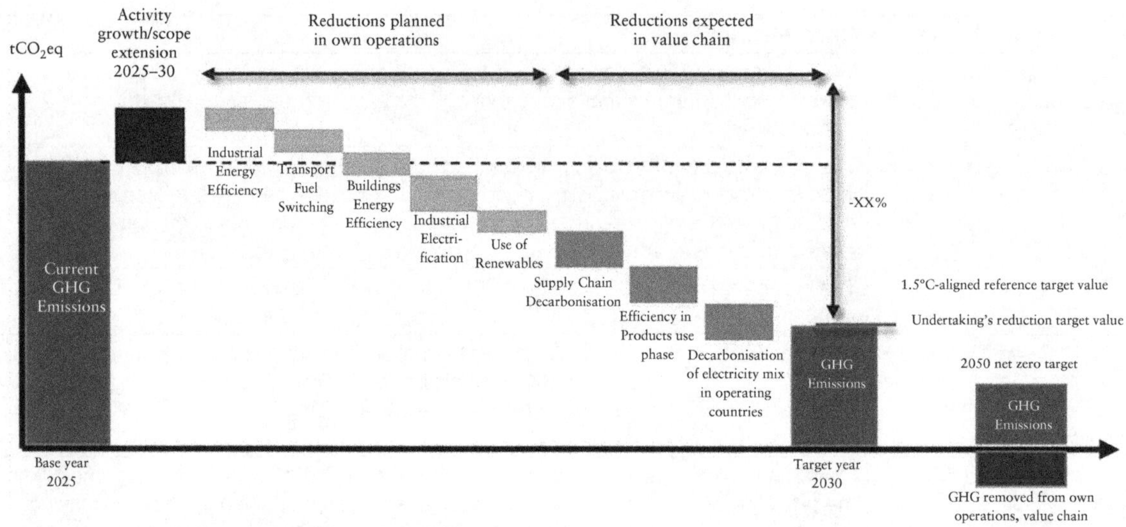

Emission reduction targets in tabular form.

	Base year (e.g., 2025)	2030 target	2035 target	...	Up to 2050 target
GHG emissions ($ktCO_2eq$)	100	60	40		
Energy efficiency and consumption reduction	-	–10	–4		
Material efficiency and consumption reduction	-	–5	-		
Fuel switching	-	–2	-		
Electrification	-	-	–10		
Use of renewable energy	-	–10	–3		
Phase out, substitution or modification of product	-	–8	-		
Phase out, substitution or modification of process	-	–5	–3		
Other	-	-			

Source: ESRS E1.AR 31

Another good example of disclosing GHG reduction targets can be found in the 2023 sustainability report of SGL Group (p. 49). With regard to actual GHG emissions that have to be reported, ESRS E1–6 (Gross Scopes 1, 2, 3 and total GHG emissions) contains the relevant reporting requirements:

- Scope 1 GHG emissions give an overview on the direct impacts on climate change and the proportion of its total GHG emissions which are regulated under emission trading schemes.
- Scope 2 GHG emissions address the indirect impacts on climate change caused by energy the organization consumes, either externally purchased or acquired.
- Scope 3 GHG emissions reflect impacts that occur in the upstream and downstream value chain beyond Scope 1 and 2 GHG emissions. Typically, for most organizations, this is the biggest group of GHG emissions.

This distinction is based on the methodology established by the Greenhouse Gas Protocol to which ESRS E1 refers. For each scope of GHG emissions, ESRS E1 specifies reporting requirements as follows:

- For Scope 1 emissions, disclosures comprise the gross Scope 1 GHG emissions in metric tonnes of CO_2 equivalents and the percentage of Scope 1 GHG emissions from regulated emission trading schemes.
- For Scope 2 emissions, disclosures comprise the gross Scope 2 GHG emissions in metric tonnes of CO_2 equivalents, based on each of the following two different methods of calculation:
    - location-based emissions, referring to energy that is physically consumed at an operations site or business facility. This is calculated using the average emission intensity of local grids.
    - Market-based emissions, addressing the individual company and its specific contract agreements in the market, i.e. energy a company purchases.

  To distinguish these two methods, the GHG Protocol issued separate GHG Protocol Scope 2 Guidance, which can be found online (GHG Protocol, 2015).
- For Scope 3 emissions, disclosures comprise the GHG emissions in metric tonnes of CO_2 equivalents from each significant Scope 3 category. These categories are defined by the GHG Protocol and require specific materiality assessments. To distinguish these two methods, the GHG Protocol issued separate GHG Protocol Scope 3 Calculation Guidance that can be found online.

These reporting requirements for Scopes 1, 2 and 3 could be presented in a company report as in Example 6.9.

ESRS E1 also addresses specific rules for setting the reporting boundaries when reporting on GHG emissions. Adding to the general requirements for setting these boundaries, organizations must include GHG emissions according to the extent of their operational control over them for:

- associates
- joint ventures
- unconsolidated subsidiaries (investment entities)
- contractual arrangements that are joint arrangements not structured through an entity (i.e. jointly controlled operations and assets).

The GHG data for these organizations is also not limited to the share of equity held but is dependent on an organization's actual impact.

ESRS 1.AR 48 contains a table that a company is required to use when reporting on its GHG emissions that you should refer to. The table requires a company report retrospective information as well as information for milestone and target years, such as 2030 and 2050.

Example 6.9

Semperit's GHG emissions report

Following a tabular representation of the GHG emission figures as required for Scope 1, 2 and 3, Semperit illustrates the data in pie charts:

EMISSIONS SCOPE 1, 2 & 3 2023

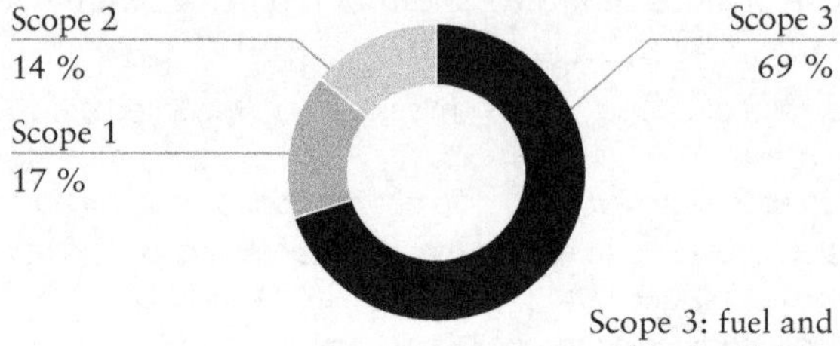

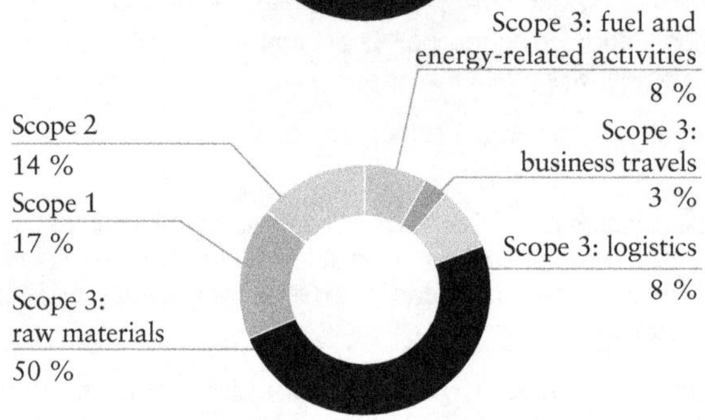

SCOPE 3 EMISSIONS 2023

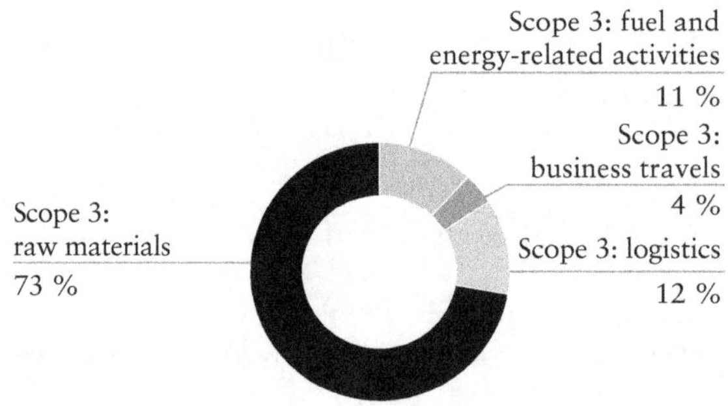

Source: Semperit (2023), p. 85

Also, organizations shall disclose their GHG emissions intensity as shown in Example 6.10. This intensity is calculated as total GHG emissions per **net revenue**.

Example 6.10

GHG INTENSITY BASED ON NET REVENUE

GHG intensity per net revenue	2021	2022	2023 (N)	% N / N-1
Total GHG emissions (location-based) per net revenue (tCO2eq/Monetary unit)	693	365	538	47%
Total GHG emissions (market-based) per net revenue (tCO2eq/Monetary unit)	693	365	538	47%

Source: SGL (2023), p. 59

The further disclosure requirements of ESRS E1 regarding metrics also relate to the disclosure requirements on GHG emissions.

ESRS E1–5 requires a detailed breakdown of an organization's energy mix as this is the main driver of Scope 1 and Scope 2 GHG emissions. This comprises the total energy consumption in MWh related to own operations disaggregated by:

- fossil sources
- nuclear sources
- renewable sources.

ESRS E1 also defines high climate impact sectors for which a further disaggregation of energy consumption by fossil sources is required (e.g. fuel consumption from coal and coal products). Also, for organizations working in such a sector, the energy intensity (total energy consumption per net revenue) has to be disclosed.

ESRS E1–7 addresses two different aspects:

- *GHG removals and storage: (Anthropogenic) removals refer to the withdrawal of GHGs from the atmosphere as a result of deliberate human activities. These include enhancing biological anthropogenic sinks of CO_2 and using chemical engineering to achieve long-term removal and storage.*
- *Carbon credits: transferable or tradable instrument that represents one metric tonne of CO_2eq emission reduction or removal and is issued and verified according to recognized quality standards.*

(ESRS G1 Annex II)

To avoid the risk of greenwashing and to incite the efforts of organizations to aim for a factual reduction of their emissions, strict requirements are in place so that GHG removals and carbon credits are reported on in a transparent way.

An organization has to disclose the total amount of GHG removals and storage in metric tonnes of CO_2eq disaggregated and separately disclosed for the amount related to the undertaking's own operations and its upstream and downstream value chain, further broken down by removal activity. With regard to carbon credits, the total amount of these carbon credits outside the undertaking's value chain in metric tonnes of CO_2eq must be disclosed, separately presenting carbon credits verified against recognized quality standards and cancelled in the reporting period or cancelled in the future.

Furthermore, ESRS E1–7 addresses two different public claims that an organization might make regarding following **net-zero targets** and GHG neutrality. In that case, organizations have to be transparent about the relevant role of GHG removals (for net-zero targets) and carbon credits (for GHG neutrality) in achieving these ambitions.

ESRS E1–8 requires organizations to disclose whether they have established internal carbon pricing schemes. If such a system is established, further information is required, for example how these schemes support decision-making and encourage the employment of climate-related policies and targets. Similar to how organizations are encouraged to report on emission reduction targets (refer to Example 6.8), ESRS E1.AR 66 recommends using a tabular format for internal carbon pricing scheme disclosures, as shown in Table 6.6.

Table 6.6 Tabular format for internal carbon pricing scheme disclosures recommended by ESRS E1.AR 66

Types of internal carbon prices	Volume at stake (tCO_2eq)	Prices applied (€/tCO_2eq)	Perimeter description
CapEx shadow price			
Research and Development (R&D) investment shadow price			
Internal carbon fee or fund			
Carbon prices for impairment testing			
Etc.			

Source: ESRS E1.66

ESRS E1 links to financial statements

Among all ESRS, ESRS E1 contains the most extensive links to financial statements, demanding that organizations reflect on the impacts of climate change on their strategy and business model. These links can originate from all relevant sub-topics of ESRS E1: climate change mitigation, climate change adaptation and energy.

ESRS E1–9 requires organizations to directly think about and report on the links between climate change and their financial statements (refer to Table 6.7). This reporting requirement demands the detailed quantification of the anticipated financial effects in monetary terms before considering climate-related actions:

- anticipated financial effects from material physical risks
- anticipated financial effects from material transition risks
- potential to benefit from material climate-related opportunities.

Table 6.7 Detailed information required for disclosures on anticipated financial effects from climate risks, ESRS E1–9, 66–67

Anticipated financial effects from material physical risks	Anticipated financial effects from material transition risks
With regard to assets and liabilities: • the monetary amount and proportion of assets at material physical risk over the short, medium and long term before considering climate change adaptation actions (disaggregated by acute and chronic physical risk) • the proportion of assets at material physical risk addressed by the climate change adaptation actions • the location of significant assets at material physical risk.	With regard to assets and liabilities: • the monetary amount and proportion of assets at material transition risk over the short, medium and long term before considering climate mitigation actions • the proportion of assets at material transition risk addressed by the climate change mitigation actions • a breakdown of the carrying value of the undertaking's real estate assets by energy-efficiency classes • liabilities that may have to be recognized in financial statements over the short, medium and long term.

Table 6.7 Detailed information required for disclosures on anticipated financial effects from climate risks, ESRS E1–9, 66–67 (Continued)

Anticipated financial effects from material physical risks	Anticipated financial effects from material transition risks
With regard to revenues: • the monetary amount and proportion (percentage) of net revenue from its business activities at material physical risk over the short, medium and long term.	With regard to revenues: • the monetary amount and proportion (percentage) of net revenue from its business activities at material transition risk over the short, medium and long term including, where relevant, the net revenue from the organization's customers operating in coal, oil and gas-related activities.

Source: ESRS E1, 66–67

The results of scenario analysis should inform the assessment. Furthermore, reconciliations to the relevant line items or notes in the financial statements are required for significant amounts of the assets and net revenue at material physical risk and material transition risk.

With regard to material climate-related opportunities, a quantification of benefits is only required if it meets the qualitative characteristics of useful information as set forth in ESRS 1 Appendix B, in essence, if estimations are possible with reasonable certainty. Possible approaches towards quantification that an organization might consider are laid out as follows by ESRS E1–9:

- expected savings from mitigation actions
- potential market sizes or expected changes to net revenue from low-carbon products and services or adaptation solutions to which the organization has or may have access.

Beyond ESRS E1–9, other disclosure requirements of ESRS E1 require similar links to financial statements and amounts included in these statements. For example:

- ESRS E1–1 on transition plans and resilience analysis often requires such links.
- ESRS E1–3 on actions taken with regard to climate change requires disclosures on significant monetary amounts of **CapEx** and **OpEx** required to implement these actions (ESRS E1.29 (c)).
- ESRS E1–6 requires a reconciliation between revenues for calculating GHG emission intensity and revenues presented in financial statements (ESRS E1.55).
- ESRS E1–8 on internal carbon pricing requires a quantification such as shadow prices applied for CapEx or **research and development (R&D)** investment decision-making, internal carbon fees or internal carbon funds (ESRS E1.63 (a)).

Activity 6.3 draws together the financial effects of climate change, sustainability reporting and financial reporting and how these separate facets of business increasingly overlap.

ACTIVITY 6.3

Outside the scope of sustainability reporting, the financial effects of climate change are also increasingly addressed in financial reporting, for example under the IFRS Sustainability Disclosure Standards. Recently, the **European Systemic Risk Board (ESRB)** conducted a study on this link between climate-related risks and financial statements.

> *The report concludes that while IFRS [Accounting Standards] generally enable entities to effectively reflect climate-related risks in their financial statements, minor amendments in the following areas would have positive implications for financial stability: (i) the application of the materiality principle under IAS 1, (ii) the addition of climate factors to the list of indicators of impairment of non-financial assets under IAS 36, (iii) how provisions and contingent liabilities should be recognised according to IAS 37 in view of climate-related risks, and (iv) additional disclosure requirements, examples and guidance on how climate-related risks should*

(Continued)

be incorporated into the estimation of expected credit losses and the fair value of financial instruments. Work on the accounting treatment of pollutant pricing (i.e., carbon pricing) mechanisms should also be prioritised.

Effective implementation of IFRS is essential for accurately reflecting climate-related risks in financial statements, in which regard regulators, microprudential supervisors, accounting enforcers and auditors all have an important role to play. They should consider developing guidance on (i) disclosures by financial institutions, (ii) how climate-related risks can affect the expected credit loss estimates of banks, and (iii) how to compute cash flows from insurance contracts directly exposed to climate factors. Besides, auditors can already assess and challenge existing disclosures on climate-related risks in the financial statements.

Choose one of the IAS/IFRS Accounting Standards mentioned in the ESRB study and explain in detail how climate change plays an important role in the relevant assessments.

Source: European Systemic Risk Board (2024)

Transitional provisions for ESRS E1

Appendix C of ESRS 1 contains phase-in provisions. The list covers two disclosure requirements of ESRS E1.

For all organizations that report on climate change based on ESRS E1, ESRS E1–9 Anticipated financial effects from material physical and transition risks and potential climate-related opportunities can be omitted in the following circumstances:

- For the first year of preparation of its sustainability statement, an organization may omit this disclosure requirements in its entirety.
- For the first three years (or for the two years after omitting the disclosure requirement in the first year), an organization may restrict itself only to qualitative disclosures. This option, however, can only be used if it is impracticable to prepare the quantitative disclosures required by ESRS E1–9.

Disclosure requirement ESRS E1–9 is considered to be challenging, requiring data and methods for valuation that may not be available to many organizations applying ESRS for the first time. The above provisions give more time to these companies so they can gather the relevant data. It is worth considering that appropriate methods for conducting these assessments might be developed in the meantime, giving more guidance and promoting more harmonized practices by organizations.

ESRS E1–6 Gross Scopes 1, 2, 3 and total GHG emissions enables an organization that does not exceed the average number of 750 employees to omit the datapoints on Scope 3 emissions and total GHG emissions for the first year of preparation of its sustainability statement. In such a case, only information on Scope 1 and Scope 2 GHG emissions is required.

However, although transitional requirements exempt organizations from covering the full scope of their value chains for their first three years of sustainability reporting, with regard to metrics, datapoints from other EU legislative bodies listed in ESRS 2 Appendix B cannot be omitted because of this exemption. Scope 3 GHG emissions are mentioned in ESRS 2 Appendix B. Thus, organizations have to disclose information on the GHG emissions in their value chain from the very first year of their reporting obligations, unless the more specific phase-in requirement for Scope 3 GHG emissions applies.

OTHER STANDARDS AND FRAMEWORKS RELATING TO ESRS E1

GRI and ESRS E1

Under GRI, two standards address those sustainability matters that are covered by ESRS E1, GRI 302: Energy 2016 and GRI 306: Emissions 2016. Disclosure requirements under all areas of ESRS E1 were influenced by the requirements of these two GRI Standards.

GRI 302: Energy 2016 directly relates to disclosure requirement ESRS E1–5. The GRI Standard shows a higher level of granularity with regards to disclosures that are required by organizations. However, with small exemptions, the requirements by GRI and ESRS are aligned to a high degree with regard to energy:

- Disclosure 302–1 Energy consumption within the organization
- Disclosure 302–2 Energy consumption outside of the organization
- Disclosure 302–3 Energy intensity
- Disclosure 302–4 Reduction of energy consumption
- Disclosure 302–5 Reductions in energy requirements of products and services

GRI 306: Emissions 2016 directly relates to ESRS E1–6. As both standards draw on the methodology of the GHG Protocol, the degree of alignment is very high once again. In part, the standards require different breakdowns of values. Furthermore, if a company applies GRI Sector Standards, it may disaggregate GHG emissions by specific gases relevant to a sector:

- Disclosure 305-1 Direct (Scope 1) GHG emissions
- Disclosure 305-2 Energy indirect (Scope 2) GHG emissions
- Disclosure 305-3 Other indirect (Scope 3) GHG emissions
- Disclosure 305-4 GHG emissions intensity
- Disclosure 305-5 Reduction of GHG emissions
- Disclosure 305-6 Emissions of ozone-depleting substances (ODS)
- Disclosure 305-7 Nitrogen oxides (NOx), sulfur oxides (SOx), and other significant air emissions

Activity 6.4 provides an opportunity to explore the differences in ESRS E1 and relevant GRI Standards.

ACTIVITY 6.4

Locate the EFRAG GRI–ESRS Interoperability Index. Compare the disclosure requirement on intensity ratio between ESRS E1 and GRI. Discuss any differences you notice.

TCFD and ESRS E1

The TCFD was initiated in response to growing recognition of the systemic risks posed by climate change to financial stability. Uncertainty about the financial implications of climate-related risks, including physical risks from climate events and transitional risks associated with policy changes, created a need for consistent and comparable disclosures. The establishment of the TCFD followed a number of international policy developments, including the Paris Agreement in 2015, which emphasized the role of financial systems in supporting climate goals.

The FSB announced the creation of the TCFD at the COP21 meeting in Paris. Chaired by Michael Bloomberg, the Task Force comprised 32 members from diverse sectors, including finance, insurance, energy and asset management, representing global perspectives. The TCFD's mandate was to develop voluntary, consistent climate-related financial risk disclosures that could be used by companies, banks and investors to make informed financial decisions.

In December 2016 the TCFD released its first recommendations for public consultation. In June 2017 they issued the final report, Recommendations of the Task Force on Climate-related Financial Disclosures. Adoption and implementation of the TCFD gained momentum, with increasing support from governments, regulators and private-sector entities. The TCFD framework emphasizes the need for climate-related financial disclosures across four core areas: governance, strategy, risk management, and metrics and targets. The recommendations are structured to be industry-agnostic, ensuring broad applicability while encouraging sector-specific supplements. Jurisdictions such as the UK and New Zealand have mandated TCFD-aligned disclosures for certain sectors, reflecting its growing role in regulatory regimes.

The TCFD recommends the following:

1 **Governance**

The governance pillar focuses on the oversight of climate-related risks and opportunities. Companies are encouraged to disclose:

- the board's role in overseeing climate-related risks and opportunities
- management's role in assessing and managing these risks.

2 **Strategy**

Under the strategy pillar, organizations are asked to report:

- climate-related risks and opportunities identified over the short, medium, and long term
- the impact of these risks and opportunities on business models, strategy, and financial planning
- resilience analysis, including the use of scenario planning to assess the potential impacts of different climate futures (e.g., 2°C or 4°C warming scenarios).

3 **Risk management**

This pillar addresses how organizations identify, assess, and manage climate-related risks. The recommendations highlight:

- processes for identifying and managing physical and transitional risks
- integration of climate risk into the organization's overall risk management framework.

4 **Metrics and targets**

The metrics and targets pillar emphasizes the importance of quantifying climate-related risks and opportunities. It recommends:

- disclosure of metrics used to assess risks and opportunities (e.g., greenhouse gas emissions, carbon intensity)
- targets set to manage these risks and opportunities, along with progress tracking. (Adapted from TCFD, 2017)

Most notably, the TCFD provided organizations with a wealth of different resources on climate-related scenario analysis that can also be used for reporting under other standards (such as ESRS). The TCFD knowledge hub, available online, is an important source for deepened understanding of relevant methods and processes.

Concurrent with the release of the TCFD 2023 status report on 12 October 2023, the TCFD has fulfilled its remit and been disbanded. The FSB has asked the IFRS Foundation to take over the monitoring of the progress of companies' climate-related disclosures.

Use Activity 6.5 to explore how the Bank of England integrates TCFD requirements into its climate-related financial disclosure.

ACTIVITY 6.5

Bank of England

The Bank of England releases yearly climate disclosures that follow the structure recommended by the Financial Stability Board's TCFD. These climate disclosures follow the four key elements: governance, strategy, risk management and metrics and targets.

Find the Bank of England's Climate-related Financial Disclosure 2023 on their website. Discuss how they report on the four key elements as suggested by the TCFD. How does the Bank of England combine the reporting disclosures under TCFD with the Bank's own five key goals? How may this affect a stakeholder reading the report?

Source: Bank of England (2023)

Science-based targets and ESRS E1

Science-based targets (SBTs) represent a critical mechanism for aligning corporate climate action with the overarching objectives of the Paris Agreement. The Science Based Targets initiative (SBTi) provides a standardized approach for organizations to develop GHG reduction targets that are grounded in the latest climate science and consistent with planetary boundaries. This framework emphasizes accountability and transparency, requiring organizations to adopt targets that meet the following key criteria:

- **Ambition:** Targets must align with a decarbonization pathway that reflects either a 1.5°C or well below 2°C scenario.
- **Comprehensiveness:** Targets must cover all relevant GHGs across Scope 1 (direct emissions), Scope 2 (indirect emissions from energy use), and, where material, Scope 3 (indirect emissions within the value chain).
- **Time-bound:** Targets must be set within a defined timeframe, typically 5–15 years, to ensure near-term accountability while contributing to long-term net-zero goals.
- **Continuous improvement:** Organizations are encouraged to periodically update targets to reflect advancements in climate science, evolving methodologies, and shifts in business operations. (Adapted from Science Based Targets, 2024)

The SBTi employs various sector-specific decarbonization pathways, recognizing the heterogeneity of industries and their unique emissions profiles. These pathways draw on robust climate models and consider factors such as technological potential, market trends and regulatory developments. Notable methodologies include the Absolute Contraction Approach, which requires companies to reduce emissions by a fixed percentage, and the Sectoral Decarbonization Approach, which tailors reductions to specific industry dynamics.

Additionally, the SBTi's Net-Zero Standard provides a comprehensive framework for achieving net-zero emissions. This standard distinguishes between near-term and long-term targets, emphasizing both immediate reductions and the eventual neutralization of residual emissions through carbon removal.

The adoption of SBTs has surged in recent years, driven by growing stakeholder expectations, regulatory pressures and the realization of climate risks. By 2023, over 4,500 organizations globally had committed to or set SBTs, spanning diverse sectors such as energy, finance, manufacturing and retail.

The cascading impacts of SBT adoption extend beyond the corporate level, influencing supply chains, investors and policymakers. By setting SBTs, organizations may signal a commitment to sustainable growth, catalyzing broader systemic changes and fostering progress towards a low-carbon economy.

Despite the progress, significant challenges persist in scaling the adoption and effectiveness of SBTs. Common barriers include data availability, methodological complexity and uncertainties in Scope 3 emissions accounting. Moreover, ensuring consistency between corporate targets and national climate policies remains a critical concern, particularly in jurisdictions with less stringent climate regulations.

Future advancements in the SBTi framework are likely to focus on deepening sectoral integration, enhancing methodologies for Scope 3 emissions and incorporating emerging scientific insights, such as tipping points and climate feedback loops. Additionally, fostering collaboration among organizations, governments and non-governmental organizations will be an important component in addressing systemic challenges and driving widespread adoption of science-based climate strategies.

Greenhouse Gas Protocol (GHGP)

The GHGP is the world's most widely used framework for measuring and managing GHG emissions. Developed through a partnership between the World Resources Institute (WRI) and the World Business Council for Sustainable Development (WBCSD) in 1998, the protocol provides standardized methodologies for companies, governments and organizations to quantify and report their GHG emissions. Its goal is to ensure consistency, transparency and comparability in GHG accounting across sectors and regions, facilitating efforts to mitigate climate change.

The GHGP has been instrumental in harmonizing GHG accounting practices globally. It is structured around three primary standards: the Corporate Standard, the Corporate Value Chain (Scope 3) Standard and the Product Life Cycle Standard. These standards provide guidance for measuring emissions within an organization's operational boundaries, across its value chain, and for individual products or services, respectively. By offering a comprehensive approach to emissions accounting, the GHGP has become the foundation for numerous climate initiatives and disclosure frameworks, including the TCFD and SBTi.

Emissions scopes

A key feature of the GHGP is its classification of emissions into three scopes, which reflect the sources of GHG emissions and their relationship to an organization (refer to Example 6.11).

Example 6.11

Lenzing's demonstration of GHGP Scopes 1, 2 and 3

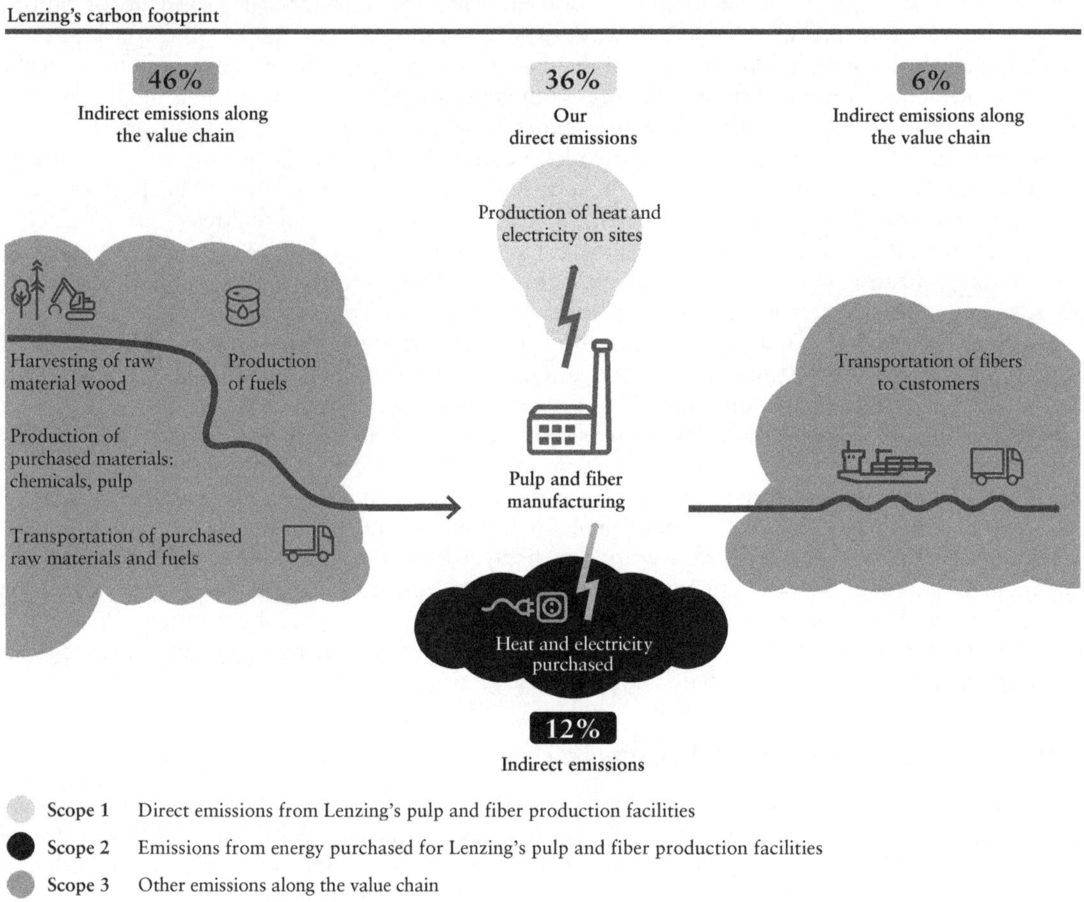

Source: Lenzing (2023), p. 81

Activity 6.6 encourages you to develop some of these concepts further.

ACTIVITY 6.6

The visualization in Example 6.11 is based on figure 3 on p. 26 in the GHGP Corporate Standard, at www.ghgprotocol.org/sites/default/files/standards/ghg-protocol-revised.pdf. Locate this standard and compare both visualizations. Discuss how and why Lenzing's illustration differs from this original visualization and the effects such may differences have.

Since its inception the GHGP has significantly influenced global climate governance. It serves as the basis for many corporate sustainability efforts and regulatory frameworks, such as the EU's Carbon Border Adjustment Mechanism and the US SEC's proposed climate disclosure rules. Its alignment with international standards such as the IPCC guidelines further enhances its credibility and applicability. Additionally, the protocol has been adapted for specific industries and regions, making it a versatile tool for addressing diverse climate-related challenges.

The GHGP continues to evolve to address emerging climate issues, including the integration of new reporting metrics and alignment with global net-zero ambitions. Its robust and adaptable framework has made it a cornerstone in the global effort to reduce GHG emissions, contributing to the transparency and accountability necessary for meaningful climate action.

ISSB and ESRS E1

IFRS Sustainability Disclosure Standard S2 requires entities to disclose material climate-related risks and opportunities, with a strong emphasis on carbon emissions reporting. This aligns with international frameworks like the TCFD and GHGP, ensuring comparability and transparency across organizations.

IFRS S2 mandates the disclosure of GHG emissions across three scopes (Scope 1, 2 and 3). In addition organizations must disclose how climate-related risks and opportunities affect their financial position and performance. The disclosures in IFRS S2 are summarized as the:

- impacts on revenue, costs and asset values due to carbon pricing mechanisms or regulatory changes
- financial risks associated with transitioning to a low-carbon economy (for example, stranded assets)
- quantitative metrics: total GHG emissions (measured in CO_2eq), carbon intensity and progress towards net-zero commitments
- targets: climate-related targets, including reductions in emissions, timelines and baselines. (Adapted from IFRS S2)

IFRS S2 builds on and consolidates other carbon reporting frameworks to create a global baseline for disclosures. While TCFD provided a principles-based framework, IFRS S2 focuses on embedding these principles into financial reporting standards, making them more actionable for investors and stakeholders.

To enhance carbon reporting, organizations must conduct and disclose scenario analyses to evaluate the resilience of their business models under different climate-related scenarios (e.g. 1.5°C or 2°C pathways). This is to support the assessment of risks related to carbon emissions, such as regulatory changes, market shifts or physical climate impacts.

Reporting requirements under IFRS S2, ESRS E1 and GRI are aligned to a very high degree. Organizations are thus able to report under those three standards at the same time if they make the appropriate accounting choices. Consider this further using Activity 6.7.

ACTIVITY 6.7

There are two relevant sets of interoperability guidelines: one linking ESRS and IFRS Sustainable Disclosure Standards, and another linking GRI and IFRS Sustainable Disclosure Standards with regard to GHG accounting. Compare the guidelines and identify the disclosure requirements where users of IFRS Sustainable Disclosure Standards would need to make accounting choices in order to align with ESRS and GRI requirements as well.

CONCLUSION

The evolving landscape of climate reporting underscores the increasing urgency for standardized, transparent and actionable disclosures to address global climate challenges. ESRS E1, the GHGP, the TCFD and the more recent standards of the ISSB collectively contribute to shaping a coherent reporting ecosystem. Each standard shares a common objective of equipping stakeholders with reliable and comparable climate-related information to guide decision-making and drive sustainability.

The ESRS E1 aligns closely with the EU's climate agenda, focusing on harmonizing sustainability reporting within its regulatory framework. The GHGP offers a widely adopted methodology for quantifying and managing emissions, serving as a critical tool for organizations to meet their climate commitments.

The TCFD's principles of governance, strategy, risk management and metrics have provided a foundation for organizations to assess and communicate climate risks and opportunities and is an integral part of ESRS E1. The TCFD has now been embedded into the work of the ISSB. The ISSB represents a global push towards consolidation and simplification, aiming to unify sustainability disclosure standards on an international scale.

While the integration of these frameworks holds the promise of greater coherence, challenges remain. These include ensuring consistency across jurisdictions, addressing data gaps and aligning corporate strategies with reporting requirements. However, the collective progress of these initiatives marks a decisive step towards fostering accountability, driving climate action and enabling the transition to a low-carbon economy.

As climate reporting evolves, the collaboration between policymakers, standard-setters and businesses will be essential in overcoming implementation challenges and enhancing the utility of disclosures.

SUMMARY

The following items relate to the learning objectives listed at the beginning of the chapter.

- **LO 1. Explain the disclosure requirements for ESRS E1 Climate change.**

  ESRS E1 requires organizations to disclose their policies, actions and targets with regard to climate change. Beyond that ESRS E1 also requires the disclosure of transition plans, which describe how organizations adapt their strategies and business models to climate change. Furthermore, the standard covers an extensive list of metrics to disclose, with the disclosure of GHG emissions and related information at its core.

- **LO 2. Understand the reporting requirements for GHG emissions.**

  ESRS E1 builds on the methodology of established international standards and frameworks, most importantly on the methodology of the GHG Protocol. Accordingly, organizations do not just have to disclose their total emissions expressed in GHG equivalents, but also their emissions for Scopes 1, 2 and 3. This gives insights into the detailed impacts regarding climate change along the entire value chain of operations.

- **LO 3. Explain the role of scenario analysis for climate disclosures.**

  Based on recent climate projections, organizations must analyse the effects of climate change on their operations. More specifically, organizations have to include the results of this analysis for their resilience analysis and to make conclusions for their transition plans. The way they have to adapt their strategies and business models will largely depend on the actual change that the climate will undergo, which will change the business environment drastically as well.
- **LO 4. Understand the different metrics and targets for climate reporting.**

  The metrics that organizations have to disclose focus on GHG emissions and related information. Energy consumption is one important driver of emissions; organizations must disclose this data in detail. Further disclosures cover aspects such as the use of GHG removals or carbon credits in order to address aims such as net zero or GHG neutrality. To also underline the financial effects of climate change on an organization, ESRS E1–9 requires detailed disclosures from an outside-in perspective, making detailed references to financial statements.
- **LO 5. Discuss the financial effects on an organization over the short, medium and long term caused by the risks and opportunities arising from the organization's impacts and dependencies on climate change.**

  Climate change already has an immediate impact on the balance sheet via investment requirements or the need to conduct impairments in case assets are physically impaired. In the long run, climate change and its impact on strategy and business models directly affect the value of organizations. It offers risks and for some companies also opportunities; risks can be distinguished into physical and transitional risks.
- **LO 6. Understand the connections between key sustainability reporting frameworks for climate reporting.**

  ESRS E1 builds on the work of the GHG Protocol. This framework is the global point of reference on GHG reporting. Another core framework is the recommendations of the TCFD that heavily influenced reporting on a corporate level. Standards such as the GRI or the ISSB Sustainability Disclosure Standards set different priorities, focusing on different perspectives (inside-out or outside-in) on climate change and different levels of breakdown. However, they are mostly interoperable, thus allowing organizations to meet the requirements of all these standards with just one report.

EXERCISES

1. Explain how the GHG Protocol and the recommendations of the TCFD have influenced the ESRS and the IFRS Sustainability Disclosure Standards. (LO 1, LO 6)
2. Sustainability reporting aims to bring about change in the behaviour of companies. How do the disclosure requirements set forth in ESRS E1 follow this aim and what mechanisms do they address? Discuss. (LO 1)
3. Discuss the significance of the three different scopes of GHG emissions that organizations have to disclose under ESRS. Why is it important to make such distinctions, and what are the different implications for GHG management with regard to each of these scopes? (LO 2)
4. Obtain the most recent sustainability reports from Shell and Total Energies. Look for the relevant sections in their reports on climate-related risks and opportunities. Are there any differences in identified physical and transitional risks? What was the role of climate scenario analysis for identifying these risks in the respective reports? (LO 3)
5. Explain the links and differences between net-zero targets, science-based targets and climate- (or GHG-) neutrality targets. (LO 4)
6. Explain the difference between carbon credits and GHG removals in the context of ESRS E1. (LO 4)
7. Obtain the sustainability reports of two real estate companies: JLL France and Immofinanz (Austria). Find the disclosures on energy consumption and mix and outline key differences as well as similarities. (LO 4)
8. Choose two different business models (e.g. real estate, energy, transportation) and compare the typical impacts of these activities on climate change. How could these impacts trigger risks and opportunities in the short, medium and long-term perspective? What are the possible financial effects as a result? (LO 5)
9. Obtain the ESRS–ISSB Standards Interoperability Guidance. Explain the decisions an EU organization has to make when preparing its sustainability report so that it can claim accordance with ESRS as well as IFRS Sustainability Disclosure Standards. To what extent do these decisions differ in the case of a non-EU organization that applies IFRS Sustainability Disclosure Standards and wants to align with ESRS as well? (LO 6)

CHAPTER 7
Environmental reporting II: Pollution, water and marine resources

Learning objectives

After studying this chapter you should be able to:

- LO 1. Discuss global and local contexts of pollution as well as water and marine resources.
- LO 2. Understand disclosure requirements for ESRS E2–E3.
- LO 3. Identify the role of stakeholder engagement in fulfilling the disclosure requirements of ESRS E2–E3.
- LO 4. Discuss the financial effects on an organization over the short, medium and long term caused by risks and opportunities arising from an organization's impacts and dependencies in the topic areas of ESRS E2–E3.
- LO 5. Explain the role of other standards for pollution and water and marine resources disclosures.

The end of plastic pollution?

On 2 March 2022, UN Member States at the UN Environment Assembly endorsed a resolution entitled 'End plastic pollution: Towards an international legally binding instrument', with resolve to create a legally binding agreement by 2024. It addresses the full lifestyle of plastics and plastic products, from design to recyclability and reusability.

The global plastic production industry is predicted to double in capacity between 2017 and 2040. Plastic is not only polluting in and of itself, but the emissions associated with plastic production, use and disposal are on track to make up 15% of all permissible global emissions by 2050.

The limitations imposed by the *End plastic pollution* resolution will have the biggest impact in the global south, which is historically disproportionately affected by climate change.

Source: UNEP (2022)

INTRODUCTION

ESRS E2 Pollution and ESRS E3 Water and marine resources aim to enhance transparency and accountability, ensuring that companies address critical environmental issues in their operations and report on their performance in a consistent and comparable manner. By adhering to ESRS E2 and E3, companies can demonstrate their commitment to environmental stewardship and sustainable development.

Pollution poses a significant environmental challenge, impacting **ecosystems**, public health and overall sustainability (Landrigan *et al.*, 2018; Rockström *et al.*, 2009). Including pollution in sustainability reports under ESRS E2 highlights an organization's commitment to mitigating its environmental footprint, while promoting transparency regarding efforts to manage and reduce harmful emissions and waste.

ESRS E3 on water and marine resources plays a critical role in advancing sustainable management practices for water and marine ecosystems, which are essential for ecological balance. Water and marine resources are increasingly under threat from pollution, overexploitation and climate change, leading to degradation of biodiversity, disruptions to food security and scarcity of clean water (Grey & Sadoff, 2007). The achievement of most SDGs is dependent on access to sufficient and safe water (Ait-Kadi, 2016).

ESRS E2 and E3 not only help in mitigating environmental impacts but also provide a framework for integrating sustainability into corporate strategy, ultimately contributing to a more resilient and sustainable economy.

ESRS E2 POLLUTION

ESRS E2 addresses the management and reduction of pollution, including air, water and soil pollution, as well as the handling of hazardous substances. Pollution control is essential for protecting public health and preserving environmental quality. Companies are required to disclose their policies, targets, actions and outcomes related to pollution prevention and control. This includes reporting on emissions of pollutants, the use of hazardous materials and measures taken to mitigate pollution-related risks.

Research indicates that effective pollution management can lead to significant health benefits and environmental improvements (European Environment Agency, 2024; World Health Organization, 2024). Furthermore, companies that proactively manage pollution risks can enhance their reputation, reduce regulatory compliance costs and improve their long-term sustainability (Porter & van der Linde, 1995). ESRS E2 focuses on pollution, including air, water and soil pollution, and the impacts of hazardous substances. It requires companies to disclose the pollutants they release into the environment, excluding greenhouse gases (GHGs) already covered by ESRS E1, as well as nitrogen oxides (NOx), sulphur oxides (SOx) and particulate matters which have direct implications for public health and environmental degradation (EFRAG, 2024d).

Pollution is at stake both in global and local contexts, creating complex challenges for organizations and policymakers alike. Globally, pollution contributes to climate change, ocean acidification and transboundary environmental issues such as air pollution crossing national borders. These global impacts require coordinated international efforts, such as treaties and frameworks such as the Paris Agreement, to mitigate the effects on ecosystems and economies. Locally, pollution has more immediate and visible effects, including water contamination, hazardous waste disposal and air quality degradation, which directly impact public health, biodiversity and local economies. For organizations, understanding these contexts is crucial for developing sustainable practices that comply with regulations while aligning with global sustainability goals. Effective pollution management must account for both the broader systemic risks and the specific regional dynamics that influence regulatory frameworks, stakeholder expectations and environmental outcomes.

Within the ESG framework, ESRS E2 plays a crucial role by prioritizing pollution management. For instance, a manufacturing company might disclose initiatives to reduce **air pollutants** through the adoption of cleaner technologies, while a chemical company could report on strategies to minimize hazardous waste, showcasing tangible actions taken to address pollution risks. Example 7.1 provides insights into how organizations have joined the movement to end plastic pollution. The example is taken from the German company SAP. More than 200 large companies have joined this movement. Example 7.1 also highlights the role of stakeholders such as The Business Coalition for a Global Plastics Treaty in advancing organizations' engagement in reducing their negative impact in regard to pollution.

Example 7.1

Plastic pollution and the role of organizations

SAP Endorses the Business Coalition

The Business Coalition for a Global Plastics Treaty was created in September 2022 and has since received support from many international organizations, financial institutions and NGOs. The coalition is focused on the *End plastic pollution* resolution adopted by the UN Environment Assembly in March of the same year (refer back to the opening example for more information on this resolution).

One of the coalition's 200+ members is German business software and solution company SAP. SAP global sustainability lead Natasha Pergl believes the organization 'understand[s] first-hand' the difficulty of understanding regulation, material flow, upstream effort and downstream solutions faced by consumers.

In May 2024, as the UN Plastics Treaty entered the final stages of negotiations, SAP emphasized the importance of 'harmonized regulations and simplified information flow' to achieve international success with the new legal guidance. SAP outlines four key cornerstones to achieving systemic change with the 'once-in-a-generation' global plastics treaty:

- *Common definitions for plastics and packaging to ensure mutual understanding and interoperability*: This applies to the categorization of various plastic polymers, how products are structured and denominated, and how they are packaged and sold.
- *Harmonization across the plastics life cycle, covering criteria for product design, extended producer responsibility schemes, and assessment for recyclability*: This will support businesses to design for circularity and recyclability, ensure that strategic decisions are guided by the capabilities of existing downstream infrastructure, and highlight where new capital investments are needed.
- *Harmonized national disclosure schemes to ensure uniformity, comparability, and information transparency*: This is essential for giving investors and regulators a base of information for policy steering and decision-making. It will also allow business to harness the full potential of AI-driven innovation to accelerate solutions at scale.
- *Recognition of the role of digital tools for traceability*: Improved data and the application of digital tracking will enable true progress.

'*The treaty goals are ambitious, but with an agreement that focuses on global rules covering product design and material fate, extended producer responsibility schemes, and chemicals of concern, we can unleash the power of global business to deliver the solutions necessary*,' says Stephen Jamieson, global head of Circular Economy Solutions, SAP.

Source: SAP (2024)

ESRS E2 specifies disclosure requirements which enable organizations to report their impacts on pollution, including air, water and soil contamination. For example, ESRS E2 covers the pollutive impacts on water and marine resources, including via microplastics, caused or generated by organizational activities. Readers of sustainability statements should, therefore, be able to understand how an organization pollutes ground and water environments and the steps they take to minimize their impact.

ESRS E2 defines these different types of pollution as follows:

- *Pollution of air* refers to the organization's 'emissions into air (both indoor and outdoor), and prevention, control and reduction of such emissions'.
- *Pollution of water* refers to the organization's 'emissions to water, and prevention, control and reduction of such emissions'.
- *Pollution of soil* refers to the organization's 'emissions into soil and the prevention, control and reduction of such emissions'.

In terms of **substances of concern,** ESRS E2 covers an organization's production, use and/or distribution and commercialization of such substances. This is extended to include what ESRS E2 calls **'substances of very high concern'**. The disclosure requirements concerning such substances aim to provide organizations with an understanding of the potential and actual impacts they cause. There is also discussion on possible use, distribution and commercialization restrictions for substances of concern.

Activity 7.1 asks you to consider a specific listed company's disclosure of water pollution-related information.

ACTIVITY 7.1

Select a listed company of your choice. Choose their most recent sustainability (or integrated) report. List all water pollution-related information disclosed by the company. As an extra, compare the list of pollution-related information disclosed by the company with that of the requirements in ESRS E2.

Sustainability matters applicable for ESRS E2 (ESRS 1.AR 16)

Appendix A of ESRS 1 contains the list of minimum sustainability matters an organization has to assess during its materiality analysis. The sub-topics that are distinguished for ESRS E2 address different types as well as different substances that might cause the pollution. As a result, there might be overlap between those different sustainability matters (refer to Table 7.1).

Table 7.1 Minimum sustainability matters applicable to ESRS E2

Topic	Sub-topic	Sub-sub-topic
Pollution	Pollution of air	
	Pollution of water	
	Pollution of soil	
	Pollution of living organisms and food resources	
	Substances of concern	
	Substances of very high concern	
	Microplastics	

The definitions of 'substances of concern' and 'substances of very high concern' refer to various other EU regulations. The latter are specified by the criteria laid down in Article 57 of Regulation (EC) No 1907/2006 (REACH) and must be identified in accordance with Article 59(1) of that regulation. Examples for such substances include carcinogenic, mutagenic or toxic substances. Example 7.2 looks at the relevant section of the 2023 Sustainability Report published by Ampleon.

Example 7.2

Ampleon reports on its policy with regard to substances of (very) high concern

Banned and restricted substances policy

To protect our customers, employees, and the environment from the use of chemicals and substances that may present a threat to the environment and human health during production, use or via disposal at the end of the product lifecycle, we have several programs in place which regulate our use of hazardous chemicals or "substances of concern". In fact, we follow some of the highest standards in the industry.

We carefully monitor our use of substances categorized as restricted, hazardous, or relevant, and have committed, as part of our near-term sustainability program, to achieve a 100 % reduction of all restricted and hazardous substances which are not critical use. We track our usage of chemicals in our company-wide chemical management program, which registers and classifies the chemical substances we handle. Any use or emission of restricted or hazardous substances must be covered by internal approval. For such substances, we are searching for alternatives to be used as quickly as possible.

Ampleon's policy "ECO-Products Substance Control for Products and Packaging" specifies substances which are not permitted in materials, parts, semi-finished goods, and products at levels above our established threshold. This is to ensure that no Ampleon product sold contains any substances which are restricted by law or other regulations. We also apply the European Union's Directive on the restriction of the use of certain hazardous substances in electrical and electronic equipment (commonly known as RoHS) and key customer requirements.

All Ampleon products produced as of March 2024 are lead free.

For additional info including our REACH statement please visit our website: www.ampleon.com/documents/quality/ampleon-reach-certificate.pdf

Source: Ampleon (2023), p. 13

Reporting area: Impacts, risks and opportunities management (IRO) for ESRS E2

ESRS E2 comprises two disclosure requirements with regard to policies and actions (refer to Table 7.2).

Table 7.2 ESRS E2 disclosure requirements for E2–1 and E2–2

Disclosure requirement	Brief description
E2–1. Policies related to pollution	The organization shall manage its material impacts, risks and opportunities related to pollution prevention and control.
E2–2. Actions and resources related to pollution	The organization shall disclose its pollution-related actions and the resources allocated to their implementation. The objective of this disclosure requirement is to enable an understanding of the key actions taken and planned to achieve the pollution-related policy objectives and targets.

Organizations are to include information on the policies they have in place to manage their material impacts, risks and opportunities related to pollution in accordance with ESRS 2 policies adopted to manage material sustainability matters. The organization thus needs to indicate, with regard to its own operations and its value chain, whether and how its policies address the following areas where material (refer to Example 7.3):

a) mitigating negative impacts related to pollution of air, water and soil including prevention and control,
b) substituting and minimizing the use of substances of concern, and phasing out substances of very high concern, in particular for non-essential societal use and in consumer products, and
c) avoiding incidents and emergency situations, and if and when they occur, controlling and limiting their impact on people and the environment.

Example 7.3

SGL Group reports on its approach towards reducing pollution-related impacts

E2-1 Policies related to pollution

SGL Group's Environmental Policy defines and communicates how we work with our environmental performance. The policy commits SGL Group to complying with applicable laws, regulations, and legislation covering areas within air quality, water quality and consumption, responsible chemical handling, sustainable resource management and waste reduction.

It also commits SGL Group to informing our customers on environmental challenges, supporting them in reducing their CO_2 footprints and influencing them and suppliers to choose solutions with low CO_2 emissions whenever possible (these actions have a corresponding reduction on air pollution in our upstream supply chain).

The policy is binding for all employees in all countries we operate in. Furthermore, all employees have mandatory training in our Environmental Policy to familiarise with the policy content, company initiatives, targets and overall responsibilities as a global organisation.

Further information on the scope and implementation of the Environmental Policy is described in E1-2.

Source: SGL (2023), pp. 69–70

Reporting area: Metrics and targets (MT) for ESRS E2

The reporting area MT comprises four disclosure requirements, with a focus on targets and metrics regarding different types of pollutions (refer to Table 7.3).

Table 7.3 Disclosure requirements for ESRS E2–3 to E2–6

Disclosure requirement	Brief description
E2–3. Targets related to pollution	The organization must discuss whether and how its targets aid in the prevention and control of air, water and soil pollutants and substances of concern.
E2–4. Pollution of air, water and soil	The organization must disclose the pollutants generated by its operations. This includes microplastics generated or used by the organization.
E2–5. Substances of concern and substances of very high concern	The organization must include every aspect of its relationship with substances of concern and substances of very high concern. This includes production, use, import and export, commercialization and distribution of such materials.
E2–6. Anticipated financial effects from material pollution-related risks and opportunities	The organization must disclose the potential financial effects of its risks and opportunities regarding pollution.

ESRS E2–4 is one key disclosure requirement under ESRS E2. ESRS 2.28(a) requires organizations to disclose the amounts of each pollutant listed in Annex II of the European Pollutant Release and Transfer Register (Regulation (EC) No 166/2006) emitted to air, water and soil. Only emissions of GHGs which are disclosed in accordance with ESRS E1 shall be omitted. Disclosures shall include the emissions from those facilities over which the organization has financial control and those over which it has operational control, if these facilities exceed certain threshold value specified in Annex II of Regulation (EC) No 166/2006. For an example, please refer to Lenzing (2023), p. 89. In contrast, further information on the reporting requirements on microplastic is given by the FAQ of the EU Commission, Question 'ID 441 – Microplastics':

> *If material, an undertaking is to provide, as a minimum, information on the microplastics amounts that it generates or uses. These refer to intentional or unintentional generation or use, both through production processes and procurement. For reporting purposes, microplastics leaving the facilities of the undertaking in the form of products, parts of products or services, or emissions are to be considered. Microplastics that stay within the facilities, that are used in production processes and that represent inventory used for business processes need not be reported, as they do not leave the facilities.*
>
> *Legislation on the matter of microplastics is currently evolving; hence, more defined requirements may be expected in the future.*

ESRS E2 draws on the concept of ecological threshold. ESRS E2.24 specifies that the organization:

> *[s]hall specify whether (local) ecological thresholds [...] and entity-specific allocations were taken into consideration when setting targets. If so, the undertaking shall specify:*
>
> *(a) the ecological thresholds identified, and the methodology used to identify such thresholds;*
> *(b) whether or not the thresholds are entity-specific and if so, how they were determined; and*
> *(c) how responsibility for respecting identified ecological thresholds is allocated in the undertaking.*

Ecological thresholds are key tipping points in natural ecosystems, where minor changes in environmental conditions can result in irreversible shifts in the ecosystem's structure or functioning. For instance, a gradual rise in pollution levels might not cause immediate damage, but once a critical threshold is crossed, the ecosystem could experience significant and lasting changes. Under ESRS E2, organizations may account for these ecological thresholds when establishing their environmental goals. These thresholds encompass a range of environmental limits, including biosphere integrity, stratospheric ozone depletion, atmospheric aerosol loading, soil degradation and ocean acidification.

Tools like the **Dynamic Global Vegetation Model (DGVM)** simulate ecosystem dynamics and predict how pollution influences factors such as biodiversity, water quality and habitat integrity. These models can identify threshold points beyond which ecosystems may experience significant damage (Quillet *et al.*, 2010).

Example 7.4 showcases how companies are preparing to implement ESRS E2. The extent of reporting will be dependent upon the topic (in this case, pollution) being material to the organization.

ESRS E2 links to financial statements

The final disclosure requirement of ESRS E2 centres on the potential financial effects of pollution-related impacts, risks and opportunities; this can be seen at the end of Example 7.4. Organizations must disclose the financial implications of material risks stemming from pollution, quantifying these effects in monetary terms wherever feasible. If quantification is not possible, qualitative information should be provided. For opportunities, quantification is only necessary when it does not compromise the quality of the disclosure.

Example 7.4

GUBI Sustainability Report 2023

Pollution

As described in section IRO-1 (page 21), GUBI conducted a thorough double materiality assessment that considered its impacts, risks and opportunities related to the topics, subtopics, and sub-sub-topics in the ESRS 1 General Requirements, including topics and subtopics related to pollution. The outcome of the assessment was that GUBI's business model may be linked to pollution of water, air and soil from the extraction of raw materials and input materials such as textiles, plastics, coatings, solvents and metal in its products as well as from the transportation of GUBI's products. The assessment also concluded that a small share of GUBI's products may contain substances of concern in for example textile materials. During 2023 GUBI has conducted a Biodiversity assessment which has impacted the score of pollution related topics. The scored Impact from water in use and pollution of water have been downgraded 5 to 2. The impact score for pollution of soil has been increased from 3 to 4.

Policies related to pollution
GUBI's sustainability policy to manage material environmental impacts, risks and opportunities is described in section E1-2.

Actions and resources related to pollution
GUBI, which imports and sells furniture and lighting, follows various legislation and directives concerning, among other things, requirements for the unpermitted use of chemicals, the content of chemicals and their limit values as well as test requirements. In addition, GUBI also follows legislation in relation to requirements for individual labelling of products for specific content of certain types of chemicals. The most important directives/requirements that GUBI is covered by are REACH, CE marking, Prop65, ROHS Law label and in the future also PFAS.

In addition, GUBI aims to have several collections certified according to the Greenguard certificate. Greenguard certification for low chemical emission products helps demonstrate both compliance with key chemical emission standards and GUBI commitment to heathier indoor environments.

See section S4-1 for the list of collections where GUBI is aiming to have certified during 2024.

Targets related to pollution
The overall target for pollution is to follow legislation and directives as described above. Currently, GUBI has not defined any other specific targets related to pollution.

Pollution of air, water and soil
GUBI is currently not able to disclose the pollutants that are generated through raw material sourcing, transformation, and use in the production of GUBI's products in its value chain (suppliers and sub-suppliers) due to lack of transparency and reliable data points.

Substances of concern and substances of very high concern
GUBI's products contain materials such as textiles, plastics, and various surface treatments. These materials carry a risk of containing hazardous substances. GUBI follows various legislation and directives concerning, among other things, requirements for the unpermitted use of chemicals, the content of chemicals and their limit values as well as test requirements. In addition, GUBI also follows legislation in relation to requirements for individual labelling of products for specific content of certain types of chemicals. The most important directives/requirements that GUBI is covered by are REACH, CE marking. Prop65, ROHS Law label and in the future also PFAS. GUBI does procure substances of concern (or of very high concern) in own operation.

Potential financial effects from pollution-related impacts, risks and opportunities
GUBI has assessed the potential financial effects from pollution-related risks to be medium. The identified risks include costs associated with changing materials driven by changing customer/consumer demand and/or regulation.

Source: GUBI (2023)

Organizations are expected to outline the financial effects of pollution-related risks and opportunities, including short-, medium- and long-term time horizons and associated uncertainties. They should also report on revenues from products containing substances of concern, costs incurred from pollution incidents and provisions made for environmental protection. Additionally, any incidents that significantly affect the environment or financial performance should be contextualized to ensure full transparency.

OTHER STANDARDS AND FRAMEWORKS RELATING TO ESRS E2

ISO standards provide specific guidance on environmental management systems, pollution control and water management, which can enhance a company's ability to comply with ESRS E2. For example, ISO 14001: Environmental Management Systems, offers a framework for organizations to manage and reduce their environmental impacts, including pollution. Implementing ISO 14001 helps companies systematize their pollution control measures and water management practices.

Going beyond such management systems, it should be noticed that ESRS E2 refers to a multitude of different standards and frameworks. The standard refers to, for example, the Industrial Emissions Directive, Seveso III Directive, the EU Taxonomy, the SFDR or REACH as well as the Chemicals Strategy for Sustainability (2020) and the EU's **zero pollution action plan for air, water and soil.** International initiatives that were considered include the recommendations of the TCFD and TNFD as well as the Natural Capital Protocol and the World Economic Forum's white paper on 'Measuring Stakeholder Capitalism' (2020).

GRI

GRI 305: Emissions 2016 also addresses matters relating to pollution. However, compared to ESRS E2, its scope of application is considerably limited: it covers air pollutants that have significant adverse impacts on ecosystems, air quality, agriculture, and human and animal health.

Besides reporting requirements on Scope 1, 2 and 3 emissions, two disclosure requirements might also be of use under ESRS E2 (refer to Table 7.4).

Table 7.4 GRI 305 disclosure requirements relevant for ESRS 2

Disclosure 305-6	Emissions of ozone-depleting substances (ODS)
Disclosure 305-7	Nitrogen oxides (NOx), sulfur oxides (SOx), and other significant air emissions

ESRS E3 WATER AND MARINE RESOURCES

ESRS E3 focuses on the sustainable management of water and marine resources. This includes the efficient use of freshwater resources, the protection of water bodies and the preservation of marine ecosystems. Water scarcity and marine degradation are critical global challenges that threaten biodiversity, human health and economic development (UNESCO, 2019; World Bank, 2016). Organizations are expected to disclose their water usage, water-related risks and strategies for managing water resources sustainably. This encompasses measures to reduce water consumption, improve water quality and protect marine habitats. Effective water management practices are vital for ensuring the availability of clean water for all users and maintaining the health of aquatic ecosystems (Gleick, 2003; Vörösmarty *et al.*, 2010).

Globally, water scarcity, marine pollution and ecosystem degradation are pressing issues that affect biodiversity, climate regulation and socio-economic stability. Locally, organizations must navigate specific water-related challenges, such as regulatory requirements on water quality, access to clean water and local community impacts.

Under ESRS E3, the term 'water' covers freshwater as well as groundwater. Freshwater comprises rainwater, lakes and rivers, surface water and water from wetlands, as well as the water in glaciers and ice sheets. ESRS E3 includes disclosure requirements on water consumption in the undertaking's activities, products and services, as well as related information on water withdrawals and water discharges. When discussing marine resources, ESRS E3 includes the extraction and use of such resources and associated economic activities.

Sustainability matters applicable for ESRS E3 (ESRS 1.AR 16)

Appendix A of ESRS 1 contains the list of minimum sustainability matters an organization has to assess during its materiality analysis. The topic of ESRS E3 is split into two main sub-topics: 'water' and 'marine resources'. The standard stresses the need to assess impacts, risks and opportunities along the entire value chain. As impacts are typically local, the standard also requires information on an appropriate detail level (refer to Table 7.5).

Table 7.5 Minimum sustainability matters for ESRS E3

Topic	Sub-topic	Sub-sub-topic
Water and marine resources	Water	Water consumption
		Water withdrawals
		Water discharges
	Marine resources	Water discharges in the oceans
		Extraction and use of marine resources

The rationale behind the structure of sub-topic 'water' is explained by the basis for conclusions to ESRS E3:

- **Water issues:** water quantity or water quality (ESRS 3.BC3(b))
- **Water flow and balance:** 'Water consumption, water storage, water use, water withdrawals and water discharge are the key concepts used to quantify inflows and outflows of water and understand water balance. Water consumption equals to water withdrawals minus water discharges.' (ESRS 3.BC3(c))

The basis for conclusions to ESRS E3 also highlights that pressures on marine resources also 'originate from issues related to the management of waste, pollution, the circular economy, biodiversity, freshwater, habitat conservation which are also covered by other standards'. (ESRS 3.BC3(d)). As a consequence, connections should be made between disclosures under the respective standards wherever possible.

Reporting area: Impacts, risks and opportunities management (IRO) for ESRS E3

The organization must describe its policies adopted to manage its material impacts, risks and opportunities related to water and marine resources (refer to Table 7.6). The objective of this disclosure requirement is to enable an understanding of the organization's policies which address the identification, assessment, management and/or remediation of its material water and marine resources-related impacts, risks and opportunities.

Table 7.6 Disclosure requirements for E3–1 and E3–2

Disclosure requirement	Brief description
E3–1. Policies related to water and marine resources	The organization shall describe its policies adopted to manage its material impacts, risks and opportunities related to water and marine resources. For example: the organization shall indicate whether and how its policies address: (a) water management including the use and sourcing of water and marine resources in its own operations, water treatment and the prevention and abatement of water pollution resulting from its activities. (b) product and service design in view of addressing water-related issues and the preservation of marine resources. (c) commitment to reduce material water consumption in areas at water risk in its own operations and along the value chain.
E3–2. Actions and resources related to water and marine resources	The organization shall disclose its water and marine resources-related actions and the resources allocated to their implementation.

With regard to disclosure requirement ESRS E3–1, it is required that organizations report on sites that are located in an area of high water stress and that are not covered by a policy. If this is the case, then the organization has to state this and provide reasons for not having adopted such a policy.

As with ESRS E2, one further disclosure requirement relates to ESRS 2: ESRS 2 IRO-1 'Description of the processes to identify and assess material water and marine resources-related impacts, risks and opportunities'. The reporting requirements are also identical to the ones set forth in ESRS E2, just referring to different sustainability matters. As a consequence, organizations have to disclose whether and how they have screened their assets and activities to identify their actual and potential water and marine resources-related impacts, risks and opportunities in their own operations and their value chains, and whether and how they have conducted consultations, including consultations with affected communities.

Reporting area: Metrics and targets (MT)

The reporting area MT comprises one disclosure requirement addressing targets and two separate disclosure requirements regarding metrics. One of these metrics addresses water-related impacts, while the other covers financial effects resulting from these impacts.

Table 7.7 provides an overview of the disclosure requirements under ESRS E3–3 to E3–5.

ESRS E3–4 only covers water consumption. Additionally, water intensity has to be disclosed as complementary information to this metric: total water consumption in its own operations in m^3 per million EUR net revenue. In contrast, information on water withdrawals and water discharges is merely optional under ESRS E3–4. If any of these two categories is associated with material impacts, risks or opportunities, it might give rise to entity-specific disclosure requirements. Hydro's Integrated Annual Report (p. 93) is an excellent example of how an organization reports on its water consumption and other types of water interactions.

In the same vein as ESRS E2, ESRS E3 asks organizations to specify if ecological thresholds and entity-specific allocations were taken into consideration when setting targets. Organizations may look at whether such thresholds are part of the contextual information, and whether the targets it has set and presented are mandatory or voluntary. Example 7.5 provides a short extract from Danone's work on water management. The extract shows how stakeholders, in this case WWF and the **International Union for Conservation of Nature (IUCN)**, are engaged to help organizations make a positive impact.

Table 7.7 Disclosure requirements for ESRS E3–3 to E3–5

Disclosure requirement	Brief description
E3–3. Targets related to water and marine resources	The organization shall disclose the biodiversity and ecosystem-related targets it has set. This includes details about the targets. For example: • how the targets relate to material impacts, risks and opportunities; • how the targets relate to water consumption, including areas of high water stress.
E3–4. Water consumption	The organization shall disclose information on its water consumption in relation to material impacts, risks and opportunities. The report shall include: • total water consumption in m^3 • total water consumption (m^3) in areas at water risk • total amount of water reused and recycled (m^3) • total amount of water stored (m^3) and any changes in water storage additional contextual information necessary to fully understand the prior metrics, such as method of data collection, water quality and whether data is calculated or estimated.
E3–5. Anticipated financial effects from material water and marine resources-related risks and opportunities.	The organization shall disclose the anticipated financial effects of material water and marine resources-related risks and opportunities.

Example 7.5

Stakeholder engagement with sustainability reporting on water: Danone

Danone's Alpro, a leading plant-based brand in Europe, has developed a pilot project called 'We only have one planet – Lead the change', with WWF and other partners such as the International Union for Conservation of Nature. In Spain, the project engages growers to cover 10% of the entire brand's almond sourcing. Rather than setting simple water efficiency targets, this project aims to establish production targets based on planetary boundary definitions. Stockholm Resilience Centre 'The planetary boundaries concept presents a set of nine planetary boundaries within which humanity can continue to develop and thrive for generations to come'. Extensive studies have been conducted to help Alpro and its suppliers better understand the watersheds where almonds are sourced, and create concrete action plans for other farms in the supply chain.

Source: Danone (n.d.)

ESRS E3 links to financial statements

As with all the other environmental standards, one of the key disclosures of ESRS E3 includes a requirement for the quantification of the anticipated financial effects in monetary terms before considering water and marine resources-related actions. Where this is not possible without undue cost or effort, only qualitative information is required. For financial effects arising from opportunities, a quantification is not required if it would result in disclosure that does not meet the qualitative characteristics of information.

OTHER STANDARDS AND FRAMEWORKS RELATING TO ESRS E3

Water is a core issue for many global and European initiatives. The EU Water Framework Directive and the EU Biodiversity Strategy aim at protecting and restoring water-related ecosystems, while the EU Floods Directive aims at reducing flood risks. The EU Drinking Water Directive aims at securing access to safe and affordable drinking water for all. With regard to oceans, the EU Marine Strategy Framework Directive provides a legal framework for the conservation and sustainable use of oceans and their resources. ISO 14046 on water footprint specifies principles, requirements and guidelines for assessing and reporting water footprints. It helps organizations evaluate their water use and its environmental impacts, promoting sustainable water management practices.

Other international standards such as the International Water Stewardship Standard serve to strengthen global stewardship of water, as discussed in Example 7.6 on the **Alliance for Water Stewardship (AWS)**.

Example 7.6

Alliance for Water Stewardship (AWS)

Stewardship is about taking care of something that we do not own. Good water stewards recognize the need for collective responses to the complex challenges facing the water resources we all rely on.

What is water stewardship? We define water stewardship as the use of water that is socially and culturally equitable, environmentally sustainable and economically beneficial, achieved through a stakeholder-inclusive process that includes both site- and catchment-based actions.

What is the Alliance for Water Stewardship? AWS is a global membership collaboration comprising businesses, NGOs and the public sector. Our members contribute to the sustainability of local water-resources through their adoption and promotion of a universal framework for the sustainable use of water – the International Water Stewardship Standard, or AWS Standard – that drives, recognizes and rewards good water stewardship performance.

Source: Alliance for Water Stewardship (n.d.)

Organizations often combine voluntary standards with that of mandatory reporting requirements. Furthermore, there is a considerable number of other voluntary frameworks and standards that assists organizations with their communication on water-related impacts, risks and opportunities. Examples include the CDSB Framework Application guidance for water-related disclosures, the CEO Water Mandate, the UN Global Compact's Communication on Progress (CoP) questionnaire and the CDP water questionnaire.

GRI

GRI 303: Water and Effluents 2018 also addresses sustainability matters related to ESRS E3. Its standard focuses on water withdrawal, water consumption, water discharge and water quality. These reporting requirements are very detailed and contain metrics on a broader range of water-related impacts, risks and opportunities than ESRS (where, for example water withdrawals and water discharges are not required under ESRS E3–4, refer to Table 7.8).

Table 7.8 GRI 303 reporting requirements

Topic management disclosures	
Disclosure 303-1	Interactions with water as a shared resource
Disclosure 303-2	Management of water discharge-related impacts
Topic disclosures	
Disclosure 303-3	Water withdrawal
Disclosure 303-4	Water discharge
Disclosure 303-5	Water consumption

TRANSITIONAL PROVISIONS FOR ESRS E2 AND E3

Appendix C of ESRS 1 contains phase-in provisions that also apply for ESRS E2 and E3. For both standards, they are restricted to one disclosure requirement: anticipated financial effects from impacts, risks and opportunities related to the respective sustainability matter (ESRS E2–6 and E3–5). Unlike the case of the corresponding phase-in regulation for ESRS E1–9, the provisions for ESRS E2 and E3 are not restricted by any further restrictions. For the first year of preparation of its sustainability statement, the disclosure requirement may be omitted in its entirety; for the first 3 years of preparation of its sustainability statement, an organization may comply with the respective disclosure requirement without reporting any quantitative information on financial effects.

CONCLUSION

In conclusion, the ESRS E2 Pollution and ESRS E3 Water and marine resources standards play an important role in advancing corporate sustainability by enhancing transparency and accountability in environmental reporting regarding their respective topics. These standards, together with international voluntary initiatives to reduce pollution and manage water and marine resources sustainably, compel organizations to assess and disclose their impacts on pollution and water-related resources, integrating environmental risks and opportunities into their strategic decision-making. GRI, ISO and other international initiatives support organizations to engage with pollution and water and marine resources in their sustainability reports and organizational work. A number of the UN SDGs relate to pollution and water and marine resource dimensions (Bebbington & Unerman, 2020). Disclosures on pollution and water management directly support SDGs 6 (Clean Water and Sanitation), 12 (Responsible Consumption and Production) and 14 (Life Below Water), aligning corporate activities with global sustainability priorities.

SUMMARY

The following items relate to the learning objectives listed at the beginning of the chapter.

- **LO 1. Discuss global and local contexts of pollution as well as water and marine resources.**

  Pollution together with water and marine resources are matters at stake both in global and local contexts, creating complex challenges for organizations and policymakers alike. Globally, pollution contributes to climate change, ocean acidification and transboundary environmental issues, such as air pollution crossing national borders. Water scarcity and marine pollution are at the global level pressing issues that affect biodiversity, climate regulation and socio-economic stability. At a local level, pollution, including water contamination, hazardous waste disposal and air quality degradation, have direct impacts on public health among other things. Local challenges with pollution and water and marine resources often have more immediate and visible effects.

- **LO 2. Understand disclosure requirements for ESRS E2–E3.**

  ESRS E2 enables organizations to report their impacts on pollution, including air, water and soil contamination. ESRS E3 focuses on the sustainable management of water and marine resources. This includes the efficient use of freshwater resources, the protection of water bodies and the preservation of marine ecosystems.
- **LO 3. Identify the role of stakeholder engagement in fulfilling the disclosure requirements of ESRS E2–E3.**

  Engaging key stakeholders, which may include employees, local communities, suppliers, investors and regulatory bodies, helps organizations identify material environmental risks, opportunities and impacts related to pollution and water resources. Organizations should consider how silent stakeholders are represented. This chapter has highlighted a number of stakeholder-driven initiatives, for example The Business Coalition for a Global Plastics Treaty and the Alliance for Water Stewardship.
- **LO 4. Discuss the financial effects on an organization over the short, medium and long term caused by the risks and opportunities arising from an organization's impacts and dependencies in the topic areas of ESRS E2–E3.**

  In regard to ESRS E2, organizations must disclose the financial implications of material risks stemming from pollution, quantifying these effects in monetary terms wherever feasible. For ESRS E3 one of the key disclosures here includes a requirement for the quantification of the anticipated financial effects in monetary terms before considering water and marine resources-related actions or, where not possible without undue cost or effort, qualitative information.
- **LO 5. Explain the role of other standards for pollution and water and marine resources disclosures.**

  ESRS E2 and E3 are supported by regulations from GRI, ISO and other international initiatives. Together, these aim to engage organizations with their polluting actions and their use of water and marine resources and provide a framework for reporting on these matters in the sustainability report.

EXERCISES

1. How do ESRS E2 (Pollution) and/or ESRS E3 (Water and Marine Resources) enhance transparency and accountability in corporate environmental reporting? Provide specific examples of how organizations might use these standards to disclose pollution and/or water-related impacts. In your analysis, you should identify which pollution and/or water matters included in the reporting are global and which are of a local nature. (LO 1, LO 2)
2. Choose an organization that has disclosed information on pollution or water-related impacts in line with ESRS E2 or E3. Analyse their disclosures and discuss how well the organization is addressing its environmental risks and opportunities. Do they make disclosures on the financial effects of pollution and/or water-related topics material to the organization? In your analysis, you may choose to include the company's alignment with the SDGs. (LO 2)
3. What might be the consequences for an organization that fails to comply with ESRS E2 and E3 standards? Discuss the potential financial, legal and reputational risks associated with non-compliance in environmental reporting. (LO 2, LO 4)
4. Select a recent corporate sustainability report from a European organization and assess its compliance with ESRS E2 or E3. Identify the strengths and weaknesses of the report. Identify potential stakeholders consulted to identify material pollution and/or water-related issues. (LO 2, LO 3)
5. Explain the role of international and national standards (voluntary standards such as the GRI) in shaping the disclosure of pollution impacts and water and marine resource management. Consider how the use of voluntary standards influences the accountability of the organization in terms of pollution and water. (LO 5)

CHAPTER 8

Environmental reporting III: Biodiversity, ecosystems, resource use and the circular economy

Learning objectives

After studying this chapter you should be able to:

- LO 1. Discuss global and local contexts of biodiversity, ecosystems, resource use and circular economy.
- LO 2. Understand disclosure requirements for ESRS E4 and ESRS E5.
- LO 3. Identify the role of stakeholder engagement in fulfilling the disclosure requirements of ESRS E4 and ESRS E5.
- LO 4. Discuss the financial effects on an organization over the short, medium and long term caused by the risks and opportunities arising from the organization's impacts and dependencies in the topic areas of ESRS E4 and ESRS E5.
- LO 5. Explain the role of TNFD and other standards for biodiversity and ecosystems as well as for resource use and circular economy disclosures.

All industries have material dependencies on nature in their value chains

As awareness of nature's essential role in the global economy grows, corporations are increasingly acknowledging that biodiversity and natural capital are vital assets, integral to their sustainability reporting and transition planning.

The significant degradation of nature and the escalating climate crisis are deeply interconnected, with climate change identified as the third largest driver of nature loss by the Intergovernmental Science-Policy Platform on Biodiversity and Ecosystem Services (IPBES).

Currently, methods for companies to assess their operational impact on nature are still in their early stages. Moreover, businesses are grappling with a flood of new and potential regulations, such as California's climate rules and the EU's **Regulation on Deforestation-free Products** set to take effect at the end of 2024. This regulatory landscape can make it challenging for compliance professionals to determine where to begin.

For many companies, the **UK Transition Plan Taskforce (TPT)** suggests that a practical starting point is to analyse how nature fits into their climate transition plans. By integrating climate and environmental goals into a single strategy, companies can adopt a coordinated approach to addressing both climate change and nature-related objectives. To do this effectively, however, companies must understand the key competencies needed to implement these plans and acknowledge the existing gaps in their capabilities.

Source: Thomson Reuters (2024)

INTRODUCTION

In December 2022, the United Nations Convention on Biodiversity held in Montreal resulted in a landmark agreement aimed at preventing further destruction of the world's terrestrial and marine ecosystems. The Global Biodiversity Framework, endorsed by 188 nations, sets forth a goal to conserve 30% of the planet by 2030 and calls for the mobilization of US$200 billion annually for biodiversity-related funding. This agreement represents the first unified global commitment to reversing biodiversity loss. It also serves as a crucial signal to businesses worldwide, highlighting the essential role of the corporate sector in biodiversity conservation efforts. These are important policy steps towards protecting nature and biodiversity. As highlighted by the International Union for Conservation of Nature (IUCN), 'nature is the system that keeps us alive. The diversity of life must be conserved for its own sake, but also in order to ensure the sustainability of our developmental model, which is entirely dependent on biodiversity' (IUCN, 2014).

The impact of business activities on biodiversity is gaining increasing societal attention, prompting companies to measure and report their interactions with ecosystems to maintain their social licence to operate (Boiral *et al.*, 2019). Biodiversity considerations have been integrated into sustainability reporting frameworks, such as GRI. Additionally, business associations are offering guidance to their members on addressing biodiversity concerns, exemplified by the World Business Council for Sustainable Development's (WBCSD) Guide to Corporate Ecosystem Valuation. The more recent international initiative is that of the Taskforce on Nature-related Financial Disclosures (TNFD). The TNFD was launched in July 2020 as a market-led initiative aimed at developing a framework for organizations to report and manage risks related to nature and biodiversity. Its creation was driven by growing awareness of the financial risks posed by nature loss, similar to the risks from climate change.

This chapter will address ESRS E4 Biodiversity and ecosystems and ESRS E5 Resource use and circular economy (EFRAG, 2023–24) and explore how organizations are required to measure, manage and report their impacts and dependencies on biodiversity (ESRS E4) and how they use resources efficiently while promoting circular economy principles (ESRS E5).

ESRS E4 focuses on the interrelations between corporate activities and biodiversity, emphasizing the need for companies to disclose their impacts and dependencies on ecosystems. Biodiversity loss, driven by deforestation, habitat degradation and pollution, represents one of the most pressing global environmental challenges. As businesses operate in ecosystems, they depend on the services these ecosystems provide, from clean water and air to raw materials and climate regulation (Sukhdev *et al.*, 2010). By aligning sustainability reporting with biodiversity conservation goals, ESRS E4 seeks to ensure that organizations measure, mitigate and transparently report their biodiversity risks and opportunities (refer also to Boiral *et al.*, 2021).

The global scope of ESRS E4 extends beyond Europe, recognizing the role of European companies in biodiversity loss in other parts of the world. Companies operating in international supply chains are expected to report on biodiversity impacts in sourcing raw materials, particularly in biodiversity-sensitive areas such as tropical forests or coral reefs. Academic literature, such as Haffar and Searcy (2017), emphasizes that global supply chains often obscure corporate impacts on biodiversity, making transparency essential.

ESRS E5 shifts the focus to resource efficiency and the circular economy, encouraging companies to adopt sustainable practices in resource use and waste management. In the context of growing resource scarcity and environmental degradation, the transition to a circular economy, where materials are reused, recycled and regenerated, is no longer optional but necessary for sustainable development (Geissdoerfer *et al.*, 2017). ESRS E5 mandates companies to report on their efforts to reduce waste, improve resource efficiency and promote circular practices that minimize environmental impact while creating long-term economic value.

ESRS E4 BIODIVERSITY AND ECOSYSTEMS

PwC (2022) noted that over half of the world's GDP is highly or moderately dependent on nature, yet very few companies know how much their operations depend on nature. Example 8.1 demonstrates how the global environmental charity World Wide Fund for Nature (WWF) defines biodiversity at a high level and how it depicts the current status of biodiversity.

Example 8.1

WWF defines and explains biodiversity

Biodiversity can be defined as the kinds of life in an area that make up our natural world: the animals, plants, fungi and microorganisms such as bacteria.

> *Each of these species and organisms work together in ecosystems, like an intricate web, to maintain balance and support life. Biodiversity supports everything in nature that we need to survive: food, clean water, medicine, and shelter.*

Humans have put pressure on the Earth by using ever increasing amounts of resources thereby upsetting the balance of ecosystems and causing a loss of biodiversity. The 2022 Living Planet Report by WWF highlighted an 'average 69% decline in global populations of mammals, fish, birds, reptiles, and amphibians since 1970'. The 2019 Global Assessment Report by the Intergovernmental Platform on Biodiversity and Ecosystem Services (IPBES, 2019) identified that a huge number – 1 million – animal and plant species are threatened with extinction.

> *Three-quarters of the land-based environment and roughly 66% of the ocean environment have been significantly altered. More than a third of the world's land surface and nearly 75% of freshwater resources are now devoted to crop or livestock production. Climate change worsens the impact of other stressors on nature and our well-being. Humans have overfished the oceans, cleared forests, polluted our water sources, and created a climate crisis. These actions are impacting biodiversity around the world, from the most remote locales to our own backyards.*

Source: WWF (2022)

The ESRS E4 standard is an important disclosure tool supporting the advancement of biodiversity conservation in corporate practices by mandating that companies disclose their impacts, dependencies and efforts related to biodiversity. This transparency encourages businesses to integrate biodiversity into their core strategies. By focusing on material risks, action plans and financial implications, ESRS E4 has the potential to foster accountability between organizational life and nature, thus addressing the global biodiversity crisis:

> *ESRS 4 defines disclosure requirements that relate to the organization's relationship to terrestrial, freshwater and marine habitats, ecosystems and populations of related fauna and flora species, including diversity within species, between species and of ecosystems and their interrelation with indigenous peoples and other affected communities.*

The terms 'biodiversity' and 'biological diversity' refer to the variability among living organisms from all sources including, inter alia, terrestrial, freshwater, marine and other aquatic ecosystems and the ecological complexes of which they are part. (ESRS E4 paras 2–3)

The objective of ESRS E4 is to specify disclosure requirements which will enable users of the sustainability statement to understand:

- **a** an organization's material, actual and potential impacts on biodiversity and ecosystems and its contributions towards drivers of biodiversity loss
- **b** an organization's actions, planned or in place, to prevent or mitigate material impact on biodiversity and ecosystem loss
- **c** an organization's ability to adapt its strategy and business model in consideration of the above.

Also, the risks and opportunities relating to biodiversity have to be reported. This includes the nature, type and extent of these risks and opportunities and how the organization manages them. Also, corresponding financial effects should be disclosed.

In doing so, organizations have to consider a number of political frameworks and legal requirements, such as the EU Biodiversity Strategy for 2030. ESRS E4 aligns with major global frameworks, such as the **Post-2020 Global Biodiversity Framework** and the **Kunming-Montreal Global Biodiversity Framework,** which set goals for no net biodiversity loss by 2030 and full recovery by 2050.

ESRS E4 also relates to the concept of 'planetary boundaries', as organizations are asked to respect biosphere integrity and land system change. Planetary boundaries are discussed in Example 8.2.

Example 8.2

Planetary boundaries

In September 2023, a team of scientists quantified, for the first time, all nine processes that regulate the stability and resilience of the Earth system.

These nine Planetary Boundaries were first proposed by former centre director Johan Rockström and a group of 28 internationally renowned scientists in 2009. The Planetary Boundaries are the safe limits for human pressure on the nine critical processes which together maintain a stable and resilient Earth.

The 2023 update not only quantified all boundaries but also concluded that six of the nine boundaries have been transgressed.

What happens when these boundaries are crossed? In short, such a breach increases the risk of triggering large-scale irreversible environmental changes. Such changes might not happen overnight, but these boundaries 'mark a critical threshold for increasing risks to people and the ecosystems we are part of'.

Planetary boundaries are interdependent and interrelated processes within the Earth's system. So, if one of these boundaries is crossed, the negative effect will be felt across other boundaries. 'We cannot consider Planetary Boundaries in isolation in any decision making on sustainability. Only by respecting all nine boundaries can we maintain the safe operating space for human civilization.'

Source: Stockholm Resilience Centre (2023)

It is important for organizations to acknowledge that biodiversity and ecosystems are intricately linked to various other environmental issues. The primary direct drivers of changes in biodiversity and ecosystems include climate change, pollution, land-use change, alterations in freshwater use and marine environments, direct exploitation of organisms and the introduction of **invasive species**. These factors interact and often exacerbate each other, leading to significant impacts on ecological balance and the sustainability of natural habitats. This interconnectedness is also reflected in the concept of planetary boundaries stated earlier.

Also, ESRS E4 makes a distinct reference to ESRS S3 Affected communities. Most often, biodiversity changes have an impact on local communities that an organization must take into account.

Sustainability matters applicable for ESRS E4 (ESRS 1.AR 16)

Appendix A of ESRS 1 contains the list of minimum sustainability matters an organization has to assess during its materiality analysis. Compared with other ESRSs, the sustainability matters linked to ESRS E4 are often only listed as examples, which underlines how complex and difficult to comprehensively outline this sustainability matter is. Also, there are links to other ESRSs – as 'climate change' is listed both as a separate topic (ESRS E1) and as a sub-sub-topic to ESRS E4. Also, similar links to other standards are present as well, which again goes to underline how the topic of 'biodiversity and ecosystem' can also be seen as an umbrella topic that encompasses all the other topics of the ESRSs.

Table 8.1 looks at the topics covered in Appendix A to ESRS 1.

Table 8.1 Discussion of ESRS E4 in ESRS 1 Appendix A

<table>
<tr><th>Topic</th><th>Sub-topic</th><th>Sub-sub-topic</th></tr>
<tr><td rowspan="9">Biodiversity and ecosystems</td><td rowspan="6">Direct impact drivers of biodiversity loss</td><td>Climate change</td></tr>
<tr><td>Land-use change, fresh water-use change and sea-use change</td></tr>
<tr><td>Direct exploitation</td></tr>
<tr><td>Invasive alien species</td></tr>
<tr><td>Pollution</td></tr>
<tr><td>Others</td></tr>
<tr><td>Impacts on the state of species</td><td>Examples:
• Species population size
• Species global extinction risk.</td></tr>
<tr><td>Impacts on the extent and condition of ecosystems</td><td>Examples:
• Land degradation
• Desertification
• Soil sealing.</td></tr>
<tr><td>Impacts and dependencies on ecosystem services</td><td></td></tr>
</table>

This interlinking with the topics of the other environmental ESRSs poses specific challenges to organizations when preparing their sustainability report. Organizations are required to make connections between these topics in order to give users of their sustainability report a holistic understanding of their environmental impacts, risks and opportunities. Consequently, it will often not be enough to outline the relevant sustainability matters for each individual standard. Instead it is important to make cross-references or to even present their disclosures together in one chapter of the report.

Reporting area: Strategy (SBM) for ESRS E4

Under this reporting area, organizations are required to disclose how their biodiversity and ecosystem impacts, dependencies, risks and opportunities are linked to their strategy and business models.

Table 8.2 sets out the disclosure requirement in ESRS E4–1.

Table 8.2 ESRS E4–1 Disclosure requirement

Disclosure requirement	Brief description
E4–1 Transition plan and consideration of biodiversity and ecosystems in strategy and business model	The organization shall disclose how its biodiversity and ecosystem impacts, dependencies, risks and opportunities originate from and trigger adaptation of its strategy and business model. The resiliency of the business model must be discussed, in terms of the model's resilience to risk, scope of resilience analysis, the involvement of stakeholders, any assumptions made and the time horizons used.

Example 8.3 uses the Annual and Sustainability Report (2023) of Lenzing to demonstrate how ESRS E4-1 can be reported on to meet disclosure requirements.

Example 8.3

Lenzing reports on its impacts and dependencies on biodiversity

Assessment: State of Lenzing's influence and dependencies on biodiversity and ecosystems

The Lenzing Group uses two different types of forestry for its wood sourcing, depending on the global region: sustainable and multi-functional forest management is applied in the Northern hemisphere by Lenzing's wood and pulp suppliers in Europe and North America. Plantation forestry with high sustainability standards is conducted mainly in the Southern hemisphere by Lenzing's pulp supplier in South Africa and by the new pulp plant in Brazil. In Lenzing's joint venture project, LD Celulose, with Dexco (formerly Duratex) in Brazil, wood is sourced from FSC®-certified plantations of currently more than 90,000 hectares. Plantation forestry can reduce deforestation pressure on natural (primary) forest areas by providing wood at very high yields per unit area as an alternative to sourcing it from natural forests. FSC® certification entails management criteria to protect biodiversity17, as determined in detail in the national standards.

Lenzing's impacts and dependencies

Wood is the most important raw material for Lenzing. The main source of potential impact from the Lenzing Group's operations and supply chain is therefore connected to land use by forestry. Lenzing also mainly depends on biodiversity and the proper functioning of healthy forest ecosystems that provide the raw material of wood. Negative effects on biodiversity can arise from over-intensified utilization of forests. On the other hand, the positive effects of sustainable forest management on biodiversity and eco-systems are well known and can be further explored and implemented.

Semi-natural forests do not require irrigation. Plantations of LD Celulose and those of Lenzing's suppliers are situated in areas with sufficient rainfall; this is a legal requirement for establishing plantations in the respective countries. Therefore, it can be assumed that groundwater levels are not significantly affected and salinity levels in soils are not increased due to wood sourcing in Lenzing's sphere of influence.

In the case of semi-natural forests, it can be assumed that impacts on native species and on biodiversity will be long lasting, since many areas have been managed in this way for several forest generations. An internal case study from 2022 commissioned by Lenzing on Austrian forests in conjunction with the Austrian environmental NGOs umbrella organization Umweltdachverband has pointed out that there are numerous species living in managed beech forests in Austria, among them also red-list species, which have adapted to the management practices. The study concluded that reversing these semi-natural forests to completely natural forests (stopping all management) could potentially harm these species. For a summary of the findings, see the 'Biodiversity and eco-systems' focus paper.

Additional potential impacts on water, soil, and air can arise from production facility emissions or from transportation. For more information, please see the chapters 'Pollution', 'Water and marine resources' and 'Raw material security'.

At the end of the value chain of textile and nonwoven products, biodiversity impacts can arise from non-degradable materials entering the environment, if those products are not correctly disposed of. For more information on biodegradability of Lenzing's fibers, please see the 'Resource use and circular economy' chapter.

Source: Lenzing (2023)

Resilience analysis is at the core of ESRS E4–1. Similar disclosure requirements are in place for ESRS E1 with regard to climate change. If any sustainability matter related to ESRS E4 is material, organizations have to make similar considerations for biodiversity and ecosystems as well. An ecosystem can be resilient, as can a business model relating to its upkeep. Resilience in both cases is defined in Example 8.4.

Example 8.4

What is resilience in the context of biodiversity and an organization's business model?

In the context of biodiversity, resilience refers to the ability of ecosystems to recover from disturbances, maintain functionality and continue providing essential services such as clean water, air and habitat for species. For an organization's business model, resilience involves recognizing dependencies on these ecosystem services and the risks associated with biodiversity loss. Businesses that incorporate biodiversity resilience into their strategies are better equipped to adapt to environmental changes, mitigate risks (such as supply chain disruptions) and safeguard long-term sustainability. By building resilience into their models, organizations can protect themselves from ecological collapse, align with regulatory requirements like the ESRS E4 and contribute to global biodiversity goals.

ESRS E4–1 also contains one optional data point. An organization may provide information on its plan to transition towards a business model and strategy that will wholly align with various sustainability disclosure frameworks, such as the Kunming-Montreal Global Biodiversity Framework and the **EU Biodiversity Strategy for 2030**. ESRS E4.AR 1–3 contain further examples for information that should be given when disclosing such a transition plan. The transition plan according to ESRS E4–1 corresponds to and complements the transition plan for climate change according to ESRS E1–1; however, the latter is a mandatory disclosure requirement (if such a transition plan has been developed by the organization).

The second disclosure requirement under the reporting area 'strategy' relates to ESRS 2 Disclosure Requirement 2 – SBM 3 Material impacts, risks and opportunities and their interaction with strategy and business model. ESRS 2 SBM 3 requires the organization to disclose a list of material sites in its own operations, including sites under its operational control, based on the assessments of its materiality analysis. For each site, detailed information must be given. Furthermore, the organization must disclose whether it has identified material negative impacts with regards to **land degradation, desertification** or **soil sealing,** and whether it has operations that affect threatened species. Example 8.5 demonstrates how this reporting may appear in practice.

Example 8.5

Ørsted gives a list of its material impacts, risks and opportunities

Biodiversity and ecosystems

	Material impact or risk	Description
Direct impact drivers on biodiversity loss		
• Negative impact (VC)	Natural resources exploitation and land-use change from mining of minerals and metals.	Almost all resources used in our supply chain, and subsequently in our renewable energy assets, are virgin materials that are mined and processed. Extraction and refinement of these materials can have adverse impacts on biodiversity. We are actively working towards managing our value chain impacts.
Impacts on the extent and condition of ecosystems and the state of species		
• Negative impact (VC)	Habitat loss from land degradation caused by mining of minerals and metals.	Habitat loss and ecotoxicity from run-off of mining leading to land degradation, which may result in an indirect impact causing a decrease in species population size (and potentially causing extinction risk). We are actively working towards managing our value chain impacts.
• Negative impact (OO)	Disturbances to habitats and displacement or loss of species.	Disturbances to habitats due to construction and operation of renewable energy assets. Construction and operation of renewable energy projects can impact habitats due to ground preparation and the presence of infrastructure and can adversely impact certain species. We scope these impacts and take appropriate avoidance, reduction, and mitigation action to manage them.
• Positive impact (OO)	Biodiversity restoration, research, and innovation initiatives.	We conduct habitat and ecosystem restoration efforts, including maximising positive impacts on wider supportive ecosystems (e.g. salt marsh). We conduct species restoration efforts, research on habitats and species, and innovation (e.g. biodiversity monitoring and tracking).

Source: Ørsted (2023), p. 74

Reporting area: Impacts, risks and opportunities management (IRO) for ESRS E4

Under this reporting area, companies have to disclose their policies and actions with regard to biodiversity and ecosystems. Table 8.3 sets out the disclosure requirements for ESRS E4–2 and E4–3.

Table 8.3 Disclosure requirements for ESRS E4–2 and E4–3

Disclosure requirement	Brief description
E4–2. Policies related to biodiversity and ecosystems	The organization must disclose the policies it has in place to manage impacts, risks and opportunities that concern biodiversity and ecosystems.
E4–3. Actions and resources related to biodiversity and ecosystems	The organization must identify the resources it allocates to actions related to biodiversity and ecosystems, so as to allow understanding of the key actions an organization takes and their impact on relevant policy targets.

As with reporting SBM, ESRS E4 relates to ESRS 2: Disclosure Requirement 2 – IRO 1 Description of processes to identify and assess material biodiversity and ecosystem-related impacts, risks, dependencies and opportunities. Organizations are required to disclose how they considered the sustainability matters related to ESRS E4 in their materiality assessment. This includes, for example, if and how the assessment was conducted at a site level by the organization, how physical and transitional risks were considered, what attention was given to systemic risks and how affected communities living next to the sites of the organization were consulted. Further requirements are in place for sites located in or near biodiversity-sensitive areas and with regard to necessary biodiversity mitigation measures. Finally, ESRS E4 recommends that organizations may disclose whether and how they have used biodiversity and ecosystems scenario analysis in their materiality assessment. Also, a reference is made to the LEAP approach which organizations are recommended to implement, which is discussed in Example 8.6.

Example 8.6

LEAP approach

LEAP stands for 'Locate, Evaluate, Assess, Prepare'. It is a guidance on the identification and assessment of nature-related matters, developed by the Taskforce on Nature-related Financial Disclosures (TNFD). However, beyond biodiversity, this method can also be applied to the other environmental matters covered by ESRS (e.g. ESRS E2.AR 1; E3.AR 1; E5.AR 1).

The following visualization gives an overview on the main elements of the LEAP approach. Most importantly, this approach requires organizations to conduct their materiality analysis on the level of geographical locations.

(Continued)

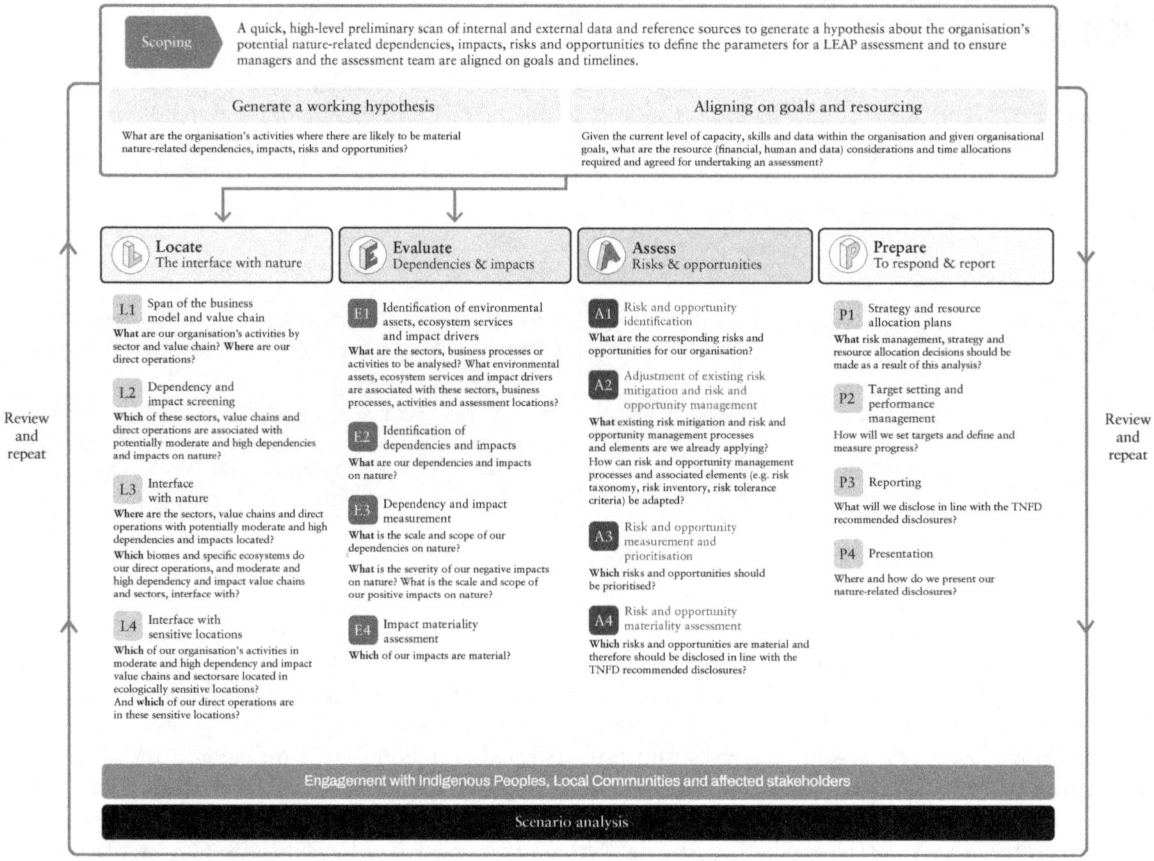

Source: TNFD (2023a)

The disclosure requirement in ESRS E4–3 refers to an important concept that also plays an important role in other disclosure requirements of this standard: the mitigation hierarchy. The mitigation hierarchy is a tool that helps organizations identify appropriate ways of mitigating negative impacts caused by their operations. The hierarchy follows a four-step approach, with the first steps always being more preferable than the later steps: avoidance, minimization, restoration and offsets. Figure 8.1 illustrates the mitigation hierarchy.

The application is recommended by the 'Basis for conclusions' (EFRAG, 2023b), which accompanies ESRS E4. Use of the mitigation hierarchy ensures organizations do not obscure relevant information pertaining to ESRS E4 in alignment with ESRS 1 Appendix B's focus on relevance and **faithful representation**. As a consequence, negative impacts have to be presented irrespective of the measures taken to mitigate these impacts. In case of offsets, ESRS E4 requires additional disclosures on actions taken regarding these offsets.

Reporting area: Metrics and targets (MT) for ESRS E4

The reporting area of metrics and targets comprises one disclosure requirement addressing targets and two separate disclosure requirements regarding metrics. As with all the other environmental standards, ESRS E4–6 requires companies to disclose financial effects from the sustainability matter under consideration. ESRS E4–5, in contrast, contains a non-exhaustive list of metrics that might be disclosed in order to meet the objective of ESRS E4.

Figure 8.1 The mitigation hierarchy

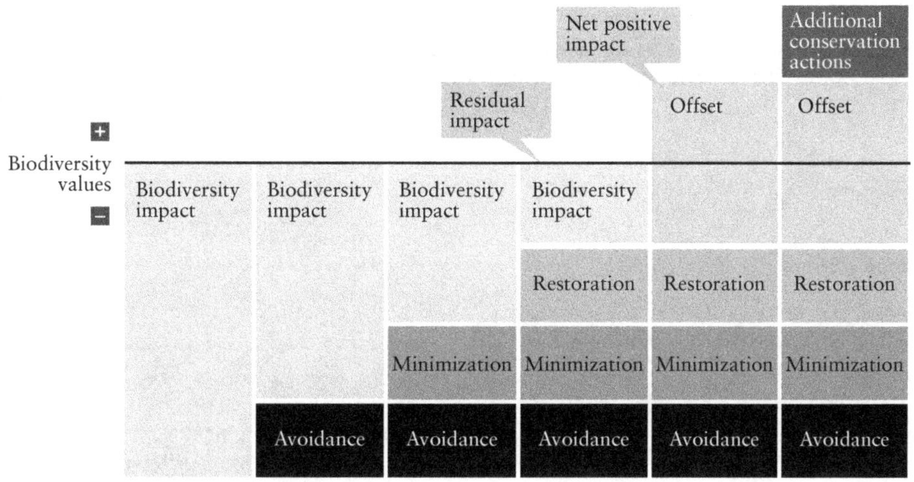

Source: Redrawn from EFRAG (2023b)

Table 8.4 sets out the disclosure requirements for ESRS E4–4 to E4–6.

Table 8.4 Disclosure requirements for ESRS E4–4 to E4–6

Disclosure requirement	Brief description
E4–4. Targets related to biodiversity and ecosystems	The organization shall disclose the biodiversity and ecosystem-related targets it has set. This includes details about the targets. For example: • whether and how ecological thresholds were considered when setting targets • whether the targets are informed by the Kunming-Montreal Global Biodiversity Framework, relevant aspects of the EU Biodiversity Strategy for 2030 and other relevant national policies and legislation • how said targets relate to the impacts, risks and opportunities of the organization's operations as well as operations in its upstream and downstream value chain.
E4–5. Impact metrics related to biodiversity and ecosystems change.	The organization shall report metrics related to its material impacts on biodiversity and ecosystems. For example: • the conversion of land cover over time, such as five years of deforestation • any change in the makeup of land, such as the fragmentation of habitats • changes in the management of the ecosystem over time • the functional connectivity of populations on the land, such as individuals' movement and the movement of genes throughout a population. An organization may also report the metrics it uses to manage the introduction and spread of invasive alien species into an ecosystem.
E4–6. Anticipated financial effects from material biodiversity and ecosystem-related risks and opportunities	The organization shall disclose the potential financial effects of its risks and opportunities regarding material biodiversity and ecosystems.

Regarding ESRS E4–5, the disclosure examples listed in Table 8.4 are just recommendations. But if the organization identified sites located in or near biodiversity-sensitive areas that are negatively affected by these sites, the number and area (in hectares) of sites owned, leased or managed in or near these protected areas or key biodiversity areas must be disclosed. Otherwise, organizations have to identify and disclose metrics that suit the nature of their impacts, risks and opportunities on an entity-specific basis. In order to do so, organizations might refer to frameworks such as the recommendations of the TNFD, as demonstrated in Example 8.7.

Example 8.7

TNFD metrics for sustainability reports

The recommendations of the TNFD list metrics that organizations might include in their sustainability reports, depending on the nature of the impact, risk or opportunity that has to be represented. The following table gives two examples of such metrics and their calculation. However, it should be noted that for a company subject to the CSRD, it is not mandatory to use any of these metrics; however, it is highly recommended and is one way to meet the reporting obligations set forth in ESRS E4 (and also other environmental standards).

Metric no.	Driver of nature change	Indicator	Metric
C2.1	Pollution/pollution removal	Wastewater discharged	Volume of water discharged (m3), split into: • Total; • Freshwater; and • Other.[1] Including: • Concentrations of key pollutants in the wastewater discharged, by type of pollutant, referring to sector-specific guidance for types of pollutants; and • Temperature of water discharged, where relevant.
C2.2		Waste generation and disposal	Weight of hazardous and non-hazardous waste generated by type (tonnes), referring to sector-specific guidance for types of waste. Weight of hazardous and non-hazardous waste (tonnes) disposed of, split into: • Waste incinerated (with and without energy recovery); • Waste sent to landfill; and • Other disposal methods. Weight of hazardous and non-hazardous waste (tonnes) diverted from landfill, split into waste: • Reused; • Recycled; and • Other recovery operations.

[1] Freshwater: (≤1,000 mg/L Total Dissolved Solids). Other: (>1,000 mg/L Total Dissolved Solids). Reference: GRI (2018) GRI 303-4 Water discharge

Source: TNFD (2023b)

Use Activity 8.1 to develop your understanding of how companies report on ESRS E4 disclosure standards within their annual or sustainability reports.

ACTIVITY 8.1

Biodiversity disclosures in practice

Using the listed company Novozymes' most recent Integrated Annual Report (or another organization of your choice), conduct the following analysis:

1. Provide a brief description of content of the sections related to biodiversity in the **integrated report** (or sustainability report if you choose to work with another organization).
2. Assess whether the report adequately addresses the disclosure requirements outlined in ESRS E4.
3. Identify potential areas for improvement or gaps in the reporting. Alternatively, state the conclusion that there is no scope for improvement.
4. Discuss how you perceive the balance between the metrics provided on own ESRS E4 biodiversity and narrative (text) disclosures.

ESRS E4 links to financial statements

Similar to the other environmental standards, ESRS E4 requires organizations to report on anticipated financial effects from biodiversity and ecosystem-related risks, actions and opportunities. Organizations are required to disclose the following information:

- **a** a quantification of the anticipated financial effects (negative or positive) in monetary terms or, if this is not possible with due effort, a qualitative information. This quantification may be given as a single amount or a range
- **b** a description of the effects considered and the impacts and dependencies to which they relate and the corresponding time horizons
- **c** a description of the critical assumptions used for quantifying the anticipated financial effects as well as the sources which this quantification is based upon and the level of uncertainty. (Adapted from ESRS E4)

OTHER STANDARDS AND FRAMEWORKS RELATING TO ESRS E4

At the European level, ESRS E4 fits within the broader EU policy on biodiversity. The EU's Biodiversity Strategy for 2030 aims to protect and restore ecosystems, halt biodiversity loss and ensure that Europe's natural capital is preserved for future generations. Organizations making ESRS E4 disclosures will report on the impacts of their operations on biodiversity, reflecting the EU's commitment to achieving climate neutrality and halting biodiversity loss.

ESRS E4 is designed to directly support the EU's goal of protecting 30% of Europe's land and sea areas by 2030, aiming to create biodiversity-positive business practices. Corporations are expected to assess how their activities affect local biodiversity hotspots, such as **Natura 2000 sites**, which are protected under EU law.

Organizations that report in accordance with ESRS E4 will address their biodiversity-related risks, dependencies and impacts, including how they interact with ecosystems at a local level. This might involve identifying endangered species or habitats affected by corporate activities, as well as the extent to which they comply with local conservation laws.

However, implementing ESRS E4 at the local level requires businesses to collaborate with local authorities and environmental organizations. It also presents challenges, such as differing regional biodiversity conditions across Europe and the need for specialized knowledge in assessing biodiversity impacts. A study by Wiersema (2022) highlights that regional biodiversity assessments often require bespoke methods, creating difficulties for companies trying to standardize their reporting practices.

Globally, ESRS E4 has the potential to contribute to the broader international effort to combat biodiversity loss, notably through alignment with frameworks such as the **Convention on Biological Diversity (CBD)** and the Kunming-Montreal Global Biodiversity Framework adopted in 2022 at the 15th meeting of the **Conference of the Parties to the Convention on Biological Diversity**. The ESRS E4 standards are not isolated but contribute to achieving the global goal of halting biodiversity loss by 2050, as outlined in the Post-2020 Global Biodiversity Framework.

Implementing ESRS E4 in a global context poses challenges, particularly in data availability and standardization. Global ecosystems differ widely, and collecting accurate, comparable biodiversity data across regions remains a significant obstacle. Additionally, the lack of enforceable global biodiversity laws means that compliance with ESRS E4 relies heavily on voluntary corporate commitment outside Europe (Ekardt *et al.*, 2023; WWF, 2024).

GRI and ESRS E4

Under GRI Standards, the sustainability matter biodiversity received much attention when standard GRI 101: Biodiversity was published in 2024. This standard replaced GRI 304: Biodiversity 2016. It has been aligned with the goals and targets of the Kunming-Montreal Global Biodiversity Framework and aims to help organizations better understand which decisions and business practices have an impact on biodiversity, where in their value chain these impacts occur, and how they can be managed by the organization.

GRI 101 contains eight disclosure requirements:

Topic management disclosures

Disclosure 101–1: Policies to halt and reverse biodiversity loss
Disclosure 101–2: Management of biodiversity impacts
Disclosure 101–3: Access and benefit-sharing

Topic disclosures

Disclosure 101–4: Identification of biodiversity impacts
Disclosure 101–5: Locations with biodiversity impacts
Disclosure 101–6: Direct drivers of biodiversity loss
Disclosure 101–7: Changes to the state of biodiversity
Disclosure 101–8: Ecosystem services

In contrast to ESRS E4, GRI 101 only focuses on impacts on biodiversity and ecosystems by an organization. Metrics required by the standard have to be given at a site level, thus requiring very granular information.

TNFD and ESRS E4

ESRS E4 aligns with global reporting frameworks such as the TNFD. This ensures that EU-based companies can contribute to global biodiversity targets, providing internationally comparable data on corporate impacts on biodiversity.

TNFD is a market-driven, science-based and government-supported initiative that equips organizations with the tools to address emerging nature-related challenges. Launched in June 2021 with the backing of the G20 Sustainable Finance Working Group and financial support from various governments and philanthropic foundations, the TNFD aims to foster greater awareness and action on nature-related issues.

In September 2023, the TNFD released a comprehensive set of disclosure recommendations and guidance designed to encourage and enable businesses and financial institutions to assess, report and act on their dependencies, impacts, risks and opportunities related to nature.

These recommendations and guidance are intended to help businesses and the finance sector integrate nature into their decision-making processes. The Taskforce's ultimate goal is to steer global financial flows away from nature-negative outcomes and towards nature-positive outcomes, in alignment with the Global Biodiversity Framework.

TNFD and wider ESRS

Since 2022, EFRAG and the TNFD have closely collaborated, facilitating a continuous exchange of ideas and information in the development of the ESRS and TNFD recommendations and guidance. This partnership has ensured a high degree of consistency in the language, approach and definitions within both the ESRS environmental standards and the TNFD's recommendations and additional guidance. This partnership led to the signing of a Memorandum of Understanding (MoU) in December 2023. This MoU emphasizes the importance of enhancing corporate sustainability assessments and reporting to address nature-related issues. It represents a shared commitment to improving corporate transparency concerning nature, including biodiversity and ecosystems. Additionally, as part of this MoU, EFRAG became the 20th knowledge partner of the TNFD (EFRAG, 2024a).

The TNFD defines nature as the natural world, highlighting the diversity of living organisms, including humans, and their interactions with each other and their environment. Both the TNFD and the ESRS address the four realms of nature: land, ocean, fresh water and atmosphere. Additionally, ESRS emphasize that within the concept of double materiality, 'nature may be considered as a silent stakeholder' (ESRS 1.AR7), and reference the 'interface with nature' in relation to the materiality assessment process of their environmental standards, excluding ESRS E1 on climate change. Both the TNFD and ESRS adopt the terms 'biodiversity' and 'ecosystems' in line with the definitions provided by the **UN Convention on Biological Diversity**. The TNFD distinguishes between 'nature' and 'biodiversity', with biodiversity specifically referring to the variability of living organisms across the four nature realms. In the ESRS, biodiversity and ecosystems are included as one of the sustainability matters addressed in the topical standards, alongside climate change, pollution, water and marine resources, and resource use and the circular economy (EFRAG, 2024a).

Table 8.5 provides an overview of the 14 disclosure recommendations of the TNFD.

Table 8.5 The disclosure recommendations of the TNFD

TNFD Disclosure recommendations	
Governance	A. Describe the board's oversight of nature-related dependencies, impacts, risks and opportunities.
	B. Describe management's role in assessing and managing nature-related dependencies, impacts, risks and opportunities.
	C. Describe the organization's human rights policies and engagement activities, and oversight by the board and management, with respect to Indigenous Peoples, Local Communities, affected and other stakeholders, in the organization's assessment of, and response to, nature-related dependencies, impacts, risks and opportunities.
Strategy	A. Describe the nature-related dependencies, impacts, risks and opportunities the organization has identified over the short, medium and long term.
	B. Describe the effect nature-related dependencies, impacts, risks and opportunities have had on the organization's business model, value chain, strategy and financial planning, as well as any transition plans or analysis in place.
	C. Describe the resilience of the organization's strategy to nature-related risks and opportunities, taking into consideration different scenarios.
	D. Disclose the locations of assets and/or activities in the organization's direct operations and, where possible, upstream and downstream value chains that meet the criteria for priority locations.

(Continued)

Table 8.5 The disclosure recommendations of the TNFD (Continued)

Risk and impact management	A(i). Describe the organization's processes for identifying, assessing and prioritizing nature-related dependencies, impacts, risks and opportunities in its direct operations.
	A(ii). Describe the organization's processes for identifying, assessing and prioritizing nature-related dependencies, impacts, risks and opportunities in its upstream and downstream value chain(s).
	B. Describe the organization's processes for managing nature-related dependencies, impacts, risks and opportunities.
	C. Describe how processes for identifying, assessing, prioritizing and monitoring nature-related risks are integrated into and inform the organization's overall risk management processes.
Metrics and targets	A. Disclose the metrics used by the organization to assess and manage material nature-related risks and opportunities in line with its strategy and risk management process.
	B. Disclose the metrics used by the organization to assess and manage dependencies and impacts on nature.
	C. Describe the targets and goals used by the organization to manage nature-related dependencies, impacts, risks and opportunities and its performance against these.

Source: Modified from TNFD (2023b)

The TNFD specifies that organizations are not limited by the additional set of metrics and are encouraged to report any other metrics that are material and relevant to them.

The EFRAG and the TNFD published a guidance document to help GRI reporters to align with the TNFD recommendations (TNFD, 2024), which supports preparers with meeting the requirements of both sets of disclosures.

ESRS E5 RESOURCE USE AND CIRCULAR ECONOMY

The objective of ESRS E5 is to specify disclosure requirements which will enable users of the sustainability statement to understand the organization's resource use and its contributions towards achieving a circular economy. The principle of resource efficiency, avoiding the depletion of resources and instead seeking sustainable sourcing and use of renewable resources, is referred to in this ESRS as 'resource use and circular economy'.

The ESRS define 'circular economy' as:

> *[A]n economic system in which the value of products, materials and other resources in the economy is maintained for as long as possible, enhancing their efficient use in production and consumption, thereby reducing the environmental impact of their use, minimising waste and the release of hazardous substances at all stages of their life cycle, including through the application of the waste hierarchy.* (ESRS E5 para. 3)

This definition refers to the circular economy principles that are part of the EU's approach towards achieving the aims of a circular economy. This comprises the following principles:

- usability
- reusability
- repairability
- disassembly
- remanufacturing or refurbishment

- recycling
- recirculation by the biological cycle
- other potential optimization of product and material use.

The waste hierarchy lays out a priority order in waste prevention and management:

- prevention
- preparing for reuse
- recycling
- other recovery (e.g. energy recovery)
- disposal. (ESRS E5, paras 35–37)

Consequently, the objective of ESRS E5 is to specify disclosure requirements which will enable users of the sustainability statement to understand:

- **a** how the organization affects resource use and the circular economy in terms of material positive and negative actual or potential impacts
- **b** any actions taken, and the result of such actions, to prevent or mitigate actual or potential negative impacts arising from resource use and to address corresponding risks and opportunities
- **c** how the organization adapts its strategy and business model in line with circular economy principles.

The risks and opportunities relating to resource use and circular economy have to be reported. This includes the nature, type and extent of these risks and opportunities and how the organization manages them. The corresponding financial effects should also be disclosed.

The physical flow of resources is of special importance to ESRS E5, which promotes the reduction of waste in order to implement the principles of a circular economic system. As a consequence, the measurement and management of resource inflows and resource outflows is at the core of this specific ESRS. Ultimately, organizations are to implement measures to help in decoupling their economic growth from the use of materials. Electronics manufacturer Samsung has conducted research into its customers' approach to sustainability while examining its own use of resources, as shown in Example 8.8.

Example 8.8

Samsung's Sustainability Consumer Survey

Mark Newton, Head of Corporate Sustainability for Samsung Electronics America, states in a Samsung Newsroom US article that '[Samsung] want[s] to empower people and educate them on practical and cost-effective ways they can join us in making a positive impact on the environment'.

A survey conducted by Samsung found that 77% of respondents wishing to act more sustainably were recycling and upcycling, while 66% were reducing food waste. Samsung responds to its consumers' desire to minimize waste in a number of ways. It encourages proper disposal of its devices to limit landfill waste, provides accessible care for its products to increase their life span, and offers trade-ins of old devices so that they can be recycled directly by Samsung. Since 2009, Samsung says it has repurposed or recycled 1.3 billion pounds in weight of e-waste in the US alone through such initiatives.

> *When it comes to food waste, the right technology can serve up a healthy portion of inspiration. Approximately 7 in 10 U.S. adults feel guilty about food waste, driven by the lack of time or motivation to cook (29%) and the tendency to order delivery despite a fully stocked fridge (26%). Gen Z feel the heat in the kitchen the most with 39% feeling guilty when they don't know what to cook.*

(Continued)

This is where the new Samsung AI Family Hub™+ steps in. Advanced AI Vision Inside™ technology uses a built-in camera to identify a variety of fresh food items and automatically generates a list of what food users have in stock, right in the SmartThings app. There, you can get recommendations for recipes that use the ingredients you have on hand. In addition to meal planning, this feature also lets you know what to buy at the grocery store, helping reduce excess purchases – or the dreaded trip back for something you missed.

Newton also states that sustainability practices at Samsung do not inhibit but enhance innovation within the company. This is demonstrated by their industry-first SolarCell Remote which recharges in indoor light and is predicted to save 200 million batteries from going to landfill by 2033.

Source: Samsung (2024)

Sustainability matters applicable for ESRS E5 (ESRS 1.AR 16)

Appendix A of ESRS 1 contains the list of minimum sustainability matters an organization has to assess during its materiality analysis. For ESRS E5, this list is rather short, only covering the three matters referred to in Table 8.6.

Table 8.6 Discussion of ESRS E5 in ESRS 1 Appendix A

Topic	Sub-topic	Sub-sub-topic
Circular economy	Resources inflows, including resource use	
	Resource outflows related to products and services	
	Waste	

The ESRS provides definitions for these three sustainability matters as follows:

- *Resources inflow: Resource that enters the undertaking's facilities.*
- *Resources outflow: Resource that leaves the undertaking's facilities.*
- *Waste: Any substance or object which the holder discards or intends or is required to discard.*

(ESRS G1 Annex II)

Accordingly, the scope of examinations required by ESRS E5 is broad. It requires organizations to have an overview of their resource flows. To meet this requirement, systems for tracking and documenting these flows need to be implemented as a prerequisite. Each of the three sub-topics related to ESRS E5 is reflected in a metric that the standard contains (ESRS E4–4, E4–5 and E4–6).

Reporting area: Impacts, risks and opportunities management (IRO) for ESRS E5

Under this reporting area, organizations have to report on their policies with regard to resource use and the circular economy, as well as on their actions with regard to this sustainability matter (refer to Table 8.7).

Table 8.7 Disclosure requirements for ESRS E5–1 and E5–2

Disclosure requirement	Brief description
E5–1. Policies related to resource use and the circular economy	The organization shall describe the policies in place that manage material impacts, risks and opportunities concerning resource use and the circular economy.
E5-2. Actions and resources related to resource use and the circular economy	The organization shall disclose the actions it takes concerning resource use and the circular economy and the resources it allocates to said actions.

Disclosures on policies shall address all material impacts, risks and opportunities within an organization's own operations as well as in its upstream and downstream value chain. The most important aspects that should be covered are:

- the transition away from virgin resources, and the organization's relative increase in the use of recycled resources
- the sustainable method by which recycled and renewable resources are sourced.

Refer to Example 8.9 for an insight into how a company may disclose the information required by ESRS E5–1.

Example 8.9

Ørsted discloses information as required by ESRS E5–1

Our approach and policies

We are reliant on significant amounts of critical raw materials to meet the scale and pace needed for the renewable energy build-out. However, renewable energy supply chains are under pressure, and bottle-necks and material scarcities are already defining the pace of the energy transition in many markets. We can reduce some of these pressures through circularity efforts. By considering the provenance and mix of materials and increasing recycling and reusing, we can reduce the demand for virgin materials and reduce volatilities in our supply chain while minimising negative impacts throughout the value chain, including carbon emissions.

The dominant share of our upstream carbon emissions comes from the extraction and processing of materials for our assets (approximately 75%) – steel alone accounts for approximately 50%. By incorporating circular principles across our business we can reduce carbon emissions to help reach our science-based net-zero target while ensuring responsible waste management. We mainly work across three circularity levers:

1 **Circular design and materials**
We take measures to reduce and optimise resource usage by rethinking the design of our new renewable energy assets. We want to engage with key suppliers to promote the use of recycled and recyclable materials, particularly in high-impact categories like steel.

2 **Operations and late-life strategies**
We strive to maximise the value of our components and assets. We investigate opportunities for repairing, refurbishing, and reusing key components to prolong their lifetime, and we aim to extend the operational lifetime of our wind farms by up to 10 years, beyond the expected lifetime.

(Continued)

3 **Resource recovery and recycling**
Our ambition is to ensure that all materials, when they reach their end-of-life stage, can be effectively recovered and recycled into new supply chains.

To support the promotion of circularity and waste management in our business, we have a resource management policy covering all Ørsted activities and locations. The objective of the policy is to address our aim of minimising the use of virgin resources and to provide the direction for sustainable sourcing of resources. Accountability for our circularity efforts lies with our Chief Operating Officer.

Source: Ørsted (2023), p. 106

Another disclosure requirement relates to ESRS 2 IRO–1 Description of the processes to identify and assess material resource use and circular economy-related impacts, risks and opportunities. In addition to the general disclosure requirements set forth in ESRS 2, an organization which reports on sustainability matters relating to ESRS E5 has to include information on:

- whether and how its assets and activities are screened for actual and potential impacts, risks and opportunities, including in its own operations, the value chain and the method of screening
- whether and how the organization has consulted affected and wider communities.

Reporting area: Metrics and targets (MT) for ESRS E5

The metrics and targets area is similarly structured to its equivalent from ESRS E4. The relevant disclosures comprise one disclosure requirement addressing targets (ESRS E5–3) and three separate disclosure requirements regarding metrics: ESRS E5–4 and E5–5 contain a – non-exhaustive – list of metrics that companies should disclose to meet the objectives of ESRS E5. The metrics of these standards are linked, as E4–4 covers resource inflows and E4–5 resource outflows. ESRS E5–6 requires companies to disclose the financial effects from resource use and the circular economy. These disclosures are discussed further in Table 8.8.

Table 8.8 Disclosure requirements for ESRS E5–3 to E5–6

Disclosure requirement	Brief description
E5–3. Targets related to resource use and the circular economy	The organization shall disclose the targets it has set in relation to resource use and the circular economy. For example, it must report on resource inflows and outflows and how these align with the targets in place.
E5–4. Resource inflows	The organization shall report on the material impacts, risks and opportunities related to resource inflows. Information regarding relevant materials must be expressed in tons or kilograms. Such information may be: • overall weight of materials used • the percentage of materials used in manufacturing that have a biological basis • the percentage and weight of secondary or recycled materials and components used throughout the manufacturing process.

Table 8.8 Disclosure requirements for ESRS E5–3 to E5–6 (Continued)

E5–5. Resource outflows	The organization shall report on the material impacts, risks and opportunities related to resource outflows. This report may include: • the expected durability of products produced • how products can be repaired, with reparability ranked against an established rating system where possible • the proportion of recyclable material in products and packaging. Further stipulation requires the organization to categorize its waste as hazardous or non-hazardous.
E5–6. Anticipated financial effects from material resource use and circular economy-related risks and opportunities	The organization shall disclose the potential financial effects of its risks and opportunities regarding material resource use and the circular economy.

A demonstration of how an organization may report on its material inflows in accordance with ESRS E5–4 is shown in Example 8.10.

Example 8.10

Hydro reports on its resource use in accordance with ESRS E5–4

Resource use per material					
1,000 metric tonnes	2023	2022	2021[1]	2020	2019
Virgin material inflows					
Alumina	2,866	3,122	3,346	3,048	2,954
Aluminium	3,939	3,927	4,103	3,478	3,880
Aluminium fluoride	29	28	32	32	31
Alloying metals	54	46	50	44	49
Lime	42	42	45	45	39
Sodium hydroxide	673	615	591	513	435
Sulphuric acid	16	19	22	22	21
Thickener	6	6	6	4	4
Petroleum coke	377	412	441	437	421
Pitch	79	81	93	96	90
Aluminium scrap inflows					
Post-consumer scrap[2]	444	321	335	104	98
Pre-consumer scrap	1,055	963	1,018	317	340
Total aluminium scrap	**1,499**	**1,285**	**1,353**	**421**	**438**

[1] 2021 is the first year we have consolidated recycling data from Hydro Extrusions, making the 2021 results not directly comparable to previous years' data

[2] 2023 including Alumetal full year

Source: Hydro (2023), p. 106

Disclosure requirements for ESRS E5–5 also cover disclosures on the sustainability matter waste. Regarding its own operations, excluding the upstream and downstream value chain, an organization has to report on:

- the total amount of waste generated (in tons or kilograms)
- the total amount by weight diverted from disposal, including:
  - a breakdown between hazardous waste and non-hazardous waste
  - a breakdown by specific recovery operation types (e.g. 'recycling').
- the amount by weight directed to disposal by waste treatment type and the total amount, summing all three types, with a breakdown between hazardous waste and non-hazardous waste
- the total amount and percentage of non-recycled waste
- the total amount of hazardous waste and radioactive waste generated by the undertaking. (ESRS E5–5 paras 37–39)

This list does not exhaust the reporting requirements concerning waste listed in ESRS E5–5. These extensive and very detailed requirements highlight the considerable challenges that companies will face regarding the collection of data within their operations. Example 8.11 shows how Austrian polymer and plastic product manufacturer Semperit AG Holding reports on its waste targets.

Example 8.11

Semperit reports on its metrics and targets with regard to recycling

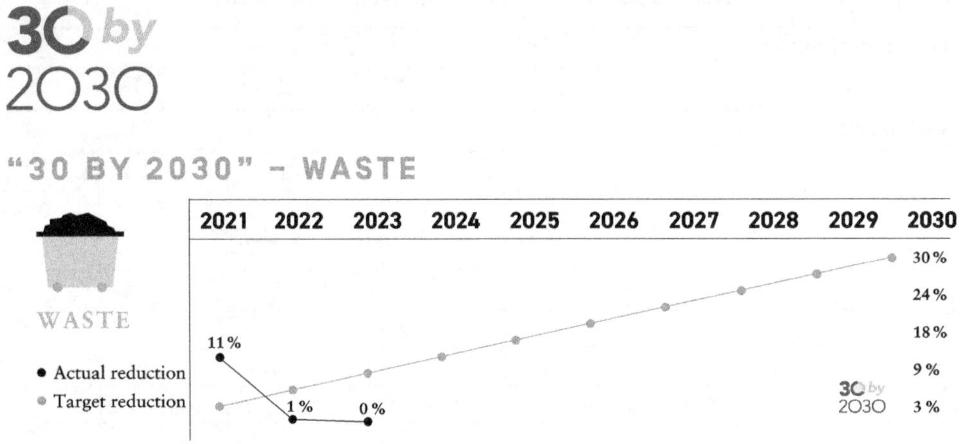

By 2030, the Group aims to save 30% of waste per production volume (target valid until the end of 2023; for further information on the target adjustment until 2030, refer to p. 49 ff.). As the reduction target relates to the quantity produced, the Semperit Group was unable to achieve the 2023 savings target of 9% in the area of waste due to the declining production output and the sale of Sempermed (both events with a negative impact on produced and marketed product quantities). The annual target for 2023 was missed by 9%. As production output decreases, the volume of rubber waste generally increases when production lines are ramped up and down, as the machines have to warm up and run empty and the use of materials cannot be completely avoided. The measures that are taken to achieve the goals vary from business to business and are accompanied by process adjustments and quality criteria as well as an innovation performance.

Source: Semperit (2023), p. 98

Now complete Activity 8.2 to further your understanding of ESRS 4 and 5 in a business context.

ACTIVITY 8.2

Using Ørsted's most recent Annual Report (or another organization of your choice), conduct the following analysis:

1. Provide a description of the sections related to resource use and the circular economy. What do they say about the overall quantity and quality of disclosures made on that sustainability matter (and any other sustainability matters covered in the report)?
2. Assess whether the report adequately addresses the disclosure requirements outlined in ESRS E5. Use Tables 8.7 and 8.8 to guide you.
3. Identify potential areas for improvements or any gaps in the reporting.
4. Discuss what you perceive to be the balance between the metrics provided in ESRS E5 and the qualitative information.

Source: Ørsted (2023)

ESRS E5 links to financial statements

As with all other environmental standards, the disclosure requirements on anticipated financial effects require organizations to disclose quantitative or, if not possible with due cost and effort, qualitative information on their risks and opportunities related to resource use and the circular economy. Further explanations have to be given on these effects as well as on any underlying assumptions, sources used and levels of uncertainty incurred.

OTHER STANDARDS AND FRAMEWORKS RELATING TO ESRS E5

Within the EU, achieving a state of circular economy is one of the main political ambitions. Following up on the Green Deal, the EU Commission published the EU Circular Economy Action Plan in March 2020. This action plan comprises a set of interrelated initiatives along the entire life cycle of products. It targets how products are designed, aiming at establishing a strong and coherent product policy framework in order to make sustainable products, services and business models the norm. As a consequence, waste should be reduced to the greatest extent possible. As part of the action plan, consumers should be empowered by cost-saving opportunities.

The EU Industrial Strategy was published in 2021. It addresses issues that materialized during the COVID-19 pandemic. Based on these learnings, the strategy aims to drive the transformation to a more sustainable, digital, resilient and globally competitive economy. As part of that strategy, consumers should receive trustworthy and relevant information to choose reusable, durable and repairable products (e.g. via a 'right to repair').

Another important framework is set forth by the **Directive 2008/98/EC (Waste Framework Directive)**. It aims at protecting the environment and human health by preventing or reducing the adverse impacts of the generation and management of waste. Also, the overall impacts of resource use are to be reduced, for example by improving the efficiency of the use of such resources.

On a global level, the most important point of reference with regard to resource use and the circular economy is set forth in the UN's SDG Goal 12 Responsible Consumption and Production. Target 12.2 in particular aims at achieving the sustainable management and efficient use of natural resources; and target 12.5 aims at substantially reducing waste generation through prevention, reduction, recycling and reuse. Both targets are supposed to be achieved by 2030.

GRI and ESRS E5

Under GRI, two standards contain reporting requirements related to ESRS E5 – GRI 301 Materials 2016, and GRI 306 Effluents and Waste 2016/Waste 2020. Both served as the main points for orientation when ESRS E5 was drafted.

Both GRI 101 and GRI 306 comprise an extended number of required metrics. They might also provide further guidance when reporting on metrics as required by ESRS E5:

GRI 301: Materials 2016
Disclosure 301–1: Materials used by weight or volume
Disclosure 301–2: Recycled input materials used
Disclosure 301–3: Reclaimed products and their packaging materials

GRI 306: Waste 2020
Disclosure 306–3: Waste generated
Disclosure 306–4: Waste diverted from disposal
Disclosure 306–5: Waste directed to disposal

GRI 306 Effluents and Waste 2016 was superseded by GRI 306 Waste 2020. However, the disclosure requirement GRI 306–3 Significant spills in the earlier version still remains in effect. Currently, the GRI is working on a separate standard for spills.

TRANSITIONAL PROVISIONS FOR ESRS E4 AND ESRS E5

For both standards, ESRS E4 and ESRS E5, Appendix C of ESRS 1 contains phase-in provisions. However, they do differ vastly in scope.

Among all environmental standards, ESRS E4 is the standard that is subject to the most extensive phase-in requirements. First, all organizations that have to report under ESRS E4 are granted the option to phase in disclosure requirement E4–6 Anticipated financial effects from biodiversity and ecosystem-related impacts, risks and opportunities. Similar to all other environmental standards, this specific disclosure requirement may be omitted in the first year of reporting entirely; in the following two years, disclosures can be restricted to qualitative information.

However, organizations that do not exceed an average number of 750 employees may omit ESRS E4 in its entirety in the first two years of preparing their sustainability reports. Nevertheless, the sustainability matters covered by both standards must be covered by the materiality analysis. In the case that such a sustainability matter is material, the organization has to disclose brief descriptions on that matter nevertheless (ESRS 2.BP 2). This strong phase-in provision was added to ESRS E4 in the latter stages of the standard's finalization. Many stakeholders fed back that they found the matter of 'biodiversity and ecosystem' difficult to understand and thus needed more time to establish relevant systems and processes to be able to report on this sustainability matter. An extended period of time to prepare was granted to smaller organizations that are subject to ESRS.

With regard to ESRS E5, only disclosure requirement ESRS E5–6 Anticipated financial effects from resource use and circular economy-related impacts, risks and opportunities is subject to a phase-in provision that is identical that of ESRS E4.

CONCLUSION

ESRS E4 on biodiversity and ecosystems operates within both local European and global contexts, supporting the EU's ambitious biodiversity goals while aligning with international frameworks. It plays a crucial role in fostering transparency about corporate impacts on biodiversity, though challenges such as data collection, local biodiversity differences and global supply chain complexities remain.

PwC (2022) argue that to adequately mitigate nature-related risks and harness opportunities, businesses must go beyond disclosure. A nature strategy provides a forward-looking plan to address nature-related risks and opportunities and contributes to transformation to increase organizational alignment with a nature-positive economy. However, the disclosure requirements of ESRS E4 might serve as a basis and orientation for organizations that want to develop such a strategy. The standard refers to international frameworks and standards and helps organizations to identify the relevant impacts, risks and opportunities that should be their priority.

From the perspective of ESRS E5, the global context of resource use and the circular economy emphasizes sustainable resource management and waste reduction, aligning with international frameworks like the UN's SDG 12. It calls for global corporate responsibility in minimizing resource consumption and adopting circular practices. Locally, especially within the EU, ESRS E5 supports the Circular Economy Action Plan, requiring companies to disclose how they manage resource efficiency, waste and material flows to promote circularity in line with the EU's broader sustainability objectives under the Green Deal.

ESRS E4 is probably the environmental standard with the broadest scope of sustainability matters to be covered. It can be considered an umbrella standard under which the other environmental standards of the ESRS sit. It is therefore important to implement a holistic approach to any policies, actions and targets an organization develops to ensure they are fully captured in reporting. Only then, can an organization adequately disclose the importance of environmental matters, not only from an impact perspective but also from a financial standpoint.

SUMMARY

The following items relate to the learning objectives listed at the beginning of the chapter.

- **LO 1. Discuss global and local contexts of biodiversity, ecosystems, resource use and circular economy.**

  The EU's policy on biodiversity and ESRS E4 align well. Any organization that discloses information in line with ESRS E4 will report their biodiversity-related impacts and risks, demonstrating by extension their commitment to the EU's climate neutrality and biodiversity recovery plans. Globally, ESRS E4 acts as a framework via which organizations can support the international efforts to halt biodiversity loss. ESRS E4 can be used in tandem with other disclosure guidance, such as the Kunming-Montreal Global Biodiversity Framework.

  This is similar to how ESRS E5 aligns with the UN's Sustainable Development Goals. Within the EU, organizations also operate under the Circular Economy Action plan, under which they must report on their circularity, waste and resource efficiency in line with the EU's Green Deal sustainability objectives.

- **LO 2. Understand disclosure requirements for ESRS E4 and ESRS E5.**

  ESRS E4 guides organizations in their disclosure of their impacts on biodiversity and their dependencies on ecosystems. ESRS E5 requires companies to report on their waste, moreover their efforts to reduce waste, improve their circular practices and increase resource efficiency.

- **LO 3. Identify the role of stakeholder engagement in fulfilling the disclosure requirements of ESRS E4 and ESRS E5.**

  Within the concept of double materiality, 'nature may be considered as a silent stakeholder' (ESRS 1.AR7). In alignment with the TNFD, ESRS calls for organizations to describe their human rights policies and engagement activities, and oversight by the board and management with respect to indigenous peoples, local communities, affected and other stakeholders in the organization's assessment of, and response to, nature-related dependencies, impacts, risks and opportunities.
- **LO 4. Discuss the financial effects on an organization over the short, medium and long term caused by the risks and opportunities arising from the organization's impacts and dependencies in the topic areas of ESRS E4 and ESRS E5.**

  Both ESRSs require organizations to report on the expected financial effects related to the underlying sustainability matters. Most organizations depend on the use of resources of any type for their operations. A lack of the availability of natural resources or the inefficient use (waste) of any type of resources in its operations could cause severe economic harm for them or even threaten their existence. Also, in order to achieve the aims related to resource use and circular economy, consumers in the EU will be empowered to raise their demands with regard to the sustainability of products and services offered to them.
- **LO 5. Explain the role of TNFD and other standards for biodiversity and ecosystems as well as for resource use and circular economy disclosures.**

  Both ESRS E4 and ESRS E5 are embedded in a broader set of standards and frameworks addressing the underlying sustainability matters. They provide an understanding for the relevant concepts as well as for the underlying political aims. With regard to disclosure requirements, additional guidance can be obtained by referring to such standards and frameworks. Whilst the corresponding disclosure requirements of the GRI influenced the work on both ESRS E4 and ESRS E5, the recommendations of the TNFD provide a major point of reference for reporting on biodiversity and ecosystems – often referred to as 'gold standard' for biodiversity reporting.

EXERCISES

1. Discuss global and local contexts of biodiversity reporting. (LO 1)
2. Select a company from the mining, agriculture or energy sectors and review its sustainability or financial report. Identify how they address biodiversity and ecosystems. Based on your analysis, draft a mock biodiversity disclosure that would be compliant with ESRS E4. (LO 2)
3. Select a company that has implemented a circular economy initiative (e.g. a company using recycled materials in its production). Review its sustainability report and identify how it has integrated circular economy principles. Draft a disclosure note that would be compliant with ESRS E5 Resource use and circular economy, highlighting resource efficiency, recycling initiatives and waste reduction efforts. (LO 1, LO 2)
4. What is the purpose of ESRS E5 Resource use and circular economy, and why is it important for companies to report on their resource use and waste management practices? How does the circular economy model contribute to sustainability in this context? (LO 1, LO 2, LO 3, LO 4)
5. Imagine you are an accountant for a company that operates in a biodiversity-sensitive area (e.g. near a national park). Perform a materiality assessment that identifies the company's potential impacts on local ecosystems. Outline how these impacts could be reported under ESRS E4. Consider factors such as habitat destruction, water usage and pollution, and describe how each should be disclosed in financial statements. (LO 1, LO 2, LO 5)
6. Research the concept of ecosystem services and discuss how a company's dependence on these services could present financial risks. Using an example company, explain how these risks could be measured and disclosed under ESRS E4. Example sectors to consider are agriculture (pollination services), forestry (deforestation impacts) or tourism (loss of natural beauty). (LO 2, LO 4, LO 5)
7. Choose a company that has successfully implemented circular economy practices. Analyse its resource use and waste reduction strategies, and discuss how the company's financial and sustainability reporting would be enhanced under ESRS E5 Resource use and circular economy. (LO 2, LO 4, LO 5)

CHAPTER 9
Social reporting I: ESRS S1 Own workforce and ESRS S2 Workers in the value chain

Learning objectives

After studying this chapter you should be able to:

- LO 1. Discuss global and local contexts of social reporting.
- LO 2. Understand disclosure requirements for ESRS S1 and ESRS S2.
- LO 3. Identify the role of stakeholder engagement, with employees and their representatives, in fulfilling the disclosure requirements of ESRS S1 and ESRS S2.
- LO 4. Discuss the financial effects on an organization over the short, medium and long term caused by the risks and opportunities arising from the organization's impacts and dependencies in the topic areas of ESRS S1 and ESRS S2.
- LO 5. Explain the role of the United Nations Universal Declaration of Human Rights, International Labour Organization (ILO) labour rules and other standards for social disclosures.

Sustainable work (Deloitte's Human Capital Trends Report)

Almost two in five Millennial and Gen Z workers have rejected job offers from companies that do not align with their personal values. Some 64% of workers state that they would be more willing to stay with an organization that has values and practices benefitting wider society, rather than those that focus solely on creating shareholder value. Such practices also increase profitability and productivity – it is a win-win for organizations. Therefore, if an organization extends its sustainability focus, it can create sustainable work.

Sustainable work embeds inclusion and wellbeing into all facets of the work environment. Sustainable work has a positive effect on employees, enabling growth and learning, rewarding them appropriately and fostering trust. As a result, employees are less stressed in and outside of work, leading to higher productivity and potential. This can be achieved if leadership teams behave like a social enterprise – they must engage with, actively manage and invest in their people and their values, such as the value of sustainable work.

Research by Deloitte indicates that organizations do not understand the wider benefits to the company of prioritizing and maintaining sustainable work. A large organization will spend approximately US$10.5 million a year on social wellbeing programmes with the intention of boosting employee engagement and productivity, but with inconclusive results on the business side of matters. Meanwhile, burnout and mental health remain among the biggest reasons for a Millennial or Gen Z worker to leave their job. A manageable work–life balance and opportunities for learning are key factors that these workers look for when seeking new employment.

Deloitte found that fewer than 15% of respondents to their Human Capital Trends Report in leadership positions were prepared to inclusively lead an expanding workforce or to consider broader societal and environmental risks when making decisions. This leadership gap must be a critical consideration when an organization is discussing implementing the first stages of sustainable work.

Considering the positive correlation between workplace diversity and employee wellbeing with business outcomes, it is surprising that organizations seem to be struggling to embed the practices of sustainable work into their businesses.

Given that there are positive and clear links between wellbeing, diversity, equity, inclusion and business outcomes – such as increased profitability, productivity and performance – it's perhaps surprising that organizations are struggling to truly embed these topics into the heart of their businesses.

Source: Deloitte (2023)

INTRODUCTION

The first two ESRSs in the package of four standards on social reporting address impacts, risks and opportunities relating to working conditions. Not only are companies required to address relevant sustainability matters within their own operations but also in the various parts of their value chain. This is consistent with the general requirements for materiality analysis and defining reporting boundaries as set forth by ESRS 1.

ESRS S1 Own workforce focuses on an organization's internal environment and more specifically its employed and non-employed workers. An organization's social responsibility embraces the physical and emotional wellbeing of its employees (Barrena-Martínez *et al.*, (2019). The integration of social responsibility principles has evolved into a fundamental aspect of organizational identity and practice. Central to this is the concept of social reporting, which encompasses the systematic disclosure of an organization's efforts and impacts concerning societal concerns. Within this expansive framework, the disclosure of information related to the internal workforce emerges as one of the most important dimensions.

ESRS S2 Workers in the value chain requires similar disclosures regarding workers who are not employed directly by an organization, but by its suppliers or customers, for example. Thus, the ESRS makes it clear that an organization shall be held accountable as well for those practices it supports via its business relationships. This is also in line with legislation such as the CSDDD, which takes a similar stance.

This chapter delves into the details of reporting on workers along the entire value chain of an organization. Relevant standards and frameworks that are also considered for a better understanding are the GRI Standards, the Universal Declaration of Human Rights and the **International Labour Organization (ILO)** international labour standards. The GRI Standards play an important role in shaping own workforce disclosure practices. GRI 401, specifically, provides a comprehensive framework for organizations to disclose information on social sustainability aspects related to their own workforce.

ESRS S1 OWN WORKFORCE

The objective of ESRS S1 is to specify disclosure requirements which will enable users of the sustainability statement to understand the organization's material impacts on its own workforce, as well as related material risks and opportunities.

The ESRS defines own workforce/own workers as follows:

> *Employees who are in an employment relationship with the undertaking ('employees') and non-employees who are either individual contractors supplying labour to the undertaking ('self-employed people') or people provided by undertakings primarily engaged in 'employment activities. (NACE Code N78)* (ESRS Annex II)

Further explanations for 'employees' and 'non-employees' are provided by the ESRS. While the former sub-group is most often straight-forward to identify, non-employees can address a variety of constellations such as contractors hired by the undertaking to perform work that would otherwise be carried out by an employee, or people who are formally employed by third parties and fill in for employees who are temporarily absent. Both sub-groups of own workers directly perform their services for the organization, the main difference being the extent to which the organization can exert control over these workers. National labour laws play an important role in further distinctions between both sub-groups and other service providers that are not own workers as defined by ESRS S1.

ESRS S1 comprises two disclosure requirements relating to ESRS 2 as well as 17 topic-specific disclosure requirements. These requirements are designed to provide an understanding of important aspects of an organization's social performance, addressing various aspects such as labour practices, human rights, diversity and inclusion, community engagement, and other social impacts. By mandating these disclosures, ESRS S1 aims to enhance transparency and accountability in corporate social responsibility reporting, enabling stakeholders to make informed assessments of an organization's social contributions and impacts.

Sustainability matters applicable for ESRS 1 (ESRS 1.AR 16)

Appendix A of ESRS 1 contains a list of the minimum sustainability matters an organization has to assess during its materiality analysis (refer to Table 9.1). The list of sustainability matters relating to an organization's own workforce is the most comprehensive of all ESRSs. They are derived from international and European human rights instruments and conventions such as the **International Bill of Human Rights**, the **International Labour Organization's Declaration on Fundamental Principles and Rights at Work** and ILO Fundamental Conventions, the European Convention of Human Rights and the revised **European Social Charter**.

Example 9.1 showcases the ILO's Tripartite Declaration of Principles concerning Multinational Enterprises and Social Policy and lays out basic definitions of several workforce-related sustainability matters listed by ESRS 1. This also exemplifies the interlinks between ESRS and other frameworks (or in this case a declaration).

Table 9.1 List of minimum sustainability matters

Topic	Sub-topic	Sub-sub-topic
Own workforce	Working conditions	Secure employment
		Working time
		Adequate wages
		Social dialogue
		Freedom of association, the existence of works councils and the information, consultation and participation rights of workers
		Collective bargaining, including rate of workers covered by collective agreements
		Work–life balance
		Health and safety
	Equal treatment and opportunities for all	Gender equality and equal pay for work of equal value
		Training and skills development
		Employment and inclusion of persons with disabilities
		Measures against violence and harassment in the workplace
		Diversity
	Other work-related rights	Child labour
		Forced labour
		Adequate housing
		Privacy

Example 9.1

The ILO's Tripartite Declaration of Principles concerning Multinational Enterprises and Social Policy lays out basic definitions of several workforce-related sustainability matters listed by ESRS 1. As a general principle, Article 33 sets forth:

> *Multinational enterprises as well as national enterprises, through active employment planning, should endeavour to provide stable employment for workers employed by each enterprise and should observe freely negotiated obligations concerning employment stability and social security. In view of the flexibility which multinational enterprises may have, they should strive to assume a leading role in promoting security of employment, particularly in countries where the discontinuation of operations is likely to accentuate long-term unemployment.*

In the case of changes in operations, for example because of mergers or acquisitions, enterprises should work together with government authorities and representatives of workers in order to mitigate adverse effects of employment to the greatest possible extent (Article 34). Also, arbitrary dismissals should be avoided at any time (Article 35).

Source: International Labour Organization (2023)

Reporting area: Strategy (SBM)

Both disclosure requirements under the reporting area 'strategy' relate to ESRS 2. They require in-depth depictions of how own workers are considered in the stakeholder dialogue. If the company identifies material impacts, risks or opportunities, they also have to be presented. Since ESRS S1 is subject to materiality assessment, these two disclosure requirements only apply in case a material sustainability matter that falls under ESRS S1 is identified.

ESRS 2 SBM–2 Interests and views of stakeholders: The organization should disclose how the interests, views and rights of people in its own workforce, including respect for their human rights, are taken into account by the organization's strategy and business model.

ESRS 2 SBM–3 Material impacts, risks and opportunities and their interaction with strategy and business model: The undertaking should disclose whether and how actual and potential impacts on its own workforce arise as a result of the organization's strategy and business model and how these impacts contribute to adapting the strategy and business model.

Example 9.2 showcases the ESRS 2 SBM–3 disclosure requirement in practice.

Example 9.2

Ørsted Annual Report 2023

The visualization in the Ørsted annual report is an integral part of their ESRS 2 SBM–3 requirement that the organization discloses whether and how actual and potential impacts on its own workforce arise as a result of the organization's strategy and business model.

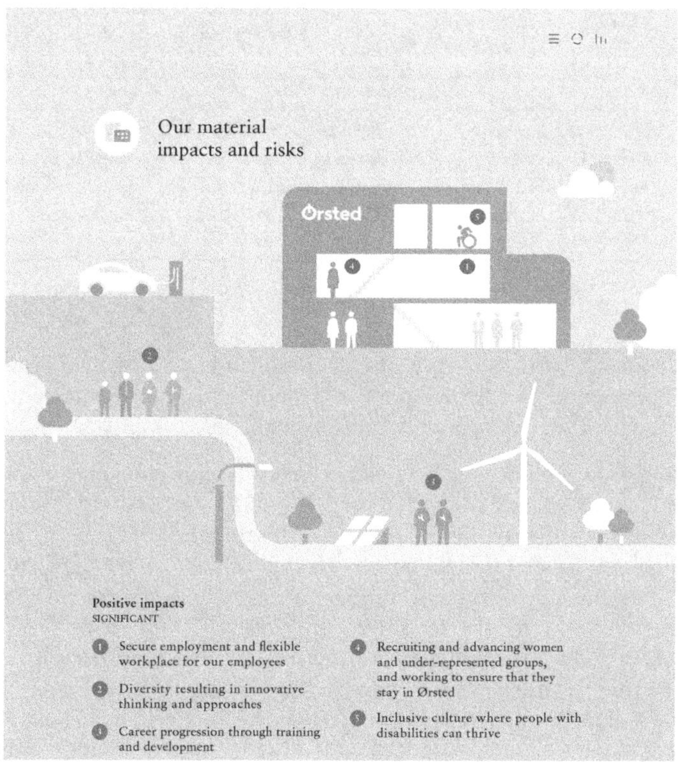

Source: Ørsted (2023), p. 112

Reporting area: Impacts, risks and opportunities management (IRO)

Under this reporting area, companies have to disclose their policies and actions with regard to their own workforce (refer to Table 9.2).

Table 9.2 Disclosure requirements under ESRS S1 for S1–1 to S1–4

Disclosure requirement	Brief description
S1–1. Policies related to own workforce	The organization should report on its policies for managing the material impacts on its own workforce and the material risks and opportunities in this context. For example, it should disclose whether there are organizational policies aimed at eliminating discrimination, including harassment, and policies regarding the promotion of equal opportunities.
S1–2. Processes for engaging with own workforce and workers' representatives about impacts	For this disclosure requirement, the organization should describe the general processes for engaging its own workforce and its representatives with respect to actual and potential material impacts on its own workforce. For example, it should disclose whether the exchange takes place directly with the workforce or with representatives of the workforce, as well as the type and frequency of the exchange.
S1–3. Processes to remediate negative impacts and channels for own workers to raise concerns	The organization should describe the processes in place to address any negative impacts on the workforce that the organization has caused or contributed to. In addition, the options available for the workforce to raise concerns must be outlined and, among other things, the specific mechanisms and processes in this regard should be disclosed.
S1–4. Taking action on material impacts and approaches to mitigating material risks and pursuing material opportunities related to own workforce, and the effectiveness of those actions and approaches	The organization should disclose how it takes action to address material negative and positive impacts, and to manage material risks and pursue material opportunities related to its own workforce, and the effectiveness of those actions.

Channels to use to raise concerns are an important element of the due diligence processes a company might employ for its own workforce – and also for all other social matters. Grievance mechanisms are an important example of such channels. The ESRSs define grievance mechanisms as follows:

> *[a]ny routinized, state-based or non-state-based, judicial or non-judicial processes through which stakeholders can raise grievances and seek remedy. Examples of state-based judicial and non-judicial grievance mechanisms include courts, labour tribunals, national human rights institutions, National Contact Points under the OECD Guidelines for Multinational Enterprises, ombudsperson offices, consumer protection agencies, regulatory oversight bodies, and government-run complaints offices. Non-state-based grievance mechanisms include those administered by the undertaking, either alone or together with stakeholders, such as operational-level grievance mechanisms and collective bargaining, including the mechanisms established by collective bargaining. They also include mechanisms administered by industry associations, international organizations, civil society organizations, or multi-stakeholder groups.*
>
> (ESRS 4 Appendix A: Defined terms)

The ESRS refer to UN Guiding Principle 31 for further specification of suitable grievance mechanisms. Accordingly, they should meet the criteria of being legitimate, accessible, predictable, equitable, transparent and rights-compatible. In order to be effective, they should also be based on engagement and dialogue with stakeholders.

Also, ESRS 1 addresses the role of workers' representatives and how an organization engages with this body. This can be of relevance with regard to stakeholder dialogue activities for materiality assessment, for formulating policies, for setting targets and for tracking the effectiveness of actions set by the organization. It should be noted that the CSRD contains a provision that requires organizations to actively engage with workers' representatives during the reporting process. So, overall, workers' representatives will play an important role for ESRS reporting. To ensure that these representatives are able to fulfil this new role, they need adequate training as well as institutionalized dialogue formats on all relevant sustainability matters.

Another disclosure requirement relates to ESRS 2 IRO-1 Description of the processes to identify and assess material resource use and circular economy-related impacts, risks and opportunities.

Reporting area: Metrics and targets (MT)

ESRS S1 comprises the longest list of metrics of any ESRS published so far (refer to Table 9.3). This also reflects the variety of sustainability matters covered by the standard. It should be noticed that organizations only have to report such metrics that provide material information on those sustainability matters that were identified as material.

Table 9.3 ESRS S1 disclosure requirements for S1–5 to S1–17

Disclosure requirement	Brief description
S1–5. Targets related to managing material impacts, advancing positive impacts, as well as to risks and opportunities	Within the scope of this disclosure requirement, the organization should explain the time-bound and outcome-oriented targets with regard to the following topics: • the reduction of negative impacts on its own workforce • advancing positive impacts on its own workforce • managing material risks and opportunities related to its own workforce. In addition, for example, the process for setting targets and the involvement of the organization's own workforce in this context should be disclosed.
S1–6. Characteristics of the undertaking's employees	The main characteristics of the workforce should be described in regard to this disclosure requirement. In the course of this, the total number of employees, by gender and by country, the full-time equivalent as well as the rate of employee turnover during the reporting period should be disclosed.
S1–7. Characteristics of non-employees in the undertaking's own workforce	In this disclosure requirement, the organization describes the key characteristics of the non-employee workers in the own workforce. This includes the total number of non-employee workers and the type of work they perform.
S1–8. Collective bargaining coverage and social dialogue	The organization shall disclose information on the extent to which the working and employment conditions of its own workforce are determined or influenced by collective bargaining agreements and the extent to which the workforce in the European Economic Area (EEA) is involved in social dialogue at organization and European level. For example, the percentage of the total workforce covered by collective agreements should be disclosed.

(Continued)

Table 9.3 ESRS S1 disclosure requirements for S1–5 to S1–17 (Continued)

S1–9. Diversity metrics	This disclosure requirement includes the number and percentage of the gender distribution in the top management level and the age distribution (under 30 years, 30–50 years, over 50 years) of the organization's own workforce.
S1–10. Adequate wages	The organization must disclose whether all employees of its own workforce receive adequate wages, which are based on corresponding benchmarks. If employees do not receive appropriate compensation, this must be disclosed.
S1–11. Social protection	As part of this disclosure requirement, the organization should state whether its own employees are protected against loss of income due to serious life events. These life events include, among others, illness, maternity leave and accidents at work. If the employees are covered within this scope, no further information is required.
S1–12. Persons with disabilities	Disclosures on the percentage of persons with disabilities in its own workforce, optionally broken down by gender.
S1–13. Training and skills development metrics	The organization shall indicate the extent to which training is provided to the workforce. For example, the following shall be disclosed: the percentage of the workforce that has participated in regular performance evaluations and the average number of hours of training per employee. This information shall be broken down by categories of employees and gender.
S1–14. Health and safety metrics	Disclosures include the reporting of information on the extent to which employees are covered by the organization's occupational health and safety management system, as well as the number of incidents related to work-related injuries, illnesses and fatalities. In addition, the organization shall disclose the number of fatalities resulting from work-related injuries and work-related illnesses of other employees working on the organization's premises.
S1–15. Work-life balance	Disclosures on the extent to which employees have the right to family-related leave and use this possibility. If due to social policy and/or collective agreements all employees have a family-related right to absence, it is sufficient for this disclosure requirement to state this.
S1–16. Remuneration metrics (pay gap and total remuneration)	Disclosure requirement on the percentage pay gap between women and men and the ratio between the remuneration of the highest paid person and the median remuneration of the employees should be disclosed by the organization.
S1–17. Incidents, complaints and severe human rights impacts	Disclosure requirements include, for example, the disclosure of the number of work-related incidents and/or complaints and severe human rights impacts and incidents within the organization's own workforce, as well as any related significant fines or sanctions for the reporting period.

Example 9.3 provides some insights from practice into how training and skills development activities can be reported upon.

Example 9.3

Hydro's detailed breakdown of its training and skills development activities (ESRS S1–S13)

S1.5 Training and development

Reporting principles

Training and development statistics is based on training that is completed and registered by Hydro employees in our human resources systems. Training, education and career development activities that are not registered by the individual employee, as well as on-the-job training activities, are not captured by the reported metrics. Instructor-led courses that are conducted locally are not always registered and thus not included in the reported metrics.

The metrics include both mandatory and voluntary training. See also Note G1.3 on compliance-related training, specifically.

Training and development

	2023	2022
Training hours completed by Hydro employees	262,647	217,958
Courses completed	15,323	16,680
of which, male	11,211	
of which, female	4,112	
Avg. training hours per participant	17.1	13.1
Avg. training hours per employee	8.2	6.8
Avg. training hours, male employees	8.0	7.1
Avg. training hours, female employees	8.7	5.7

* Training statistics do not cover employees at the four recyclers acquired from Alumetal in 2023

Top five training types by number of participants

#	2023	2022	2021
1	HSSE	Compliance	Cyber security
2	Administrative systems	HSEE	All lifecycle
3	Compliance	Sustainability	IT systems training
4	Human resources	Human resources	IT
5	Sustainability	Employee lifecycle	Human resources

In 2023, 52 percent of the conducted training that are registered as completed were conducted online, while 25 percent was instructor-led. The most common categories of mandatory training were HSSE, compliance, human resources and sustainability. HSSE and compliance are also among the top categories for completed courses of voluntary training. Other common categories of voluntary training are administrative systems, team leadership and self leadership.

Training initiatives can vary from year to year based on business needs and initiatives.

Source: Hydro (2023), p. 133

Example 9.4 is another example from practice. It exemplifies the reporting targets and actual achievements regarding health and safety.

Example 9.4

SGL Group's combined overview on its targets and actual achievements concerning health and safety (ESRS S1–S14)

	TARGET	2023	2022
Total Lost Time Incident Frequency (LTIF)	0.00	0.6	1.19
Total Recordable Case Frequency (TRCF)	1.50	1.45	1.55
Proportion of all employees covered by H&S management system	100%	100%	100%
Incidents			
Number of fatalities		0	0
Number of work-related accidents		10	12
Number of cases of work-related ill health		0	1
Number of days lost due to work-related injuries and fatalities		69	-

SAFETY PERFORMANCE IN 2023

S1-14 Health & safety metrics

Note on health & safety metrics

The proportion of the workforce is given as a percentage, in headcount terms, of SGL Group's own employees and is based on Danish legal requirements.

We do not have any data restrictions or limitations to data on work-related ill health and therefore we are reporting the number for the entire global organisation.

Source: SGL (2023), p. 85

Activity 9.1 allows you to conduct your own analysis of the coverage of workforce data with the company Novozymes. You can also apply the same exercise questions to a company of your choice.

ACTIVITY 9.1

Using the listed company Novozymes' most recent Integrated Annual Report (or another organization of your choice), conduct the following analysis:

1 Provide a description of the sections related to own workforce (e.g. diversity data, occupational health and safety measures, training programmes) of Novozymes. What is said at an overall level about the organization's own workforce?
2 Assess whether the report adequately addresses the disclosure requirements outlined in ESRS S1. Use the table from Example 9.4 and also S1–S17 in ESRS S1 as a guide, or just use a selection of the disclosure requirements.
3 Identify potential areas for improvement or gaps in the reporting. Alternatively, draw the conclusion that there is no scope for improvement.
4 Discuss how you perceive the balance to be between the metrics provided on own workforce versus the positive impact the organization is achieving in this area.

As many of the metrics set forth in ESRS S1 are very specific, they often involve very technical issues. Not all of them are addressed by the standard itself in a satisfying way. As a consequence, EFRAG has published several FAQs that try to provide further guidance on questions raised in practice.

Example 9.5 provides one such question that asks if the metric 'family-related leave' presumes that an employee is entitled to every concept of family-related leave.

Example 9.5

ID 340 Entitlement to family-related leave addresses the disclosure requirement ESRS S1–15 Work-life balance. The following question was asked: Does the metric 'family-related leave' presume that an employee is entitled to every concept of family-related leave?'

> EFRAG replied: *'Yes, family-related leave is defined as including maternity leave, paternity leave, parental leave and carer's leave (ESRS S1.AR 96). The focus of the Disclosure Requirement is whether family-related leave is covered by regulations (e.g. government's social protection), organizational policies, agreements, contracts or collective agreements (ESRS S1.AR 97) that contain family-related leave entitlements. Such entitlements may differ at a country level.*
>
> *Being entitled to take family-related leave would thus mean, based on national law or collective agreements, for female employees to be entitled to take maternity, parental and carer's leave, and for male employees to be entitled to paternity, parental and carer's leave. The scope of family leave may vary across countries, and such contextual information may be relevant to users (e.g. that employees are entitled to maternity leave but not to paternity leave in a given country). If based on national law or collective agreements, female/male employees are not entitled to all of the respective female/male types of family-related leave, then they would not qualify to be considered in the nominator of the metric.'*

Consider also Activity 9.2.

ACTIVITY 9.2

ESRS S1 asks organizations to disclose the gender pay gap (ESRS S1–16), defined as the difference in average pay levels between female and male employees, expressed as percentage of the average pay level of male employees.

Should the organization include variable components of salary or only gross wage?

ESRS S1 link to financial statements

An example of linkage between ESRS S1 and the financial statements relates to the number of employees in an organization. ESRS S1–6 cross-checks the number of employees required against the most appropriate amount disclosed in the financial statements. This includes the average number of employees during the year, disclosed according to Article 16 of the Directive 2013/34/EU (Official Journal of the European Union, 2013) and other relevant data if they are disclosed in the financial statements.

Since ESRS S1–6 provides some flexibility in terms of methodology for calculating the head count number of employees (i.e. average or at the end of the year), the undertaking is required to disclose the methodology used. If an organization applied a different methodology for calculating the head count between the disclosure note to the financial statements and this datapoint in ESRS S1–6 (e.g. average for the former, end of the year for the latter), it shall explain the difference in the basis for calculation following the principle of connectivity defined in ESRS 1.

In more explicitly financial terms, most disclosures required by ESRS S1 can be traced to either specific positions in the income statement (such as personnel expenses) or in the balance sheet (e.g. personnel provisions). ESRS S1 also requires companies to make these linkages when items from financial statements are included in one of the disclosures required by ESRS (e.g. ESRS S1–16) or when this linkage is important for the understanding of the users of sustainability reports on material risks and opportunities.

Example 9.6 shows disclosures on the number of courses held and the people trained, but also total expenditures incurred.

Example 9.6

In its Annual and Sustainability Report 2023, Lenzing not only lists the number of courses held and the people trained but also total expenditures incurred.

Learning and development

[ESRS S1-13; GRI 404-1, 404-3]
Around 67,168 times courses from Learn@Lenzing were completed in the reporting year. This results in a total training time of 45,707 hours and therefore an average training time of 5.5 hours per employee. Total expenditure on lifelong learning and personnel development decreased to EUR 5.76 million in 2023, after increases from EUR 6.19 million in 2021 to EUR 6.75 million in 2022. The numbers include group-wide expenses by Bildungszentrum Lenzing (BZL). Therefore, the group-wide consolidated expenses for training courses in 2023 were EUR 2.25 million (2022: EUR 2.48 million, 2021: EUR 2.46 million).

Source: Lenzing (2023), p. 137

ESRS S2 WORKERS IN THE VALUE CHAIN

ESRS S2 mandates reporting on all workers, both upstream and downstream in the organization's value chain, who are or could be significantly affected by the organization's operations. ESRS S2 mirrors the requirements in ESRS S1 but extends them down to the workers in the value chain. ESRS S2 thus introduces a comprehensive framework for organizations to report on the social impacts within their value chain.

The ESRS defines workers in the value chain/value chain workers as follows:

> *An individual performing work in the value chain of the undertaking, regardless of the existence or nature of any contractual relationship with the undertaking. In the ESRS, the scope of workers in the value chain includes all workers in the undertaking's upstream and downstream value chain who are or can be materially impacted by the undertaking. This includes impacts that are connected to the undertaking's own operations, and value chain, including through its products or services, as well as through its business relationships. This includes all workers who are not in the scope of 'Own Workforce'.*

As a consequence, workers according to ESRS S1 and ESRS S2 are complementary groups. If workers are already in the scope of ESRS S1, they do not have to be included under the scope of ESRS S2 again. In the presence of personnel leasing agreements or similar situations, this implies the need for critical analyses in order to make the correct classification. Stakeholders falling under ESRS S2 are distinguished from those in the two other social ESRSs by their work relationship with direct or indirect clients or suppliers; for those entities, in turn, they are typically part of their own workforce.

Sustainability matters applicable for ESRS 1 (ESRS 1.AR 16)

Again, companies are confronted with an extensive list of sustainability matters that they have to cover in their materiality analyses (refer to Table 9.4).

Table 9.4 Sustainability matters requiring coverage in materiality analyses

Topic	Sub-topic	Sub-sub-topic
Workers in the value chain	Working conditions	Secure employment
		Working time
		Adequate wages
		Social dialogue
		Freedom of association, including the existence of work councils
		Collective bargaining
		Work-life balance
		Health and safety
	Equal treatment and opportunities for all	Gender equality and equal pay for work of equal value
		Training and skills development
		The employment and inclusion of persons with disabilities
		Measures against violence and harassment in the workplace
		Diversity
	Other work-related rights	Child labour
		Forced labour
		Adequate housing
		Water and sanitation
		Privacy

The lists of sustainability matters applicable to ESRS S1 and ESRS S2 are mostly identical. This is consistent with the overall approach the ESRS take with regard to the responsibility of organizations for workers in their entire value chains. There are only the following exceptions:

- Only with regard to an organization's own workforce, working conditions comprise 'the information, consultation and participation rights of workers' as well as the 'rate of workers covered by collective agreements'
- In contrast, 'water and sanitation' is only included in the list for workers in the value chain.

Activity 9.3 allows you to work with questions regarding materiality of social impacts on workers in the value chain of an organization.

ACTIVITY 9.3

How should companies determine the materiality of social impacts on workers in their value chain? What factors should be considered when deciding which impacts to report on?

Reporting area: Strategy (SBM)

Similar to ESRS S1, this only includes two disclosure requirements related to ESRS 2. They have to be made in case a related sustainability matter is assessed to be material.

- ESRS 2 SBM–2 Interests and views of stakeholders: The organization should disclose how the interests, views and rights of value chain workers, including respect for their human rights, are taken into account by the organization's strategy and business model.
- ESRS 2 SBM–3 Material impacts, risks and opportunities and their interaction with strategy and business model: Under this disclosure requirement, the undertaking should disclose whether and how actual and potential impacts on its value chain workers arise as a result of the organization's strategy and business model and how these impacts contribute to adapting the strategy and business model.

Reporting area: Impacts, risks and opportunities management (IRO)

The disclosure requirements on IRO are also mostly identical to the requirements set forth in ESRS S1. They follow the same rationales, but there are differences in their subject matter (refer to Table 9.5).

Table 9.5 ESRS disclosure requirements for S2–1 to S2–4

S2–1. Policies related to value chain workers	This outlines strategies to address significant impacts on workers, including risks, opportunities, adherence to human rights and compliance with international standards. Organizations should disclose any incidents of non-compliance and their planned remedies.
S2–2. Engagement with value chain workers	This details how organizations interact with workers or their representatives, addressing actual and potential impacts. It covers how worker input influences decisions, responsibility allocation, worker rights agreements and the inclusion of vulnerable workers. If no such practices exist, a timeline for their implementation should be provided.
S2–3. Remediation and grievance mechanisms	Organizations disclose how they address adverse impacts on workers and the channels available for raising concerns. This includes how workers report issues, the effectiveness of these channels, remedial actions taken and measures to ensure trust and non-retaliation.
S2–4. Actions on material impacts	This details the actions taken to manage significant impacts, risks and opportunities related to value chain workers. This includes prevention strategies for negative impacts, initiatives for positive outcomes and tracking of action plan effectiveness. Responses to identified negative impacts should also be disclosed, including mitigation and prevention measures.

ESRS S2 thus marks a significant shift in corporate responsibility, expanding the scope of care and accountability to encompass the entire value chain. Organizations are encouraged to adopt a holistic approach to sustainability, recognizing their responsibilities to all workers in their network.

Example 9.7 provides a practice example of ESRS 2 disclosures on workers in the value chain. You will encounter a reference to the OECD due diligence guideline. As the CSDDD comes into force, it will be the overriding reference for due diligence.

Example 9.7

Ørsted Annual Report (2023). Extract of disclosure on ESRS S2 workers in the value chain

Responsible sourcing of minerals and metals

Our approach and policies

Our renewable energy assets are dependent on metals, including rare earth elements for wind turbine magnets, copper for transportation cables, and lithium for batteries. A significant share of these metals is mined in countries where the likelihood of adverse impacts on human and labour rights is high, and we must therefore do everything we can to avoid harmful effects. Therefore, we have a specific focus on striving to respect and protect the rights of workers and communities involved in the minerals and metals supply chain.

Our efforts within sourcing of minerals and metals focus on the responsible supply chain of metals, acknowledging the challenges inherent in the mining industry's long and complex supply chains. We focus on ten key metals with the highest risk of adverse social and environmental impacts, operating through three strategic pillars:

1. **Supplier engagement**
   We work closely with key suppliers, aligning with the OECD due diligence guidance on responsible mining. This involves assessing suppliers' management systems and supply chain risks and implementing response strategies.
2. **Supply chain transparency**
   Addressing the challenge of transparency, we collaborate with first-tier suppliers and industry partners, exploring technological solutions to enhance traceability of supply chains for metals.
3. **Industry partnerships**
   Engaging with multi-stakeholder initiatives such as the Initiative for Responsible Mining Assurance (IRMA) and the International Responsible Business Conduct (IRBC) Agreement for the Renewable Energy Sector, we leverage partnerships to work on shared solutions to industry-wide impacts and risks.

Actions

In 2023, we continued our engagement with suppliers and industry associations, reinforcing our efforts of mapping our supply chains and enhancing our influence to mitigate social and environmental risks within our minerals and metals supply chain. Key initiatives include:

1. **Continued engagement with IRMA**
   Building on our membership since the end of 2022 as the first renewable energy company, we actively participated in the Buyers Group alongside leaders in the automotive, electronics, and gemstone industries. This collaborative effort aims to collectively promote responsible supply chains of minerals and metals and advocate for ethical mining practices.
2. **Advancements in transparency**
   We have started a pilot project applying blockchain technology to enhance the transparency of copper usage at one of our UK wind farms. Also, we have agreed with a supplier to initiate reporting on the origin of steel used in foundations for upcoming projects, a significant step towards increased transparency.
3. **Signing the IRBC for the Renewable Energy Sector**
   We joined forces with other wind developers, industry partners, civil society, and governmental stakeholders to address and mitigate risks and impacts on people and the environment in the operations and supply chains of the renewable energy sector. The aim of the agreement is to promote international responsible business conduct (IRBC), including collaborating with trade unions to address impacts on workers in our minerals and metals supply chain.

As part of our ongoing commitment to transparency and accountability, we plan to evaluate the results of our blockchain pilot in 2024, exploring potential applications to other suppliers and metals. Moving forward, we will also explore the reporting of the origin of steel for foundations and wind turbines with selected suppliers.

Source: Ørsted (2023), p. 121

Reporting area: Metrics and targets (MT)

In stark contrast to ESRS S1, the disclosure requirements of ESRS S2 just require companies to report on their targets with regard to workers in the value chain. No explicit requirements are stipulated with regard to metrics, however, but this does not exempt organizations from disclosing such metrics. Following the requirements for entity-specific disclosures, organizations have to identify which metrics are suitable for depicting its material impacts, risks and opportunities related to workers in the value chain. They might refer to other standards and frameworks to produce such metrics; in many cases, they will be very similar to the ones reported under ESRS S1:

- S2–5 Targets related to impacts, risks and opportunities: Organizations are expected to disclose specific, time-bound targets for managing negative impacts, promoting positive outcomes and addressing risks and opportunities for value chain workers. These targets help to track progress and guide actions in line with ESRS S2's objectives.

However, in contrast to metrics reported under ESRS S1, data availability will be a considerable issue when reporting under ESRS S2. For that reason, many organizations will make use of the transitional provisions for disclosures concerning value chain information. However, at the same time, concrete steps have to be taken to secure the relevant data in order to meet the organization's disclosure obligations in the future. Activity 9.4 allows you to consider either in Ørsted's integrated report or an organization of your choice the metrics and targets in terms of social data.

ACTIVITY 9.4

Locate what information Ørsted (or another organization of your choosing) discloses under the reporting area 'Metrics and targets' in terms of its social data.

TRANSITIONAL PROVISIONS FOR ESRS S1 AND ESRS S2

The disclosure requirements set out in ESRS S1 and ESRS S2 require considerable efforts in data collection. In addition, already existing metrics have to be evaluated in terms of how far they meet the new definitions of the ESRS. Processes have to be established in order to obtain and report data in an efficient way to the relevant bodies within a company. For that reason, in order to provide organizations with more time for the relevant transition towards ESRS reporting, ESRS 1 includes several transitional provisions, most often phase-in regulations.

For ESRS S1, several metrics or at least specific data points of metrics covered by the standard can be omitted for their first year of preparing sustainability reports in accordance with ESRS.

Even more flexibility is granted to organizations that do not exceed the average number of 750 employees: they can omit ESRS S1 for their first year of preparing sustainability reports in accordance with ESRS. Regarding ESRS S2, the entire standard may be omitted for the first two years under the same conditions. However, in both cases, the sustainability matters covered by both standards must be covered by the materiality analysis. If a sustainability matter is material, the organization has to disclose brief descriptions on that matter nevertheless (ESRS 2.BP 2).

With regard to ESRS 2, the transitional provisions concerning information related to an organization's value chain apply. For their first year of preparing sustainability reports in accordance with ESRS, organizations can restrict the information provided mostly on publicly or otherwise available information on policies, actions or targets. No information on metrics is required at all. However, this transitional provision only refers to disclosures that can be omitted. With regard to materiality analysis, an organization has to obtain all information necessary for making its assessments, including using qualified estimations where necessary.

OTHER STANDARDS AND FRAMEWORKS

A number of the UN SDGs relate to the social dimensions of sustainability transformation. Examples include SDG 3 on good health and wellbeing, SDG 4 on quality education, SDG 5 on gender equality and SDG 10 on reduced inequalities. The United Nations Human Rights framework and the ILO labour rules are both critical pillars in the promotion and protection of human rights and labour standards globally. Activity 9.5 allows you to explore what other standards an organization may refer to in regard to sustainable sourcing of minerals and metals.

ACTIVITY 9.5

Locate what other standards and initiatives Ørsted uses in its 2023 integrated report when providing disclosures on the responsible sourcing of minerals and metals.

The United Nations Universal Declaration of Human Rights (UDHR)

The **Universal Declaration of Human Rights (UDHR)**, adopted by the United Nations General Assembly in 1948, stands as a landmark document in the history of human rights. Emerging from the ashes of World War II and its atrocities, the UDHR aimed to establish a universal framework of fundamental rights inherent to all human beings. This framework includes landmark documents such as the Universal Declaration of Human Rights, the **International Covenant on Civil and Political Rights**, and the **International Covenant on Economic, Social and Cultural Rights**. These instruments establish the foundation for a range of rights, including the rights to life, liberty and security, as well as economic, social and cultural rights such as the right to work, fair wages and safe working conditions. Here is a look at the UDHR:

- **Inherent dignity and equality:** Every individual is born free and equal in dignity and rights, regardless of their race, colour, sex, language, religion or any other status.

  The UDHR emphasizes the universality of human rights and prohibits discrimination based on any arbitrary ground.
- **Right to life, liberty and security of person:** The document affirms the fundamental right to life and freedom from arbitrary detention, torture and cruel, inhuman or degrading treatment.
- **Civil and political rights:** These encompass freedoms of expression, assembly, religion and participation in government.
- **Economic, social and cultural rights:** The UDHR recognizes the right to work, social security, education and an adequate standard of living.

While not a legally binding treaty, the UDHR has exerted immense influence on international human rights law. It serves as a common standard of achievement for all nations and inspires national and regional legal frameworks that further elaborate and enforce these fundamental rights.

CSRD and ESRS S1 provide an explicit reference to the UDHR and an extract of this is provided in Example 9.8.

Example 9.8

Disclosure requirement S1-1 from ESRS S1.AR 12

When disclosing the alignment of its policies with the UN Guiding Principles on Business and Human Rights, the undertaking shall consider that the Guiding Principles refer to the International Bill of Human Rights, which consist of the Universal Declaration of Human Rights and the two Covenants that implement it, as well as the International Labour Organization's Declaration on Fundamental Rights and Principles at Work and the core conventions that underpin it, and may report on alignment with these instruments.

ESRS S1 delves deeper into specific aspects of the UDHR related to the workforce. The standard focuses on the following areas:

- **Non-discrimination:** Organizations must disclose policies and practices to ensure a diverse and inclusive workplace.
- **Fair working conditions:** Reporting on working hours, health and safety measures, and parental leave reflects adherence to fair working conditions.
- **Just compensation:** Disclosure of wage structures and equal pay practices aligns with the UDHR's right to fair remuneration.

The CSRD emphasizes reporting on material sustainability aspects. The UDHR plays a role here by informing organizations of what workforce issues can be considered material. For instance, an organization with a global supply chain might identify preventing forced labour as a material issue due to the potential human rights violations and reputational risks (this is a focus in ESRS S2–S4).

In essence, the UDHR provides the broad framework of human rights, while the CSRD and ESRS S1 translate those principles into concrete reporting requirements for organizations regarding their workforce management practices. To enhance your understanding of the UDHR try Activity 9.6.

ACTIVITY 9.6

Discuss the challenges and advantages with bringing UDHR principles into the external disclosures of organizations.

The International Labour Organization (ILO) international labour standards

The ILO sets international labour standards through conventions and recommendations. These cover a wide range of topics, such as working hours, occupational safety and health, child labour and freedom of association. ESRS S1 explicitly references these ILO standards, essentially using them as a benchmark for organizations to measure their own workforce practices.

The ILO's labour rules provide a foundation for ESRS S1. Organizations that comply with ESRS S1 reporting requirements are demonstrating their commitment to upholding internationally recognized labour standards and fostering a sustainable and responsible approach to workforce management.

GRI

While there is no one-to-one correlation between GRI social standards and ESRS S1, there is a significant overlap and high level of interoperability between them. GRI Standards outline detailed disclosures related to labour practices, occupational health and safety, training and development, diversity and inclusion, and worker engagement.

By adhering to GRI 401, organizations are required to demonstrate their commitment to responsible labour practices, transparently report on social impacts on their own workforce and contribute to broader efforts towards promoting decent work and human rights within the global workforce. Here is an example of GRI 401 disclosure requirements:

- Disclosure 402–1: New employee hires and employee turnover
- Disclosure 402–2: Benefits provided to full-time employees that are not provided to temporary or part-time employees
- Disclosure 402–3: Parental leave

Activity 9.7 allows you to explore the GRI–ESRS Interoperability Index and specifically tease out the data points and disclosure requirements on parental leave. This will give you an understanding of the level of harmonization on this particular topic between the ESRS and GRI.

ACTIVITY 9.7

Locate the EFRAG GRI–ESRS Interoperability Index (EFRAG, 2023a). Compare the data points and disclosure requirements on parental leave between ESRS S1 and GRI.

Beyond GRI 401, there is an abundance of further GRI social standards that cover sustainability matters that are of relevance to report. GRI 402 focuses on minimum notice periods regarding operational changes, GRI 403 Occupational health and safety, GRI 404 Training and education, GRI 405 Diversity and equal opportunity and GRI 406 Non-discrimination.

Three GRI social standards are typically used more frequently with regard to workers in the value chain: GRI 407 Freedom of association and collective bargaining, GRI 408 Child labour and GRI 409 Forced or compulsory labour.

CONCLUSION

The examination of ESRS S1 and ESRS S2 in this chapter underscores their role in advancing corporate social responsibility. ESRS S1 mandates comprehensive disclosure on an organization's own workforce, encompassing aspects such as diversity, equal opportunities and working conditions. Meanwhile, ESRS S2 extends this scrutiny to the entire value chain, addressing potential adverse impacts on workers beyond the company's direct employees.

Collectively, these standards herald a new era of transparency and accountability, compelling businesses to acknowledge and address their social impacts comprehensively. While the implementation of these standards presents challenges, particularly regarding data collection and verification, their potential to drive positive change in working conditions globally is undeniable.

SUMMARY

The following items relate to the learning objectives listed at the beginning of the chapter.

- **LO 1. Discuss global and local contexts of social reporting.**

  Working with ESRS S1 Own workforce and ESRS S2 Workers in the value chain takes us from the local to global (or regional) context of social reporting. ESRS S1 Own workforce focuses on an organization's internal environment and its employed and non-employed workers, thus focusing on the local workforce (note that firms may have an own workforce in multiple countries). ESRS S2 Workers in the value chain requires similar disclosures with regard to workers that are not employed directly by an organization, but, for example, by its suppliers or customers. ESRS E2 mandates that organizations are held responsible for the practices it supports via its business relationships. Therefore this ESRS touches on social issues that lie beyond the local boundaries of the organization.

- **LO 2. Understand disclosure requirements for ESRS S1 and ESRS S2.**

  ESRS S1 consists of two disclosure requirements relating to ESRS 2 and a further 17 topic-specific disclosure requirements. These requirements allow for an organization's social performance to be evaluated. Labour practices, human rights, diversity and inclusion, and community engagement all fall within the disclosure requirements of ESRS S1. The lists of sustainability matters applicable to ESRS S1 and ESRS S2 are mostly identical. This is consistent with the overall approach the ESRS take with regard to the responsibility of organizations for workers in their entire value chains. However, there are differences between the two with regards to certain rights relating to an organization's own workforce as well as water and sanitation.

- **LO 3. Identify the role of stakeholder engagement, with employees and their representatives, in fulfilling the disclosure requirements of ESRS S1 and ESRS S2.**

  Both disclosure requirements under the reporting area 'strategy' in ESRS S1 relate to ESRS 2, and they mandate that the consideration of own workers is described in-depth in the stakeholder dialogue. ESRS S1 is subject to materiality assessment. Materiality assessment in itself requires stakeholder engagement. Stakeholders falling under ESRS S2 are distinguished from those in the two other social ESRS by their work relationship with direct or indirect clients or suppliers; for those entities, in turn, they are typically part of their own workforce.
- **LO 4. Discuss the financial effects on an organization over the short, medium and long term caused by the risks and opportunities arising from the organization's impacts and dependencies in the topic areas of ESRS S1 and ESRS S2.**

  Most of the disclosures that ESRS S1 requires can be linked to an organization's income statement or balance sheets, such as personnel expenses. It is required that an organization makes these linkages when financial information is included in a disclosure under ESRS, or when the linkage will provide key context to the users of the sustainability report on material risks and opportunities.
- **LO 5. Explain the role of United Nations Universal Declaration of Human Rights, International Labour Organization (ILO) labour rules and other standards for social disclosures.**

  The United Nations Declaration of Human Rights, the ILO labour rules and similar standards and frameworks provide protection and promotion for workers' human rights. Several UN SDGs relate to social dimensions of sustainability transformation such as SDG 3 on good health and wellbeing.

EXERCISES

1 ESRS S1 (Disclosure Requirement S1–11 – Social protection, para. 74) specifies that, 'The undertaking shall disclose whether all its employees are covered by social protection, through public programs or through benefits offered by the undertaking, against loss of income due to any of the following major life events', hereunder (d) parental leave. You are asked to do the following:

   a Identify two different countries (for example Italy and Sweden) and investigate differences in the countries' public programs for parental leave.

   b Identify two companies, one in each of these countries, and locate their disclosures on parental leave.

   Discuss your findings and what this means for companies operating in the different countries you chose to analyse, with regards to their disclosures on para. 74 and specifically point (d). (LO 1)

2 Using an organization of your choice, identify potential material social impacts related to the organization's own workforce (e.g. high employee turnover, gender pay gap, safety hazards). (LO 2)

3 Discuss potential challenges organizations might face in complying with ESRS S1, such as data collection and reporting complexities. (LO 2)

4 How might the implementation of ESRS S2 differ across different industries? What are the unique challenges and opportunities for different sectors (e.g. you may compare apparel, agriculture and technology)? (LO 2)

5 Select two organizations operating in the same industry and compare their 'own workforce' reporting practices based on available information or sustainability reports (comparative analysis). Identify if the reporting is harmonized or whether there is divergence. If differences exist, discuss the potential factors influencing these variations in reporting practices. (LO 1, LO 2)

6 Choose a company that had to comply with CSRD–ESRS as of 1 January 2024 (for example Mærsk Annual Report 2024 available at //investor.maersk.com/static-files/31bf05a1-6f0c-4fbd-a3c7-3f58e044f668). On pages 70–71 of the report the company discloses stakeholder engagement. You are asked to do the following:

   a Identify the stakeholder groups Mærsk engaged with in the context of preparing its sustainability report and thus its sustainability work.

   b Identify which stakeholder groups bring forth issues relating to ESRS S1 and S2.

   c Are there ways in which you would like to improve the disclosures on stakeholder engagement in regards to the social matters covered in ESRS S1 and S2? (LO 3)

7 You are asked to identify 1–2 potential financial benefits of adhering to ESRS S1 over the short, medium and/or long term. In working with this exercise you can choose any of the disclosure requirements of ESRS S1 (for example parental leave, employee turnover, etc). (LO 4)

8 How does ESRS S2 impact executive compensation and incentives? Should executive pay be linked to the achievement of social targets related to workers in the value chain? (LO 4)

9 The following table illustrates an extract of data points in ESRS S1. Locate which one of these correlates with the disclosure requirements in GRI. Write in the corresponding requirements that you located in the GRI. Note down which GRI you located the requirement in. (LO 5)

Data point description ESRS S1	Narrative/metric	Corresponding requirement in GRI
Description of relevant human rights policy commitments relevant to own workforce	narrative	
Disclosure of general approach in relation to respect for human rights including labour rights, of people in its own workforce	narrative	
Disclosure of general approach in relation to engagement with people in its own workforce	narrative	
Disclosure of general approach in relation to measures to provide and (or) enable remedy for human rights impacts	narrative	
Disclosure of whether and how policies are aligned with relevant internationally recognized instruments	narrative	
Policies explicitly addressing trafficking in human beings, forced labour or compulsory labour and child labour	semi-narrative	
Workplace accident prevention policy or management system in place	semi-narrative	
Specific policies aimed at elimination of discrimination are in place	semi-narrative	
Grounds for discrimination are specifically covered in policy	semi-narrative	
Disclosure of specific policy commitments related to inclusion and (or) positive action for people from groups at particular risk of vulnerability in own workforce	narrative	
Disclosure of whether and how policies are implemented through specific procedures to ensure discrimination is prevented, mitigated and acted upon once detected, as well as to advance diversity and inclusion	narrative	

CHAPTER 10

Social reporting II: ESRS S3 Affected communities and ESRS S4 Consumers and end-users

Learning objectives

- LO 1. Discuss global and local contexts of social reporting in terms of affected communities and end-users.
- LO 2. Understand disclosure requirements for ESRS S3 and ESRS S4.
- LO 3. Identify the role of stakeholder engagement with employees and their representatives in fulfilling the disclosure requirements of ESRS S3 and ESRS S4.

- LO 4. Discuss the financial effects on an organization over the short, medium and long term caused by the risks and opportunities arising from the organization's impacts and dependencies in the topic areas of ESRS S3 and ESRS S4.
- LO 5. Explain the role of the United Nations Declaration of Human Rights, International Labour Organization (ILO) labour rules and other standards for social disclosures.

Communities and social performance: An example from the mining sector

In May 2020, British-Australian mining company Rio Tinto destroyed culturally significant rock shelters at Juukan Gorge, Australia. The company describes this event as 'a breach of [their] values', and the following statement from Chief Executive Jakob Stausholm is available on their website:

> *Since the tragic destruction of the rock shelters at Juukan Gorge, on the land of the Puutu Kunti Kurrama and Pinikura people in Western Australia, we have been changing the way we work in every part of our business. While we have made progress, we know it will take time to transform our culture and regain trust. But, together with the Indigenous peoples of the lands on which we operate, we are committed to ensuring cultural heritage is respected, valued and conserved for future generations.*

In 2021 and 2022, Rio Tinto released Communities and Social Performance Commitments Disclosure Reports which detail the progress made since the destruction of Juukan Gorge rock shelters. In 2023 there was an update entitled Progress on our communities and social performance commitments, and this progress is also detailed in Rio Tinto's Annual Reports.

Source: Rio Tinto (2023)

INTRODUCTION

This chapter focuses on two ESRSs: ESRS S3 Affected communities and ESRS S4 Consumers and end-users. ESRS S3 addresses the impact of organizational activities on communities, emphasizing the need for transparency and accountability in how businesses interact with and affect communities along their entire value chain. This standard highlights the importance of understanding and mitigating adverse impacts while promoting positive contributions to community development. It encourages organizations to engage with local stakeholders, assess social risks and report on their community-focused initiatives and outcomes. ESRS S4, on the other hand, focuses on the impact of organizational activities on consumers and end-users. It underscores the responsibility of businesses to ensure that their products and services are safe, reliable and beneficial to those who use them. This standard calls for detailed reporting on issues such as product safety, customer satisfaction and the ethical implications of marketing and sales practices. It aims to foster trust and accountability between businesses and their consumers, ultimately contributing to sustainable consumption patterns and enhanced consumer welfare.

By adhering to these standards, organizations can demonstrate their commitment to social responsibility and ethical practices, thereby enhancing their reputation and building stronger relationships with stakeholders. This chapter will delve into the principles, requirements and implementation strategies of ESRS S3 and ESRS S4, providing a comprehensive understanding of how businesses can effectively report on their social impacts and contribute to sustainable development. Through exploring these standards, the chapter aims to equip you with the knowledge and tools necessary to navigate the evolving landscape of social reporting.

International standards such as the GRI, ISO 26000, the United Nations Guiding Principles on Business and Human Rights (UNGPs) and the OECD Guidelines for multinational enterprises provide complementary guidance that supports and expands the principles outlined in ESRS S3 and ESRS S4.

ESRS S3 AFFECTED COMMUNITIES

The aim of ESRS S3 Affected communities is to specify disclosure requirements that will enable users of the sustainability statement to understand the material impacts on affected communities connected with the undertaking's own operations and value chain. This includes impacts through its products or services, business relationships and the related material risks and opportunities. ESRS S3 defines affected communities as follows:

> *People or group(s) living or working in the same area that have been or may be affected by a reporting undertaking's operations or through its upstream and downstream value chain. Affected communities can range from those living adjacent to the undertaking's operations (local communities) to those living at a distance. Affected communities include actually and potentially affected indigenous peoples.*

More specifically, ESRS S3 requires an explanation of the general approach the organization takes to identify and manage any material actual and potential impacts on affected communities in relation to:

> *a) communities' economic, social and cultural rights (for example, adequate housing, adequate food, water and sanitation, land-related and security-related impacts);*
> *b) communities' civil and political rights (for example, freedom of expression, freedom of assembly, impacts on human rights defenders); and*
> *c) particular rights of indigenous peoples (for example, free, prior and informed consent, self-determination, cultural rights).*
>
> (ESRS 3, Objective 2(a))

ESRS S3 gives special consideration to indigenous peoples and their specific rights; they should enjoy special protection as such. However, the standard outlines that there is no clear definition of this group of affected communities. Instead, international conventions outline that it is the people who identify themselves as 'indigenous'. This makes identifying indigenous people along their entire value chain a challenging task for organizations. Accordingly, organizations have to engage in dialogue with their affected communities and further refer to inputs, for example by local NGOs.

The ESRSs refer to ILO Convention No. 169 in order to outline the principle of self-identification:

> *An important criteria for defining indigenous people is related to their connection to a traditional area, as defined in ILO Convention No. 169, Article 1, which states that the convention applies to: '(a) tribal peoples in independent countries whose social, cultural and economic conditions distinguish them from other sections of the national community, and whose status is regulated wholly or partially by their own customs or traditions or by special laws or regulations; (b) peoples in independent countries who are regarded as indigenous on account of their descent from the populations which inhabited the country, or a geographical region to which the country belongs, at the time of conquest or colonisation or the establishment of present state boundaries and who, irrespective of their legal status, retain some or all of their own social, economic, cultural and political institutions'. ILO Convention 169 also states in Article 1(2) that: 'self-identification as indigenous or tribal shall be regarded as a fundamental criterion for determining the groups to which the provisions of this Convention apply'.*
>
> (ILO Convention, 1989)

Affected communities are a key group of affected stakeholders. Activity 10.1 presents a realistic scenario in which ESRS S3 may be applied.

ACTIVITY 10.1

The organization called ABC identifies local communities within a 50 km radius of their mining sites, including Indigenous groups and small villages that rely on natural resources from the environment. This environment is impacted by ABC's business activities. Discuss how this correlates with the objectives of ESRS S3.

Sustainability matters applicable for ESRS S3 (ESRS 1.AR 16)

Appendix A of ESRS 1 contains the list of minimum sustainability matters an organization has to assess during its materiality analysis. For the first two sub-topics, sustainability matters are derived from similar sources as the ones already discussed for ESRS S1 and S2, especially international and European human rights instruments. Regarding indigenous people, however, the specific pronouncements of ILO Declaration 169 ('Indigenous and Tribal Peoples Convention') and the **UN Declaration on the Rights of Indigenous Peoples** are referenced on a sub-topic and sub-sub-topic level, as demonstrated in Table 10.1.

Table 10.1 Breakdown of affected communities

Topic	Sub-topic	Sub-sub-topic
Affected communities	Communities' economic, social and cultural rights	Adequate housing
		Adequate food
		Water and sanitation
		Land-related impacts
		Security-related impacts
	Communities' civil and political rights	Freedom of expression
		Freedom of assembly
		Impacts on human rights defenders
	Rights of indigenous peoples	Free, prior and informed consent
		Self-determination
		Cultural rights

Source: Appendix A 8 AR 16, ESRS 1

Example 10.1 looks at what the UN stipulates as free, prior and informed consent, a sub-sub-topic in Table 10.1.

Example 10.1

'Free, prior and informed consent' is one of the fundamental principles set forth by the UN Declaration on the Rights of Indigenous Peoples. They are expanded upon by a multitude of additional guidelines, such as the Manual on 'Free Prior and Informed Consent' by the Food and Agriculture Organization (FAO) of the UN:

> *All elements within FPIC are interlinked, and they should not be treated as separate elements. The first three elements (free, prior and informed) qualify and set the conditions of consent as a decision-making process. In short, consent should be sought before any project, plan or action takes place (prior), it should be independently decided upon (free) and based on accurate, timely and sufficient information provided in a culturally appropriate way (informed) for it to be considered a valid result or outcome of a collective decision-making process.*
>
> [...]
>
> *Consent refers to the collective decision made by the rights-holders and reached through the customary decision-making processes of the affected Indigenous Peoples or communities. Consent must be sought and granted or withheld according to the unique formal or informal political-administrative dynamic of each community. Indigenous peoples and local communities must be able to participate through their own freely chosen representatives, while ensuring the participation of youth, women, the elderly and persons with disabilities as much as possible.*

Source: FAO (2016), p. 15

Reporting area: Strategy (SBM)

Both disclosure requirements under the reporting area 'strategy' relate to ESRS 2. Similar to ESRS S1 and S2, they require in-depth depictions of how affected communities are considered in the stakeholder dialogue. If the company identifies material impacts, risks or opportunities, they also have to be presented. Since ESRS S3 is subject to materiality assessment, these two disclosure requirements only apply in case a material sustainability matter that falls under ESRS S3 is identified.

ESRS 2 SBM–2 Interests and views of stakeholders: The organization should disclose how the interests, views and rights of its affected communities are taken into account by the organization's strategy and business model.

ESRS 2 SBM–3 Material impacts, risks and opportunities and their interaction with strategy and business model: Under this disclosure requirement, the undertaking should disclose whether and how actual and potential impacts on affected communities arise as a result of the organization's strategy and business model and how these impacts contribute to adapting the strategy and business model. Furthermore, a detailed description of affected communities is required, also with regard to whether these communities are affected by an organization's own operations or through its value chain. In addition, indigenous peoples that are affected have to be identified.

Reporting area: Impacts, risks and opportunities (IRO) management

Under ESRS S3, organizations are required to disclose detailed information on affected communities. Organizations must thus provide data on the assessments conducted to identify the impacts of their operations on local communities. This includes the methodologies used, the scope of the assessments and the findings regarding both positive and negative impacts. Table 10.2 outlines the high-level disclosure requirements.

Table 10.2 Disclosure requirements in ESRS S3

Disclosure requirement	Brief description
S3–1. Policies related to affected communities	The organization shall describe its policies adopted to manage its material impacts on affected communities, as well as associated material risks and opportunities.
S3–2. Processes for engaging with affected communities about impacts	The organization shall disclose its general processes for engaging with affected communities and their representatives about actual and potential impacts on them.
S3–3. Processes to remediate negative impacts and channels for affected communities to raise concerns	The organization shall describe the processes it has in place to provide for or cooperate in their mediation of negative impacts on affected communities that the undertaking is connected with, as well as channels available to affected communities to raise concerns and have them addressed.
S3–4. Taking action on material impacts and approaches to mitigating material risks and pursuing material opportunities related to affected communities, and effectiveness of those actions	The organization shall disclose how it takes action to address material impacts on affected communities, and to manage material risks and pursue material opportunities related to affected communities and the effectiveness of those actions.

Source: Adapted from EFRAG (2022a)

The disclosure requirements on IRO are mostly identical to ESRS S1 and S2. However, organizations face specific challenges when reporting under ESRS S3. This is due to the heterogeneity of affected communities that might be relevant for organizations – highly depending on the business model and value chain – and how an appropriate interaction is set up accordingly. Thus, reporting practices on this group of stakeholders are expected to vary greatly in contrast to the more homogenous groups of own workers and workers in the value chain. Example 10.2 demonstrates how SGL Group reports on its work with a local NGO from an affected community.

Example 10.2

SGL Group

Based on its business model, SGL Group reports on humanitarian logistics services provided to affected communities, in close collaboration with a local NGO.

S3–2 Processes for engaging with affected communities about impacts

SGL Group's Aid & Relief logistics teams engage with partner organisations and government entities to understand the needs of beneficiary communities and the complexities of providing humanitarian aid and government logistics support. By listening to their concerns, we can be aware of the vulnerabilities of communities and can incorporate their perspectives into the logistics planning. This allows Aid & Relief to adapt its provisions to better reach beneficiaries in all regions of the world. By involving local stakeholders, we create a better, more inclusive logistics system, especially in areas where communities suffer from lack of infrastructure and basic humanitarian needs.

The Executive Vice President of Aid & Relief and Government Logistics is the most senior role responsible for conducting this engagement.

Another way we engage with affected communities is by hiring individuals with local knowledge and expertise of key regions of focus. For example, we hired experienced Ukrainian logisticians to work on projects in Ukraine and develop new solutions. Leveraging these individuals' expertise allowed us to effectively address the many logistical challenges inherent in providing aid and relief services in a conflict-affected area, in co-ordination with local authorities in Ukraine.

Source: SGL (2023), p. 92

In contrast, OMV – a large integrated oil, gas and chemicals company – focuses its disclosures on affected communities on interaction with local communities adversely affected by its various (exploration) activities. This is expanded on in Example 10.3.

Example 10.3

OMV

Disclosure regarding affected communities by OMV.

Community Consultation and Social Impact Assessments

Our community relations and development management process is based on centralized policies and targets, and is implemented by locally responsible persons using local resources. In line with our community relations and development procedure, which is in effect for all countries in which we are active, we engage with local communities through tailored programs. For instance, all projects from OMV's Energy segment require community consultation in the development phase. In 2023, 5 out of 13 development projects were in the process of community consultation.

(Continued)

We start by conducting a Social Impact Assessment (SIA), which includes the free, prior, and informed consent (FPIC) of local stakeholders. Sometimes, an SIA is integrated into an Environmental and Social Impact Assessment (ESIA) to foster synergies and efficiencies. The purpose of an SIA is to ensure that the views of the local communities, especially of indigenous peoples, are incorporated into and addressed throughout all phases of the project life cycle: commissioning, operation, and decommissioning or abandonment. We also pay particular attention to any possible impact on human rights.

Based on the internal guidelines for conducting SIAs, we include a baseline study, community needs assessments, stakeholder analyses, and a study of social risks associated with the project. Where possible, SIAs are conducted in a participatory manner by directly consulting with potentially affected communities. Our standards require the outcomes of the SIA to be communicated to affected stakeholders. Based on the outcome of the SIA, site-specific strategies for community relations and development, stakeholder engagement plans, and Community Grievance Mechanisms are developed and implemented.

Source: OMV (2023), p. 129

Reporting area: Metrics and targets (MT)

ESRS S3 only comprises one disclosure requirement on targets, as demonstrated in Table 10.3. No disclosure requirement on metrics exists. Flexibility is granted to organizations in their reporting practices here as well. However, this does not mean that an organization does not have to report on such metrics; instead, an organization has to assess whether entity-specific metrics must be disclosed in order to depict its IRO with regard to affected communities.

Table 10.3 Further disclosure requirement in ESRS S3

Disclosure requirement	Brief description
S3–5. Targets related to managing material impacts, advancing positive impacts, as well as to risks and opportunities	The organization shall disclose the time-bound and outcome-oriented targets it may have set related to: • reducing negative impacts on affected communities • advancing positive impacts on affected communities • managing material risks and opportunities related to affected communities.

Source: Adapted from EFRAG (2022a)

An illustration of how a company may disclose its targets and metrics simultaneously is provided in Example 10.4.

Example 10.4

Lenzing

Lenzing discloses its targets for affected communities as well as related metrics.

Sustainability targets, measures and progress

- Complaints of community members around sites: 49
- 'Community engagement' target: To continuously support the development of local communities near Lenzing production sites and support social welfare programs to 2025 and beyond.

Source: Lenzing (2023), p. 147

It is expected that sector-specific ESRSs cover some disclosure requirements on metrics that refer to affected communities. Until these standards are issued, existing standards and frameworks such as the GRI Standards provide guidance on how to define and report on relevant metrics. Use Activity 10.2 to further your understanding of the GRI Standards.

ACTIVITY 10.2

Look up the GRI Standards that related to affected communities – they are part of the '400 series' of standards. Which metrics can you identify that might also be helpful for organizations to meet reporting obligations under ESRS?

ESRS S3 link to financial statements

Financial effects and affected communities can be related. For example, should a natural disaster have a substantial effect on a company's operations, this could indirectly but severely harm the local affected communities.

Example 10.5 provides an illustration of how GUBI provided a short narrative disclosure on affected communities, stating that in this case this was a topic not material to them.

Example 10.5

GUBI Sustainability Report 2023

Affected communities

Affected communities have not been identified as material through the materiality assessment described in section SBM-3 and GUBI are therefore not obliged to disclose any information according to ESRS 1 General requirements appendix E.

Policies related to affected communities

GUBI is committed to the Ten Principles of the UNGC for responsible business conduct within the areas of human rights, labour, environment, and anti-corruption. GUBI has general processes and mechanisms in place like GUBI's speak up culture and whistle-blower scheme. It does not, however, have dedicated processes and mechanisms to monitor and engage with potentially affected communities and indigenous peoples. This is due to the size of GUBI and the nature of its business whereby through the materiality assessment GUBI has concluded that its risk of adversely impacting communities and indigenous peoples is low. GUBI considers its Code of Conduct, Sustainability policy and related policies to be aligned with internationally recognized standards. GUBI has no knowledge of potential violations in its upstream and downstream value chain in relation to UN Global Compact principles. Nor has GUBI received any reports related to human rights issues and incidents connected to affected communities.

Source: GUBI (2023), p. 61

Other standards and frameworks

According to ESRS S3, the organization must disclose whether and how its policies related to affected communities are aligned with internationally recognized standards, particularly those relevant to communities and indigenous peoples such as the United Nations Guiding Principles on Business and Human Rights.

Additionally, the undertaking must report any instances where there has been a failure to respect the UN Guiding Principles on Business and Human Rights, the International Labour Organization (ILO) Declaration on Fundamental Principles and Rights at Work, or the OECD Guidelines for Multinational Enterprises. These reports should cover both the organization's operations and its upstream and downstream value chains, including, where applicable, the nature of such cases.

GRI

Affected communities are also covered extensively under GRI reporting. However, in contrast to ESRS S3, the relevant disclosure requirements are split over several individual standards.

The disclosure requirements in ESRS S3 are closely related to GRI 413 Local Communities 2016. GRI 413 only covers 'individuals or groups of individuals living or working in areas that are affected or that could be affected by the organization's activities'. Because of the heterogeneity of these local communities, organizations are required to assess the vulnerabilities these local communities suffer as a result of the organization's activities. Table 10.4 provides an example of GRI 401 disclosure requirements.

Table 10.4 GRI 413 disclosure requirements

Disclosure 413–1	Operations with local community engagement, impact assessments and development programmes.
Disclosure 413–2	Operations with significant actual and potential negative impacts on local communities.

GRI 411 Rights of indigenous peoples 2016 focuses on disclosures on impacts on indigenous peoples. Organizations should depict how they manage the rights of indigenous people. The UN Declaration on the Rights of Indigenous Peoples and the ILO Convention 169 are referred to as documents that should guide organizations in their reporting and, more importantly, in their sustainability due diligence. GRI 411 also comprises one metric, Disclosure 411–1 Incidents of violations involving rights of indigenous peoples. You can compare GRI Standards and ESRS S3 in Activity 10.3.

ACTIVITY 10.3

Locate the EFRAG GRI–ESRS Interoperability Index (EFRAG, 2023a). Compare the data points and disclosure requirements on parental leave between ESRS S3 and GRI Standards.

Beyond GRI 411 and 413, two other standards that cover sustainability matters are closely related to affected communities. GRI 410 Security practices 2016 addresses specific matters with regard to the conduct of security personnel towards third parties, as it might negatively impact local communities. GRI 414 Supplier social assessment 2016 covers disclosures on how an organization manages social impacts through its supply chain, especially via screening new suppliers using social criteria.

ESRS S4 CONSUMERS AND END-USERS

The purpose of ESRS S4 on consumers and end-users is to outline disclosure requirements that will allow users of the sustainability statement to comprehend the significant impacts on consumers and end-users associated with the undertaking's products or services, either through own operations or its value chain. This includes the related material risks and opportunities.

ESRS S4 Appendix A gives the following definitions for consumers and end-users:

Consumer: Individuals who acquire, consume or use goods and services for personal use, either for themselves or for others, and not for resale, commercial or trade, business, craft or profession purposes.

End-user: Individuals who ultimately use or are intended to ultimately use a particular product or service.

(ESRS S4, Appendix A: Defined terms)

ESRS S4 thus focuses on the downstream value chain of an organization. However, it only covers individuals, that is natural persons who are consumers or end-users. This understanding is based on the Consumer Rights Directive. Also, ESRS S4 directly relates to Article 38 of the EU Charter of Fundamental Rights which addresses consumer protection. As a consequence, for organizations that merely engage in B2B activities, ESRS S4 is of limited relevance.

Besides focusing on a different group of stakeholders, ESRS S4 is aligned in structure and content with ESRS S1 to ESRS S3. Customers and end-users are a key group of affected stakeholders.

Sustainability matters applicable for ESRS S4 (ESRS 1.AR 16)

Again, the relevant sustainability matters that must be covered by materiality analysis can be found in Appendix A of ESRS 1. These matters focus on human rights and are consequently founded on general instruments such as the Charter of Fundamental Rights of the European Union and the UN Guiding Principles on Business and Human Rights. More specifically, with regard to the rights of consumers and end-users, Article 29b of the CSRD contains requirements that were further specified by EFRAG (refer to Table 10.5).

Table 10.5 Topics covered by Article 29b of the CSRD

Topic	Sub-topic	Sub-sub-topic
Consumers and end-users	Information-related impacts for consumers and/or end-users	Privacy
		Freedom of expression
		Access to (quality) information
	Personal safety of consumers and/or end-users	Health and safety
		Security of a person
		Protection of children
	Social inclusion of consumers and/or end-users	Non-discrimination
		Access to products and services
		Responsible marketing practices

Privacy is one important sustainability matter that is addressed by several topics under ESRS, such as own workforce (ESRS S1) and workers in the value chain (ESRS S2). In the context of ESRS S4, privacy is considered to be part of 'information-related impacts', that is those most often linked with data collected by an organization on its customers and end-users. Consequently, relevant questions include which data an organization is allowed to collect, how to inform their customers and end-users about this data and which rights to give their stakeholders in order to make specific claims on how this data is used. Example 10.6 demonstrates how the **European Convention on Human Rights** protects the right to individual privacy.

Example 10.6

European Convention on Human Rights

Article 8 of the European Convention on Human Rights protects the right to privacy by individuals:

1. *Everyone has the right to respect for his* [sic] *private and family life, his home and his correspondence.*
2. *There shall be no interference by a public authority with the exercise of this right except such as is in accordance with the law and is necessary in a democratic society in the interests of national security, public safety or the economic well-being of the country, for the prevention of disorder or crime, for the protection of health or morals, or for the protection of the rights and freedoms of others.*

While this definition focuses on the relationship between states and individuals, important legal acts that are derived from it, more clearly addressing the requirements for private organizations, include the General Data Protection Regulation (GDPR). Here, the right to privacy is understood as the ability of individuals to control their personal information.

Source: European Convention on Human Rights (1950–2021)

ESRS S4.4 contains one important exemption: 'The unlawful use or misuse of the undertaking's products and services by consumers and end-users fall outside the scope of this standard.' This limits the scope of analyses that are required by an organization. However, the use or misuse of third parties clearly is relevant, thus addressing aspects such as data security and protection.

Reporting area: Strategy (SBM)

As for ESRS S1 to ESRS S3, both disclosure requirements under the reporting area 'strategy' relate to ESRS 2. Disclosure requirements in ESRS S4 only differ in as far as the group of affected stakeholders is changed.

ESRS 2 SBM–2 Interests and views of stakeholders: The organization should disclose how the interests, views and rights of its consumers and end-users are taken into account by the organization's strategy and business model.

ESRS 2 SBM–3 Material impacts, risks and opportunities and their interaction with strategy and business model: Under this disclosure requirement, the undertaking should disclose whether and how actual and potential impacts on its consumers and end-users arise as a result of the organization's strategy and business model and how these impacts contribute to adapting the strategy and business model. Also, detailed descriptions of these stakeholders and their location in the value chain are required. ESRS S4 highlights the need to outline which customers or end-users might be specifically vulnerable to certain business practices by the organization. Example 10.7 highlights some of these vulnerable people.

Example 10.7

Potentially vulnerable populations within the consumer base

Examples of particular characteristics of consumers and/or end-users that may be considered by the undertaking when responding to paragraph 11 include young consumers and/or end-users who may be more susceptible to impacts on their physical and mental development, or who lack financial literacy and may be more susceptible to exploitative sales or marketing practices. They may also include women in a context where women are routinely discriminated against in their access to particular services or in the marketing of particular products.

Source: Annual reporting (n.d.)

Now use Activity 10.4 to discuss the responsibility of organizations to vulnerable groups of consumers and end-users.

ACTIVITY 10.4

Why should organizations be held accountable for their impacts on vulnerable groups of customers and end-users? How could this be reflected in business practices – in policies, actions and targets set by an organization? Are there any trade-offs between specific measures to address the needs of these stakeholders, and the rights as well as freedoms granted to them and the organization?

Reporting area: Impacts, risks and opportunities (IRO) management

Under ESRS S4, organizations must disclose detailed information on product and service safety and customer satisfaction and feedback (refer to Table 10.6). For example, organizations need to report on measures taken to ensure the safety and reliability of their products and services. This includes information on safety assessments, compliance with safety regulations, and any incidents of non-compliance or safety-related issues. Regarding customer satisfaction and feedback, organizations must disclose how they measure and address customer satisfaction. This involves reporting on customer feedback mechanisms, satisfaction surveys and actions taken to respond to consumer concerns and improve the customer experience.

Table 10.6 Disclosure requirements in ESRS S4

Disclosure requirement	Brief description
S4–1. Policies related to consumers and end-users	The organization shall describe its policies adopted to manage its material impacts of its products and/or services on consumers and end-users, as well as associated material risks and opportunities.
S4–2. Processes for engaging with consumers and end-users about impacts	The organization shall disclose its general processes for engaging with consumers and end-users and their representatives about actual and potential impacts on them.
S4–3. Processes to remediate negative impacts and channels for consumers and end-users to raise concerns	The organization shall describe the processes it has in place to provide for or cooperate in their mediation of negative impacts on consumers and end-users that the undertaking is connected with, as well as channels available to consumers and end-users to raise concerns and have them addressed.
S4–4. Taking action on material impacts and approaches to mitigating material risks and pursuing material opportunities related to consumers and end-users, and effectiveness of those actions	The organization shall disclose how it takes action to address material impacts on consumers and end-users, and to manage material risks and pursue material opportunities related to consumers and end-users, and the effectiveness of those actions.

Compared to ESRS S1 to ESRS S3, the disclosure requirements under the reporting area IRO are once again generic and only involve switching the stakeholder group under consideration. For organizations directly – or indirectly via their value chain – engaging in B2C business activities, many of the disclosure requirements can be addressed by existing quality management and customer relationship management practices. Example 10.8 shows how Lenzing acts to take care of its customers and end-users.

Example 10.8

Lenzing reports on actions taken with regard to product safety for customers and end-users

Product assurance for (in)direct customers

Independent third-party certifications are in place to certify standards, products, and management systems to ensure compliance with customer and regulatory requirements and to assess strategic fit with Lenzing's corporate strategy.

In this respect, Lenzing operates a quality management system based on ISO 9001:2015. Additional quality management systems such as FAMI-QS and Hazard Analysis Critical Control Points (HACCP), are in place for specific business segments. All form the basis for the relevant work processes and reinforce efforts to achieve complete customer satisfaction.

The PSRA department manages a variety of external third-party certifications on a global level in relation to product safety for different applications (e.g. food contact, skin contact compliance) and sustainability (e.g. biodegradability) and assesses new certification requests. These certificates serve to ensure transparency and demonstrate the safety and compliance of Lenzing fibers as well as their compatibility in their application fields.

[...]

Product safety for consumers and end-users

As mentioned above, the PSRA department is globally responsible for the safety of Lenzing fibers in their intended uses and for compliance with the laws, regulations, and standards that apply to the fiber businesses.

Therefore, in addition to the external third-party certifications, risk assessments for intentional ingredients are carried out and the impact of business-specific regulations, standards, and requirements is continuously monitored and assessed. PSRA prepares appropriate declarations/confirmations for customer enquiries on relevant topics and is either personally in contact with industrial associations or informed by Lenzing representatives on new topics and developments having an impact on business and product safety.

Source: Lenzing (2023), p. 152

Reporting area: Metrics and targets (MT)

Like ESRS S2 and ESRS S3, ESRS S4 only comprises one disclosure requirement on targets with regard to customers and end-users (Table 10.7). As well, organizations applying ESRS S4 have to identify relevant metrics and report on them on an entity-specific basis.

Table 10.7 Further disclosure requirement of ESRS S4

Disclosure requirement	Brief description
S4–5. Targets related to managing material impacts, advancing positive impacts, as well as to risks and opportunities	The organization shall disclose the time-bound and outcome-oriented targets it may have set related to: **a** reducing negative impacts on consumers and/or end-users **b** advancing positive impacts on consumers and/or end-users **c** managing material risks and opportunities related to consumers and/or end-users.

Example 10.9 demonstrates the metrics that Hydro discloses regarding its customers and end-users.

Example 10.9

Hydro metrics with regard to relevant certifications for consumers and end-users

S4.2 Certifications

Reporting principles

According to Hydro's policy, all operational sites shall comply with, but not necessarily be certified according to ISO 9001, ISO 14001 and ISO 45001. Certification according to these standards is a decentralized responsibility based on identified business needs. OHSAS 18001 is discontinued and has been replaced by ISO 45001.

Hydro's power plants in Norway have chosen not to be certified. However, they are fulfilling the requirements given in the mentioned standards. In addition, the power plants need to comply with the requirements given by the Norwegian Water Resource and Energy Directorate (NVE), i.e. concessions for operations as well as environmental, third person safety, security and emergency preparedness regulations. The table below shows the distribution of certification of the other operational sites in Hydro.

In addition to the mentioned ISO, several sites are also certified according to different sector and customer specific standards. Examples of such certifications are the IATF 16949 for the automotive industry, and the Aluminium Stewardship Initiative (ASI). In 2023, 29 new sites received the ASI certification.

Share of relevant operational sites certified				
	ISO 9001	**ISO 14001**	**ISO 45001**	**ASI**
Eligible	96	94	91	91
Certified	89	89	72	79
Percentage certified	**93%**	**95%**	**79%**	**87%**

IATF 16949 is fully aligned with the structure and requirements of ISO 9001 and is required by customers that produce service parts or parts for car assembly. Of our sites delivering to the automotive industry, 86 percent are certified according to the IATF 16949.

All fully-owned smelters, 6 remelters and 19 Extrusion sites are also certified according to the ISO 50001 Energy Management systems, representing 62 percent of Hydro's total electricity consumption.

Source: Hydro (2023), p. 152

Explore the Hydro Integrated Annual Report (2023) in Activity 10.5.

ACTIVITY 10.5

Refer to the Integrated Annual Report 2023 of Hydro from which Example 10.9 is taken. Go to the chapter on ESRS S4 and try to identify the definition of 'consumers and end-users' Hydro uses. Is it reporting about B2C or B2B business? To what extent is this definition aligned with the definition in ESRS S4?

ESRS S4 link to financial statements

Arguably, the link to financial statements is even more clearly visible for ESRS S4 than it is for many of the other social ESRSs. Risks for an organization can arise because of the organization's dependency on consumers and/or end-users for its core business. Issues with regard to any of the sustainability matters covered by the standards can directly impact the relationship between an organization and its customers, leading to revenue decline or additional costs for these organizations in order to compensate for any such issues.

Besides such problems that might directly relate to the business activities of an organization, other effects must be considered. An external effect could be a low likelihood but high impact external event that may trigger financial effects, for example a global pandemic. Such an event could lead to severe impacts on certain consumers' livelihoods, resulting in major changes in patterns of consumption.

OTHER STANDARDS AND FRAMEWORKS

In fulfilling the requirements set out by certain disclosure criteria of ESRS S4, the organization may be guided by a multitude of existing standards.

ESRS S4 frequently refers of the UN Guiding Principles on Business and Human Rights and the OECD Guidelines for Multinational Enterprises focused on remediation and grievance mechanisms. For example, ESRS S4 requires organizations to consider 'effectiveness criteria for nonjudicial grievance mechanisms', as laid out in the UN Guiding Principles on Business and Human Rights in describing the effectiveness of channels for consumers and/or end-users to raise concerns. ESRS S4.AR 24 lists guiding questions that an organization might follow. This guidance is supported by ISO 26000, which acts as guidance for organizations that are integrating social responsibility practices into their strategy, policy and culture. The end goal of this integration is for all facets of an organization to be contributing to sustainable development as much as possible.

GRI

Showing a narrower scope than ESRS S4, GRI Standards focus on customers. There are three standards that address the relevant aspects: GRI 416 Customer health and safety 2016, GRI 417 Marketing and labelling 2016 and GRI 418 Customer privacy 2016. While, in turn, these standards address aspects that fall under ESRS S4 as well, an important addition lies again with the addition of topical metrics that might be employed for ESRS reporting purposes. Table 10.8 provides an example of GRI 416 disclosure requirements.

Table 10.8 Disclosure requirements for GRI 416

Disclosure 416–1	Assessment of the health and safety impacts of product and service categories.
Disclosure 416–2	Incidents of non-compliance concerning the health and safety impacts of products and services.

TRANSITIONAL PROVISIONS FOR ESRS S3 AND ESRS S4

Given the generic and, in contrast to ESRS S1 and the environmental as well as governance ESRSs, rudimentary nature of disclosure requirements set forth in ESRS S3 and ESRS S4, there is also no need for extensive transitional provisions. For each of the two standards, only one phase-in regulation is included in Appendix C of ESRS 1.

Organizations that not exceed the average number of 750 employees can omit all disclosure requirements of ESRS S3 and ESRS S4 in their first two years of preparing sustainability reports in accordance with ESRSs.

However, the sustainability matters covered by both standards must be included in the materiality analysis. If such a sustainability matter is material, the organization has to disclose brief descriptions on that matter nevertheless (ESRS 2.BP 2).

Also, with regard to both standards, the transitional provisions concerning information related to an organization's value chain will play an important role. Accordingly, for their first three years of preparing sustainability reports in accordance with ESRSs, organizations can restrict the information provided mostly on publicly or otherwise available information on policies, actions or targets. No information on metrics is required at all. Nevertheless, the relevant sustainability matters of ESRS S3 and ESRS S4 must be included in the materiality analysis as well.

A GLOBAL OUTLOOK

Taking a global outlook, and considering disclosures on affected communities beyond ESRS S3, brings us to global frameworks such as the GRI and the United Nations Guiding Principles on Business and Human Rights (UNGP). These frameworks emphasize transparency and accountability for organizations operating in sectors with significant community impacts, such as mining, energy and construction. Organizations with global activities increasingly face scrutiny for their operations in the global south, where affected communities are at higher risk of marginalization or lack resources to defend their rights (Jamali & Mirshak, 2007). NGOs often advocate for transparency and hold organizations accountable for disclosing their social impacts. With regards to consumers and end-users, these are increasingly aware of and concerned about the ethical, social and environmental implications of their purchases.

Academic research during the last decades has broadly addressed social reporting, often as an integral part of sustainability reporting. In 2013, however, Eccles and Serafeim (2013) highlight that social reporting, particularly on community relations, is becoming a central element in the evolving ESG landscape, as investors and stakeholders increasingly seek transparency on corporate social performance.

At the local level, effective community engagement is crucial for accurate social reporting. Organizations are expected to involve communities in their reporting processes, ensuring that their voices are represented and their concerns addressed in official reports. Muthuri *et al.* (2012) propose that participatory approaches in social reporting help organizations build trust and mitigate conflict with affected communities. Reporting on affected communities can improve stakeholder engagement and help mitigate conflicts between organizations and local populations. When organizations disclose information about their impacts, it facilitates dialogue, trust-building and better problem-solving. Studies have highlighted that corporate social disclosures, including those related to affected communities, foster a sense of accountability and encourage constructive engagement, which can reduce tensions and conflicts with communities, especially in industries such as mining and energy (Owen & O'Dwyer, 2008). Other interesting contributions in research include that of the concept of shared value. Studies have proposed that the concept of creating shared value, where organizations that report on and actively address community issues align their business interests with social progress, can support sustained success for both the organization and the community (Porter & Kramer, 2011).

CONCLUSION

ESRS S3 and ESRS S4 represent significant broadening of the social dimension of sustainability reporting. The operationalization of ESRS S3 necessitates robust methodologies for conducting impact assessments and engaging with diverse communities. The varying socio-economic, cultural and environmental contexts require tailored engagement strategies which can be resource-intensive and complex to manage. Moreover, ensuring the genuine inclusion of marginalized voices in these processes is critical but often difficult to achieve. There is a risk that engagement efforts may be superficial or tokenistic, failing to address the deeper systemic issues affecting these communities.

Similarly, ESRS S4 demands comprehensive reporting on consumer impacts, including product safety, customer satisfaction and data privacy. The increasing complexity of global supply chains and the rapid pace of technological advancement exacerbate these challenges. For instance, ensuring product safety and compliance across diverse markets with different regulatory standards can be daunting. Furthermore, the rise of digital products and services introduces new dimensions of consumer impact, particularly concerning data protection and privacy. Organizations must navigate the intricate web of global data privacy laws while maintaining consumer trust.

The requirement for detailed disclosures on material risks and opportunities associated with community and consumer impacts underscores the need for sophisticated risk management frameworks. However, integrating these frameworks into existing corporate structures can be challenging. Organizations may struggle to align their traditional risk management approaches with the nuanced and often qualitative nature of social and environmental risks. Additionally, the dynamic nature of these risks, influenced by evolving societal expectations and regulatory landscapes, adds another layer of complexity.

There is also the issue of assurance and verification. Ensuring the accuracy and reliability of sustainability reports is paramount, yet the lack of standardized metrics and methodologies for assessing social impacts can undermine this process. The subjectivity involved in evaluating qualitative data related to community and consumer impacts poses a significant challenge for auditors and assurance providers.

ESRS S3 and ESRS S4 necessitate a nuanced understanding of diverse community and consumer contexts, sophisticated risk management and robust assurance mechanisms. As organizations strive to meet these requirements, it is essential to continuously evaluate and refine the frameworks to ensure they drive meaningful and authentic engagement with affected communities and consumers, rather than merely fulfilling regulatory obligations. This iterative process will be critical in realizing the full potential of ESRS S3 and ESRS S4 in promoting sustainable and equitable business practices.

SUMMARY

The following items relate to the learning objectives listed at the beginning of the chapter.

- **LO 1. Discuss global and local contexts of social reporting in terms of affected communities and end-users.**

  Adopting a global perspective and extending the focus on disclosures about affected communities and end-users beyond ESRS S3 and ESRS S4, leads us to global frameworks like the Global Reporting Initiative (GRI) and the United Nations Guiding Principles on Business and Human Rights (UNGPs). These frameworks stress the importance of transparency and accountability for organizations operating in sectors such as mining, energy, and construction, where community impacts can be profound. Organizations with global operations, especially in the Global South, often face increased scrutiny due to the heightened vulnerability of local communities, who may lack the resources to protect their rights or avoid marginalization. NGOs play a crucial role in advocating for transparency and ensuring that organizations disclose their social impacts. In relation to end-users, including consumers, there is growing awareness and concern about the ethical, social, and environmental consequences of their purchasing decisions. As a result, consumers are increasingly demanding more responsible and transparent business practices, pushing organizations to be more open about their impacts and sustainability efforts.

- **LO 2. Understand disclosure requirements for ESRS S3–S4.**

  The aim of ESRS S3 Affected communities is to specify disclosure requirements that will enable users of the sustainability statement to understand the material impacts on affected communities connected with the undertaking's own operations and value chain. The purpose of ESRS S4 on consumers and end-users is to outline disclosure requirements that will allow users of the sustainability statement to comprehend the significant impacts on consumers and end-users associated with the undertaking's own operations and value chain. For both standards this includes impacts through its products or services, business relationships, and the related material risks and opportunities. This chapter has provided tables that give insights into the detailed disclosure requirements.

- **LO 3. Identify the role of stakeholder engagement, with employees and their representatives, in fulfilling the disclosure requirements of ESRS S3–S4.**

  Both standards encourages organizations to engage with local stakeholders, assess social risks, and report on their community-focused initiatives and outcomes. ESRS S4, on the other hand, focuses on the impact of organizational activities on consumers and end-users. It underscores the responsibility of businesses to ensure that their products and services are safe, reliable, and beneficial to those who use them.

- **LO 4. Discuss the financial effects on an organization over the short, medium and long term caused by the risks and opportunities arising from the organization's impacts and dependencies in the topic areas of ESRS S3–S4.**

  Material risks may emerge from the undertaking's reliance on affected communities, where low-probability but high-impact events could lead to significant financial consequences. For instance, a natural disaster triggering a catastrophic industrial accident within the organisation's operations could result in severe damage to both the business and the surrounding communities, with far-reaching financial and social impacts. Risks to an organization can also arise because of the organization's dependency on consumers and/or end-users where low likelihood but high impact events may trigger financial effects, for example, where a global pandemic leads to severe impacts on certain consumers' livelihoods resulting in major changes in patterns of consumption.

- **LO 5. Explain the role of the Universal Declaration of Human Rights, International Labour Organization (ILO) labour rules and other standards for social disclosures.**

  International standards such as the Global Reporting Initiative (GRI), ISO 26000, the United Nations Guiding Principles on Business and Human Rights (UNGPs), and the OECD Guidelines for Multinational Enterprises provide complementary guidance that supports and expands the principles outlined in ESRS S3 and ESRS S4.

EXERCISES

1 Select two organizations from different industries and compare the disclosure practices of these organizations with the disclosure requirements of ESRS S3 and ESRS S4. Identify any gaps or areas for improvement in their reporting practices. Discuss how far differences in the business models of these two organizations are responsible for the different reporting practices that you found. (LO 2)

2 Select an organization of your choice and summarize the methodologies used by the organization to engage with affected communities. (LO 2, LO 3)

3 Choose one organization with accessible sustainability reports. With the reports, complete the following tasks:

  a Identify how the organization engages with the topic of affected communities (ESRS S3).

  b Analyse the differences in their impact assessments and mitigation strategies (ESRS S3).

  c Identify and analyse the organization's approach to product safety, customer satisfaction, ethical marketing and data protection (ESRS S4). Identify if the organization makes reference to the Universal Declaration of Human Rights, the ILO labour rules and other standards for social disclosures. (LO 4)

  d Assess the strengths and weaknesses of the selected organization's reporting on ESRS S3 and ESRS S4. (LO 3, LO 4)

  e Identify whether the organization makes any disclosures about the potential financial effects on its plans for the short, medium and long term with regard to ESRS S3 and/or ESRS S4. (LO 1, LO 2, LO 3, LO 4, LO 5)

CHAPTER 11
Governance and business conduct reporting: ESRS G1

Learning objectives

After studying this chapter you should be able to:

- LO 1. Understand disclosure requirements for ESRS G1 Business conduct.
- LO 2. Discuss the financial effects on an organization over the short, medium and long term caused by the risks and opportunities arising from the organization's impacts and dependencies in the topic areas of ESRS G1.
- LO 3. Explain the role of OECD Guidelines for Multinational Enterprises and other standards relevant for governance and business conduct disclosures.
- LO 4. Contrast key differences between other relevant reporting frameworks that address business conduct (for example, United Nations Global Compact and the OECD guidelines).
- LO 5. Distinguish between the reporting requirements for ESRS G1 and ESRS 2 with regard to sustainability governance.

Governance reporting at Siemens

Operating with integrity and in compliance with laws and regulation is fundamental to stakeholder trust and our company's continued success. Siemens and its roughly 320,000 employees operate in multiple countries around the world. Our customers in both the private and public sectors serve a vast array of industries. Our global business operations are governed by numerous national legal systems and take place in a variety of political, social, and cultural settings that are constantly changing. Therefore, Siemens' business and compliance environment is correspondingly complex. The way that Siemens and our partners do business impacts the markets and societies where we operate. Unethical and unlawful conduct like corruption, cartel arrangements, and money laundering can distort competition, hinder economic development, and threaten human rights and democracy. As a global player, Siemens is responsible for setting an example in all its operations and in collaboration with all its stakeholders. By building alliances against corruption and promoting fair competition together with stakeholders from politics, business, and society, Siemens can through Collective Action help establish the conditions for fair competition and thereby promote innovation.

Source: Siemens (2023)

INTRODUCTION

ESRS G1 on business conduct outlines specific disclosure requirements focused on business conduct, emphasizing transparency, ethical behaviour and governance practices. These requirements mandate organizations to report on various aspects such as anti-corruption policies, bribery prevention measures, ethical supply chain management and stakeholder engagement.

The term governance as employed in the ESRSs pertains to the mechanisms through which organizations monitor, manage and oversee sustainability-related impacts, risks and opportunities. Governance encompasses the processes by which an organization defines its procedures, controls and operations to ensure effective decision-making. This includes the allocation of responsibilities, the establishment of clear communication channels, adherence to laws and regulations, and the maintenance of integrity and accountability across all organizational levels.

At the overarching level, key components of robust governance structures of organizations are addressed in ESRS 2. This includes disclosures on the risk and compliance management system and the internal control system in so far as they relate to sustainability reporting. Additionally, due diligence processes, incentive systems and the roles and responsibilities of the administrative, management and supervisory bodies fall under the umbrella term governance. ESRS 2 comprises five governance-related disclosure requirements on these essential aspects (refer to Chapter 4).

ESRS G1 on business conduct, the focus of this chapter, contains eight disclosure requirements explicitly targeting business conduct issues. Other frameworks and initiatives such as GRI, **United Nations Global Compact** (**UNGC**) and the OECD Guidelines for Multinational Enterprises support voluntary disclosures in the area of governance and business conduct of organizations (EFRAG, 2022b).

SUSTAINABILITY GOVERNANCE: INTERACTION BETWEEN ESRS 2 AND ESRS G1

Governance can play a key role in promoting sustainability and ethical business practices (Rinaldi, 2019). Effective governance frameworks enable organizations to identify and manage ESG risks, thereby safeguarding their long-term viability and societal licence to operate. Strong governance seeks to support that sustainability goals are integrated into the strategic vision of the organization, driving consistent and transparent reporting on ESG performance. In addition, it supports fostering a culture of ethical behaviour, where decision-making processes are guided by a commitment to legal compliance and moral principles. By embedding sustainability into the core governance structures, organizations can enhance their reputation, build stakeholder trust and achieve competitive advantage.

Governance under ESRS also emphasizes the need for robust risk management systems that identify potential threats to sustainability and implement proactive measures to mitigate them. It requires the establishment of internal controls that provide accurate and reliable financial and non-financial information, essential for informed decision-making and accountability. Moreover, governance frameworks support continuous improvement through regular monitoring and evaluation of governance practices, ensuring they evolve in response to emerging challenges and stakeholder expectations.

ESRS G1 is intrinsically linked to other ESRS standards, particularly ESRS 2, which provides overarching guidelines on governance, risk management and internal control. While ESRS G1 focuses specifically on business conduct issues, including corporate culture, whistleblower protection and anti-corruption strategies, ESRS 2 establishes the foundational governance principles that underpin these areas (Gerwing *et al.*, 2022).

ESRS 2 sets out general requirements for the governance structures and processes that companies must adopt to ensure effective oversight of sustainability-related issues. It outlines the roles and responsibilities of the administrative, management and supervisory bodies, emphasizing the importance of their commitment to sustainability goals. ESRS 2 also mandates the development of clear communication channels to facilitate transparent sustainability reporting and stakeholder engagement.

By adhering to the principles laid out in ESRS 2, organizations can create a robust governance framework that supports the specific requirements of ESRS G1. This interconnection ensures a cohesive approach to governance, where general principles guide the implementation of specific practices, fostering a comprehensive and integrated system for managing sustainability and ethical conduct.

In summary, the definition and scope of governance as per ESRS guidelines highlight the essential role governance plays in sustainability and ethical business practices. The interconnectedness between ESRS G1 and ESRS 2 underscores the importance of a unified governance approach, ensuring that organizations are well equipped to navigate the complexities of organizational responsibility.

ESRS G1 BUSINESS CONDUCT

ESRS G1 focuses on business conduct as a core element of governance. ESRS G1 encompasses a broad array of elements including, but not limited to, compliance with legal requirements, corporate culture and ethical conduct. The CSRD refers to 'business ethics'; EFRAG decided to rename ESRS G1 'to present the topic in a more neutral manner' (ESRS G1.BC 4). However, only some topics are covered of those which are generally considered to be related to 'business conduct'.

The ESRS G1 defines the scope of business conduct as including the following topics:

a) business ethics and corporate culture, including anti-corruption and anti-bribery, the protection of whistleblowers, and animal welfare;
b) the management of relationships with suppliers, including payment practices, especially with regard to late payment to small and medium-sized undertakings.
c) activities and commitments of the undertaking related to exerting its political influence, including its lobbying activities.

The scope of ESRS G1 thus is very different from the other topical ESRS. They do not directly relate to environmental or social impacts of an organization, some of the topics are even clearly financial in nature. Also, these topics covered by ESRS G1 are relatively heterogeneous in their nature.

ESRS G1 follows a slightly different structure than the other topical ESRS. Whilst these show a focus on reporting on policies, actions, metrics and targets, relating to specific sustainability matters (which are defined in Appendix A of ESRS 1). In contrast, ESRS G1 sets forth different disclosure requirements explicitly addressing sustainability matters. Furthermore, these disclosure requirements cover policies and actions in an integrated way. Different to all other topical ESRS, ESRS G1 does not contain an explicit disclosure requirement on targets; however, disclosure requirements on metrics also are relevant for targets that thus become mandatory to disclose.

This structure of ESRS G1 raises questions with regard to the application of minimum disclosure requirements (ESRS). EFRAG has addressed these in its FAQ document shown in Example 11.1.

Example 11.1

Question "Question ID 479 – Minimum disclosure requirements and ESRS G1" addresses this issue. The following question was asked: 'Do MDRs have to be applied for matters that are to be reported following the ESRS G1?'

EFRAG answered this question as follows: 'The MDRs from paragraphs 63 to 81 in ESRS 2 shall be applied with respect to Policies, Actions, Targets and Metrics in G1 irrespective of the fact that there is no cross-reference in the topical standard.'

Source: EFRAG (2024c)

Sustainability matters applicable for ESRS G1 (ESRS 1.AR 16)

Appendix A of ESRS 1 contains the list of minimum sustainability matters an organization has to assess during its materiality analysis. The list of sustainability matters relating to ESRS G1 is heterogeneous. These matters are derived from a multitude of different standards or frameworks like the **EU Whistleblowing Directive,** the UN Guiding Principles on Business and Human Rights and the OECD guidelines. Table 11.1 provides an overview of the sub-topics of business conduct listed in ESRS G1.

Table 11.1 Breakdown of topics within Business conduct

Topic	Sub-topic	Sub-sub-topic
Business conduct	Corporate culture	
	Protection of whistle-blowers	
	Animal welfare	
	Political engagement and lobbying activities	
	Management of relationships with suppliers including payment practices	
	Corruption and bribery	Prevention and detection including training
		Incidents

In the EU, many organizations are already subject to specific requirements with regard to these matters (e.g., the EU Whistleblowing Directive). This is the case especially for large and listed corporations. However, the CSRD extends the scope of organizations that have to address these matters and to report about them considerably.

The list of sustainability matters related to ESRS G1 underwent several changes during the drafting of the ESRS. Many topics that were considered relevant for business conduct but not for every type of organization where removed and left for future reporting requirements of sector-specific ESRS. One important example for this is fair competition amongst market participants. In contrast, other topics that are closely related to business conduct are covered by other ESRS, e.g. "privacy" in ESRS S4 (ESRS G1.BC 3).

Reporting area: Strategy (SBM)

ESRS G1 only contains one disclosure requirement under the reporting area "strategy". It relates to ESRS 2. This disclosure requirement only applies in case a material sustainability matter that falls under ESRS G1 is identified.

ESRS 2 GOV-1 – The role of the administrative, supervisory and management bodies: The organization should disclose

- the role of the administrative, management and supervisory bodies related to business conduct
- the expertise of the administrative, management and supervisory bodies on business conduct matters.

While disclosure requirement GOV-1 in ESRS 2 mainly relates to processes of managing and overseeing sustainability reporting in general, ESRS G1 requires organizations to add specific statements that address the sustainability matters covered by this topical standard.

Reporting area: Impacts, risks and opportunities management (IRO)

Under this reporting area, companies have to disclose their policies and actions with regard to their business conduct. As already mentioned, ESRS G1 follows a topical structures with its disclosure requirements on IRO. The standard addresses several key areas, collectively referred to as 'business conduct matters', which include (a) business ethics and corporate culture; (b) supplier relationship management and (c) political influence and lobbying – this is shown in Table 11.2.

Table 11.2 Overview of ESRS G1

Disclosure requirement	Brief description
G1-1 Business conduct policies and corporate culture	This encompasses anti-corruption and anti-bribery measures, protection of whistleblowers, and animal welfare practices.
G1-2 Management of relationships with suppliers	This involves managing relationships with suppliers, including payment practices, with particular emphasis on addressing late payments to small and medium-sized enterprises (SMEs).
G1-3 Political engagement	This covers the activities and commitments related to the organization's political influence, including its lobbying efforts.

BUSINESS CONDUCT POLICIES AND CORPORATE CULTURE

The organization is required to disclose its policies on business conduct matters, including how it cultivates its corporate culture. This disclosure aims to shed light on the organization's measures to identify, assess, manage, and mitigate material impacts, risks, and opportunities associated with business conduct. It also seeks to illuminate the organization's approach to fostering a positive corporate culture.

ESRS G1 requires that organizations disclose its policies with respect to business conduct matters, and how it fosters its corporate culture. The reporting shall include how the organization establishes, develops, promotes and evaluates its corporate culture. (ESRS-G1, paragraph 242-7). Example 11.2 provides an extract of the narrative of an organization's disclosures on business conduct.

Example 11.2

Disclosures on business conduct – Nokian Tyres 2023 Sustainability Report

The governance actions at Nokian Tyres are described in the Corporate Governance Statement annually. At the heart of the corporate culture at Nokian Tyres are the key policies defined within the compliance framework of Nokian Tyres, and annually reviewed by The Board of Directors and the management of Nokian Tyres.

These policies include financial policies, such as Tax Policy and Risk Management Policy, as well as policies targeting for good corporate ethics, such as Code of Conduct, Anti-Bribery and Conflict of Interest Code of Conduct, Data Protection Policy, and the Supplier Code of Conduct, among others.

The Policies present the principles to be followed in the Nokian Tyres' business, as well as further operative guidelines and controls to ensure the policies are followed. Nokian Tyres' business is guided by the ethical principles presented in the Board-approved Code of Conduct that can be found on the company website at company.nokiantyres.com/sustainability/responsible-business/corporate-culture-and-business-conduct/code-of-conduct/. The document specifies the principles for Nokian Tyres' business, including instructions for various matters related to ethics and antibribery guidelines. Nokian Tyres does not condone any form of bribery within the company's operations. Every employee needs to adhere to the Code, and Nokian Tyres has an online training for all personnel. The majority of employees conducted the training in 2019 when it was introduced, and the training is included in the induction for new employees.

Source: Nokian Tyres (2023), p. 75

Use Activity 11.1 to expand your knowledge on the corporate culture content of sustainability reports.

ACTIVITY 11.1

Locate the sustainability report of Nokian Tyres (or an organization of your choice). Discuss how its sustainability report explains how the organization cultivates its corporate culture.

Specific requirements from ESRS G1 (p. 5) regarding disclosures of the organization's policies with respect to business conduct matters and how it fosters its corporate culture, cover:

1) *A description of the mechanisms for identifying, reporting and investigating concerns about unlawful behaviour or behaviour in contradiction of its code of conduct or similar internal rules; and whether it accommodates reporting from internal and/or external stakeholders*
2) *Where an organisation has no policies on anti-corruption or anti-bribery consistent with the United Nations Convention against Corruption, it shall state this and whether it has plans to implement them and the timetable for implementation*
3) *How the organisation protects whistleblowers and if the organisation has no policies on the protection of whistleblowers, it shall state this and whether it has plans to implement them and the timetable for implementation*
4) *Where applicable, whether the organisation has in place policies with respect to animal welfare*
5) *The organisation's policy for training within the organisation on business conduct, including target audience, frequency and depth of coverage*
6) *The functions within the undertaking that are most at risk in respect of corruption and bribery.*

(ESRS G1, p. 5)

Corporate culture, in the sense of how it is referred to in ESRS G1, has a very narrow meaning. It addresses many of the other matters covered by ESRS G1 and how an organization makes sure that incidents related to various factors, such as corruption, are avoided. Example 11.3 contains an extract from BASF's Integrated Report (2023) which discusses how it acts to ensure any animal-based studies in its operating chain meet the required legal standards.

Example 11.3

BASF 2023 Integrated Report

Before launching products on the market, we subject them to a variety of tests, including environmental and toxicological tests using state-of-the-art knowledge and technology. If these tests include animal studies, this is generally required by law and necessary to reliably evaluate the safety and efficacy of our products. If we employ animal studies, we adhere to the specifications laid down by the German Animal Welfare Act as well as the requirements of the Association for Assessment and Accreditation of Laboratory Animal Care (AAALAC) – the highest standard for laboratory animals in the world. We develop and are continuously optimizing alternative methods to experimentally assess the safety and tolerance of our products without animal studies. In addition, we are involved in networks such as the European Partnership for Alternative Approaches to Animal Testing (EPAA) to further develop alternative methods across sectors. Our aim is to replace, reduce or refine animal studies to minimize the impact on them. For example, we use an OECD-certified alternative testing strategy developed jointly with Givaudan for animal-free testing of allergic skin reactions. We also use other alternative methods wherever possible. In 2022, BASF SE's Experimental Toxicology and Ecology became the first institute in the world to be certified for Good In Vitro Method Practices (GIVIMP). GIVIMP is a standard published by the OECD. It increases the quality of data generated by in vitro test methods and confidence in newly developed nonanimal testing methods.

Source: BASF (2023), p. 152

Try Activity 11.2 to closer examine the BASF Integrated Report (2023) discussed in Example 11.3.

ACTIVITY 11.2

Does BASF meet the disclosure requirements of ESRS G1 on animal welfare?

Discuss the extent of the BASF disclosure requirements and the other frameworks and regulations that they make reference to.

MANAGEMENT OF RELATIONSHIPS WITH SUPPLIERS

Under ESRS G1, an organization is required to provide information about the management of its relationships with its suppliers and its impacts on its supply chain (refer to Figure 11.1). Transparency on fair behaviour in the procurement process is one main aim of the standard. Consequently, special attention is given to late payments to SME suppliers.

The information required by ESRS G1–2 comprises:

- **a** the organization's approach to its relationships with its suppliers from a double materiality perspective
- **b** whether and how it considers social and environmental criteria for the selection of its suppliers.

Prevention and detection of corruption and bribery

Under ESRS G1, an organization must provide information about its systems to prevent and detect, investigate and respond to allegations or incidents relating to corruption and bribery, including the related training.

The required disclosure must include the following information according to ESRS G1.18:

a) a description of the procedures in place to prevent, detect and address allegations or incidents of corruption and bribery

b) whether the investigators or investigating committee are separate from the chain of management involved in the matter

c) the process, if any, to report outcomes to the administrative, management and supervisory bodies.

Figure 11.1 High level description of relationship with suppliers, animal welfare and business conduct at GUBI

Business conduct *(relationship with suppliers)*	**Business conduct** *(animal welfare)*	**Business conduct** *(GUBI)*
(10)	(11)	(12)
GUBI's way of managing procurement relationships impacts the suppliers' behaviour both from a sustainability point of view and an ethical perspective. Suppliers and sub-suppliers are impacted in GUBI's value chain. The time horizon is expected to be short-term, medium and long-term.	Proper treatment of animals mainly through GUBI's engagement with suppliers and sub-suppliers in relation to sourcing animal by-products such as wool. The time horizon is expected to be short-term, medium and long-term.	GUBI's corporate culture has a direct impact on people it employs and on the organisations and people GUBI engage with. Value chain impact is mainly identified within our own operations and partners (customers). The time horizon is expected to be short-term, medium and long-term.

Source: GUBI (2023), p. 21

Deutsche Bank discusses its corruption and bribery prevention training in its non-financial reports, as illustrated in Example 11.4.

Example 11.4

Deutsche Bank reports on the training to prevent incidents of corruption and bribery

Regular (at least annual) training is conducted for all employees and contractual workers across all locations and businesses, as well as the members of the Management Board, covering all financial crime risks including anti-fraud bribery & corruption, and testing their policy knowledge. This mandatory curriculum is accompanied by other additional facultative training offerings. The training modules highlight the importance of identifying financial crime risks and raising concerns or suspicions including the use of the anonymous whistleblowing hotline. Modules articulate personal, professional, financial, regulatory, and societal consequences of failing to manage financial crime risks. For example, the mandatory anti-bribery and corruption trainings cover relevant regulatory requirements and key areas of Deutsche Bank's risk exposure as well as the corresponding prevention measures and applicable minimum standards and policies. A training completion rate of 99.97% (99.97% for money laundering and terrorist financing, 99.96% for anti-fraud, bribery, and corruption, and 99.96% for sanctions and embargoes) has been achieved for the learners required to complete the mandatory anti-financial crime training by end of the fourth quarter 2023. Learners who have not completed the training within the required due date are subject to potential disciplinary action and reported to the Compliance red flag team for investigation.

Source: Deutsche Bank (2023), p. 114

Reporting area: Metrics and targets (MT)

Each ESRS includes a component on metrics and targets. ESRS G1 has three subject categories that require metrics and targets: incidents of corruption or bribery, political influence and lobbying activities, and payment practices. Table 11.3 provides examples of selected metrics and targets per topic.

Table 11.3 Examples of metrics and targets in ESRS G1 topics

Topic	Examples of metrics and targets
G1–4. Incidents of corruption or bribery	• The number of convictions and the amount of fines for violation of anti-corruption and anti-bribery laws • The number of confirmed incidents in which own workers were dismissed or disciplined for corruption or bribery-related incidents.
G1–5. Political influence and lobbying activities	• The total monetary value of financial and in-kind political contributions made directly and indirectly to political parties, aggregated by country or geographical area where relevant, as well as type of recipient/beneficiary • Where appropriate, how the monetary value of in-kind contributions is estimated.
G1–6. Payment practices	• The average time the undertaking takes to pay an invoice from the date when the contractual or statutory term of payment starts to be calculated, in number of days • The number of legal proceedings currently outstanding for late payments.

Source: EFRAG (2022c)

Refer to Example 11.5 for an example of how an organization may choose to disclose its political engagements.

Example 11.5

ESRS G1 Political engagement disclosure

The annex of ESRS G1 provides an illustrative example on how an organization might make disclosures on political engagement:

> *During the 20XY financial year ABC was involved in activities around the proposed regulation XXX which could have significant negative impacts on its business model if implemented in the current format. ABC's considers that while the proposed regulation will realise some improvements to the regulatory regime such as xxx, in its current format the costs relating to xxx will outweigh the benefits. ABC and its peers continue to work with XXX (the regulator) to improve this balance.*

Source: EFRAG (2022c), AR 15

ESRS G1 link to financial statements

Many of the disclosure requirements of ESRS G1 are directly or indirectly financial in nature:

- they comprise monetary disclosure, for example on payments to political parties or fines paid by the organization
- many matters that are covered might be associated with risk that can have considerable financial effects for the organization, for example as a consequence of changes in payment practices.

In that respect, ESRS G1 might be even more 'financial' in nature than are the other ESRSs. Many of the sustainability matters covered stress risks an organization faces for improper business conduct. As a consequence, matters linked to ESRS G1 are frequently also discussed in the financial statements and in the management commentary. A good example would be how Porr reports on cartel proceedings with the Federal Competition Authority in Austria in its management report (Porr, 2021, p. 82).

TRANSITIONAL PROVISIONS FOR ESRS G1

ESRS G1 is the only standard for which Appendix C of ESRS 1 does not contain any phase-in regulations. So, every organization which applies ESRS has to include all relevant disclosures in its sustainability statement. This underlines that business conduct is considered to be a sustainability matter of high urgency and relevance for all organizations applying ESRS.

As EFRAG also stresses that relevant sustainability matters related to business conduct differ from sector to sector, the transitional provision in chapter 10.1 of ESRS 1 (relating to entity-specific disclosures) is of high importance for ESRS G1. Organizations have to analyse other existing sector-specific standards and frameworks for disclosure requirements that might also apply to their business model. This can add to the list of matters that organizations have to consider when reporting on their business conduct.

OTHER RELEVANT FRAMEWORKS IN THE AREA OF BUSINESS CONDUCT

In the topical area of business conduct, various international frameworks complement the principles and standards established by ESRS G1. These frameworks collectively aim to promote ethical, transparent and sustainable business practices across organizations at a global level. They provide comprehensive guidelines that address governance, transparency, ethical conduct, stakeholder engagement, and environmental and social responsibilities. A key convention is that of the United Nations Convention against Corruption (UNCAC), while other important frameworks include the OECD Guidelines for Multinational Enterprises, the GRI Standards and the SDGs. In addition, the UN Global Compact and ISO 26000 on Social Responsibility also provide guidance on governance and business conduct of organizations. These frameworks intersect in various ways with ESRS G1, with the aim of reinforce strengthened organizational behaviour and contributing to a coherent global approach to sustainable development and accountability. This section provides an overview of the United Nations Convention against Corruption and the OECD Guidelines for Multinational Enterprises.

United Nations Convention against Corruption

UNCAC represents a landmark international treaty that aims to address the pervasive issue of corruption globally. Adopted by the United Nations General Assembly on 31 October 2003, and entering into force on 14 December 2005, UNCAC is a comprehensive, legally binding instrument that provides a global framework for combatting corruption in both public and private sectors.

ESRS G1 and UNCAC intersect in their objectives and principles. UNCAC encompasses a wide range of measures to prevent and combat corruption more effectively:

- **Prevention:** Emphasizing the importance of preventative measures, UNCAC advocates for the establishment of anti-corruption bodies, the promotion of transparency in public administration and the implementation of effective codes of conduct for public officials.

- **Criminalization and law enforcement:** The convention requires member states to criminalize various forms of corruption, including bribery, embezzlement and money laundering. It also mandates measures to enhance law enforcement cooperation, ensuring the prompt and effective prosecution of corrupt activities.
- **International cooperation:** Recognizing the transnational nature of corruption, UNCAC fosters international collaboration through mutual legal assistance, extradition and information exchange among state parties. This cooperation is crucial for tracking and recovering assets illicitly transferred across borders.
- **Asset recovery:** One of the most innovative aspects of UNCAC is its focus on asset recovery. It obliges states to adopt measures for the direct recovery of property through international cooperation, emphasizing the return of assets to countries of origin as a fundamental principle of the convention.
- **Technical assistance and information exchange:** The convention calls for the provision of technical assistance to developing countries, aiding them in building the capacity to implement anti-corruption measures. It also promotes the sharing of knowledge and best practices among state parties.

OECD Guidelines for Multinational Enterprises

The OECD guidelines (OECD, 2023) provide recommendations for responsible business conduct in a global context. Key areas of overlap with ESRS G1 include:

- **Disclosure:** transparency in business activities and operations.
- **Human rights:** respect for human rights in business practices.
- **Anti-corruption:** prevent bribery and corruption.

The OECD guidelines have evolved since their inception, reflecting the changing landscape of international business and the growing emphasis on corporate responsibility. The guidelines were first adopted in 1976 as part of the Declaration on International Investment and Multinational Enterprises, aiming to promote positive contributions by multinational enterprises to economic, environmental and social progress worldwide.

Over the decades the guidelines have undergone several revisions to adapt to emerging challenges and developments in the global economy. Updates have occurred in 2000, 2011 and 2023, each iteration expanding and refining the scope of responsible business conduct expected of multinational enterprises. These updates have incorporated contemporary issues such as human rights, environmental sustainability and anti-corruption measures.

The OECD guidelines comprise a set of voluntary principles and standards for responsible business conduct in a global context. The guidelines are divided into chapters, each addressing specific areas of corporate responsibility. Examples include policies for sustainable development, due diligence and stakeholder engagement. In terms of disclosures, the OECD guidelines ask that organizations provide accurate and timely information on all material matters, including financial performance, governance, and environmental and social impacts and that they adhere to high-quality standards of accounting, disclosure and audit. They also provide guidelines on human rights, fair labour practices and collective bargaining.

On the environmental side the guidelines ask for environmental management information and the application of a precautionary approach to environmental challenges and enhanced environmental performance through innovation. The OECD guidelines also address combatting bribery, bribe solicitation and extortion, consumer interests, science and technology, and competition and taxation. ESRS G1 and the OECD guidelines both include principles and guidelines to ensure responsible and transparent business practices. The intersection of these two frameworks is evident in their shared emphasis on governance, transparency, ethical conduct and sustainable business operations. Table 11.4 outlines key areas where ESRS G1 intersects with the OECD guidelines.

Table 11.4 Intersection of ESRS G1 and OECD guidelines

Topic	ESRS G1	OECD guidelines
Governance and accountability	• Focuses on the disclosure of governance structures and processes, including the roles and responsibilities of boards, committees and management. • Emphasizes accountability and transparency in decision-making processes.	• Advocates for clear governance structures that strengthen accountability and ethical conduct within multinational enterprises. • Encourages the adoption of effective corporate governance frameworks that align with international standards and best practices.
Transparency and disclosure	• Requires detailed disclosures on various aspects of governance, including risk management, internal controls and the oversight of ethical practices. • Mandates transparency in financial and non-financial reporting, highlighting the importance of clear and accurate information for stakeholders.	• Stresses the importance of transparency in business operations, urging enterprises to provide timely, accurate and comprehensive information on all material matters, including financial performance, governance, and environmental and social impacts. • Promotes high standards of accounting, disclosure and audit practices to enhance stakeholder trust and confidence.
Ethical conduct and anti-corruption	• Emphasizes the need for companies to implement robust policies and procedures to prevent corruption, bribery and other unethical behaviours. • Encourages companies to disclose their anti-corruption measures and the effectiveness of their implementation.	• Provides comprehensive recommendations for combatting bribery, bribe solicitation and extortion. • Encourages enterprises to establish internal controls, ethics and compliance programmes to prevent and detect corruption and to foster a culture of integrity and transparency.
Stakeholder engagement	• Highlights the importance of engaging with stakeholders, including employees, customers, suppliers and communities, to ensure their interests and concerns are considered in governance processes. • Requires organizations to disclose their stakeholder engagement practices and how stakeholder feedback influences corporate decision-making.	• Advocates for meaningful stakeholder engagement, emphasizing the role of stakeholders in shaping responsible business conduct. • Encourages enterprises to engage with stakeholders regularly and transparently, ensuring that their operations reflect the interests and expectations of those affected by their activities.
Human rights and labour practices	• Focuses on the disclosure of policies and practices related to human rights, labour standards and workplace conditions. • Requires organizations to report on measures taken to ensure respect for human rights and fair labour practices within their operations and supply chains.	• Emphasizes the responsibility of organizations to respect human rights and uphold fair labour practices. • Encourages organizations to adopt and implement due diligence processes to identify, prevent and mitigate adverse human rights impacts associated with their activities.

(Continued)

Table 11.4 Intersection of ESRS G1 and OECD guidelines (Continued)

Topic	ESRS G1	OECD guidelines
Environmental responsibility	• While primarily focused on governance, it also acknowledges the need for governance structures to oversee environmental management and sustainability efforts. • Encourages organizations to integrate environmental considerations into their governance frameworks and report on their environmental performance and impact.	• Provides recommendations for environmental management, urging enterprises to adopt practices that minimize environmental harm and promote sustainable resource use. • Encourages organizations to apply the precautionary principle and enhance their environmental performance through continuous improvement and innovation.

Example 11.6 provides the illustration of BASF applying the OECD guidelines. The terms **Tripartite Declaration of Principles Concerning Multinational Enterprises and Social Policy, The Responsible Care® Global Charter** and **The German Corporate Governance Code** are explained in the glossary at the end of the textbook.

Example 11.6

BASF's list of human rights guidance promoted by the company in its Combined Management's Report

We are committed to conducting our business activities in a responsible and respectful manner, guided by our corporate values and global standards (see page 33). Our actions are based on the applicable laws and regulations. Some of our voluntary commitments go above and beyond these. In doing so, we take internationally recognized principles into account. We respect and promote:

- The Universal Declaration of Human Rights and the two U.N. Human Rights Covenants
- The 10 principles of the U.N. Global Compact
- The core labor standards of the International Labour Organization (ILO) and the Tripartite Declaration of Principles Concerning Multinational Enterprises and Social Policy
- The OECD Guidelines for Multinational Enterprises
- The Responsible Care® Global Charter
- The German Corporate Governance Code

Source: BASF (2023), p. 153

It should be noted that the OECD has also published the OECD Due Diligence Guidance for Responsible Business Conduct (OECD, 2018). This guidance contains many instructive examples and helps organizations to implement the requirements of the more abstract OECD Guidelines for Multinational Enterprises.

CONCLUSION

ESRS G1, the OECD guidelines and UNCAC represent examples of conventions, standards and frameworks that are available to foster responsible and ethical business conduct. Closely related to ESRS 2, ESRS G1 emphasizes the importance of governance, transparency and accountability in corporate operations, setting a high standard for sustainability reporting within the EU. The OECD guidelines extend these principles globally, providing a comprehensive blueprint for multinational enterprises to navigate the complexities of responsible business conduct, encompassing areas such as human rights, labour practices, environmental sustainability and anti-corruption measures. UNCAC complements these frameworks by addressing the critical issue of corruption, promoting preventative measures, law enforcement, international cooperation and asset recovery.

Collectively, these frameworks create a robust foundation for businesses to operate ethically and transparently, ensuring their activities contribute positively to societal and economic progress while mitigating adverse impacts. The integration and alignment of these standards highlight the global consensus on the necessity for corporate responsibility and integrity, reinforcing the commitment to sustainable development and the rule of law. By adhering to these guidelines, businesses can build trust with stakeholders, enhance their reputational capital and contribute to a fairer and more sustainable global economy.

SUMMARY

The following items relate to the learning objectives listed at the beginning of the chapter.

- **LO 1. Understand disclosure requirements for ESRS G1 Business conduct.**

  ESRS G1 establishes disclosure requirements that enable users of an organization's sustainability statements to comprehensively understand its strategy, approach, processes, procedures, and performance concerning business conduct. addresses several key areas, collectively referred to as 'business conduct matters', which include (a) business ethics and corporate culture; (b) supplier relationship management and (c) political influence and lobbying. Topics such as the protection of whistleblowers and animal welfare are to be found in ESRS G1.

- **LO 2. Discuss the financial effects on an organization over the short, medium and long term caused by the risks and opportunities arising from the organization's impacts and dependencies in the topic areas of ESRS G1.**

  Governance under ESRS G1 emphasizes the need for robust risk management systems that identify potential threats to sustainability and implement proactive measures to mitigate them. It requires the establishment of internal controls that provide accurate and reliable financial and non-financial information, essential for informed decision-making and accountability.

- **LO 3. Explain the role of OECD Guidelines for Multinational Enterprises and other standards relevant for governance and business conduct disclosures.**

  ESRS G1's focus on board accountability, anti-corruption measures, risk management, and stakeholder engagement reflects the principles enshrined in the OECD guidelines and other global governance frameworks.

- **LO 4. Contrast the key differences between other relevant reporting frameworks that address business conduct (for example, United Nations Global Compact and the OECD guidelines).**

  This chapter has outlined the content of UNGC and the OECD Guidelines for Multinational Enterprises in order to allow for an understanding of the contrast between the frameworks. It has, for example, been highlighted that ESRS G1 and the OECD guidelines both set forth principles and guidelines to ensure responsible and transparent business practices. The intersection of these two frameworks is evident in their shared emphasis on governance, transparency, ethical conduct, and sustainable business operations.

- **LO 5. Distinguish between the reporting requirements of ESRS G1 and ESRS 2 with regard to sustainability governance.**

  Both standards, ESRS G1 and ESRS 2, address matters that are directly related to sustainability governance – in essence how an organization engages in responsible business practices. ESRS G1 addresses concrete sustainability matters on which an organization has to report and on which it sets policies, actions and targets. ESRS 2, in turn, addresses structures and processes within an organization that embeds ESG in risk management, internal control and in the work of the administrative, management, and supervisory bodies.

EXERCISES

1 Explain the significance of protecting whistleblowers in maintaining corporate integrity. (LO 1)

2 Locate metrics and targets that align with those of ESRS G1 in the BASF 2023 Combined Management's Report (or an organization of your choice). (LO 1)

3 Outline the specific disclosure requirements related to whistleblower protection according to ESRS G1. (Additionally, you could compare the disclosure requirements on whistleblowers in GRI with those of ESRS G1.) (LO 1)

4 ESRSs do not elaborate much on what specific actions should be taken to foster corporate culture. Locate two companies of your choice and identify and compare what disclosures they provide on this matter. (LO 1)

5 Discuss the financial effects on an organization over the short term and long term of risks and opportunities arising from the organization's impacts and dependencies in the topic areas of ESRS G1 Business conduct. (LO 2)

6 Outline the anti-corruption disclosure requirements and guidelines and make reference to other standards, frameworks and/or laws that are relevant for organizations to consult with regards to anti-corruption. (LO 3, LO 4)

7 Analyse real-world examples of Santander and Société Générale. Compare and contrast their approaches towards sustainability governance (ESRS 2 and ESRS G1). Identify best practices, and highlight areas for improvement. (LO 5)

PART THREE

Subject-specific themes under sustainability reporting

Sustainability reporting is moving towards becoming an essential aspect of modern business and governance, reflecting a growing global emphasis on transparency, accountability and sustainable development. In this Part, selected themes are covered addressing certain nuances across sectors, emerging trends and the professional competencies required for the future.

This Part of the book delves into the financial sector, where sustainability reporting plays a transformative role in shaping responsible investment and financing practices. Topics such as sustainability reporting in financial institutions, green bonds and the Sustainable Finance Disclosure Regulation (SFDR) underline the sector's efforts to align financial flows with global sustainability goals. Frameworks like the Principles for Responsible Banking (PRB) illustrate the ethical commitments shaping the industry's reporting standards.

Part Three also examines assurance and audit practices in sustainability reporting, emphasizing the importance of credibility and reliability in disclosures. This is followed by a chapter dedicated to data solutions for sustainability reporting, focusing on the CSRD's requirement for digital tagging of sustainability reporting, as well as how technological innovations enable organizations to track, report and improve their sustainability performance. A discussion on sustainability reporting in the public sector highlights its unique challenges and opportunities, including accountability to diverse stakeholders. Finally, the Part addresses the evolving role of the accounting profession, emphasizing the competencies required for future accountants to navigate sustainability imperatives effectively. As sustainability becomes increasingly integrated into financial decision-making, accountants will play a pivotal role in shaping a more sustainable future.

Through these themes, Part Three of this book aims to provide a comprehensive understanding of the multifaceted nature of sustainability reporting and its implications across selected sectors.

In closing, it is worthwhile highlighting that the worsening ecological degradation and growing social challenges underscore the urgency of reimagining current business practices. Advancing accounting and reporting practices that create transparency on the impact of organizations across topical dimensions under ESG can serve to strengthen opportunities.

CHAPTER 12
The financial sector and sustainability reporting

Learning objectives

After studying this chapter you should be able to:

- LO 1. Discuss the international regulatory landscape for sustainability reporting in the financial sector.
- LO 2. Understand disclosure requirements in the EU Sustainable Finance Disclosure Regulation (SFDR).
- LO 3. Describe what the Principles for Responsible Banking are.
- LO 4. Describe what an EU green bond is.
- LO 5. Contrast key differences between reporting frameworks and sustainability efforts in the financial sector.

Counting on it...

While business is largely shifting to mandatory sustainability reporting, the financial services sector has not followed suit at the same pace. The reasons are manifold, including:

- Business models of financial institutions are complex and diverse, so their environmental and social impacts are challenging to determine, as they are often indirect and difficult to measure.
- A vast and diverse client base makes tracking emissions and environmental impact across the value chain difficult.
- Regulatory compliance often trumps voluntary sustainability reporting.
- For decades, financial performance has taken priority over all other aspects. Culture change is slow.

The financial services sector is experiencing increasing pressure for sustainability reporting to become mandatory. In the European Union (EU), the Sustainable Finance Disclosure Regulation (SFDR) requires financial market participants to disclose information on how they integrate sustainability risks into their investment decision-making. The EU's Taxonomy Regulation provides a framework for identifying sustainable economic activities, which is expected to have implications for financial institutions. In many jurisdictions, there are already regulations requiring companies to disclose ESG information in their financial reporting.

Source: KPMG (2023a)

INTRODUCTION

Sustainable finance involves incorporating ESG factors into financial decision-making, promoting long-term investments in sustainable activities and projects. Environmental considerations include climate change mitigation, biodiversity preservation, pollution prevention and the circular economy. Social considerations address inequality, inclusiveness, labour relations, human rights and community investment. Governance involves the management structures, employee relations and executive remuneration of institutions, ensuring the integration of social and environmental factors in their decision-making processes (World Bank, 2018).

In addition to the CSRD and accompanying ESRS and the Taxonomy Regulation, the EU has also released the **Sustainable Finance Disclosure Regulation (SFDR)**, which is focused on the disclosure obligations of financial market participants and financial advisers. More explicitly, the EU introduced the SFDR to reduce the risks of greenwashing, by requiring more disclosure and standardized reporting by asset managers on sustainable investment practices, as of March 2021 (Dikolli *et al.*, 2022). The SFDR is the first comprehensive sustainability disclosure requirement imposed on investment funds (Dai *et al.*, 2023).

The SFDR requires the provision of comparable information on how an organization integrates sustainability risks and considerations into its investment decision and advisory processes. The regulation is designed to combat greenwashing, promote transparency and enable investors to make more informed choices about sustainable investments.

Overall, the introduction of the SFDR marks a significant shift in the regulatory landscape for sustainability reporting in the financial sector. In addition, it should be highlighted that there are other global initiatives aimed at stimulating sustainable finance practices. These initiatives include, for example, the Principles for Responsible Banking (PRB), launched by the **United Nations Environment Programme Finance Initiative (UNEP FI)**, to guide banks in aligning their strategies with the SDGs and the Paris Agreement.

This chapter considers the impact of the CSRD and SFDR on the financial sector, exploring the challenges and opportunities they present. It examines the historical context and theoretical underpinnings of sustainability reporting and provides an overview of the regulatory requirements.

FRAMEWORK FOR SUSTAINABLE FINANCE

Sustainable finance integrates ESG factors into investment decisions, fostering long-term capital allocation towards projects and activities that benefit both society and the environment. Environmental considerations encompass mitigating and adapting to climate change, preserving biodiversity, preventing pollution and promoting a circular economy. Social considerations address issues such as inequality, inclusiveness, labour relations, human capital development, community well-being and human rights. Governance focuses on the structures and practices of public and private institutions, ensuring that social and environmental concerns are embedded in decision-making processes.

THE EUROPEAN UNION

Within the EU, sustainable finance is a strategic tool aimed at driving economic growth while minimizing environmental impact, aligning with the climate and environmental goals of the European Green Deal. It also involves transparently disclosing ESG-related financial risks and mitigating them through effective governance of financial and corporate actors. Sustainable finance practices seek to direct private capital, alongside public funds, towards a climate-neutral, climate-resilient, resource-efficient and equitable economy.

The SFDR, as an integral part of the move towards sustainable finance, aims to reduce information asymmetry regarding sustainability risks, impacts, the promotion of environmental or social characteristics, and sustainability investment (Dai *et al.*, 2023). Schoenmaker (2017) proposed a model (refer to Table 12.1) as an attempt to consider the evolution of sustainable finance over time.

Table 12.1 The evolution of sustainable finance over time

Sustainable finance typology	Value created	Ranking of factors	Horizon
Sustainable Finance 1.0	Shareholder value	F > S and E	Short-term
↓	↓	↓	↓
Sustainable Finance 2.0	Stakeholder value	T = F + S + E	Medium-term
↓	↓	↓	↓
Sustainable Finance 3.0	Common good value	S and E > F	Long-term

Note: F = financial value; S = social impact; E = environmental impact; T = total value. At Sustainable Finance 1.0, the maximization of F is subject to minor S and E constraints.

Source: Adapted from Schoenmaker (2017)

Within the EU, the concept of 'transition finance' is also highlighted. Sustainable finance encompasses both green finance (financing inherently environmentally friendly activities) and transition finance (financing activities transitioning towards environmental sustainability). Transition finance focuses on funding private investments that reduce current high greenhouse gas emissions or other environmental impacts, ultimately leading to a climate-neutral and sustainable economy. This could involve investments in green production methods or minimizing environmental footprints where green technologies are not yet available.

The EU states that transition finance is crucial to achieving its 2030 targets of reducing greenhouse gas emissions by 55% and minimizing environmental impacts. It is particularly relevant for companies that aspire to become sustainable but require a phased approach due to varying starting points on their sustainability journey. On 13 June 2023, the European Commission issued non-binding recommendations on how companies can voluntarily leverage EU sustainable finance tools to seek or provide transition finance (refer to European Commission, 2023c). The EU's sustainable finance toolbox caters not only to companies with exemplary sustainability records but also to those at different stages of their sustainability journey, as long as they have clear sustainability targets. It also enables smaller companies to access financing for their transition in a proportionate manner.

It is important to note that research studies highlight the importance of exercising caution in regard to the sustainable financing mechanisms leading to actual changes in financing practices (Dikolli *et al.*, 2022).

Sustainable Finance Disclosure Regulation (SFDR)

The SFDR has applied since March 2021 and requires financial market participants (FMPs) and financial advisers to disclose at entity and product level how they integrate sustainability risks and principal adverse impacts in their investment decision-making processes. It also introduces additional product disclosures for financial products making sustainability claims. Table 12.2 provides the overarching structure of the SFDR.

Table 12.2 Overarching structure of the SFDR

Article	Text
Article 1 Subject matter	This Regulation lays down harmonized rules for financial market participants and financial advisers on transparency with regard to the integration of sustainability risks and the consideration of adverse sustainability impacts in their processes and the provision of sustainability-related information with respect to financial products.
Article 2 Definitions	This Article provides definitions for 'financial market participants'.
Article 3 Transparency of sustainability risk policies	Financial market participants shall publish on their websites information about their policies on the integration of sustainability risks in their investment decision-making processes. Financial advisers shall publish on their websites information about their policies on the integration of sustainability risks in their investment advice or insurance advice.
Article 4 Transparency of adverse sustainability impacts at entity level	This Article prescribes that financial market participants shall publish and maintain on their websites: (a) where they consider principal adverse impacts of investment decisions on sustainability factors, a statement on due diligence policies with respect to those impacts, taking due account of their size, the nature and scale of their activities and the types of financial products they make available; or (b) where they do not consider adverse impacts of investment decisions on sustainability factors, clear reasons for why they do not do so, including, where relevant, information as to whether and when they intend to consider such adverse impacts. Further details on the content are provided in Article 4.
Article 5 Transparency of remuneration policies in relation to the integration of sustainability risks	Financial market participants and financial advisers shall include in their remuneration policies information on how those policies are consistent with the integration of sustainability risks, and shall publish that information on their websites.
Article 6 Transparency of the integration of sustainability risks	Article 6 requires that financial market participants shall include descriptions of the following in pre-contractual disclosures: (a) the manner in which sustainability risks are integrated into their investment decisions; and (b) the results of the assessment of the likely impacts of sustainability risks on the returns of the financial products they make available. The Article also provides details in regard to what financial market participants need to disclose if sustainability risks are not considered to be relevant. It highlights that the descriptions for sustainability risks not being relevant shall include a clear and concise explanation of the reasons therefor.
Article 7 Transparency of adverse sustainability impacts at financial product level	By 30 December 2022, for each financial product where a financial market participant applies point (a) of Article 4 (1) or Article 4(3) or (4), the disclosures referred to in Article 6(3) shall include the following: (a) a clear and reasoned explanation of whether, and if so, how a financial product considers principal adverse impacts on sustainability factors; and (b) a statement that information on principal adverse impacts on sustainability factors is available in the information to be disclosed pursuant to Article 11(2).
Article 8 Transparency of the promotion of environmental or social characteristics in pre-contractual disclosures	Where a financial product promotes, among other characteristics, environmental or social characteristics, or a combination of those characteristics, provided that the companies in which the investments are made follow good governance practices, the SFDR prescribes the information requirements to be disclosed.
Article 9 Transparency of sustainable investments in pre-contractual disclosures	Where a financial product has sustainable investment as its objective and an index has been designated as a reference benchmark, the information to be disclosed pursuant to Article 6(1) and (3) shall be accompanied by the list of topics prescribed in Article 9.

(Continued)

Table 12.2 Overarching structure of the SFDR (Continued)

Article 10 Transparency of the promotion of environmental or social characteristics and of sustainable investments on websites	Financial market participants shall publish and maintain on their websites information prescribed in Article 10 for each financial product referred.
Article 11 Transparency of the promotion of environmental or social characteristics and of sustainable investments in periodic reports	This Article outlines that where financial market participants make available a financial product as referred to in Article 8(1) or in Article 9(1), (2) or (3), they shall include a description of listed information in their periodic reports.
Article 12 Review of disclosures	Financial market participants shall ensure that any information published in accordance with Articles 3, 5 or 10 is kept up to date. Where a financial market participant amends such information, a clear explanation of such amendment shall be published on the same website.
Article 13 Marketing communications	Without prejudice to stricter sectoral legislation, in particular Directives 2009/65/EC, 2014/65/EU and (EU) 2016/97 and Regulation (EU) No 1286/2014, financial market participants and financial advisers shall ensure that their marketing communications do not contradict the information disclosed pursuant to this Regulation.
Article 14 Competent authorities	Member States shall ensure that the competent authorities designated in accordance with sectoral legislation, in particular the sectoral legislation referred to in Article 6(3) of this Regulation, and in accordance with Directive 2013/36/EU, monitor the compliance of financial market participants and financial advisers within the requirements of this Regulation. The competent authorities shall have all the supervisory and investigatory powers that are necessary for the exercise of their functions under this Regulation.
Article 15 Transparency by Institutions for Occupational Retirement Provision (IORPs) and insurance intermediaries	IORPs shall publish and maintain the information referred to in the SFDR.
Article 16 Pension products covered by Regulations (EC) No 883/2004 and (EC) No 987/2009	Member States may decide to apply this Regulation to manufacturers of pension products operating national social security schemes which are covered by specified EU Regulations.
Article 17 Exemptions	This Regulation shall neither apply to insurance intermediaries which provide insurance advice with regard to **Insurance-based Investment Products (IBIPs)** nor to investment firms which provide investment advice that are enterprises irrespective of their legal form, including natural persons and self-employed persons, provided that they employ fewer than three persons.
Article 18 Report	The ESAs shall take stock of the extent of voluntary disclosures in accordance with point (a) of Article 4(1) and point (a) of Article 7(1). By 10 September 2022 and every year thereafter, the ESAs shall submit a report to the Commission on best practices and make recommendations towards voluntary reporting standards.

Article 19 Evaluation	By 30 December 2022, the Commission evaluated the application of this Regulation. In December 2024 the Summary Report of the Open and Targeted Consultations on the SFDR assessment was published. Available at finance.ec.europa.eu/document/download/0f2cfde1-12b0-4860-b548-0393ac5b592b_en?filename=2023-sfdr-implementation-summary-of-responses_en.pdf.
Article 20 Entry into force and application	This regulation applied from 10 March 2021.

Source: Regulation (EU) 2019/2088 of the European Parliament and of the Council of 27 November 2019 on sustainability-related disclosures in the financial services sector

Activities 12.1 and 12.2 ask you to do a deeper dive into the SFDR and search for the definition of financial market participants while engaging with the more explicit disclosure criteria.

ACTIVITY 12.1

Download the full text of the SFDR. Locate the definitions of financial market participants (Article 2).

ACTIVITY 12.2

Using the SFDR you downloaded in Activity 12.1, select a few of the disclosure criteria and screen them against a financial institution of your choice.

Example 12.1 from Deutsche Bank Wealth Management, Sustainability Disclosures includes an illustration of their sustainability risk policy and shows how SFDR can be translated into practice.

Example 12.1

Deutsche Bank Wealth Management, Sustainability Disclosures – Deutsche Bank Luxembourg S.A. – Example of Sustainability Risk Policy

Introduction

SFDR came into effect on March 10, 2021. SFDR imposes new transparency obligations (Website disclosures, Pre-Contractual disclosures) & periodic reporting requirements on investment management firms at both a product and entity/manager level. This section relates to the 'Website Disclosure' regulatory obligations arising out of SFDR Articles 3-10. More information can be found on the below links. [...]

1.1 Sustainability Risk Policy

Article 3: *Transparency of sustainability risk policies for financial market participants and financial advisors for Deutsche Bank Luxembourg S.A., March 2021*

Introduction / Summary

On March 10, 2021 the Regulation (EU) 2019/2088 of November 27, 2019 on sustainability-related disclosures in the financial sector (Disclosure Regulation) has entered into force. This regulation aims to support sustainable investments by requiring Financial Market Participants (FMPs) and Financial Advisers (FAs) to disclose information regarding sustainability risks to investors and clients.

(Continued)

Article 3 of this regulation requires information to be shared with regards to the integration of sustainability risks within investment decision-making processes and investment advice. The approach taken by Deutsche Bank Luxembourg S.A. is further detailed below.

Deutsche Bank AG applies an overarching approach to the management of sustainability that is set out in a number of group level policies and procedures, which also apply to Deutsche Bank Luxembourg S.A. as member of Deutsche Bank Group. The group-wide Sustainability Policy delineates our main sustainability principles as well as the key requirements and responsibilities in connection with sustainability-related enquiries, non-financial sustainability reporting and ratings, environmental and social due diligence in the context of reputational risk management, and, together with relevant risk frameworks and broader commitments, provides relevant context regarding the Bank's view on sustainability topics.

Whilst Deutsche Bank AG does not currently apply an overarching formal policy regarding the integration of sustainability risks in the investment decision-making and advisory processes, Deutsche Bank AG still takes sustainability risks into account, as further described in following sections. In addition, business areas are working towards inclusion of the integration of sustainability risks within relevant policies and guidelines. These will be further enhanced on an ongoing basis as more sustainability related data becomes available over time.

Definition of sustainability risks

Sustainability risks ('ESG risks') are designated as incidents or conditions in the areas of the Environment, Social or Corporate Governance, whose occurrence could have actual or potential significantly negative effects on the value of the investment. These risks can occur both separately and cumulatively; they can affect individual companies or also entire sectors/branches or regions and can have very different characteristics.

The following examples can help to clarify sustainability risks:

As a result of the occurrence of extreme weather events as a consequence of climate change (known as physical risks), for example, production locations of individual companies or entire regions can be impaired or destroyed, leading to production stoppages, rising costs to restore the production locations and higher insurance costs. Furthermore, extreme weather events as a consequence of climate change, such as long periods of low water during droughts, can impair the transport of goods or even make it impossible.

There are also risks in connection with the changeover to a low-carbon economy (known as transition risks): for example, political measures can lead to fossil fuels becoming more expensive and/or scarcer (examples: fossil-fuel phase-out, CO2 tax) or to high investment costs as a result of requirements to renovate buildings and plant. New technologies can displace familiar technologies (e.g. electric mobility), and changes in customer preferences and expectations in society can endanger companies' business models if they do not react in time and take counter measures (by adjusting their business model, for example).

A substantial increase in physical risks would require a more abrupt changeover in the economy, which in turn would lead to higher transition risks.

Social risks arise from aspects such as non-compliance with labour law standards (for example, child labour and forced labour) and compliance with occupational health and safety regulations.

Examples of risks that arise within the scope of corporate management due to inadequate corporate governance and that can lead to high fines include non-compliance with taxpayer honesty and corruption.

Sustainability risks affect the following traditional risks of investments in securities in particular, and if they occur, could have a significantly negative effect on the yields of an investment in securities:

- Sector risk
- Price change risk
- Issuer/Credit risk
- Dividend risk
- Liquidity risk
- Currency risk

Method of including sustainability risks for Financial Markets Participants and Financial Advisors

In order to evaluate sustainability risks, Deutsche Bank AG uses information such as that from external service providers that have specialised in the qualitative evaluation of ESG factors.

Because sustainability risks can have different effects on individual companies, sectors, investment regions, currencies and investment classes (for example, equities or bonds), when recommending financial instruments in the Bank follows the approach of diversifying investments as broadly as possible in order to reduce the effects of the occurrence of sustainability risks on the client's portfolio. The Bank generally recommends distribution across a variety of investment classes in order to establish an individual client opportunity/risk profile. In addition, investment advice pursues a policy of a broad spread of investment classes in a variety of branches/sectors, investment regions and currencies.

In addition to diversification, for Financial Market Participants, sustainability risks are taken into account at various points in the investment process when making investment decisions within the framework of financial portfolio management. Sustainability risks are taken into account during the macro-economic consideration and development of market opinion, when allocating assets to individual investment strategies and when selecting individual financial instruments.

Source: Deutsche Bank (2024)

Having acquainted yourself with a practice example of the application of the SFDR, Activity 12.3 asks you to identify the 'adverse sustainability impacts statement' of Deutsche Bank Luxembourg so you can gain a deeper understanding of what this entails.

ACTIVITY 12.3

Visit the page for Sustainability Disclosures of Deutsche Bank Luxembourg S.A. (www.deutschewealth.com/en/articles/sustainability-related-disclosures/sustainability-related-disclosures-db-luxembourg.html) and locate their disclosures on adverse sustainability impacts statement. Discuss the content and clarity of this statement.

During May 2024, the European Commission facilitated a comprehensive assessment of the framework, looking at issues such as legal certainty, usability and how the Regulation can play its part in tackling greenwashing (EU, 2024b).

EU green bonds

The **European Green Bond Standard (EUGBS)** is a set of requirements for bonds that want to be labeled as 'European green bonds'. EU green bonds are financial instruments designed to fund projects with positive environmental benefits. These bonds are part of the broader green finance initiative aimed at supporting sustainable development by directing capital towards environmentally friendly projects. The voluntary green bond standard uses the EU Taxonomy's detailed criteria to define green economic activities, ensures transparency in line with market best practices, and sets up supervision for organizations conducting pre- and post-issuance reviews at the European level. The ESMA will oversee these external reviewers. Creating this standard was recommended in the final report of the Commission's High-Level Expert Group (HLEG) on sustainable finance (refer to EU, 2018b).

Funds raised through green bonds must be exclusively used for projects and activities that meet the **EU Taxonomy** criteria for environmental sustainability. Green bonds typically fund projects related to renewable energy, energy efficiency, clean transportation, sustainable water management and climate change adaptation, among others.

Issuers must publish a Green Bond Framework outlining the alignment with the EU Taxonomy, the use of the proceeds and the process for selecting projects. Post-issuance, issuers are required to publish annual allocation reports until the proceeds are fully allocated, detailing how the funds have been used and their environmental impact. In addition, issuers must provide impact reports at least once during the lifetime of the bond, describing the environmental benefits achieved.

EUGBS come with requirements for external review. An external reviewer must verify that the bond's framework aligns with the EU Taxonomy and EUGBS requirements before issuance. External reviewers also verify the allocation reports and impact reports to ensure ongoing compliance. The ESMA supervises these external reviewers to maintain high standards of integrity and consistency. Activity 12.4 looks at the work of the ESMA.

ACTIVITY 12.4

Visit the ESMA website (www.esma.europa.eu/esmas-activities/investors-and-issuers/external-reviewers-european-green-bonds). Read about external reviewers for EUGBS and discuss your findings.

EUGBS must contribute to at least one of the EU's six environmental objectives:

- climate change mitigation
- climate change adaptation
- sustainable use and protection of water and marine resources
- transition to a circular economy
- pollution prevention and control
- protection and restoration of biodiversity and ecosystems.

Figure 12.1 illustrates the implementation phases of the EUGBS and Table 12.3 looks at the interaction between the SFDR and other sustainable finance legislations.

Figure 12.1 ESMA timeline of EU Green Bond Regulation

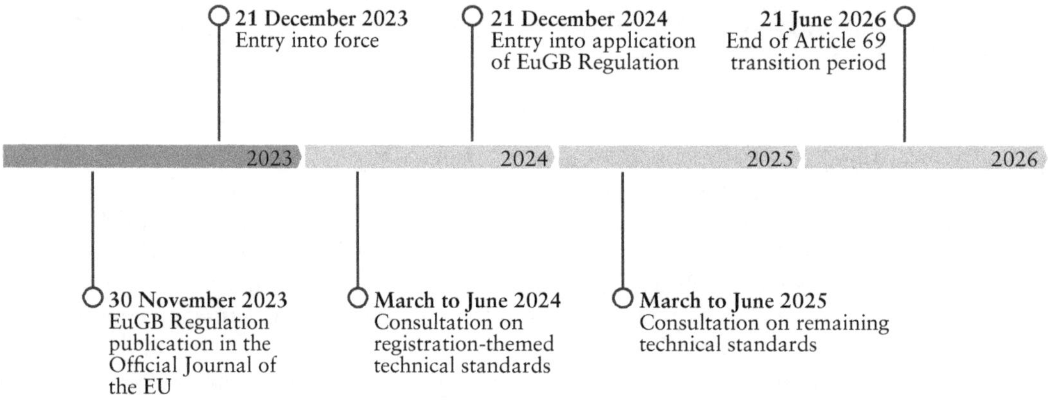

Source: Adapted from finance.ec.europa.eu/sustainable-finance/tools-and-standards/european-green-bond-standard-supporting-transition_en

Table 12.3 Interaction between the SFDR and other sustainable finance legislations

CSRD	The CSRD mandates that organizations provide more detailed and standardized sustainability information. This includes data on ESG factors that are crucial for assessing the sustainability performance of an organization. For organizations issuing green bonds, the enhanced disclosure requirements under the CSRD ensure that they provide comprehensive information about the environmental impact of the projects funded by these bonds. This transparency is critical for maintaining investor confidence and ensuring the credibility of green bonds.
EUGBS and the Taxonomy	The CSRD requires organizations to report on how their activities align with the EU Taxonomy, which is a classification system for environmentally sustainable economic activities. Green bonds issued by organizations will need to demonstrate alignment with the EU Taxonomy to ensure that the projects they finance contribute to the EU's environmental objectives. This alignment helps investors identify truly sustainable investments and supports the EU's green finance agenda.

The EU green bonds, SFDR, Taxonomy Regulation and the CSRD are linked through their shared goal of promoting transparency, accountability and sustainability in the corporate sector.

THE UNITED STATES

The Securities and Exchange Commission (SEC) is proposing to amend the rules and forms under the Investment Advisers Act of 1940 and the Investment Company Act of 1940 (SEC, 2022). These changes would require registered investment advisers, exempt advisers, registered investment organizations and business development organizations to provide more comprehensive information about their ESG investment practices.

The proposed amendments aim to enhance transparency and disclosure of ESG factors to clients and shareholders. By creating a consistent, comparable and decision-useful regulatory framework for ESG advisory services and investment companies, the SEC seeks to empower investors and safeguard their interests while fostering continued innovation in the asset management industry's evolving ESG landscape.

Activity 12.5 asks you to consider a quote from a response to the US SEC's Enhanced Disclosures by Certain Investment Advisers and Investment Companies about Environmental, Social and Governance Investment Practices, File Number S7-17-22.

ACTIVITY 12.5

The unprecedented growth in sustainable investing in the US, starting in 2019, including a dramatic expansion in the number and variety of sustainable investing products, and proliferation in the number of firms offering such products, has contributed to confusion and misunderstanding on the part of investors as well as other stakeholders regarding the various types of sustainable investing strategies and their financial and non-financial outcomes. [...] With some modifications, the proposed fund categories, definitions, and the enhanced layered disclosure approach proposed by the SEC will address some of these core concerns and create a more consistent, comparable, and decision-useful regulatory framework to inform and protect investors.

Consider this quote and discuss the importance of clarity and accessibility within ESG regulations, particularly when regulations are changed.

Source: Shilling (2023)

OTHER INTERNATIONAL INITIATIVES

This section introduces other initiatives that influence sustainability and sustainability reporting more broadly in the financial sector, namely the **Principles for Responsible Banking (PRB)** and the **Principles for Responsible Investment (PRI)**.

Principles for Responsible Banking (PRB)

The PRB were established to align the banking industry with the objectives of sustainable development and the Paris Agreement. Launched in September 2019 by the United Nations Environment Programme Finance Initiative (UNEP FI), these principles aim to ensure that banks take a leading role in fostering a sustainable future. UNEP FI uses PRB too while actively working alongside the banking community with the aim of facilitating global transition to the practice.

The history of the PRB can be traced back to 2018 when UNEP FI, in collaboration with 28 banks globally, began developing a comprehensive framework for responsible banking. This effort was driven by a recognition of the critical role that banks play in the global economy and their potential to influence sustainable development. After wide-spanning consultations and iterations, the PRB were formally introduced in 2019, with the endorsement of over 130 banks.

The PRB consist of six key principles designed to guide banks in integrating sustainability into their operations and strategies:

- **Alignment:** Banks commit to aligning their business strategies with the SDGs and the Paris Agreement. This principle underscores the importance of aligning banking practices with global sustainability targets to contribute to the achievement of these goals.
- **Impact and target setting:** Banks are required to continuously increase their positive impacts while reducing the negative impacts of their activities, products and services. They must set and publish targets to manage and mitigate significant impacts on people and the environment, focusing on areas where they can have the most substantial influence.
- **Clients and customers:** Banks commit to working responsibly with their clients and customers to encourage sustainable practices and enable economic activities that create shared prosperity for current and future generations. This principle emphasizes the role of banks in promoting sustainability through their client and customer relationships.
- **Stakeholders:** Banks pledge to proactively and responsibly consult, engage and partner with relevant stakeholders to achieve society's goals. This principle recognizes the importance of collaboration and stakeholder engagement in driving sustainable change.
- **Governance and culture:** Banks commit to implementing their commitment to these principles through effective governance and a culture of responsible banking. This includes embedding sustainability into governance structures, business strategies and decision-making processes.
- **Transparency and accountability:** Banks are required to periodically review their individual and collective implementation of these principles and be transparent about and accountable for their positive and negative impacts. They must publicly report on their progress and engage in continuous improvement.

Since the launch of the PRB, the initiative has garnered widespread support within the banking industry, with numerous banks worldwide committing to the principles. The framework has facilitated a shift towards more responsible banking practices, encouraging banks to take a proactive role in addressing global sustainability challenges. Table 12.4 illustrates how PRB is used in practice by a bank.

Table 12.4 BNP Paribas report in accordance with PRB

Reporting and Self-Assessment Requirements	High-level summary of bank's response	Reference(s)/Link(s) to bank's full response/ relevant information
Principle 1: Alignment **We will align our business strategy to be consistent with and contribute to individuals' needs and society's goals, as expressed in the Sustainable Development Goals, the Paris Climate Agreement and relevant national and regional frameworks.**		
1.1 *Describe* (high-level) your bank's business model, including the main customer served, types of products and services the main sectors and types of activities, where relevant the technologies financed across the main geographies in which your bank has operations or provides products and services.	BNP Paribas, Europe's leading provider of banking and segments financial services, has four domestic Retail Banking markets provided, in Europe, namely in France, Belgium, Italy and Luxembourg. and It operates in 65 countries and has nearly 190,000 employees, including more than 145,000 in Europe. BNP Paribas serves millions of clients around the world, from individual customers, to entrepreneurs and small businesses, corporates and civil society organisations. It offers them a wide array of financial solutions adapted to their needs: financing, payment, wealth and asset management, insurance. BNP Paribas is also a provider of real estate services and leasing solutions. The organization of BNP Paribas evolved in 2021, with three operational divisions: • Commercial, Personal Banking & Services (CPBS),comprised of: ○ Commercial banks of the Euro zone (BCEF, BNL, BCB, BCL), ○ Commercial banks outside the Euro zone (Mediterranean Europe, BancWest in the USA), ○ Specialized businesses (Arval, Leasing Solutions, Personal Finance, Personal Investors, Nickel, Floa, Lyf) • Investment and Protection Services (IPS)	See **'Presentation of operating divisions and business lines'** (*2021 URD*, p. 7 to 18) **'A diversified and integrated model, creating value'** (*2021 URD*, p. 650)

Source: BNP Paribas (2018, 2022)

Activity 12.6 allows you to explore the initiative called **Net-Zero Banking Alliance (NZBA)** in the context of PRB. Following this, Activity 12.7 demonstrates how UNEP FI incorporates PRB and other sustainability related frameworks.

ACTIVITY 12.6

Find out what the Net-Zero Banking Alliance (NZBA) is about and the scope of the PRB initiative. In doing so, identify how PRB relates to the Net-Zero Banking Alliance. Reflect upon the impact this kind of alliance might have and the role of the PRB in this context.

Source: UNEP (2019)

ACTIVITY 12.7

With the launch of the ESRS Interoperability Package, UNEP FI aims to leverage the similarities between PRB and CSRD.

Examine the UNEP FI ESRS Interoperability Package. Analyse if (or how) CSRD and the PRB can supplement each other.

Source: UNEP (2024)

Principles for Responsible Investment (PRI)

The PRI are an initiative launched in 2006 by the United Nations to encourage investors to adopt sustainable and responsible investment practices. The initiative is grounded in the understanding that ESG factors can significantly impact investment performance and that integrating these factors into investment decisions is essential for long-term value creation.

The PRI were developed through a collaboration between institutional investors, the UN Environment Programme Finance Initiative (UNEP FI) and the UN Global Compact. Over 20 institutional investors from 12 countries, representing approximately $2 trillion in assets under management, were involved in the drafting of the Principles.

The PRI consists of six voluntary and aspirational principles:

- **Incorporation of ESG issues:** Investors commit to incorporating ESG issues into their investment analysis and decision-making processes. This principle emphasizes the importance of integrating ESG factors to better manage risks and uncover opportunities that may not be apparent through traditional financial analysis alone.
- **Active ownership:** Signatories pledge to be active owners and incorporate ESG issues into their ownership policies and practices. This involves engaging with companies to improve their ESG performance, voting on shareholder resolutions and advocating for better ESG practices.
- **Disclosure and transparency:** Investors commit to seeking appropriate disclosure on ESG issues by the entities in which they invest. This principle supports the need for enhanced transparency from companies regarding their ESG practices and performance, enabling investors to make more informed decisions.
- **Promotion of PRI in the investment industry:** Signatories commit to promoting acceptance and implementation of the principles within the investment industry. This includes encouraging other investors to adopt the PRI, sharing best practices and collaborating to advance responsible investment.
- **Collaboration to enhance effectiveness:** Investors agree to work together to enhance their effectiveness in implementing the principles. This principle recognizes the value of collective action and collaboration in addressing ESG challenges and driving systemic change in the investment industry.
- **Reporting on activities and progress:** Signatories commit to reporting on their activities and progress towards implementing the principles. This accountability mechanism ensures that investors are transparent about their responsible investment practices and progress, fostering trust and continuous improvement.

Since its launch the PRI has grown significantly, with thousands of signatories representing tens of trillions of dollars in assets under management. The initiative has played a role in mainstreaming responsible investment, providing a framework for investors to integrate ESG considerations into their investment processes and promoting a more sustainable global financial system.

Key differences between PRB and PRI

As illustrated, the financial sector utilizes various reporting frameworks to guide sustainability efforts, with prominent examples being the PRI and the PRB. While both frameworks aim to integrate sustainability into financial practices, they differ significantly in focus, scope and implementation.

PRI primarily target investors, including asset owners and investment managers. The framework emphasizes responsible investment practices to promote a sustainable global financial system, encouraging signatories to integrate ESG issues into investment analysis and ownership practices.

In terms of implementation, PRI signatories commit to six principles guiding them in embedding ESG factors into their investment practices. These principles include incorporating ESG issues into investment analysis, being active owners, seeking appropriate disclosure on ESG issues from entities in which they invest, and promoting the acceptance and implementation of the principles within the investment industry. Reporting under PRI involves an annual assessment where signatories disclose their responsible investment activities and progress, fostering transparency and accountability while encouraging continuous improvement.

The audience for PRI primarily consists of institutional investors, asset managers and other financial market participants. Its impact is largely on investment strategies and portfolio management, influencing how capital is allocated and managed with a focus on long-term sustainability.

On the other hand, the PRB are designed specifically for banks and financial institutions involved in lending, deposit-taking and other banking activities. The focus of PRB is on aligning banking practices with SDGs and the Paris Agreement, ensuring that banks' business strategies and operations contribute to sustainable development. The framework emphasizes the role of banks in financing the transition to a sustainable economy.

Signatories to the PRB commit to six principles that require them to align their business strategy with society's goals as expressed in the SDGs and other relevant frameworks. These principles include aligning strategy to be consistent with and contribute to society's goals, continuously increasing their positive impact while reducing negative impacts, and working responsibly with clients and customers. Banks must conduct an impact analysis to identify the most significant impacts resulting from their activities, set targets in areas where they have the most significant impact and publicly report on their progress. This process ensures that banks are transparent about their contributions to sustainable development.

The audience for PRB includes banks, regulators, customers and society at large. The PRB impact extends to the core banking operations, influencing how banks finance projects, engage with clients and develop products and services that support sustainable development.

In summary, the key differences between these frameworks lie in their target audiences and areas of influence. The PRI focus on investors and impact investment decisions and portfolio management, while the PRB target banks and influence core banking operations, including lending and product development. Both frameworks have principles guiding sustainability efforts, but PRI emphasize responsible investment, whereas PRB emphasize alignment with societal goals and sustainable development. Furthermore, PRI require the annual disclosure of responsible investment activities, while PRB require impact analysis, target setting and public reporting on progress towards SDGs. These differences reflect the unique roles and responsibilities of investors and banks in promoting sustainability within the financial sector.

CONCLUSION

The integration of sustainable finance principles into the financial sector is gaining momentum, driven by regulatory frameworks such as the SFDR in the EU, enhanced disclosure practices in the US, and the adoption of voluntary frameworks such as the PRI and PRB globally. The SFDR mandates transparency and accountability for financial market participants, ensuring that sustainability risks are adequately disclosed and managed. In the US, evolving disclosure standards are increasing investor access to ESG information. Meanwhile, the PRB provide a voluntary framework for banks to align their strategies with global sustainability goals, fostering responsible investment and operational practices. Together, these initiatives can reshape the financial landscape, promoting greater transparency, accountability and alignment with sustainable development objectives. Research must continue to study how the collective impact of these regulatory and voluntary measures underscores the financial sector's pivotal role in driving the transition to a more sustainable and resilient global economy.

SUMMARY

The following items relate to the learning objectives listed at the beginning of the chapter.

- **LO 1. Discuss the international regulatory landscape for sustainability reporting in the financial sector.**

  Sustainable finance integrates ESG factors into financial decision-making, encouraging long-term investments in sustainable projects and activities. In addition to the CSRD, ESRS and the Taxonomy Regulation, the EU introduced the SFDR, focusing on the disclosure requirements for financial market participants and advisors to mitigate greenwashing risks. Globally, other initiatives also aim to advance sustainable finance practices. Notably, the PRB, launched by the UNEP FI, guide banks in aligning their strategies with the SDGs and the Paris Agreement.

- **LO 2. Understand disclosure requirements in the EU Sustainable Finance Disclosure Regulation (SFDR).**

  The SFDR started applying in March 2021 and requires financial market participants and financial advisers to disclose at entity and product level how they integrate sustainability risks and principal adverse impacts in their investment decision-making processes. It also introduces additional product disclosures for financial products making sustainability claims. This means that the SFDR mandates different levels of disclosure: at the entity level, firms must report on their policies regarding adverse sustainability impacts, while at the product level, they must classify financial products according to their sustainability characteristics (Article 6, 8 or 9). This classification reflects the degree to which products integrate ESG factors or pursue specific sustainable objectives. By standardizing these disclosures, the SFDR aims to provide investors with consistent, comparable information, supporting informed decision-making and fostering accountability in sustainable finance practices across the EU.

- **LO 3. Describe what the Principles for Responsible Banking are.**

  These were established to align the banking industry with the objectives of sustainable development and the Paris Agreement. Launched in September 2019 by the UNEP FI, these principles aim to ensure that banks take a leading role in fostering a sustainable future.

- **LO 4. Describe what an EU green bond is.**

  EU green bonds (EUGB) are financial instruments designed to fund projects that deliver environmental benefits, supporting sustainable development by channelling capital into eco-friendly initiatives. Part of the EU's green finance agenda, this voluntary green bond standard utilizes the EU Taxonomy's detailed criteria to define environmentally sustainable economic activities, ensuring transparency aligned with market best practices. It also establishes oversight mechanisms, with the ESMA supervising external reviewers responsible for pre- and post-issuance evaluations. This standard was recommended in the final report from the European Commission's High-Level Expert Group (HLEG) on sustainable finance.

- **LO 5. Contrast key differences between reporting frameworks and sustainability efforts in the financial sector.**

  Key differences between sustainability frameworks aimed at the financial sector lie in their target audiences and areas of influence. The PRI focus on investors and impacts investment decisions and portfolio management, while the PRB target banks and influences core banking operations, including lending and product development. Both frameworks have principles guiding sustainability efforts, but the PRI emphasize responsible investment, whereas the PRB emphasize alignment with societal goals and sustainable development.

EXERCISES

1 What are the implications of the EU's SFDR and CSRD for sustainable finance regulations and practices in other jurisdictions? Can these regulations serve as a model for global sustainable finance initiatives? (LO 1 and LO 2)

2 Discuss to what extent the SFDR and CSRD effectively address the challenges of greenwashing and promote genuine sustainable investments. What are the potential unintended consequences of these regulations? (LO 2)

3 Analyse real-world examples of SFDR and CSRD disclosures by different FMPs. Compare and contrast their approaches, identify best practices and highlight areas for improvement. (LO 2)

4 How does the EU's SFDR approach to categorizing sustainable investment products and mandating specific disclosures compare to the proposed amendments by the US Securities and Exchange Commission (SEC) in terms of their potential effectiveness in promoting transparency, preventing greenwashing and empowering investors in the ESG landscape? (LO 2 and 5)

5 Discuss the future role in terms of advantages and disadvantages of voluntary frameworks such as the Principles for Responsible Banking. (LO 3 and 5)

6 Discuss the role of EU green bonds for the financial market in Europe. (LO 4)

CHAPTER 13

Assurance and audit of sustainability reporting

Learning objectives

After studying this chapter, you should be able to:

- LO 1. Outline and discuss contemporary developments relating to audit and assurance of sustainability reporting.
- LO 2. Understand the difference between limited and reasonable assurance.
- LO 3. Explain which standards can be used for assurance of sustainability reporting.
- LO 4. Discuss challenges in regard to conducting assurance and/or audit of CSRD and ESRS compliant reports.

A global standard...

Though sustainability reporting and assurance practices are becoming increasingly mandatory, for example in the EU, the **International Federation of Accountants (IFAC)** states that 'a global best practice has yet to emerge' (IFAC, 2024a).

Reviews like those carried out by IFAC provide detail on how many companies obtain assurance and what they obtain assurance in. For example, in 2024 IFAC observed that 60% of companies obtaining assurance over their greenhouse gas (GHG) emissions did so over all three of the scopes incorporated therein. These reports solidify IFAC's belief that 'the goal of sustainability disclosure must be information [...] that is on par with financial reports'.

The future of sustainability disclosure will rely on accountants. An accountant's understanding of the sustainability standards will help to standardize reporting across all companies and will furthermore facilitate the ongoing transition from voluntary to mandatory requirements for reporting and assurance.

Source: IFAC (2024b)

INTRODUCTION

This chapter focuses on the key aspects of assurance and audit under the CSRD, exploring its implications for organizations, auditors and stakeholders. All organizations within the scope of CSRD are required to seek limited assurance over their compliance of the sustainability reporting with ESRS disclosure standards, the process carried out by the undertakings to identify the information reported pursuant to the sustainability disclosure standards and whether the organizations are in compliance with the requirement to electronically tag the sustainability reporting. This chapter is focused on providing insights into the requirements of the CSRD and contrasts it with the US Climate Disclosure Act. In addition, the chapter touches upon the recent development of International Standard on Sustainability Assurance (ISSA) 5000. ISSA 5000 marks an advancement in building global credibility and trust in sustainability reporting, as it offers essential consistency for accountants and assurance professionals as they work within the complex landscape of sustainability disclosures.

THE EVOLUTION OF SUSTAINABILITY REPORTING ASSURANCE

Voluntary and unregulated practices of sustainability reporting have over the last decades raised concerns about the reliability and credibility of the information provided (Boiral & Heras-Saizarbitoria, 2020). In response, external independent verifications have grown considerably since the 2010s (KPMG, 2020). The discussions surrounding the assurance of sustainability reporting in policy arenas, coupled with the growing market for assurance services, have heightened interest and calls for further research in this field since that time (Sonnerfeldt and Pontoppidan, 2020). Previous research (Farooq & De Villiers, 2017) categorizes existing sustainability assurance literature into five broad areas. These areas are research focused on the characteristics of the sustainability assurance field, country and organizational factors driving the demand for sustainability assurance, the role of accountants in assurance markets, compliance with standards, and the impact of these factors on enhancing the credibility of sustainability reports. The CSRD brings change to this field by requiring limited external assurance over reported sustainability information prepared in accordance with ESRS. With the move to mandatory limited assurance multiple new questions arise with regard to auditors' efforts to expand their work into this field. It highlights the need for further research that extends our understanding of applying concepts from the financial audit arena into these new audit sustainability reporting spaces (Canning *et al.*, 2019).

THE CSRD AND ASSURANCE REQUIREMENTS

The CSRD introduces a mandatory limited assurance requirement for sustainability reporting, marking a significant shift from the previous voluntary approach. This means that an independent auditor must review the sustainability information and provide a conclusion on whether it is materially misstated. Example 13.1 looks at the differences between limited and reasonable assurance.

Example 13.1

The difference between limited and reasonable assurance

Limited assurance provides moderate confidence with less rigorous procedures, is less costly and time-consuming, and results in a negative form of expression (e.g. 'nothing has come to our attention…'). More specifically, limited assurance is an engagement in which the practitioner aims to gather sufficient appropriate evidence to provide a moderate level of assurance. This assurance is expressed in the form of a negative assurance conclusion whereby the practitioner states that based on the procedures performed, nothing has come to their attention that causes them to believe that the subject matter is materially misstated. The procedures performed in a limited assurance engagement are less extensive than those conducted in a reasonable assurance engagement and typically involve inquiries, analytical procedures and limited testing of the subject matter. Consequently, the level of confidence provided to the intended users of the report is moderate, reflecting the limited nature of the procedures undertaken.

Reasonable assurance provides high confidence with more extensive procedures, is more costly and time-consuming, and results in a positive form of expression (e.g. 'in our opinion…'). Reasonable assurance is thus an engagement in which the practitioner seeks to obtain sufficient appropriate evidence to provide a high level of assurance. This assurance is expressed in the form of a positive assurance conclusion whereby the practitioner asserts that in their opinion, the subject matter is, in all material respects, fairly presented in accordance with the applicable criteria. The procedures conducted in a reasonable assurance engagement are extensive and comprehensive, involving detailed testing, verification of evidence and in-depth analysis of the subject matter. The objective is to achieve a high level of confidence for the intended users of the report, ensuring that the information is free from material misstatement. This higher level of assurance necessitates a greater commitment of time and resources compared to a limited assurance engagement.

Under the CSRD, all organizations within its scope are required to obtain limited assurance over several key aspects: the compliance of their sustainability reporting with EU sustainability reporting standards, the process undertaken to identify the information reported according to these standards, and the adherence to the requirement for electronically tagging sustainability reporting in the specified electronic format (EU, 2019).

Limited assurance is mandatory for all implementation phases of the CSRD, which means organizations must obtain this assurance in their first year of reporting. Additionally, the assurance provider must assess whether the organization's reporting complies with Article 8 of the EU Taxonomy Regulation.

The European Commission will conduct an assessment to determine the feasibility of transitioning from limited to reasonable assurance for both auditors and organizations. Following this assessment, the Commission will adopt assurance standards for limited assurance by 1 October 2026, and for reasonable assurance by 1 October 2028. Under the CSRD, the company's statutory auditor may provide this assurance. The assurance provider will issue a report containing a conclusion on whether the company has disclosed its sustainability information in accordance with the specified criteria.

The CSRD aligns with the **International Standard on Assurance Engagements (ISAE) 3000** (Revised), discussed next, which sets out the principles and procedures for assurance engagements on non-financial information. This harmonization aims to ensure the quality and credibility of sustainability reporting across the EU.

STANDARDS AND FRAMEWORKS FOR ASSURANCE

Several standards and frameworks guide the assurance of sustainability reporting. ISAE 3000 (Revised) offers a widely accepted framework for assurance engagements beyond audits or reviews of historical financial information. It applies to a wide range of non-financial disclosures, including sustainability reports, and outlines principles and procedures to ensure consistency and reliability in the assurance process. ISAE 3000 (Revised) is designed to accommodate supplemental standards, such as **ISAE 3410** ***Assurance Engagements on Greenhouse Gas Statements***.

In addition, the **AccountAbility AA1000 Assurance Standard (AA1000AS)** emphasizes inclusivity, materiality and responsiveness in sustainability reporting. It focuses on stakeholder engagement and the significance of reported information, aligning closely with the principles underpinning the CSRD. Together, these standards provide a foundation for assurance of sustainability reports.

ISSA 5000 *General Requirements for Sustainability Assurance Engagements*

The International Auditing and Assurance Standards Board (IAASB) has approved a new standard titled **International Standard of Sustainability Assurance (ISSA) 5000** ***General Requirements for Sustainability Assurance Engagements***. This standard aims to enhance the trust and confidence investors, regulators and other stakeholders have in sustainability information by providing comprehensive guidelines on conducting assurance engagements. ISSA 5000 is designed as a standalone standard applicable to any sustainability assurance engagements and can be applied to sustainability information across various topics and frameworks, such as IFRS S1, IFRS S2 and GRI.

Example 13.2 looks at the key role played by external assurance.

Example 13.2

External assurance plays a key role in enhancing trust and confidence in financial and non-financial reporting

To engage investors, regulators and other stakeholders, the IAASB has developed a global sustainability assurance standard. In doing so, it hopes to increase the trust and confidence stakeholders have in sustainability reporting.

> *The proposed International Standard on Sustainability Assurance (ISSA) 5000, General Requirements for Sustainability Assurance Engagements, will serve as a comprehensive, standalone standard suitable for any sustainability assurance engagements. It will apply to sustainability information reported across any sustainability topic and prepared under multiple frameworks, including the recently released IFRS Sustainability Disclosure Standards S1 and S2. The proposed standard is profession agnostic, supporting its use by both professional accountant and non-accountant assurance practitioners.*

Source: IAASB (2024)

The primary goal of ISSA 5000 is to ensure that disclosed sustainability information is accurate and trustworthy. Assurance practitioners will design and perform procedures to obtain evidence that the sustainability information is free from material misstatement. Their objective is to verify the reliability of sustainability information, thereby helping stakeholders understand an entity's ESG impacts. ISSA 5000 covers a wide range of sustainability topics, including climate, biodiversity, human rights and labour practices, addressing aspects such as risks and opportunities, governance, metrics and key performance indicators.

The standard aims to:

- Respond to the public interest need for a timely standard that supports the consistent performance of quality sustainability assurance engagements.
- Be suitable across all sustainability topics, the information disclosed about those topics, and the various reporting frameworks.
- Be implementable by all assurance practitioners.

Key priority areas considered during the development of ISSA 5000 include:

- Differentiating the work effort between limited and reasonable assurance, including the sufficiency of evidence.
- Ensuring the suitability of the reporting criteria, including concepts such as double materiality.
- Defining the scope of the assurance engagement.
- Addressing the reliability of information and what constitutes sufficient appropriate evidence.
- Evaluating the entity's system of internal control and its impact on obtaining sufficient appropriate evidence.
- Considering materiality in the context of the assurance engagement, including narrative and qualitative information.

ISSA 5000 will be adopted and implemented at the jurisdictional level, meaning each jurisdiction and regulatory body will decide whether sustainability reporting and assurance are mandatory and, if so, for which entities. Countries like the UK, Australia and Singapore have announced plans to require listed companies and large private companies to report climate-related disclosures. The UK has been a strong supporter of the ISSB since its launch and has recommended the UK endorsement of IFRS S1 and IFRS S2 in December 2024. The creation of the first two UK Sustainability Reporting Standards (SRS), which will be based on IFRS S1 and IFRS S2, is under way. These standards will form part of a wider Sustainability Disclosure Reporting framework led by HM Treasury.

While ISAE 3000 (Revised) will continue to be used for assurance engagements other than audits or reviews of historical financial information, ISSA 5000 was finally approved in October 2024.

THE ROLE OF AUDITORS AND ASSURANCE PROVIDERS

The role of auditors and assurance providers in the context of the CSRD is multifaceted. These professionals are responsible for conducting thorough evaluations of sustainability reports, verifying the accuracy of disclosed information and assessing the adequacy of the reporting processes. Their expertise in both financial and non-financial reporting standards enables them to provide a balanced and informed perspective on an organization's sustainability performance (refer to Chapter 16 for a discussion on the future competency requirements of auditors).

Furthermore, auditors and assurance providers play a critical role in identifying areas for improvement in sustainability reporting. Through their evaluations, they can highlight deficiencies in data collection, reporting processes and adherence to standards, providing valuable insights for companies seeking to enhance their sustainability practices.

CHALLENGES FOR ORGANIZATIONS

The CSRD's assurance requirement places a greater onus on companies to ensure the accuracy and reliability of their sustainability data. This necessitates robust internal controls, data management systems and expertise in sustainability reporting. Organizations must also prepare for increased scrutiny from auditors and stakeholders, as the assurance process enhances the credibility of their sustainability claims.

SEC US CLIMATE DISCLOSURE ACT

All SEC registrants must now include a narrative discussion of their identification, management and oversight of climate-related risks. The final rule updates regulation S-K to require organizations to report on the material impacts of climate-related financial risks, their strategies to address those risks and their governance structures, all in alignment with the recommendations of the TCFD.

Under the rule, Large Accelerated Filers (LAFs) and Accelerated Filers (AFs) must share their Scope 1 and 2 emissions, when those emissions are deemed material. The SEC draws from the **Greenhouse Gas Protocol** (GHGP) categories of emissions. The SEC Climate Rule is grounded in the concept of financial materiality.

The SEC US Climate Disclosure Act requires LAFs and AFs (excluding SRCs and EGCs) to submit attestation reports for their Scope 1 and 2 emissions data. Starting three years after they begin disclosing, both groups will have to submit attestation reports based on limited assurance. In 2033, LAFs will have to upgrade to more rigorous reasonable assurance.

The rule stipulates that assurance can be performed by providers as long as they are 'expert' and 'independent', which means that the service will not be limited to auditing firms. Providers will have to apply standards that are publicly available at no cost or widely accepted and subject to public comment. Activity 13.1 explores the SEC US Climate Disclosure Act to find out about the assurance and/or **audit requirements** that will be required for companies that have to adhere to the Act.

ACTIVITY 13.1

Discuss the assurance or audit requirements for organizations that have to adhere to SEC US Climate Disclosure Act.

CONCLUSION

The assurance and audit of sustainability reporting are critical components of the CSRD, enhancing the credibility and reliability of disclosed information. By mandating independent assurance, the CSRD addresses longstanding challenges in sustainability reporting, promoting greater transparency and stakeholder trust. While the implementation of these requirements presents certain challenges, it also offers significant opportunities for companies to improve their sustainability practices and gain competitive advantages. As the landscape of sustainability reporting continues to evolve, robust assurance and audit processes will play an increasingly important role in driving corporate accountability and sustainable development.

The CSRD mandates disclosure and assurance on a significantly broader range of ESG topics compared to the SEC's proposed rule on climate-related disclosures. While the CSRD encompasses non-climate-related environmental issues and various social topics, the SEC's proposed rule focuses solely on climate impacts and risks. Additionally, the CSRD requires assurance over all sustainability information, whereas the SEC's proposed rule mandates assurance only for Scope 1 and 2 GHG emissions.

Refer to Appendix 13.1 for an example of an independent limited assurance report on selected ESG data in the sustainability statements.

SUMMARY

The following items relate to the learning objectives listed at the beginning of the chapter.

- **LO 1. Outline and discuss contemporary developments relating to audit and assurance of sustainability reporting.**

  As the adoption of IFRS Sustainability Disclosure Standards progresses and mandatory reporting and assurance begin in the EU, corporate governance within reporting entities must become a priority. A global best practice has yet to emerge.

  While the number of organizations obtaining assurance still lags behind those reporting, a 2022 study saw a 5% increase, with 69% of reviewed organizations securing assurance for at least some of their ESG disclosures. The scope of assurance engagements has also broadened, with 59% of companies obtaining assurance for disclosures in GHG emissions, other environmental categories, social and governance areas. A more detailed review of GHG emissions found that 60% of organizations obtaining assurance over their emissions did so for all three scopes: Scope 1, Scope 2 and Scope 3.

- **LO 2. Understand the difference between limited and reasonable assurance.**

  Limited assurance provides moderate confidence through less rigorous procedures, making it less costly and time-consuming. It results in a negative expression (e.g. 'nothing has come to our attention'). In a limited assurance engagement, the practitioner seeks to obtain enough evidence to offer a moderate level of assurance. In contrast, reasonable assurance offers high confidence through more extensive procedures, resulting in a positive expression (e.g. 'in our opinion'). In this type of engagement, the practitioner gathers sufficient evidence to provide a high level of assurance, concluding with a positive statement that in their opinion, the subject matter is fairly presented in all material respects according to the applicable criteria.

- **LO 3. Explain which standards can be used for assurance of sustainability reporting.**

  Multiple standards and frameworks support the assurance of sustainability reporting. ISSA 5000 is the first comprehensive international standard dedicated to sustainability assurance. It builds on the IAASB's existing standards, particularly the International Standard on Assurance Engagements 3000 (Revised), and is designed to be adaptable to the diverse range of sustainability information organizations report – from climate-related risks and emissions data to social and governance metrics.

  Another standard, the AccountAbility AA1000 Assurance Standard (AA1000AS), emphasizes the principles of inclusivity, materiality and responsiveness in sustainability reporting. Recently, the IAASB introduced a proposed standard called the International Standard of Sustainability Assurance (ISSA) 5000 *General Requirements for Sustainability Assurance Engagements*.

- **LO 4. Discuss challenges in regard to conducting assurance and/or audit of CSRD and ESRS compliant reports.**

  The CSRD's assurance requirement places a greater onus on companies to ensure the accuracy and reliability of their sustainability data. This necessitates robust internal controls, data management systems and expertise in sustainability reporting. Organizations must also prepare for increased scrutiny from auditors and stakeholders, as the assurance process enhances the credibility of their sustainability claims.

EXERCISES

1. Why has the CSRD opted for limited assurance initially, with the possibility of moving to reasonable assurance in the future? Discuss the potential rationale behind this phased approach, considering factors like data availability, reporting maturity and stakeholder expectations. (LO 1)
2. What are the implications for global harmonization of sustainability reporting from the diverging requirements in regard to assurance on sustainability data between the EU and the US? (LO 1)
3. What is limited assurance, and how does it differ from reasonable assurance in the context of sustainability reporting? (LO 2)

4 Imagine you are providing assurance for a large multinational organization that publishes extensive sustainability reports, including data on greenhouse gas emissions, water usage and community engagement. Based on the characteristics of each standard, recommend which standards you would apply for different sections of the report and explain why. (LO 3)

5 What are the implications for companies preparing sustainability reports under the CSRD? Discuss the need for robust internal controls, data management systems and expertise in sustainability reporting. (LO 4)

6 Is limited assurance sufficient to meet the needs of stakeholders in terms of reliable and trustworthy sustainability information? Discuss the arguments for and against, considering the trade-offs between assurance level and cost. (LO 4)

7 What are the potential unintended consequences of mandating limited assurance on sustainability reporting? Discuss issues like greenwashing, increased compliance burden for companies and the risk of audits becoming a mere 'box-ticking' exercise. (LO 4)

Appendix 13.1 – Ørsted AR (2023)

Independent limited assurance report on selected ESG data in the Sustainability statements

To the stakeholders of Ørsted A/S

Ørsted A/S engaged us to provide limited assurance on selected ESG data as described below for the period 1 January – 31 December 2023 as stated on pages 81–130 and 141 in tables marked with a 'blue eye icon' ( ) (the 'Selected ESG Data').

Our conclusion
Based on the procedures we performed and the evidence we obtained, nothing came to our attention that causes us not to believe that the Selected ESG Data in tables marked with a 'blue eye icon' ( ) for the period 1 January – 31 December 2023 for Ørsted A/S are prepared, in all material respects, in accordance with the applied accounting policies developed by Ørsted A/S as stated on pages 81–130 and 141 (the 'Accounting policies').

This conclusion is to be read in the context of what we state in the remainder of our report.

What we are assuring
The scope of our work was limited to assurance over the Selected ESG Data as defined in the first paragraph of our report.

Regarding reporting on article 8 of Regulation (EU) 2020/852 (EU Taxonomy Regulation) on pages 81–85 we only provide limited assurance on whether the included data have been stated in accordance with the EU Taxonomy related accounting policies as stated on pages 81 and 85, and not whether the data are in compliance with the EU regulation.

We express limited assurance in our conclusion.

Professional standards applied and level of assurance
We performed a limited assurance engagement in accordance with International Standard on Assurance Engagements 3000 (Revised) 'Assurance Engagements other than Audits and Reviews of Historical Financial Information' and, in respect of the greenhouse gas emissions, in accordance with International Standard on Assurance Engagements 3410 'Assurance engagements on greenhouse gas statements'. The quantification of greenhouse gas emissions is subject to inherent uncertainty because of incomplete scientific knowledge used to determine the emissions factors and the values needed to combine emissions of different gasses.

A limited assurance engagement is substantially less in scope than a reasonable assurance engagement in relation to both the risk assessment procedures, including an understanding of internal control, and the procedures performed in response to the assessed risks; consequently, the level of assurance obtained in a limited assurance engagement is substantially lower than the assurance that would have been obtained had a reasonable assurance engagement been performed.

Our independence and quality control
We have complied with the independence requirements and other ethical requirements in the International Ethics Standards Board for Accountants' International Code of Ethics for Professional Accountants (IESBA Code), which is founded on fundamental principles of integrity, objectivity, professional competence and due care, confidentiality and professional behavior, and ethical requirements applicable in Denmark.

PricewaterhouseCoopers applies International Standard on Quality Management 1, ISQM 1, which requires the firm to design, implement and operate a system of quality management including policies or procedures regarding compliance with ethical requirements, professional standards, and applicable legal and regulatory requirements.

Our work was carried out by an independent multidisciplinary team with experience in sustainability reporting and assurance.

Understanding reporting and measurement methodologies
The Selected ESG Data needs to be read and understood together with the accounting policies. The accounting policies used for the preparation of the Selected ESG Data are the applied accounting policies developed by Ørsted A/S which Management is solely responsible for selecting and applying.

The absence of a significant body of established practice on which to draw to evaluate and measure ESG data allows for different, but acceptable, measurement techniques and can affect comparability between entities and over time.

Work performed
We are required to plan and perform our work in order to consider the risk of material misstatement of the Selected ESG Data. In doing so and based on our professional judgement, we:

- evaluated the appropriateness of the accounting policies used, their consistent application and related disclosures
- made inquiries and conducted interviews with Group functions with responsibility for management and reporting of the Selected ESG Data to assess reporting and consolidation processes, use of company-wide systems, and controls performed
- checked the Selected ESG Data on a sample basis to underlying documentation and evaluated the appropriateness of quantification methods and compliance with the accounting policies for preparing the Selected ESG Data
- performed analytical review and trend explanation of the Selected ESG Data
- considered the disclosure and presentation of the Selected ESG Data
- evaluated the obtained evidence.

Management's responsibilities
Management of Ørsted A/S is responsible for:

- designing, implementing, and maintaining internal control over information relevant to the preparation of Selected ESG Data that are free from material misstatement, whether due to fraud or error
- establishing objective accounting policies for preparing the Selected ESG Data
- measuring and reporting the information in the Selected ESG Data based on the accounting policies
- the content of the Selected ESG Data.

Our responsibility
We are responsible for:

- planning and performing the engagement to obtain limited assurance about whether the Selected ESG Data for the period 1 January – 31 December 2023 are prepared, in all material respects, in accordance with the accounting policies
- forming an independent conclusion, based on the procedures performed and the evidence obtained
- reporting our conclusion to the stakeholders of Ørsted A/S.

Hellerup, 7 February 2024

PricewaterhouseCoopers
Statsautoriseret Revisionspartnerselskab
CVR no. 3377 1231

Anders Stig Lauritsen
State Authorised Public Accountant
mne32800

Thomas Wraae Holm
State Authorised Public Accountant
mne30141

CHAPTER 14

Digital tagging, data and data solutions for sustainability reporting

Learning objectives

After studying this chapter you should be able to:

- LO 1. Outline and discuss contemporary developments relating to digital technologies and sustainability reporting.
- LO 2. Understand the digital tagging requirements of the CSRD.
- LO 3. Discuss challenges and opportunities in regard to data handling for CSRD and ESRS compliance.

Implementing sustainability reporting: Technology as an enabler

The available technology options will depend on the size and complexity of the organization and its activities, as will the extent to which they can aid the organization in its data collection efforts to facilitate sustainability reporting. An organization may start by capturing data for sustainability reporting with the technology that is readily available, such as spreadsheet-based templates hosted on web-based collaborative platforms (e.g. Microsoft Excel spreadsheets hosted on SharePoint, or Microsoft Forms), and subsequently move to applications with enhanced data analytics capabilities to support homogeneity. On the scalability and flexibility of a technology, consider whether the system and its vendor(s) will grow in tandem with the organization.

Set a clear strategy for using technology to facilitate sustainability reporting

There should be a clear purpose for using technology, taking into account the following points when selecting the technologies for an organization's reporting platform:

- the reporting objectives and the organization's needs that the technology is intended to address
- the data that will be collected, processed and reported on
- the scalability and flexibility of the technology to meet the organization's future needs
- integration with existing systems (e.g. financial reporting, payroll, enterprise resource planning (ERP)) or other technology with which it needs to work in unison, akin to the concept of digital core.

Before deciding on a technology, it is important to understand the reporting framework or standards applied and the data that will eventually be reported on. The technology should have the flexibility to adapt to changes as the reporting frameworks or standards evolve. Having a clear view of the following criteria will help in selecting the right technology:

- the types of data that need to be collected, for example structured or unstructured data
- the right level of granularity to meet both internal and external reporting needs
- where the data is sourced
- who will collect and input the data from within the organization, across the consolidated group and along the value chain
- the internal controls over the data vs how the data can be assured
- the gaps in the organization's data collection and processing infrastructure.

Source: ACCA (2023a)

INTRODUCTION

The CSRD and ESRS represent a significant evolution in the landscape of corporate sustainability reporting within the EU. Central to these regulatory initiatives is the integration of data and digital tagging, which facilitates dissemination of sustainability information.

Digital tagging, particularly through the use of the **European Single Electronic Format (ESEF)** and **Inline XBRL (iXBRL)**, is a key component of the CSRD. This approach not only standardizes the presentation of sustainability data but also ensures its interoperability and machine-readability, thereby enhancing accessibility and utility. The shift towards digital tagging underscores the growing recognition of the importance of robust data management practices in achieving compliance with sustainability reporting requirements (refer to ESMA, 2024).

The journey towards effective CSRD and ESRS compliance presents challenges and opportunities. Organizations must navigate the complexities of data collection, integration and validation while ensuring the accuracy and security of their sustainability information. At the same time, digital transformation presents opportunities to harness advanced technologies, such as artificial intelligence and blockchain, to streamline reporting processes and drive sustainability performance.

This chapter aims to equip readers with an introduction to the **CSRD digital tagging requirements** and explore the challenges and opportunities associated with data handling for CSRD and ESRS compliance.

DIGITAL TRANSFORMATIONS

Research has identified key concepts in digital transformation that include: digitization, digitalization and digital transformation (Verhoef *et al.*, 2021). Digitization refers to converting analogue data into digital format. Digitalization involves implementing digital technologies to manage business processes. Digital transformation, the final concept, encompasses both digitization and digitalization to achieve overarching strategic goals. These processes necessitate that organizations develop digital agility, that is the ability to adapt swiftly to technological changes (Lee *et al.*, 2015). As an organization advances in its digital transformation journey, digital agility becomes increasingly vital (Verhoef *et al.*, 2021).

Research suggests that digital transformation can enhance an organization's sustainability. Digitalization may enable organizations to track and meet their sustainability goals effectively (Irimiás & Mitev, 2020). Another example is the use of digitization to monitor ESG performance. Empirical studies have found that organizations in China substantially improved their ESG performance through enterprise digitization, although this did not necessarily translate into better environmental performance (Fang *et al.*, 2023). Other studies assert that the complete benefits on sustainability of big data and other aspects of digital evolution are not yet fully understood (Ghobakhloo, 2020). These technologies will assist organizations in digitizing data to assess and enhance their sustainability practices.

UNDERSTANDING THE DIGITAL TAGGING REQUIREMENT OF THE CSRD

A component of the CSRD is the digital tagging requirement, which mandates organizations to use standardized digital formats for their sustainability disclosures. This aims to enhance the transparency, accessibility and comparability of sustainability information, enabling stakeholders, including investors, regulators and the public, to make more informed decisions.

To advance the digitalization of sustainability data in accordance with the CSRD guidelines, EFRAG is progressing with the introduction of a digital XBRL taxonomy for the ESRS. This ESRS XBRL Taxonomy reflects the human-readable version of the ESRS and has been developed following its structure and methodology. In 2024, EFRAG approved the draft for the ESRS XBRL Taxonomy and submitted it to ESMA for further work and consultation.

In the context of ESRS, an XBRL taxonomy refers to a directory or classification scheme that defines and structures data elements for sustainability reporting according to the standard. The aim of digital reporting using the ESRS XBRL Taxonomy is to enhance the accessibility, analysability and comparability of sustainability data. Additionally, the standardized format simplifies compliance with ESRS.

The European Single Electronic Format (ESEF) will be used to publish sustainability disclosures, comprising both a substantive and a technical component. The first component is dictated by the taxonomy, which establishes the reporting-relevant contents (data points) and thus reflects the legal requirements. Consequently, the ESRS XBRL Taxonomy includes the overarching ESRS General Requirements and Disclosures (ESRS 1 and ESRS 2) as well as the ten subtopics of the topic-specific standards (Environmental, Social and Governance). The second component is defined by the Inline XBRL (iXBRL) reporting language, which specifies precisely how and where the report-relevant contents (data points) are to be disclosed.

Furthermore, the CSRD stipulates that disclosures must be labelled (tagged) with iXBRL, meaning that each sustainability data point requires precisely specified digital labelling. Reporters will need to focus on cross-cutting standard topics to ensure the highest possible clarity of reports and avoid redundancies. Once all tagged information has been validated according to both technical and content components, the report will be made available in XHTML format.

Issuers whose securities are admitted to trading on a regulated market are already familiar with iXBRL from financial reporting, where they are required to tag basic information or primary financial statement components. This should provide a solid foundation for digital sustainability reporting. It is likely that the implementation of digital sustainability reporting will be structured similarly to financial reporting. However, at the time of publication, no further information on this technical aspect is available.

To implement these technical requirements, including the labelling of data points and the visualization of reports, specialized 'viewer' and 'tagger' software will be required, similar to financial reports.

Organizations should be preparing for digital tagging as part of the CSRD implementation journey. Depending on the reporting process, digital tagging information can be integrated during the report preparation process or added at the end. Organizations need to build in time into their planning and implementation timelines to consider the assurance of tagged sustainability data.

CHALLENGES AND OPPORTUNITIES IN DATA HANDLING FOR CSRD AND ESRS COMPLIANCE

In a 2023 PwC report, the lack of data was noted as a central challenge for organizations in their CSRD implementation process (PwC, 2023a). PwC explicitly states that 'volatile regulatory environment and inadequate access to data are the biggest reported challenges'. The requirements set out by the CSRD, which mandate requirements for reporting on the organizational value chain, including its upstream and downstream activities (Directive 2022/2464), create new and complex requirements for data. The value chain-based perspective represents an increased **reporting boundary**, as traditional reporting does not consider suppliers and customers. To address this challenge, organizations should begin evaluating how to enhance their digital and data capabilities throughout the value chain. This approach will enable them to use data not only for regulatory reporting but also to significantly improve operational performance. Figure 14.1 provides a visual illustration of the digital tagging process of ESRS compliant data.

Figure 14.1 The draft digital tagging process

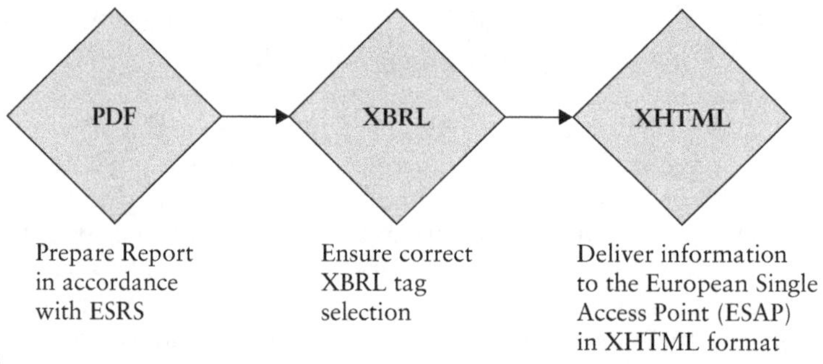

Source: KPMG (2023b)

DATA AND MATERIALITY ASSESSMENTS

Materiality assessments and maturity and gap analysis have been outlined as key steps for organizations that wish to be CSRD compliant. Conducting a materiality assessment is done in order to establish what firm-specific topics need to be reported on. The process of conducting, and the topics of, a double materiality assessment have been established by EFRAG (EFRAG, 2024b). Double materiality assessments create and require more data than organizations may be used to collecting for reporting purposes.

Existing data, or more data collected through surveys or interviews with key stakeholders can be used to conduct a materiality assessment. Organizations should conduct a gap assessment to assess whether or not they comply with both the mandatory reporting and the topics identified in their double materiality assessment. This helps organizations identify where documentation and data are missing, or how data collection and documentation processes can be improved. Data collection and documentation can be done through enterprise performance management software. One example of this is Oracle's 'Oracle Fusion Cloud Enterprise Performance Management' software, which is representative of many of EPM's functionalities (these include SAP, IBM, Workday, etc.).

Oracle's EPM allows for several steps: 1) connect and collect data, 2) prepare and validate data, 3) transform and calculate, 4) model and align sustainability initiatives, 5) predict and plan, 6) analyse and act, and 7) report and comply. The contents of each step are outlined in Table 14.1 (Oracle, n.d.). Cloud-based software can be the solution to several of the challenges outlined above (Oracle, 2024 a,b). Many of the data challenges mentioned above may require organizations to examine their master data management (MDM). The requirement to digitally tag ESG data in XBRL can also be done using cloud services such as Oracle (Oracle, n.d.).

Table 14.1 Steps in Oracle's EPM

Step	Description
Connect and collect	*Populate a purpose-built ESG data model* Oracle's enterprise sustainability management solution features a data model designed to handle diverse pre-transformed ESG activity data, such as energy use, fleet mileage, spending and workforce data. *Collect all ESG data* The account structure is based on a combination of the IFRS, ESRS (CSRD) and GRI Standards, and is separated by topic to easier align to the various reporting requirements. *Easily track source data* Unique identifiers from source documentation are captured for all systems, ensuring data integrity, and an ESG data validation log is created where needed for auditability and assurance.
Prepare and validate data	*Prepare, validate, and enrich data and metadata* Easily prepare the data and metadata by data transforming and mapping. Convert units of measure and currency with **Oracle Cloud EPM**'s various data processing capabilities. *Validate the required metrics* Identify the data that is required for your organization and run validation rules to control data quality. *Adapt Oracle to your industry* Cloud EPM sustainability can be configured for any type of organization, in any industry to satisfy multiple ESG reporting requirements.

(Continued)

Table 14.1 Steps in Oracle's EPM (Continued)

Step	Description
Transform and calculate	*Calculate key performance indicators* Environmental impact metrics often require complex calculations, whereas social and governance do so to a lesser extent. With Oracle Cloud EPM, these distinct transformations are all configurable. *Provide your preferred ratios* Oracle Cloud EPM allows flexible mapping for scope 1, 2 and 3 activities in the GHG Protocol Corporate Standard, linking data to adjustable emission factors for carbon accounting calculations. The emissions calculator then automates all unit conversions and calculations. *Get full transparency* Built-in process management helps to ensure improved clarity of calculations, identify errors and reconcile discrepancies. This allows drill back for any reported KPI for full transparency.
Model and align sustainability initiatives	*Align across your organization* Different parts of the business will have different requirements. Cloud EPM scenario modelling helps line-of-business leaders understand the impacts of their decisions and how they will affect an organization's overall sustainability goals. *Model sustainability initiatives* Scenario modelling capabilities help business leaders simultaneously evaluate multiple plans and scenarios, enhancing their understanding of ESG risks and opportunities. *Accurately allocate carbon fees* Activity-based calculations boost reporting accuracy, while advanced models incorporate carbon recharging and internal carbon fees for a more comprehensive financial and ESG performance reflection.
Predict and plan	*Operationalize sustainability plans* Turn sustainability goals into short- and long-term plans, aligning initiatives across your operations. With Cloud EPM, you can make decisions based on an integrated understanding of sustainability, finance and operations. *Predict likely performance* Using predictive planning, create and validate your forecasts and predict future performance. Data-driven predictive forecasts help you predict performance so you can take early corrective actions. *Learning to validate assumptions* Use machine learning (ML) by importing existing ML model investments into your ESG plans. Use external and operational data to validate assumptions or drivers to keep on track with ESG goals.
Analyse and act	*Monitor performance* Easily visualize ESG data in interactive dashboards so business leaders can review, explore and understand their impact on sustainability initiatives in an easier-to-understand format. *Quickly communicate ESG performance* Communicate ESG performance by combining narrative with ESG data in a collaborative, managed reporting process with approvals, progress monitoring and change tracking. *Get instant AI-powered alerts* Native AI can help to monitor ESG data, with built-in pattern recognition to provide alerts on anomalies or material variances, so you can take corrective action in a timely manner.

Table 14.1 Steps in Oracle's EPM (Continued)

Step	Description
Report and comply	*Communicate to stakeholders* Easily communicate sustainability performance to all stakeholders. Combine data, visuals and textual narratives in a single report, enabling ESG teams to author sustainability reports. *Comply with multiple frameworks* Changing rules and regulations requires flexible reporting methods. Oracle Cloud EPM allows adaptable reporting across CSRD, TCFD, IFRS, CDP and all other frameworks that can easily be changed. *Global ESG view* With a central store of ESG data, you can use Oracle Cloud EPM to create a consolidated and comprehensive global sustainability report that brings in live data as well as narrative contributions.

Source: Adapted from Oracle (n.d.)

Having gained an introductory understanding of the digital tagging process as well as data management in regard to ESRS compliant data, Activity 14.1 discusses the importance of digital tagging. You can consider the importance through a variety of angles, for example enforcement, different stakeholders or a combination of perspectives.

ACTIVITY 14.1

Evaluate the importance of digital tagging in sustainability reporting.

CONCLUSION

Digital tagging, particularly through the use of the ESEF and iXBRL, is a key component of the CSRD. This chapter has explored the requirements of this digital transformation in sustainability reporting. ESEF and iXBRL technologies enable organizations to embed machine-readable tags within human-readable reports, facilitating efficient data extraction and analysis. This technological innovation not only ensures compliance with regulatory standards but also empowers stakeholders to make more informed decisions based on reliable and standardized sustainability information.

The challenges of implementing digital tagging are significant, ranging from the complexity of data integration to the necessity for robust data governance and assurance practices. However, these challenges are accompanied by opportunities. Organizations that effectively leverage digital tagging can achieve greater operational efficiency, potentially enhancing their sustainability performance.

Moreover, the future landscape for sustainability reporting is set to evolve further with the establishment of the European Single Access Point (ESAP) by 2027, providing a centralized repository for digital financial and sustainability information across the EU. This initiative will further streamline access to corporate data, fostering greater accountability and transparency.

Individual EU member state regulators will need to publish information on how to file these reports.

In conclusion, the integration of digital tagging within the framework of the CSRD represents a transformative step towards more effective sustainability reporting. Organizations must proactively develop their digital capabilities to meet these new requirements, ensuring that their sustainability reports are not only compliant but also serve as a strategic tool for driving sustainability performance. As we move towards a more digitalized and transparent corporate reporting environment, the role of technologies like ESEF and iXBRL will be an important step in shaping the future of corporate sustainability.

SUMMARY

The following items relate to the learning objectives listed at the beginning of the chapter.

- **LO 1. Outline and discuss contemporary developments relating to digital technologies and sustainability reporting.**

  An organization may start by capturing data for sustainability reporting with the technology that is readily available, such as spreadsheet-based templates hosted on web-based collaborative platforms. Digital tagging, particularly through the use of the ESEF and iXBRL, is a key component of the CSRD. This approach not only standardizes the presentation of sustainability data but also ensures its interoperability and machine-readability, thereby enhancing accessibility and utility.

- **LO 2. Understand the digital tagging requirement of the CSRD.**

  The digital tagging requirement requires organizations to adopt standardized digital formats for their sustainability disclosures. This is aimed at enhancing transparency, accessibility and comparability of sustainability information. It is to facilitate more informed decision-making for stakeholders, including investors, regulators and the public. To support the digitalization of sustainability data in line with the CSRD, EFRAG is developing a digital XBRL Taxonomy for the ESRS. This ESRS XBRL Taxonomy mirrors the human-readable version of the ESRS, following its structure and methodology. In January 2024, EFRAG approved the draft ESRS XBRL Taxonomy.

- **LO 3. Discuss challenges and opportunities in regard to data handling for CSRD and ESRS compliance.**

  A central challenge for organizations in implementing the CSRD is the lack of comprehensive data. The CSRD introduces complex data requirements by mandating reporting on the organizational value chain, covering both upstream and downstream activities. This value chain-based approach expands traditional reporting boundaries, as it includes suppliers and customers which are often outside standard reporting scopes. To meet these demands, organizations should focus on strengthening their digital and data capabilities across the value chain. By doing so, they can leverage data not only for regulatory compliance but also to significantly enhance operational performance.

EXERCISES

1. Explain the role of ESMA and EFRAG in regard to the requirements of digital tagging of sustainability data in accordance with CSRD and ESRS. (LO 1)
2. Conduct a digital tagging simulation. Use a digital tagging tool (such as Tagging XBRL or a similar software) to tag sample financial and sustainability data. For example, tag the following data points: greenhouse gas emissions, energy consumption, water usage and waste management. (LO 2)
3. Discuss the process and any difficulties encountered during the tagging process in Exercise 2. (LO 3)

CHAPTER 15
Sustainability reporting in the public sector

Learning objectives

After studying this chapter you should be able to:

- LO 1. Understand the unique context and challenges of sustainability reporting in the public sector, including recognizing the diverse stakeholders, varying mandates and specific performance indicators relevant to public sector entities.
- LO 2. Identify the key frameworks and guidelines for public sector sustainability reporting.
- LO 3. Consider the broader implications of public sector sustainability reporting for governance, decision-making and accountability.

Why the public sector must take the lead in sustainability reporting

The case for vigorously pursuing the development and adoption of sustainability reporting standards for the public sector has never been stronger. NASA's Goddard Institute of Space Studies revealed that summer 2023 marked the Earth's highest temperatures since global records were initiated in 1880. In fact, 2023 was the warmest year ever recorded in history, according to scientists from the National Oceanic and Atmospheric Administration's National Centers for Environmental Information.

The United Nations report, The Global Climate 2011–2020, observed that every successive decade since the 1990s has been warmer than all previous decades. Extreme weather events have had devastating impacts around the world, hindering efforts towards the UN SDGs. A UN Intergovernmental Panel on Climate Change report recently emphasized both near-term risks of global warming through to 2040, as well as longer-term risks to 2100, including biodiversity loss, elevated extinction risks, diminished water availability and increased exposure to, and frequency of, extreme weather events. As the world prepares for the implementation of sustainability reporting standards from the ISSB, the need for public sector leadership is pronounced.

While governments around the world have collaborated on vital policy and regulatory solutions, they have yet to provide sustainability reporting for their own government reporting entities. This presents a major obstacle to global sustainability ambitions, particularly considering the vast physical infrastructure, non-renewable resources, rare earth elements, water and natural assets controlled by governments around the world. Olivier Boutellis-Taft, CEO of Accountancy Europe, expressed this urgency succinctly, in noting that 'There will be no sustainability transition without the public sector taking the lead.' Simply put, the public sector needs to be out in front in the journey towards sustainability reporting.

Source: KPMG (2024a)

INTRODUCTION

Sustainability reporting in the public sector has emerged as a critical practice for enhancing transparency, accountability and long-term strategic planning. As governments and public institutions face increasing pressure to demonstrate their commitment to environmental, social and economic sustainability, comprehensive reporting frameworks are often seen as essential (refer to ACCA, 2023b).

While traditionally associated with the private sector, the importance of sustainability reporting in **public sector organizations (PSOs)** has gained increasing recognition. PSOs play a vital role in addressing societal challenges, from environmental protection to social equity and economic stability. Through sustainability reporting, PSOs can enhance transparency, demonstrate accountability and inform stakeholders about their contributions to sustainable development.

In the public sector context, sustainability reporting serves multiple purposes. It provides a framework for PSOs to measure and disclose their sustainability performance, ensuring alignment with national and international sustainability goals. Moreover, it supports informed decision-making by providing comprehensive data on the environmental and social impacts of public sector activities. This practice not only fosters greater public trust and stakeholder engagement but also promotes the integration of sustainability considerations into public policy and governance.

This chapter explores the unique challenges and opportunities associated with sustainability reporting in the public sector. By integrating sustainability into their reporting practices, PSOs can improve stakeholder trust, ensure responsible resource management and contribute to broader societal goals.

Sustainability reporting in the public sector often aligns with global frameworks such as the GRI and the UN SDGs, promoting a holistic approach to governance and accountability. Furthermore, the International Public Sector Accounting Standards Board (IPSASB) has emphasized the importance of sustainability disclosures in enhancing the decision-making processes and operational transparency of public entities. With support from the World Bank, the IPSASB is developing a climate-related disclosures standard specifically for the public sector. In June 2023, the IPSASB, known for creating international reporting standards for governments and public sector entities worldwide, announced its initiative to develop this climate-related disclosures standard, the first of its kind for the public sector (IPSASB, 2023, 2024).

This chapter aims to equip you with an overview of the current state of sustainability reporting in the public sector. By understanding the principles and practices of sustainability reporting, future accountants can play a key role in advancing public sector accountability and contributing to sustainable development.

EVOLUTION OF SUSTAINABILITY REPORTING IN THE PUBLIC SECTOR

The evolution of sustainability reporting in the public sector has been shaped by a complex interplay of global initiatives, regulatory frameworks and the growing recognition of the importance of transparency and accountability in public governance. Actors such as the World Bank, the IMF and the IPSASB have played a role in advancing sustainability reporting practices.

Sustainability reporting has predominantly (up until recent times) been a concern of the private sector, with public sector entities largely focused on financial reporting. However, the recognition of the public sector's significant role in sustainable development began to gain traction in the late 20th century. Governments and international organizations started to emphasize the need for public entities to report on their environmental and social impacts alongside traditional financial metrics.

International institutions such as the **World Bank** and the **International Monetary Fund (IMF)** have strengthened their focus on sustainability matters during the last few years. The World Bank has, for example, explicitly promoted sustainability reporting within the public sector. Through its various initiatives and funding programmes, the World Bank has encouraged countries to adopt comprehensive sustainability practices. One notable initiative is the GRI, which, although initially aimed at the private sector, has been adapted for public sector use with support from the World Bank. Example 15.1 provides an illustration of the World Bank's pursuit to promote an increasing demand and need for public reporting by governments on the measures taken to combat the negative impacts of, in particularly, climate change.

Example 15.1

World Bank and public sector sustainability work

An estimated 10,000 companies in 100 countries apply GRI sustainability standards. This practice, often referred to as sustainability reporting, is becoming relatively common in the private sector, even on a voluntary basis. [...] Since 2020, signatories to the international treaty on climate change, the Paris Agreement, have been submitting national climate action plans (known as nationally determined contributions or NDCs). In NDCs, governments indicate actions taken to reduce greenhouse gas emissions to meet the goals of the Paris Agreement as well as actions to build resilience to the negative impacts of climate change. Under the enhanced transparency framework (ETF) of the Paris Agreement, governments will be expected to report on progress in mitigating climate change from 2024. The global development agenda, the Sustainable Development Goals (SDGs), also calls on governments to take urgent action on climate change and to manage natural resources sustainably.

Source: World Bank (2023)

Activity 15.1 allows you to further explore the role of the World Bank in regard to sustainability reporting in the public sector.

ACTIVITY 15.1

World Bank

Identify the following:

1. Key programmes and projects initiated by the World Bank that support sustainability reporting.
2. Specific guidelines or frameworks developed or endorsed by the World Bank for public sector entities' sustainability reporting.
3. Examples of public sector entities that have implemented World Bank-supported sustainability reporting practices.

The IMF's focus on fiscal transparency and accountability has also influenced the evolution of sustainability reporting in the public sector. The IMF's Fiscal Transparency Code, revised in 2014, emphasizes the importance of including environmental and social considerations in public financial management. This strengthens awareness and adoption of sustainability reporting practices among IMF member countries, aligning fiscal policies with broader sustainability goals.

GLOBAL FRAMEWORKS AND STANDARDS

As already highlighted in this chapter, there are a number of frameworks that provide guidelines that help public sector entities disclose their environmental, social and economic impacts in a consistent and comparable manner. Key organizations such as the GRI, the IPSASB and the UN have developed standards that guide public sector entities in their sustainability reporting efforts. In contrast to the private sector, the public sector is in most jurisdictions engaging with sustainability reporting on a voluntary basis.

International Public Sector Accounting Standards (IPSAS) – IPSASB

A significant milestone in the evolution of public sector sustainability reporting was the establishment of the IPSASB in 1997. The IPSASB develops **International Public Sector Accounting Standards (IPSAS)**, which provide guidance on accounting and financial reporting for public sector entities. Over time, the IPSASB has increasingly integrated sustainability considerations into its standards. For instance, IPSAS 1 and IPSAS 24 require disclosures related to sustainability and non-financial performance, promoting a more comprehensive approach to public sector reporting.

The IPSASB, supported by the World Bank, is developing a climate-related disclosures standard specifically for the public sector. In June 2023, the IPSASB announced the initiation of its first Sustainability Reporting Standard (IPSASB SRS™), focusing on climate-related disclosures. This standard aims to enhance transparency, enabling governments and public sector entities to make more informed decisions regarding their climate-related actions, hold them accountable for their interventions and build public trust in their efforts to address the climate emergency. The IPSASB intends to leverage the existing IFRS S2 *Climate-related Disclosures Standard* and the GRI Climate-related Topic Standard as a foundation for developing the first public sector-specific sustainability reporting standard. While acknowledging the complexities in adapting private sector guidance for public sector use, the IPSASB believes this approach can optimize efficiency and enhance compatibility with other established sustainability frameworks, such as the principles of the TCFD and GRI.

The World Bank has a history of providing financing, policy advice and technical assistance to governments in developing countries and is backing this initiative. The initial draft of the Climate-related Disclosures Standard is expected to be released for feedback in the fourth quarter of 2024.

Example 15.2 lists the links to other IPSASB practice guidelines.

Example 15.2

Links to other IPSASB practice guidelines

1 Current financial reporting project on natural resources
2 Recommended Practice Guidelines (RPGs):
- RPG 1, Reporting on the Long-Term Sustainability of an Entity's Finances
- RPG 2, Financial Statement Discussion and Analysis, Sustainability Reporting – Climate-related Disclosures Project Brief
- RPG 3, Reporting Service Performance Information

3 Current project to review IPSAS 1, Presentation of financial statements.

Source: ipsasb.org

The IPSASB has released an exposure draft (ED) on **natural resources** (IPSASB, 2023) that considers the issues relating to the recognition, measurement and presentation of natural resources by public sector entities (Aggestam Pontoppidan *et al.*, 2024). The topic of natural resource accounting has also been emphasized by the World Bank. The World Bank (2022) explicitly highlights that governments can leverage natural capital accounting to enhance the measurement of their natural resources and, in turn, incorporate them into national planning and development strategies.

It should be noted that projects in the public sector that engage with strengthening sustainability reporting shall often consider the link to government finance statistics, for example considering ongoing developments around sustainability in the statistical community, as well as UN SDG 13 Climate Action and the **UN System of Environmental Economic Accounting (UN SEEA)**.

Global Reporting Initiative (GRI)

Considering the importance of transparency and accountability in the public sector, the GRI extended its framework to include guidelines specifically tailored for public sector entities. This adaptation acknowledges the unique nature of public sector operations and the critical role these entities play in sustainable development. The GRI guidelines for the public sector provide a framework for disclosing sustainability performance, covering aspects such as governance, stakeholder engagement and service provision. The GRI's 2005 Public Sector Supplement pilot provides a foundational blueprint for impact reporting in the public sector. However, its partial implementation has led to the creation of alternative frameworks by organizations, including public universities. Numerous research studies add to our understanding of the extent to which different public sector organizations in different jurisdictions comply with the GRI framework (Greiling & Grüb, 2014).

The implementation of GRI guidelines in the public sector faces challenges. These include the complexity of data collection, the need for **capacity building** and the potential for increased administrative burden. Addressing these challenges requires ongoing support and training for public sector entities, as well as continued development and refinement of the guidelines to ensure they remain relevant and practical (Larrinaga-Gonzélez & Pérez-Chamorro, 2008). More recently the Global Sustainability Standards Board (GSSB) published a paper on impact reporting in the public sector (GSSB, 2024). The report recommends that GRI strengthens its work targeted towards the public sector.

United Nations Sustainable Development Goals (SDGs)

The integration of SDGs into public sector sustainability reporting can play a role in promoting transparency, accountability and effective governance. By aligning their efforts with the SDGs, public sector entities can contribute to global sustainability objectives while enhancing their own performance and stakeholder trust. The implementation of SDG reporting requires strategic integration, robust data management, stakeholder collaboration and transparent disclosure practices. Ultimately, the role of SDGs in public sector sustainability reporting is vital in driving sustainable development and achieving a better future for all. Example 15.3 illustrates how the City of New York embraced the SDGs for communicating sustainability information.

Example 15.3

City of New York, US, and OneNYC

The SDGs were reflected in OneNYC, a groundbreaking sustainable development plan that charts a path forward to lifting 800,000 New Yorkers out of poverty, expanding access to nutritious and affordable food, and ensuring that those on the front lines of climate change – often the most vulnerable New Yorkers – are protected.

In 2015, the City of New York Mayor's Office developed a booklet to map the connection between NYC's sustainable development plan, OneNYC, and the SDGs through *A City with Global Goals*.

In 2016, the Office released Part II of the *A City with Global Goals* booklet, which looked at the link between the SDGs and New York City's local sustainability and development initiatives contained within OneNYC.

In July 2018, the NYC became the first city in the world to report to the UN on local progress towards the global SDGs. The Mayor's Office for International Affairs coined this process the 'Voluntary Local Review'.

In September 2019, during the United Nations General Assembly, NYC launched the Voluntary Local Review (VLR) Declaration for local and regional governments worldwide to formally commit to report their local progress towards the SDGs.

In December 2021, the NYC Mayor's Office for International Affairs released a report created in collaboration with UN-Habitat about the origins and impact of the VLR.

Activity 15.2 allows you to engage with a city of your choice and identify which standards they may be using to prepare sustainability reports.

ACTIVITY 15.2

Select a city of your choice and download their sustainability report. Review the report to investigate if it makes reference to either GRI and/or SDGs.

AUDIT AND ASSURANCE OF PUBLIC SECTOR SUSTAINABILITY REPORTS

The **International Organization of Supreme Audit Institutions (INTOSAI)** Working Group on Environmental Auditing (INTOSAI WGEA), established in 1992, aims to enhance expertise in environmental auditing and improve environmental governance through high-quality contributions and visibility from both its members and non-member **Supreme Audit Institutions (SAIs)**. Currently, the INTOSAI WGEA is the largest working group under the INTOSAI, comprising 86 member SAIs. Example 15.4 provides an extract of INTOSAI's work with sustainability reporting in the public sector.

Example 15.4

INTOSAI and sustainability reporting

In 2013, the INTOSAI WGEA finalized a project on sustainability reporting. The publication reviewed experiences from private sector reporting and emerging examples from public sector reporting. The report considered it probable that similar development will take place in the public sector and that it would be advisable for SAIs to keep an eye on developments in the reporting and assurance field, especially as the role of assurance of the reports is likely to be increasingly important.

This project aims to increase the transparency and reporting by exploring the role of SAIs in sustainability reporting in [the] public sector. This role could be, for instance, encouraging the implementation or providing external assurance to sustainability reporting. Sustainability reporting in [the] public sector also emphasizes the link between financial and non-financial performance in order to address the double materiality (financial and impact materiality) as well as affects long-term management strategy, policy and plans. Therefore, sustainability reporting makes the management of an organization more environmentally and societally sustainable and impactful.

As the role of external assurance is critical to the credibility of sustainability report as a feedback process to increase the quality of the reporting, SAIs could also support in overseeing these processes. Thereby, the project explores the current reporting practices and standards and frameworks in [the] public sector. The project also discusses the benefits of sustainability reporting, and analyses the challenges faced in [the] public sector and SAIs. The project includes collaborative actions with key stakeholders such as accounting firms, GRI, UN Global Compact, CIPFA, IPSASB, etc. as well as a workshop or webinar to share knowledge and experiences between SAIs, international organizations, and experts.

Source: INTOSAI (n.d.)

PUBLIC SECTOR SUSTAINABILITY REPORTING IMPLICATIONS FOR GOVERNANCE, DECISION-MAKING AND ACCOUNTABILITY

Many PSOs regulate their environment and influence the behaviour of other organizations and individuals through laws, policies and regulations. Mandating sustainability reporting in the public sector presents several challenges due to its unique characteristics and the complexity of its operations. PSOs vary widely in terms of size, function and scope. This diversity makes it difficult to create a one-size-fits-all reporting framework that accommodates the specific needs and capacities of different PSOs. Unlike the private sector, where there are established standards for sustainability reporting, the public sector lacks universally accepted frameworks and metrics. Developing and implementing such standards across diverse PSOs is a complex task.

Nevertheless, public sector sustainability reporting has important implications extending beyond mere compliance and transparency, affecting how public institutions operate, make decisions and are held accountable by their stakeholders. Sustainability reporting in the public sector fosters greater transparency, enabling citizens and other stakeholders to understand how public resources are being used to address environmental and social challenges. This transparency builds trust between the public sector and the community.

Sustainability information can support improved policymaking. By systematically reporting on sustainability metrics, public sector entities can identify gaps and areas for improvement. This data-driven approach supports the development of more effective policies and initiatives aimed at sustainable development.

Sustainability reporting encourages a holistic view of governance, where economic, social and environmental dimensions are considered together. This integration helps in balancing various interests and in making decisions that promote long-term sustainability. Access to comprehensive sustainability reports allows policymakers and public officials to make more informed decisions. They can better assess the potential impacts of their actions on sustainability goals and adjust their strategies accordingly. Sustainability reporting helps identify risks related to environmental and social factors. By understanding these risks, public sector entities can develop mitigation strategies, ensuring more resilient and sustainable operations. Furthermore, detailed sustainability reporting provides insights into the effectiveness of current programmes and initiatives. This information can guide the allocation of resources towards the most impactful and sustainable projects. In addition, regular sustainability reporting holds public sector entities accountable for their environmental and social impacts. Stakeholders, including the public, can scrutinize the reports and demand accountability for any shortcomings or failures to meet sustainability targets. By engaging with stakeholders through sustainability reporting, public sector entities can better understand and respond to the needs and concerns of the community. This engagement fosters a collaborative approach to achieving sustainability goals.

In conclusion, public sector sustainability reporting has profound implications for governance, decision-making and accountability. It promotes transparency, informed policymaking and resource allocation, while also enhancing accountability and stakeholder engagement. These practices not only improve the sustainability performance of public sector entities but also contribute to broader societal and environmental benefits.

Example 15.5 looks at some of the challenges facing public sector organizations in their sustainability reporting.

Example 15.5

Challenges for sustainability reporting in the public sector

The public sector contributes significantly to the economy across OECD countries and is consequently a substantial source of sustainability impacts. Excluding it from sustainability reporting would limit the assessment of human activity on the environment, economy and society, including human rights. However, certain characteristics of the public sector present potential challenges for sustainability reporting:

- Many PSOs follow policies and regulations with the explicit intention of having an impact on people, the environment and the economy. Therefore the policy impacts as well as their operational impacts are likely to be material, which presents some challenges when it comes to reporting impacts, as the boundary between operational impacts and policy impacts might be unclear.
- There are gaps between sustainability reporting and accountability mechanisms with the content as well as the form of reporting being a challenge. Rules, often defined in law or custom, govern the accountability of PSOs to each other, that is ministries or government departments must give parliament an account of their activities.
- Thus far there are very limited initiatives for mandatory sustainability reporting in the public sector. A fully developed obligation to provide information on sustainability, and a set of detailed standards such as the ESRS, are currently lacking for most governments.

Source: GRI (2024b)

CONCLUSION

It is imperative for public sector sustainability reporting to evolve. In this process it is key that the public sector leverage existing standards and recommendations to enhance consistency and avoid duplicating efforts (Adams, 2023). In recent years, the harmonization of public sector accounting has accelerated, aiming to establish a unified global accounting framework. Leading this effort, the IPSASB has developed international accounting standards based on accrual accounting principles for public sector entities. However, it is crucial to recognize that the IPSASB does not possess legislative authority and, therefore, must achieve consensus and legitimacy in formulating its standards to encourage their widespread adoption (Bisogno *et al.*, 2022).

There is significant potential for advancements in guidance and standards from organizations such as the IPSASB, GRI and others.

In addition, the public sector, in similar vein to that of the private sector, needs to support the requirements for skills development and improving the quality and quantity of sustainability disclosures. While there is always more work to be done, new areas of focus for public sector sustainability reporting include:

- Assessing organizations' impacts, both positive and negative, on their contributions to the UN SDGs and outlining plans to enhance these contributions.
- Evaluating the impact of sustainable development risks and opportunities on an organization's strategy.
- Identifying the financial implications of sustainable development risks and opportunities for the reporting organization.
- Analysing the impact of policies and programmes on sustainable development.

Although this endeavour requires resources and upskilling, it offers substantial benefits, such as improved decision-making information and enhanced relationships with stakeholders. Policymakers should ensure interoperability with existing approaches. To assist report preparers, the principles of public sector sustainability reporting, along with how various standards and recommendations address these principles, are detailed in the section 'Concepts and principles of public sector sustainability reporting' of the CIPFA report 'Public sector sustainability reporting: Time to step it up' (Adams, 2023).

SUMMARY

The following items relate to the learning objectives listed at the beginning of the chapter.

- **LO 1. Understand the unique context and challenges of sustainability reporting in the public sector, including recognizing the diverse stakeholders, varying mandates and specific performance indicators relevant to public sector entities.**

  Sustainability reporting in the public sector has been influenced by a dynamic mix of global initiatives, regulatory frameworks and an increasing emphasis on transparency and accountability in governance. Organizations such as the World Bank, IMF and the IPSASB have worked to promote sustainability reporting practices. However, mandating sustainability reporting in the public sector is challenging due to the sector's unique attributes and operational complexities. Public sector organizations vary significantly in size, function and scope, making it difficult to create a universal reporting framework that meets the diverse needs and capabilities of these entities.
- **LO 2. Identify the key frameworks and guidelines for public sector sustainability reporting.**

  Sustainability reporting in the public sector often aligns with global frameworks such as the GRI and the UN SDGs, promoting a holistic approach to governance and accountability. Furthermore, the IPSASB has emphasized the importance of sustainability disclosures in enhancing the decision-making processes and operational transparency of public entities.
- **LO 3. Consider the broader implications of public sector sustainability reporting for governance, decision-making and accountability.**

  Sustainability reporting promotes an overarching approach to governance, integrating economic, social and environmental considerations to balance diverse interests and support decisions for long-term sustainability. Access to comprehensive sustainability reports enables policymakers and public officials to make more informed choices, as they can evaluate the potential impact of their actions on sustainability goals and adjust strategies accordingly. It also helps identify environmental and social risks, allowing public sector entities to develop mitigation strategies for more resilient and sustainable operations. Regular reporting enhances accountability, as stakeholders, including the public, can review and hold entities responsible for their environmental and social impacts, pushing for improvements where targets are not met. By engaging with stakeholders through sustainability reporting, public sector entities can gain a deeper understanding of community needs and concerns, fostering collaboration in achieving shared sustainability goals.

EXERCISES

1 Develop recommendations for improving sustainability reporting practices in the public sector. This could involve suggesting specific metrics, reporting formats or communication strategies that enhance transparency and accountability. (LO 1)

2 Discuss the role of accountants in ensuring the accuracy, reliability and relevance of sustainability information in public sector reporting. (LO 1)

3 Select a public sector organization that publishes sustainability report(s).
  - **a** Analyse their latest report, focusing on how they integrate sustainability practices into their operations.
  - **b** Identify which sustainability frameworks and standards they follow (e.g. GRI, SDGs, IPSASB).
  - **c** What are the key areas of sustainability the organization focuses on (e.g. environmental, social, economic)?
  - **d** How does the organization measure and report its sustainability performance? (LO 2)

4 Role-playing activity: Imagine you are part of a public sector entity's sustainability reporting team. (Note you can select a public sector entity of your choice.) Prepare a presentation for a stakeholder meeting, outlining your organization's sustainability initiatives and progress towards the SDGs. You are asked to do the following:
  - **a** Identify key stakeholders and their concerns.
  - **b** Present your organization's sustainability goals and how they align with the SDGs.
  - **c** Describe the measures taken to achieve these goals and the progress made so far. (LO 1 and 3)

CHAPTER 16
Competencies of the future accountant

Learning objectives

After studying this chapter you should be able to:

- LO 1. Understand the competency requirements of the CSRD that seeks to carry out assurance of sustainability reports.
- LO 2. Reflect on future competencies of accountants globally, regionally and locally.
- LO 3. Understand the role of the accountant and required accounts competencies to ensure a sustainable future.

Accountants, competencies and sustainability reporting

Accountants poised to play key role in sustainability reporting

The task of sustainability reporting will fall to accountancy and finance experts, who are best equipped to take on the responsibility due to their existing skillset. Experts are able to apply standards and report fairly and comprehensively. Further skills in data collection and analysis are common among accountants and will provide significant advantages to those going into sustainability reporting.

A joint study by digital automation and energy management company Schneider Electric and the **Institute of Singapore Chartered Accountants (ISCA)** examines how senior business managers involved in sustainability strategies at their organizations measure and analyse Scope 3 GHG emissions. This comes ahead of upcoming requirements for all listed companies and large non-listed companies in Singapore to make climate-related disclosures from 2025 and 2027, respectively.

The study found that 94% of Singapore organizations are not fully measuring and analysing Scope 3 emissions, thereby affecting their readiness to report. Furthermore, it noted a positive correlation between greater seniority and greater knowledge, which was attributed to the increased access to company information that senior executives have. ISCA emphasized the importance of equitable distribution of knowledge among all divisions of an organization.

Kang Wai Geat, divisional director, Professional Standards at ISCA, stated:

> *Sustainability is a megatrend that is reshaping the accountancy profession. Increasingly, organisations are turning to the accountancy profession for sustainability reporting and assurance. To take full advantage of the opportunity to help organisations advance their emissions agenda, accountants must upskill and reskill to keep up with the latest developments in sustainability.*

Source: FutureCFO (2024)

INTRODUCTION

Recent years have seen a marked increase in stakeholder expectations for transparent and trustworthy sustainability disclosures, reporting and assurance. To meet these demands and address societal needs, the accounting profession has been working to equip its members with the necessary skills. This expanded role for accountants implies a need for adequate training and development, yet there is little consensus on the specific content of such training. Additionally, while sustainability reporting has global implications, mandatory disclosure and assurance requirements currently vary across jurisdictions.

Stakeholders such as investors, regulators and the public depend on accountants for accurate and transparent sustainability reports. Accountants ensure these reports comply with established standards and accurately represent the organization's ESG performance. Accountants facilitate communication between the organization and its stakeholders by preparing reports and disclosures that address stakeholder concerns. Their work ensures that the organization's sustainability narrative is coherent, credible and aligned with stakeholder expectations (for example, double materiality).

The ISSB, the IAASB and other organizations are working towards developing globally aligned sustainability standards to support sustainability reporting as well as the assurance audit of such reports.

Research has explicitly argued that one significant obstacle to businesses contributing to a more sustainable future is the '**ecological illiteracy**' of both managers and employees within organizations (Cooper *et al.*, 2014). Rockström *et al.* (2009) notably estimate that humanity has already transgressed three **planetary boundaries**: climate change, the rate of biodiversity loss and changes to the global nitrogen cycle. This underscores the importance of ensuring that no profession, including accounting, remains ecologically illiterate. Business schools and universities play a critical role in supporting the requirements of Agenda 2030.

A EUROPEAN APPROACH TO STANDARDIZING ACCOUNTANTS' COMPETENCE – THE CSRD

The CSRD addresses the educational qualifications required by those who are to carry out assurance and audit engagements on CSRD compliant sustainability reports. The CSRD more specifically introduces new educational requirements for statutory auditors that require them to acquire both theoretical and practical knowledge in providing assurance on sustainability information and to pass a requisite examination. This marks a significant shift for the accountancy profession, highlighting the importance of adequate training (Accountancy Europe, 2022a,b). Many small practitioners will depend on their professional institutes to prepare them for this new challenge.

Approval to conduct a statutory audit requires individuals to have achieved university entrance qualifications or equivalent, completed theoretical instruction, undertaken practical training and successfully passed a professional competence examination at a university final level or equivalent, recognized by the relevant EU Member State.

The competent authorities in the respective EU Member States are to cooperate with each other with a view to achieving a convergence of the requirements set out in the CSRD. When engaging in such cooperation, those competent authorities shall take into account developments in auditing and in the audit profession and, in particular, convergence that has already been achieved by the profession. They are to cooperate with the **Committee of European Auditing Oversight Bodies** (CEAOB).

Examination of professional competence

The professional competence examination outlined in the CSRD is designed to ensure a sufficient level of theoretical understanding and practical application of knowledge relevant to statutory audits. The CSRD specifies that this examination must include a written component. Additionally, to be approved for sustainability reporting assurance, the statutory auditor's professional competence examination must guarantee the necessary theoretical knowledge and practical application skills specific to sustainability reporting assurance, with at least part of this examination also conducted in writing.

In order for the statutory auditor to also be approved to carry out the assurance of sustainability reporting, the test of theoretical knowledge shall cover at least the following subjects:

- **a** legal requirements and standards relating to the preparation of annual and consolidated sustainability reporting
- **b** sustainability analysis
- **c** due diligence processes with regard to sustainability matters
- **d** legal requirements and assurance standards for the sustainability reporting referred to in Article 26a of the CSRD.

In order for the statutory auditor or the trainee to also be approved to carry out the assurance of sustainability reporting, at least eight months of practical training shall be on the assurance of annual and consolidated sustainability reporting or on other sustainability-related services. Activity 16.1 allows you to consider the educational requirements in your local context and whether they are adequate to undertake an assurance or audit engagement of sustainability report.

ACTIVITY 16.1

Locate the educational requirements in your local country context for carrying out either an assurance or audit engagement of sustainability report.

To support accounting education in Europe, **Professional Accountancy Education Europe (PAEE)** serves as a collaboration between European accountancy bodies that strives to provide a high-quality education framework at an international level.

International Education Standards (IESs)

The **International Education Standards (IESs)**, issued by the International Federation of Accountants (IFAC), establish the principles that professional accountancy organizations should adhere to in order to develop a national accountancy profession capable of meeting the complex demands of economies and societies.

The IESs set requirements for entry into professional accounting education programmes, the **initial professional development (IPD)** of aspiring accountants and the **continuing professional development (CPD)** of practising accountants. These standards are published for use by IFAC member organizations and other stakeholders, including education providers, employers, regulators and the public sector. IESs are not yet adjusted to the requirements of sustainability reporting and accompanying competency challenges. Example 16.1 provides an insight into IFAC's proposed updates to cover these important topics.

Example 16.1

Equipping accountants for sustainability reporting: IFAC proposes enhancements to International Education Standards

The International Federation of Accountants (IFAC) has proposed updates to the International Education Standards (IESs) to integrate sustainability throughout the training of aspiring professional accountants. IFAC CEO Lee White highlighted the importance of these changes, arguing that investors and other stakeholders need sustainability reports and disclosures that are as high quality and decision useful as the financial reports already provided by accountants. To remain relevant, accountants must build the competencies required to meet this demand. These proposals provide a solid framework to prepare accountants to produce, report and assure sustainability information effectively.

The main proposals include:

- promoting collaboration with experts and multi-disciplinary teams
- introducing fundamental concepts in sustainability reporting, such as systems thinking, value chains and scenario analysis
- referring to relevant standards for sustainability reporting and assurance
- establishing a new competence area and learning outcomes focused on assurance.

Source: IFAC (2024c)

Bringing sustainability reporting into the core curriculum at university

Christensen *et al.* (2021) emphasize the need for knowledge on the sustainability and ESG standard-setting process, the materiality of ESG disclosures and the enforcement or assurance of ESG reporting. Course curriculums need to delve into the mandatory sustainability and ESG disclosure requirements, complemented by real-life case studies. Students will learn to navigate non-financial information and voluntary reporting frameworks, such as those developed by the GRI, the Greenhouse Gas Protocol and the ISSB.

In a European-based university course, an example of a key component of such courses could involve solving a case study on the implementation of the CSRD. The curriculum would address the interlinkages between financial reporting, sustainability reporting and ESG data. Students would gain a robust theoretical understanding of sustainability and ESG accounting and reporting, coupled with technical knowledge of leading reporting frameworks and mandatory reporting requirements. This comprehensive approach will equip students with the skills to understand carbon accounting, the concepts of double and financial materiality in sustainability and ESG reporting, and the distinctions between voluntary and mandatory ESG disclosures.

CONCLUSION

Accounting educators play a crucial role in equipping students with the knowledge demands of sustainability data and reporting. Embracing the evolution of sustainability practices within organizations is essential in accounting education. Studies, such as those by Jorge and Peña (2014), suggest that educators must enhance students' understanding of the significant societal impacts of business decisions and the potential 'collateral damage' they can cause. Adams (2022) further underscores the importance of redefining sustainability reporting in accounting to go beyond financial materiality and incorporate impact materiality and an integrated understanding of financial and sustainability matters. Transforming accounting education will likely necessitate changes in the curriculum, as well as innovations in teaching methods, learning processes and assessment strategies (Boyce *et al.*, 2019).

SUMMARY

The following items relate to the learning objectives listed at the beginning of the chapter.

- **LO 1. Understand the competency requirements of the CSRD that seeks to carry out assurance of sustainability reports.**

  The CSRD outlines the educational qualifications needed for professionals conducting assurance and audit engagements on CSRD-compliant sustainability reports. Specifically, it introduces new requirements for statutory auditors, mandating that they acquire both theoretical and practical knowledge in providing assurance on sustainability information and pass a required examination.

- **LO 2. Reflect on future competencies of accountants globally, regionally and locally.**

  Researchers, international standard-setters, such as IFAC, and global organizations emphasize the growing need for knowledge in the sustainability and ESG standard-setting process, the materiality of ESG disclosures and the enforcement or assurance of ESG reporting. Course curricula should address mandatory sustainability and ESG disclosure requirements, supported by real-world case studies. This approach enables students to understand non-financial information and explore voluntary reporting frameworks, including those from, for example, GRI, the Greenhouse Gas Protocol and ISSB. Regionally, as seen in the EU, explicit competencies are required by the CSRD. Transforming accounting education will likely involve curriculum updates, innovative teaching methods, new learning approaches and revised assessment strategies to prepare future professionals for the evolving demands of ESG and sustainability reporting.

- **LO 3. Understand the role of the accountant and required accounts competencies to ensure a sustainable future.**

  Investors, regulators and the public rely on accountants to deliver accurate and transparent sustainability reports. Accountants play a key role in ensuring these reports comply with established standards and accurately represent the organization's ESG performance. As sustainability reporting becomes more critical, accountants have a role to play in bridging financial and non-financial information to align with stakeholders' growing demands for transparency.

EXERCISES

1. Evaluate the strengths and weaknesses of the competency requirements of the CSRD that seeks to carry out assurance of sustainability reports. (LO 1)
2. Compare and contrast the mandatory disclosure and assurance requirements for sustainability reporting in three different jurisdictions (i.e. include only one EU based country in your assessment). Identify the jurisdictions' approaches to accounting competencies in the light of sustainability reporting assurance/audit. (LO 2)
3. Why have stakeholder expectations for transparency and trustworthy sustainability disclosures increased in recent years? Provide at least three reasons and discuss their implications for businesses. (LO 3)

References

AAASB (2023) Australian Sustainability Reporting Standards: Disclosure of Climate-related Financial Information. Available at www.aasb.gov.au/admin/file/content105/c9/AASBED_SR1_10-23.pdf#:~:text=URL%3A%20https%3A%2F%2Fwww.aasb.gov.au%2Fadmin%2Ffile%2Fcontent105%2Fc9%2FAASBED_SR1_10.

Abbott, K.W. (2012) Engaging the Public and the Private in Global Sustainability Governance. *International Affairs*, *88*(3), 543–564.

ACCA (2023a) Sustainability Reporting: The Guide to Preparation. Available at www.accaglobal.com/content/dam/ACCA_Global/professional-insights/sustainability-reporting/PI-SUSTAINABILITY-REPORTING-THE-GUIDE-TO-PREPARATION.pdf.

ACCA (2023b) Sustainability Reporting in the Public Sector: Anchor Frameworks, Adoption and Implementation. Available at www.accaglobal.com/gb/en/technical-activities/technical-resources-search/2023/april/sustainability-reporting-public-sector.html#:~:text=The%20second%20roundtable%20explored%20the%20reporting%2C%20but%20with%20appropriate%20adaptations.

Accountancy Europe (2022a) Sustainability Education. Available at accountancyeurope.eu/publications/sustainability-education/.

Accountancy Europe (2022b) Sustainability Assurance under the CSRD. Available at accountancyeurope.eu/wp-content/uploads/2022/12/220401-Sustainability-assurance-under-the-CSRD-1-1.pdf.

Adams, C. (ed.) (2022) *Handbook of Accounting and Sustainability*. Edward Elgar Publishing.

Adams, C. (2023) Public Sector Sustainability Reporting: Time to Step it Up. CIPFA. Available at www.environmental-auditing.org/media/dktkxb5x/cipfa-report-sustainability-reporting-time-to-step-it-up-april-2023.pdf.

Aggestam Pontoppidan, C., Bisogno, M., Caruana, J. and Dabbicco, G. (2024) Safeguarding Our Roots: Natural Resources Accounting and Reporting in the Public Sector. *Meditari Accountancy Research*, *32*(7), 147–170.

AGRANA (2024) The Sustainable AGRANA Value Chain 2023/24. Available at wsk-mini.agrana.com/index-en.html.

AICPA (1994) Improving Business Reporting: A Customer Focus. Available at www.aicpa.org/content/dam/aicpa/interestareas/frc/accountingfinancialreporting/downloadabledocuments/jenkins-committee-report.pdf.

Ait-Kadi, M. (2016) Water for Development and Development for Water: Realizing the Sustainable Development Goals (SDGs) Vision. *Aquatic Procedia*, *6*, 106–110.

Alawattage, C. and Azure, J.D.-C. (2021) Behind the World Bank's Ringing Declarations of 'Social Accountability': Ghana's Public Financial Management Reform. *Critical Perspectives on Accounting*, *78*.

Alawattage, C. and Fernando, S. (2017) Postcoloniality in Corporate Social and Environmental Accountability. *Accounting, Organizations and Society*, *60*, 1–20.

Alliance for Water Stewardship (n.d.) Website. a4ws.org/about/.

Ampleon (2023) Sustainability Report. Available at www.ampleon.com/sustainability/annual-report.

Annual Reporting (n.d.) Website. annualreporting.info/esrs/esrs-s4-consumers-and-end-users/.

Aragòn-Correa, J.A., Marcus, A.A. and Vogel, D. (2020) The Effects of Mandatory and Voluntary Regulatory Pressures on Firms' Environmental Strategies: A Review and Recommendations for Future Research. *Academy of Management Annals*, *14*(1), 339–365.

Arjaliès, D. and Gibassier, D. (2022) Can Financialization Save Nature? The Case of Endangered Species. *Contemporary Accounting Research*, 1911–3846.12810.

Ball, A. and Milne, M.J. (2005) Sustainability and Management Control, in A.J. Berry, J. Broadbent and D. Otley (eds) *Management Control: Theories, Issues and Performance*, Palgrave Macmillan.

Bank of England (2023) The Bank of England's Climate-related Financial Disclosure 2023. Available at www.bankofengland.co.uk/climate-change/the-bank-of-englands-climate-related-financial-disclosure-2023.

Barrena-Martínez, J., López-Fernández, M. and Romero-Fernández, P.M. (2019) Towards a Configuration of Socially Responsible Human Resource Management Policies and Practices: Findings from an Academic Consensus. *The International Journal of Human Resource Management*, *30*(17), 2544–2580.

Barry Callebaut (2023) Barry Callebaut's Approach to Double Materiality. Available at www.barry-callebaut.com/system/files/2023-11/Barry%20Callebaut%20Double%20Materiality%20Report%202023.pdf.

BASF (2023) Combined Management's Report. Available at report.basf.com/2023/en/combined-managements-report/overview-combined-management-s-report.html.

Baumüller, J. and Leitner-Hanetseder, S. (2023) Accounting for a Green Economy: Sustainable Finance and the Harmonisation of Sustainability Reporting, in O.M. Lehner, T. Harrer, H. Silvola and O. Weber (eds) *The Routledge Handbook of Green Finance*. Routledge, pp. 23–40.

Baumüller, J. and Schönauer, K. (2023) Die neue Wesentlichkeit in der europäischen Nachhaltigkeits-berichterstattung. Darstellung und Diskussion der Wesentlichkeitsanalyse gem. ESRS (Teil 1), *Praxis der internationalen Rechnungslegung*, *19*(3), 88–95.

Baumüller, J., Lopatta, K. and Hrinkow, M. (2024) § 3: ESRS 1 – Allgemeine Anforderungen, in J. Georg (eds): *ESRS Kommentar*. 2nd edition. Haufe, pp. 111–240.

Baumüller, J. and Sopp, K. (2022) Double Materiality and the Shift from Non-financial to European Sustainability Reporting: Review, Outlook and Implications. *Journal of Applied Accounting Research*, *23*(1), 8–28.

Bebbington, J. and Larrinaga, C. (2000) Environmental and Social Accounting in Europe. *European Accounting Review*, *9*(1), 3–6.

Bebbington, J. and Larrinaga, C. (2014) Accounting and Sustainable Development: An Exploration. *Accounting, Organizations and Society*, *39*(6), 395–413.

Bebbington, J. and Unerman, J. (2020) Advancing Research into Accounting and the UN Sustainable Development Goals. *Accounting, Auditing & Accountability Journal*, *33*(7), 1657–1670.

Becker-Olsen, K. and Potucek, S. (2013) Greenwashing, in S.O. Idowu, N. Capaldi, L. Zu and A.D. Gupta (eds) *Encyclopedia of Corporate Social Responsibility*. Springer.

Bénabou, R. and Tirole, J. (2010) Individual and Corporate Social Responsibility. *Economica*, *77*(305), 1–19.

Betti, G., Consolandi, C. and Eccles, R. (2018) The Relationship between Investor Materiality and the Sustainable Development Goals: A Methodological Framework. *Sustainability*, *10*(7), 2248.

Bisogno, M., Manes-Rossi, F. and Sicilia, M. (2022) Designing International Public Sector Accounting Standards: An Analysis of Constituents' Participation through Comment Letters. *Financial Accountability & Management*, *38*(4), 661–685.

BMW (2023) BMW Group Report 2023, p. 275. Available at www.bmwgroup.com/en/report/2023/downloads/BMW-Group-Report-2023-en.pdf?page=1.

BNP Paribas (2018) BNP Paribas Supports the United Nations Principles for Responsible Banking. Available at group.bnpparibas/en/news/bnp-paribas-supports-united-nations-principles-responsible-banking.

BNP Paribas (2022) Principles for Responsible Banking. Available at cdn-group.bnpparibas.com/uploads/file/bnp_paribas_2022_prb_reporting.pdf.

Boiral, O. (2016) Accounting for the Unaccountable: Biodiversity Reporting and Impression Management. *Journal of Business Ethics*, *135*(4), 751–768.

Boiral, O. and Heras-Saizarbitoria, I. (2020) Sustainability Reporting Assurance: Creating Stakeholder Accountability through Hyperreality? *Journal of Cleaner Production*, *243*, 118596.

Boiral, O., Heras-Saizarbitoria, I. and Brotherton, M.C. (2019) Professionalizing the Assurance of Sustainability Reports: The Auditors' Perspective. *Accounting, Auditing & Accountability Journal*, *33*(2), 309–334.

Boiral, O., Heras-Saizarbitoria, I. and Brotherton, M.C. (2021) Corporate Biodiversity Management and Reporting: Perspectives from the Field. *Environmental Science & Policy*, *123*, 84–96.

Borregaard (2023) Double Materiality Assessment Report 2023. Available at www.borregaard.com/media/ayeppznf/double-materiality-assessment-report-2023.pdf.

Bowen, H.R. (1953) *Social Responsibilities of the Businessman*. HarperCollins.

Boyce, G., Narayanan, V., Greer, S. and Blair, B. (2019) Taking the Pulse of Accounting Education Reform: Liberal Education, Sociological Perspectives, and Exploring Ways Forward. *Accounting Education*, *28*(3), 274–303.

Brundtland, G.H. (1987) Our Common Future: Report of the World Commission on Environment and Development. Geneva, UN-Dokument A/42/427. Available at www.un-documents.net/ocf-ov.htm.

Calabrese, A., Costa, R., Gastaldi, M., Levialdi Ghiron, N. and Villazon Montalvan, R.A. (2021) Implications for Sustainable Development Goals: A Framework to Assess Company Disclosure in Sustainability Reporting. *Journal of Cleaner Production*, *319*, 128624.

Canning, M., O'Dwyer, B. and Georgakopoulos, G. (2019) Processes of Auditability in Sustainability Assurance: The Case of Materiality Construction. *Accounting and Business Research*, *49*(1), 1–27.

CapitaLand Investment (2024) Climate Resilience Report 2024, p. 13. Available at www.capitaland.com/content/dam/capitalandinvestment/sustainability/old_CLI_Climate_Resilience_Report_2023.pdf.

Cheng, I-H., Hong, H. and Shue, K. (2014) Do Managers do Good with other Peoples' Money? *National Bureau of Economic Research*, Working Paper No. 19432. Available at www.nber.org/papers/w19432.

Christensen, H.B., Hail, L. and Leuz, C. (2021) Mandatory CSR and Sustainability Reporting: Economic Analysis and Literature Review. *Review of Accounting Studies*, *26*(3), 1176–1248.

Cooper, S.M. and Michelon, G. (2022) Conceptions of Materiality in Sustainability Reporting Frameworks: Commonalities, Differences and Possibilities. In Carol A. Adams (ed.) *Handbook of Accounting and Sustainability*. Edward Elgar Publishing.

Cooper, S., Parkes, C. and Blewitt, J. (2014) Can Accreditation Help a Leopard Change its Spots?: Social Accountability and Stakeholder Engagement in Business Schools. *Accounting, Auditing & Accountability Journal*, *27*(2), 234–258.

CSRD (2021) Available at eur-lex.europa.eu/legal-content/EN/TXT/PDF/?uri=CELEX:52021PC0189.

Dai, J., Ormazabal, G., Penalva, F. and Raney, R.A. (2023) Imposing Sustainability Disclosure on Investors: Does it Lead to Portfolio Decarbonization? European Corporate Governance Institute, Finance Working Paper 945/2023. Available at SSRN: ssrn.com/abstract=4564890.

Danone (n.d.) Water Stewardship. Available at www.danone.com/impact/planet/protecting-water-cycles.html#preserve.

Dechow, P.M. (2023) Understanding the Sustainability Reporting Landscape and Research Opportunities in Accounting. *The Accounting Review*, *98*(5), 481–493.

Del Gesso, C. and Lodhi, R.N. (2024) Theories Underlying Environmental, Social and Governance (ESG) Disclosure: A Systematic Review of Accounting Studies. *Journal of Accounting Literature*.

Deloitte (2020) Statement of Intent to Work Together Towards Comprehensive Corporate Reporting. Available at www.iasplus.com/en/publications/sustainability/statement-intent.

Deloitte (2023) Sustainable Work: How Organisations Can Extend the Sustainability Focus to the Work, Workplace and Workforce. Available at www.deloitte.com/mt/en/issues/work/sustainable-work.html.

Deloitte (2024) China Consults on Corporate Sustainability Disclosure Standard. Available at www.iasplus.com/en/news/2024/may/china-sustainability-consultation.

Deng, X., Kang, J-K. and Low, B.S. (2013) Corporate Social Responsibility and Stakeholder Value Maximization: Evidence from Mergers. *Journal of Financial Economics*, *110*(1), 87–109.

Deutsche Bank (2023) Sustainability Report. Available at www.deutschewealth.com/en/articles/sustainability-related-disclosures/sustainability-related-disclosures-db-luxembourg.html.

De Villiers, C. and Marques, A. (2016) Corporate Social Responsibility, Country-level Predispositions, and the Consequences of Choosing a Level of Disclosure. *Accounting and Business Research*, *46*(2), 167–195.

Dikolli, S.S., Frank, M.M., Guo, Z.M. and Lynch, L.J. (2022) Walk the Talk: ESG Mutual Fund Voting on Shareholder Proposals. *Review of Accounting Studies*, *27*(3), 864–896.

Doni, F., Martini, S.B., Corvino, A. and Mazzoni, M. (2020) Voluntary versus Mandatory Non-financial disclosure: EU Directive 95/2014 and Sustainability Reporting Practices Based on Empirical Evidence from Italy. *Meditari Accountancy Research*, *28*(5), 781–802.

EBRD (2022) Paris Alignment. Available at 2022.sr-ebrd.com/paris-alignment/.

Eccles, R.G. and Krzus, M.P. (2020) *Corporate Reporting: What Will it Take to Change?* Palgrave Macmillan.

Eccles, R.G. and Serafeim, G. (2013) The Performance Frontier: Innovating for a Sustainable Strategy. *Harvard Business Review*, *91*(5), 50–60.

Eccles, R.G., Krzus, M.P., Rogers, J. and Serafeim, G. (2012) The Need for Sector-Specific Materiality and Sustainability Reporting Standards. *Journal of Applied Corporate Finance*, *24*(2), 65–71.

Edmans, A. (2011) Does the Stock Market Fully Value Intangibles? Employee Satisfaction and Equity Prices. *Journal of Financial Economics, 101*(3), 621–640.

Edmans, A. (2020) *Grow the Pie: How Great Companies Deliver both Purpose and Profit*. Cambridge University Press.

European Reporting Lab (2021) Proposal for a Relevant and Dynamic EU Sustainability Reporting Standard-Setting. Final Report. February 2021. Available at finance.ec.europa.eu/system/files/2021-03/210308-report-efrag-sustainability-reporting-standard-setting_en.pdf.

EFRAG (2022a) ESRS 3 Affected Communities: Exposure Draft. Available at www.efrag.org/sites/default/files/sites/webpublishing/SiteAssets/ED_ESRS_S3.pdf.

EFRAG (2022b) Explanatory Note. Available at www.efrag.org/sites/default/files/sites/webpublishing/SiteAssets/03%20Explanatory%20note%20Fist%20set%20of%20ESRS%20Article%2029%20b_last.pdf.

EFRAG (2022c) Draft ESRS G1 BUSINESS CONDUCT. Available at www.efrag.org/sites/default/files/sites/webpublishing/SiteAssets/17%20Draft%20ESRS%20G1%20Business%20Conduct%20November%202022.pdf.

EFRAG (2023a) Draft GRI-ESRS Interoperability Index. Available at www.efrag.org/system/files/sites/webpublishing/Meeting%20Documents/2305101050307353/04-02%20draft%20ESRS-GRI%20Interoperability%20Index%20SR%20TEG%20meeting%205%20December.pdf.

EFRAG (2023b) Basis for Conclusions. Available at www.efrag.org/sites/default/files/sites/webpublishing/SiteAssets/BC%20ESRS%20E4%20Biodiversity%20and%20Ecosystems.pdf.

EFRAG (2023c) SMEs. Available at https://www.efrag.org/en/sustainability-reporting/esrs-workstreams/smes.

EFRAG (2023–24) ANNEX I to Commission Delegated Regulation (EU) 2023/2772 Supplementing Directive 2013/34/EU of the European Parliament and of the Council as Regards Sustainability Reporting Standards, published in the Official Journal of the European Union on 22 December 2023 and Including the Corrigendum published on 18 April 2024. Available at xbrl.efrag.org/e-esrs/esrs-set1-2023.html#d1e16555-3-1.

EFRAG (2024a) TNFD–ESRS Correspondence Mapping. Available at tnfd.global/wp-content/uploads/2024/06/Correspondence-mapping-ESRS-and-TNFD.pdf.

EFRAG (2024b) EFRAG IG 1: Materiality Assessment Implementation Guidance. Available at www.efrag.org/sites/default/files/sites/webpublishing/SiteAssets/IG%201%20Materiality%20Assessment_final.pdf.

EFRAG (2024c) ESRS Implementation Q&A Platform: Compilation of Explanations. Available at www.efrag.org/en/news-and-calendar/news/efrag-releases-new-esrs-qa-explanations-covering-the-januaryjuly-2024-period.

EFRAG (2024d) EFRAG SRB Meeting 10 July 2024, Paper 06-02 EFRAG Secretariat. Available at www.efrag.org/system/files/sites/webpublishing/Meeting%20Documents/2311031511250179/06-02%20Explanations%20SRB%20meeting%20240710.pdf.

Ekardt, F., Günther, P., Hagemann, K., Garske, B., Heyl, K. and Weyland, R. (2023) Legally Binding and Ambitious Biodiversity Protection under the CBD, the Global Biodiversity Framework, and Human Rights Law. *Environmental Sciences Europe*, *35*, 80.

ESMA (2023) Report: 2023 Corporate Reporting Enforcement and Regulatory Activities. Available at www.esma.europa.eu/sites/default/files/2024-03/ESMA32-193237008-8269_2023_Corporate_reporting_enforcement_and_regulatory_activities_report.pdf.

ESMA (2024) ESEF Reporting Manual: Preparation of Annual Financial Reports in ESEF Format. Available at www.esma.europa.eu/sites/default/files/library/esma32-60-254_esef_reporting_manual.pdf.

EU (2013) Directive 2013/34/EU of the European Parliament and of the Council of 26 June 2013 on the Annual Financial Statements, Consolidated Financial Statements and Related Reports of Certain Types of Undertakings, amending Directive 2006/43/EC of the European Parliament and of the Council and repealing Council Directives 78/660/EEC and 83/349/EEC Text with EEA Relevance. Available at eur-lex.europa.eu/eli/dir/2013/34/oj.

EU (2018a) Financing a Sustainable European Economy. Available at finance.ec.europa.eu/document/download/2e65cb1e-bd47-4441-816a-d89ec61eef45_en?filename=180131-sustainable-finance-final-report_en.pdf.

EU (2018b) Financing a Sustainable European Economy. Final Report 2018 by the High-Level Expert Group on Sustainable Finance Secretariat Provided by the European Commission. Available at finance.ec.europa.eu/system/files/2018-01/180131-sustainable-finance-final-report_en.pdf.

EU (2019) Commission Delegated Regulation (EU) 2018/815 of 17 December 2018 Supplementing Directive 2004/109/EC of the European Parliament and of the Council with Regard to Regulatory Technical Standards on the Specification of a Single Electronic Reporting Format (Text with EEA relevance). Available at eur-lex.europa.eu/legal-content/EN/TXT/?uri=CELEX%3A32019R0815.

EU (2022) Directive (EU) 2022/2464 of the European Parliament and of the Council of 14 December 2022 amending Regulation (EU) No 537/2014, Directive 2004/109/EC, Directive 2006/43/EC and Directive 2013/34/EU, as regards corporate sustainability reporting (Text with EEA relevance). Available at eur-lex.europa.eu/eli/dir/2022/2464/oj/eng.

EU (2024a) Regulation (EU) No 575/2013 of the European Parliament and of the Council of 26 June 2013 on Prudential Requirements for Credit Institutions and Amending Regulation (EU) No 648/2012 (Text with EEA relevance). Available at eur-lex.europa.eu/legal-content/EN/TXT/?uri=CELEX%3A02013R0575-20240709#art_4.

EU (2024b) Summary Report of the Open and Targeted Consultations on the SFDR Assessment 14 September 2023 – 22 December 2023. Available at finance.ec.europa.eu/document/download/0f2cfde1-12b0-4860-b548-0393ac5b592b_en?filename=2023-sfdr-implementation-summary-of-responses_en.pdf.

European Commission (2011) Communication from the Commission to the European Parliament, the Council, the European Economic and Social Committee and the Committee of the Regions: A Renewed EU Strategy 2011–14 for Corporate Social Responsibility, Brussels, 25.10.2011, COM(2011) 681 final. Available at eur-lex.europa.eu/legal-content/EN/TXT/PDF/?uri=CELEX:52011DC0681.

European Commission (2023a) Questions and Answers on the Adoption of European Sustainability Reporting Standards. Available at ec.europa.eu/commission/presscorner/detail/en/qanda_23_4043.

European Commission (2023b) Explanatory Memorandum. Available at eur-lex.europa.eu/legal-content/EN/TXT/HTML/?uri=PI_COM:C(2023)5303.

European Commission (2023c) Summary Report of the Open and Targeted Consultations on the SFDR Assessment. Available at finance.ec.europa.eu/document/download/0f2cfde1-12b0-4860-b548-0393ac5b592b_en?filename=2023-sfdr-implementation-summary-of-responses_en.pdf.

European Commission (2025) Directive of the European Parliament and of the Council amending Directives 2006/43/EC, 2013/34/EU, (EU) 2022/2464 and (EU) 2024/1760 as regards certain corporate sustainability reporting and due diligence requirements. Available at finance.ec.europa.eu/document/download/161070f0-aca7-4b44-b20a-52bd879575bc_en?filename=proposal-directive-amending-accounting-audit-csrd-csddd-directives_en.pdf.

European Convention on Human Rights (1950–2021) Available at fra.europa.eu/en/law-reference/european-convention-human-rights-article-8-0#:~:text=Article%208.%201%20Everyone%20has%20the%20right%20to.

European Council (2024) Council and Parliament Agree to Delay Sustainability Reporting for Certain Sectors and Third-country Companies by Two Years. Press release 7 February 2024. Available at www.consilium.europa.eu/en/press/press-releases/2024/02/07/council-and-parliament-agree-to-delay-sustainability-reporting-for-certain-sectors-and-third-country-companies-by-two-years.

European Environment Agency (2024) Air pollution. Available at www.eea.europa.eu/en/topics/in-depth/air-pollution.

European Systemic Risk Board (2024) ESRB Publishes Report on How Climate-related Risks are Reflected in IFRS Financial Standards. Available at www.esrb.europa.eu/news/pr/date/2024/html/esrb.pr240403~000aa7d19f.en.html.

Fama, E.F. and Jensen, M.C. (1983) Separation of Ownership and Control. *Journal of Law and Economics*, *26*(2), 301–325.

Fang, M., Nie, H. and Shen, X. (2023) Can Enterprise Digitization Improve ESG Performance? *Economic Modelling*, *118*, 106101.

FAO (2016) Free Prior and Informed Consent: An Indigenous Peoples' Right and a Good Practice for Local Communities. Available at openknowledge.fao.org/server/api/core/bitstreams/8a4bc655-3cf6-44b5-b6bb-ad2aeede5863/content.

Farooq, M.B. and De Villiers, C. (2017) The Market for Sustainability Assurance Services: A Comprehensive Literature Review and Future Avenues for Research. *Pacific Accounting Review*, *29*(1), 79–106.

Freeman, R.E. (1984) *Strategic Management: A Stakeholder Approach*. Cambridge University Press.

Friedman, M. (1970) The Social Responsibility of Business is to Increase its Profits. *New York Times Magazine*, 13 September.

Frishkoff, P. (1970) An Empirical Investigation of the Concept of Materiality in Accounting. *Journal of Accounting Research*, *8*, 116–129.

Fuchs, C. (2017) Critical Social Theory and Sustainable Development: The Role of Class, Capitalism and Domination in a Dialectical Analysis of Un/Sustainability. *Sustainable Development*, *25*(5), 443–458.

FutureCFO (2024) Accountants Poised to Play Key Role in Sustainability Reporting. Available at futurecfo.net/accountants-poised-to-play-key-role-in-sustainability-reporting/.

GEA (2024) Climate Transition Plan 2040, pp. 13ff. Available at cdn.gea.com/-/media/sustainability/climate-transition-plan2040-en.pdf?rev=9c64bffbd63e411b893994d9de1ebe09.

Geissdoerfer, M., Savaget, P., Bocken, N.M.P. and Hultink, E.J. (2017) The Circular Economy: A New Sustainability Paradigm? *Journal of Cleaner Production*, *143*, 757–768.

Gerwing, T., Kajüter, P. and Wirth, M. (2022) The Role of Sustainable Corporate Governance in Mandatory Sustainability Reporting Quality. *Journal of Business Economics*, *92*(3), 517–555.

GHG Protocol (2015) GHG Protocol Scope 2 Guidance. Available at ghgprotocol.org/sites/default/files/2023-03/Scope%202%20Guidance.pdf.

Ghobakhloo, M. (2020) Industry 4.0, Digitization, and Opportunities for Sustainability. *Journal of Cleaner Production*, *252*, 119869.

Gibassier, D. and Schaltegger, S. (2015) Carbon Management Accounting and Reporting in Practice: A Case Study on Converging Emergent Approaches. *Sustainability Accounting, Management and Policy Journal*, *6*(3), 340–365.

Girón, A., Kazemikhasragh, A., Cicchiello, A.F. and Panetti, E. (2021) Sustainability Reporting and Firms' Economic Performance: Evidence from Asia and Africa. *Journal of the Knowledge Economy*, *12*(4), 1741–1759.

Givaudan (2023) 2023 Integrated Report, p. 197. Available at www.givaudan.com/sites/givaudanweb.int/files/2024-02/GIV_%202023_IntegratedReport.pdf.

Gleick, P.H. (2003) Water Use. *Annual Review of Environment and Resources*, *28*(1), 275–314.

Gray, R. (2010) Is Accounting for Sustainability Actually Accounting for Sustainability ... And How Would We Know? An Exploration of Narratives of Organisations and the Planet. *Accounting, Organizations and Society*, *35*(1), 47–62.

Greenomy (2023) Simplified ESRS for SMEs under CSRD: What You Need to Know. Available at www.greenomy.io/blog/simplified-esrs-smes-under-csrd-what-you-need-to-know.

Greiling, D. and Grüb, B. (2014) Sustainability Reporting in Austrian and German Local Public Enterprises. *Journal of Economic Policy Reform*, *17*(3), 209–223.

Grewal, J. and Serafeim, G. (2020) Research on Corporate Sustainability: Review and Directions for Future Research. *Foundations and Trends® in Accounting*, *14*(2), 73–127.

Grey, D. and Sadoff, C.W. (2007) Sink or Swim? Water Security for Growth and Development. *Water Policy*, *9*(6), 545–571.

GRI (2022) The Materiality Madness: Why Definitions Matter. Available at www.globalreporting.org/media/r2oojx53/gri-perspective-the-materiality-madness.pdf.

GRI (2024a) GRI Standards: Visuals. Available at www.globalreporting.org/media/s4cp0oth/gri-gristandards-visuals-fig1_family-2021-print-v19-01.png.

GRI (2024b) Impact Reporting in the Public Sector, State of Play and Recommendations. Available at www.globalreporting.org/media/uwef1ja0/item-02-gri-project-for-public-sector-discussion-paper.pdf.

Grober, U. (2007) Deep Roots: A Conceptual History of 'Sustainable Development' (Nachhaltigkeit). Discussion Papers, Presidential Department P 2007-002, WZB Berlin Social Science Center. Available at ideas.repec.org/p/zbw/wzbpre/p2007002.html.

GSSB (2024) Impact Reporting in the Public Sector: State of Play and Recommendations. Available at www.globalreporting.org/media/uwef1ja0/item-02-gri-project-for-public-sector-discussion-paper.pdf.

GUBI (2023) GUBI Sustainability Report 2023. Available at gubi.com/en/int/company/company-information.

Haffar, M. and Searcy, C. (2017) Classification of Trade-Offs Encountered in the Practice of Corporate Sustainability. *Journal of Business Ethics*, *140*, 495–522.

Hess, D. (2007) Social Reporting and New Governance Regulation: The Prospects of Achieving Corporate Accountability through Transparency. *Business Ethics Quarterly*, *17*(3), 453–476.

Higgins, C. and Coffey, B. (2016) Improving how Sustainability Reports Drive Change: A Critical Discourse Analysis. *Journal of Cleaner Production*, *136*, 18–29.

Hopwood, B., Mellor, M. and O'Brien, G. (2005) Sustainable Development: Mapping Different Approaches. *Sustainable Development*, *13*(1), 38–52.

Hydro (2023) Integrated Annual Report 2023. Available at www.hydro.com/en/global/investors/reports-and-presentations/annual-reports/annual-report-2023/.

IAASB (2024) Understanding the International Standard on Sustainability Assurance 5000. Available at www.iaasb.org/focus-areas/understanding-international-standard-sustainability-assurance-5000.

IFAC (2021) International Standard on Assurance Engagements 3000 (Revised). Available at ifac.org.

IFAC (2024a) Equipping Accountants for Sustainability Reporting: IFAC Proposes Enhancements to International Education Standards. Changes Also Proposed to Modernize Standard on Assessing Professional Competence. Available at www.ifac.org/news-events/2024-04/equipping-accountants-sustainability-reporting-ifac-proposes-enhancements-international-education.

IFAC (2024b) The State of Play: Sustainability Disclosure and Assurance 2019–2022 Trends & Analysis. Available at ifacweb.blob.core.windows.net/publicfiles/2024-02/IFAC-State-Play-Sustainability-Disclosure-Assurance-2019-2022_0.pdf.

IFAC (2024c) Educating Accountants for a Sustainable Future. Available at www.ifac.org/knowledge-gateway/education/publications/educating-accountants-sustainable-future.

IFRS Foundation (n.d.) ESRS–ISSB Standards: Interoperability Guidance. Available at www.ifrs.org/content/dam/ifrs/supporting-implementation/issb-standards/esrs-issb-standards-interoperability-guidance.pdf.

IFRS Foundation (2021) Speech by Chair of the IFRS Foundation Trustees. Available at www.ifrs.org/news-and-events/news/2021/11/global-sustainability-disclosure-standards-for-the-financial-markets/.

IFRS Foundation (2024) Jurisdictions Representing over Half the Global Economy by GDP Take Steps Towards ISSB Standards. Available at www.ifrs.org/news-and-events/news/2024/05/jurisdictions-representing-over-half-the-global-economy-by-gdp-take-steps-towards-issb-standards/.

Igwe, M.N., Khatib, S.F.A. and Bazhair, A.H. (2023) Sustainability Reporting in Africa: A Systematic Review and Agenda for Future Research. *Corporate Social Responsibility and Environmental Management*, *30*(5), 2081–2100.

ILO Convention (1989) C169 – Indigenous and Tribal Peoples Convention, 1989 (No. 169). Available at normlex.ilo.org/dyn/nrmlx_en/f?p=NORMLEXPUB:12100:0::NO::P12100_ILO_CODE:C169.

International Labour Organization (2023) Tripartite Declaration of Principles Concerning Multinational Enterprises and Social Policy. Available at www.ilo.org/publications/tripartite-declaration-principles-concerning-multinational-enterprises-and-3.

INTOSAI (n.d.) Sustainability Reporting. Available at www.environmental-auditing.org/projects/sustainability-reporting/.

Ioannou, I. and Serafeim, G. (2017) The Consequences of Mandatory Corporate Sustainability Reporting (May 1). Harvard Business School Research Working Paper No. 11-100. Available at SSRN: ssrn.com/abstract=1799589.

IPBES (2019) Global Assessment Report on Biodiversity and Ecosystem Services. Available at www.ipbes.net/global-assessment.

IPCC (1992) Climate Change 1992. Available at www.ipcc.ch/site/assets/uploads/2018/05/ipcc_wg_I_1992_suppl_report_full_report.pdf.

IPCC (2024) IPCC Global Warming Potential Values, Greenhouse Gas Protocol 2024, p. 2. Available at ghgprotocol.org/sites/default/files/2024-08/Global-Warming-Potential-Values%20%28August%20 2024%29.pdf.

IPSASB (2023) Exposure Draft: Natural Resources. Available at www.ipsasb.org/_flysystem/azure-private/2023-08/14.3.1%20Draft%20IPSAS%20X%2C%20 Natural%20Resources.pdf.

IPSASB (2024) IPSASB Developing the First Public Sector Sustainability Reporting Standard with Support from the World Bank. Available at www.ipsasb.org/news-events/2024-06/ipsasb-developing-first-public-sector-sustainability-reporting-standard-support-world-bank.

Irimiás, A. and Mitev, A. (2020) Change Management, Digital Maturity, and Green Development: Are Successful Firms Leveraging on Sustainability? *Sustainability*, *12*(10), 4019.

IUCN (2014) Corporate Biodiversity Reporting and Indicators: Situation Analysis & Recommendations. Available at www.cbd.int/business/doc/IUCN-reporting.pdf.

Jamali, D. and Mirshak, R. (2007) Corporate Social Responsibility (CSR): Theory and Practice in a Developing Country Context. *Journal of Business Ethics*, *72*(3), 243–262.

Jensen, M.C. (2001) Value Maximization, Stakeholder Theory, and the Corporate Objective Function. *Journal of Applied Corporate Finance*, *14*(3), 8–21.

Jorge, M.L. and Peña, F.J.A. (2014) Determinants of Corporate Social Responsibility and Business Ethics Education in Spanish Universities. *Business Ethics: A European Review*, *23*(2), 139–153.

Jørgensen, S., Mjøs, A. and Pedersen, L.J.T. (2022) Sustainability Reporting and Approaches to Materiality: Tensions and Potential Resolutions. *Sustainability Accounting, Management and Policy Journal*, *13*(2), 341–361.

Khan, H.Z., Bose, S. and Johns, R. (2020) Regulatory Influences on CSR Practices Within Banks in an Emerging Economy: Do Banks Merely Comply? *Critical Perspectives on Accounting*, *71*, 102096.

Kinderman, D. (2020) The Challenges of Upward Regulatory Harmonization: The Case of Sustainability Reporting in the European Union. *Regulation & Governance*, *14*(4), 674–697.

Knudsen, J.S. and Moon, J. (2022) Corporate Social Responsibility and Government: The Role of Discretion for Engagement with Public Policy. *Business Ethics Quarterly*, *32*(2), 243–271.

Kolk, A. (2004) A Decade of Sustainability Reporting: Developments and Significance. *International Journal of Environment and Sustainable Development*, *3*(1), 51.

KPMG (2020) The Time Has Come: The KPMG Survey of Sustainability Reporting 2020, KPMG's Global Center of Excellence for Climate Change and Sustainability. Available at assets.kpmg/content/dam/kpmg/xx/pdf/2020/11/the-time-has-come.pdf.

KPMG (2022) Big Shifts, Small Steps. Survey of Sustainability Reporting, 2022. Available at kpmg.com/xx/en/home/insights/2022/09/survey-of-sustainability-reporting-2022.html.

KPMG (2023a) Counting On It: Sustainability Reporting in Financial Services. Available at assets.kpmg.com/content/dam/kpmg/xx/pdf/2023/06/esg-fs-spotlight-web-pdf.pdf.

KPMG (2023b) Get Ready for the Corporate Sustainability Reporting Directive: Understanding the CSRD. Available at assets.kpmg.com/content/dam/kpmg/nl/pdf/2023/services/faq-csrd-2023.pdf.

KPMG (2024a) Why the Public Sector Must Take the Lead in Sustainability Reporting. Available at assets.kpmg.com/content/dam/kpmg/xx/pdf/2024/04/why-the-public-sector-must-take-the-lead-in-sustainability-reporting.pdf.

KPMG (2024b) Time to Take a Broader View: Why Sustainability-linked Executive Pay is a Work in Progress, p. 7. Available at assets.kpmg.com/content/dam/kpmg/nl/pdf/2024/services/remuneration-paper-kpmg.pdf.

Krueger, P. (2015) Corporate Goodness and Shareholder Wealth. *Journal of Financial Economics*, *115*(2), 304–329.

Landrigan, P.J., Fuller, R., Acosta, N.J.R., Adeyi, O., Arnold, R., Basu, N., Baldé, A.B., … Zhong, M. (2018) The Lancet Commission on Pollution and Health. *The Lancet*, *391*(10119), 462–512.

Larcker, D.F., Seru, A. and Tayan, B. (2024) Is ESG a Luxury Good? (May 3). Rock Center for Corporate Governance at Stanford University Working Paper, Forthcoming. Available at SSRN: ssrn.com/abstract=4816562.

Larrinaga, C. and Bebbington, J. (2021) The Pre-history of Sustainability Reporting: A Constructivist Reading. *Accounting, Auditing & Accountability Journal*, *34*(9), 162–181.

Larrinaga-Gonzélez, C. and Pérez-Chamorro, V. (2008) Sustainability Accounting and Accountability in Public Water Companies. *Public Money & Management*, *28*(6), 337–343.

Lee, O.-K., Sambamurthy, V., Lim, K.H. and Wei, K.K. (2015) How Does IT Ambidexterity Impact Organizational Agility? *Information Systems Research*, *26*(2), 398–417.

Lenzing (2023) Annual and Sustainability Report 2023. Available at reports.lenzing.com/annual-and-sustainability-report/2023/_assets/downloads/entire-lenzing-ar23.pdf.

Leuz, C. and Wysocki, P.D. (2016) The Economics of Disclosure and Financial Reporting Regulation: Evidence and Suggestions for Future Research. *Journal of Accounting Research*, *54*(2), 525–622.

Malaysian Institute of Accountants (2023) Sustainability Reporting in Malaysia. October 2023. Available at www.at-mia.my/2023/10/04/sustainability-reporting-in-malaysia/.

Masulis, R.W. and Reza, S.W. (2015) Agency Problems of Corporate Philanthropy. *Review of Financial Studies, 28*(2), 592–636.

Mayer, C. (2019) *Prosperity: Better Business Makes the Greater Good*. Oxford University Press.

Mayer, C. (2020) *Firm Commitment: Why the Corporation is Failing Us and How to Restore Trust in It*. Oxford University Press.

McArthur, J.W. and Rasmussen, K. (2018) Change of Pace: Accelerations and Advances during the Millennium Development Goal Era. *World Development*, *105*, 132–143.

Meadows, H., Meadows, D.L., Randers, J. and Behrens, W.W. (1972) *The Limits to Growth*. *Universe Books*.

Michelin (n.d.) Natural Rubber at a Glance. Available at natural-rubber.michelin.com/natural-rubber-by-michelin/natural-rubber-at-a-glance.

Michelin (2022) All-Sustainable, Anchored in Michelin's Strategy. Available at www.michelin.com/en/sustainability/company.

Michelon, G., Pilonato, S. and Ricceri, F. (2015) CSR Reporting Practices and the Quality of Disclosure: An Empirical Analysis. *Critical Perspectives on Accounting*, *33*, 59–78.

Michelon, G., Rodrigue, M. and Trevisan, E. (2020) The Marketization of a Social Movement: Activists, Shareholders and CSR Disclosure. *Accounting, Organizations and Society*, *80*, 101074.

Miles, S. and Ringham, K. (2019) The Boundary of Sustainability Reporting: Evidence from the FTSE 100. *Accounting, Auditing & Accountability Journal*, *33*(2), 357–390.

Muthuri, J.N., Moon, J. and Idemudia, U. (2012) Corporate Innovation and Sustainable Community Development in Developing Countries. *Business & Society*, *51*(3), 355–381.

Nestlé (2023) Know More about Materiality. Available at www.nestle.com/sites/default/files/asset-library/documents/creating-shared-value/material-issues-across-value-chain-2017.pdf.

Nokian Tyres (2023) Sustainability Report. Available at company.nokiantyres.com/investors/reports-and-presentations/.

Novozymes (2023) The Novozymes Report 2023. Available at investors.novozymes.com/investors/financial-reports/annual-reports/default.aspx.

OECD (2018) *OECD Guide to Due Diligence for Responsible Business Conduct: The Essentials*. Available at www.oecd.org/en/publications/oecd-due-diligence-guidance-for-responsible-business-conduct_15f5f4b3-en.html.

OECD (2023) *OECD Guidelines for Multinational Enterprises on Responsible Business Conduct*. Available at www.oecd.org/en/publications/oecd-guidelines-for-multinational-enterprises-on-responsible-business-conduct_81f92357-en.html.

Official Journal of the European Union (2013) Review of Directive 2013/34/EU of the European Parliament and of the Council. Available at eur-lex.europa.eu/legal-content/EN/TXT/HTML/?uri=CELEX:32013L0034.

OMV (2023) Sustainability Report 2023. Available at reports.omv.com/en/sustainability-report/2023/.

Oracle (n.d.) Website. Available at www.oracle.com/performance-management/esg/#report.

Oracle (2024a) Delivering Sustainability with Oracle Cloud EPM. Available at www.oracle.com/a/ocom/docs/applications/epm/oracle-cloud-epm-esg-sb.pdf.

Oracle (2024b) Oracle Financial Services Climate Change Analytics. Available at www.oracle.com/a/ocom/docs/industries/financial-services/climate-change-analytics-data-sheet.pdf.

Ørsted (2023) Annual Report 2023. Available at orsted.com/en/investors/ir-material/annual-reporting-2023.

Owen, D.L. and O'Dwyer, B. (2008) Corporate Social Responsibility: The Reporting and Assurance Dimension, in A. Crane *et al*. (eds) *The Oxford Handbook of Corporate Social Responsibility*. Oxford University Press, pp. 384–409.

Paris Agreement (2015) Available at unfccc.int/process-and-meetings/the-paris-agreement.

Pesci, C., Vola, P. and Gelmini, L. (2023) Flattening or Addressing Complexity? The Future Role of GRI in Light of the Sustainability Accounting (R)evolution. *Sustainability Accounting, Management and Policy Journal*, *14*(4), 792–814.

Planet Tracker (2023) The Greenwashing Hydra. Available at planet-tracker.org/wp-content/uploads/2023/01/Greenwashing-Hydra-3.pdf.

Porr (2021) Annual Report. Available at porr-group.com/fileadmin/s_porr-group/IR/Konzernberichte/2021/PORR_annual_report_2021.pdf.

Porter, M.E. and Kramer, M.R. (2011) Creating Shared Value: How to Reinvent Capitalism – and Unleash a Wave of Innovation and Growth. *Harvard Business Review*, *89*(1–2), 62–77.

Porter, M.E. and van der Linde, C. (1995) Toward a New Conception of the Environment-competitiveness Relationship. *Journal of Economic Perspectives*, *9*(4), 97–118.

Prewave on LinkedIn (n.d.) CSDDD Chain of Activities: Scope of Risk Assessment. Available at www.linkedin.com/pulse/welcome-supply-chain-superintelligence-newsletter-prewave-cn2mf?trk=public_post.

PwC (2022) It's Now for Nature. Available at www.pwc.co.uk/issues/esg/now-for-nature.html.

PwC (2023a) Corporate Sustainability Reporting Directive (CSRD) 2023: An Analysis. Available at www.pwc.ch/en/insights/sustainability/csrd-already-has-an-impact.html.

PwC (2023b) Get Ready for the Corporate Sustainability Reporting Directive: Understanding the CSRD. Available at assets.kpmg.com/content/dam/kpmg/nl/pdf/2023/services/faq-csrd-2023.pdf.

PwC (2024) Guidelines on Self-Regulation of Listed Companies: Sustainability Report (Trial) of the People's Republic of China. Available at viewpoint.pwc.com/dt/gx/en/pwc/in_briefs/in_briefs_INT/in_briefs_INT/exposure-drafts-on-listed-company-self-regulatory.html.

Quillet, A., Peng, C. and Garneau, M. (2010) Toward Dynamic Global Vegetation Models for Simulating Vegetation–Climate Interactions and Feedbacks: Recent Developments, Limitations, and Future Challenges. *Environmental Reviews*, *18*.

Rinaldi, L. (2019) Accounting for Sustainability Governance: The Enabling Role of Social and Environmental Accountability Research. *Social and Environmental Accountability Journal*, *39*(1), 1–22.

RioTinto (2023) Juukan Gorge. Available at www.riotinto.com/en/news/trending-topics/juukan-gorge.

Rockström, J., Steffen, W., Noone, K., Persson, Å., Chapin, F.S.I., Lambin, E., Lenton, T., ... Foley, J. (2009) Planetary Boundaries: Exploring the Safe Operating Space for Humanity. *Ecology and Society*, *14*(2), Article 32.

Rosati, F. and Faria, L.G.D. (2019) Addressing the SDGs in Sustainability Reports: The Relationship with Institutional Factors. *Journal of Cleaner Production*, *215*, 1312–1326.

Russel, S., Milne, M.J. and Dey, C. (2017) Accounts of Nature and the Nature of Accounts: Critical Reflections on Environmental Accounting and Propositions for Ecologically Informed Accounting. *Accounting, Auditing & Accountability Journal*, *30*(7), 1426–1458.

Samsung (2024) Consumers Get Real about Sustainability Issues that Matter Most. Available at news.samsung.com/us/consumers-get-real-about-sustainability-issues-that-matter-most/.

SAP (2024) UN Plastics Treaty: Good for Business and the Planet. Available at news.sap.com/2024/05/un-plastics-treaty-good-for-business-and-planet/.

Schoenmaker (2017) Investing for the Common Good: A Sustainable Finance Framework, Bruegel. Available at aei.pitt.edu/88435/1/From-traditional-to-sustainable-finance_ONLINE.pdf.

Science Based Targets (2024) Getting Started Guide for Science-Based Target Setting, Version 1.1 March 2024. Available at sciencebasedtargets.org/resources/files/Getting-Started-Guide.pdf.

SEC (2022) Resubmission of Comments and Reopening of Comment Periods for Several Rulemaking. Available at www.sec.gov/files/rules/proposed/2022/33-11117.pdf.

Securities Commission Malaysia (2024) ACSR Invited Public Feedback on Proposed Use of ISSB Standards in Malaysia, February 2024. Available at www.sc.com.my/resources/media/media-release/acsr-invites-public-feedback-on-proposed-use-of-issb-standards-in-malaysia.

Semperit (2023) Sustainability Report 2023. Available at www.semperitgroup.com/fileadmin/user_upload/MediaLibrary/SemperitGroup/Company/Sustainability/Nachhaltigkeitsbericht/Semperit_Sustainability_Report_2023_EN.pdf.

SGL (2023) Group Sustainability Report 2023. Available at www.scangl.com/media/jgtoalmb/sgl-group-sustainability-report-2023.pdf.

Shilling, H. (2023) SEC Response to the SEC's Enhanced Disclosures by Certain Investment Advisers and Investment Companies about Environmental, Social and Governance Investment Practices, File Number S7-17-22. Available at www.sec.gov/comments/s7-17-22/s71722-20137895-308201.pdf.

Siemens (2023) Sustainability Report. Available at assets.new.siemens.com/siemens/assets/api/uuid:00095b96-4712-4cd1-b045-19d5df704358/sustainability-report-fy2023.pdf.

Sonnerfeldt, A.L.L. and Pontoppidan, C.A. (2020) The Challenges of Assurance on Non-Financial Reporting. *Accounting, Economics, and Law: A Convivium*, *10*(2), 20180050.

Stockholm Resilience Centre (2023) Planetary Boundaries. Available at www.stockholmresilience.org/research/planetary-boundaries.html.

Suchman, M.C. (1995) Managing Legitimacy: Strategic and Institutional Approaches. *The Academy of Management Review*, *20*(3), 571.

Sukhdev, P., Wittmer, H. and Miller, D. (2010) The Economics of Ecosystems and Biodiversity (TEEB): Mainstreaming the Economics of Nature. Available at www.teebweb.org/wp-content/uploads/2014/09/TEEB-Challenges-and-Responses.pdf.

Sulkowski, A. and Jebe, R. (2022) Evolving ESG Reporting Governance, Regime Theory, and Proactive Law: Predictions and Strategies. *American Business Law Journal*, 59(3), 449–503.

Sunhat (2023) Navigating the Interplay of GRI Standards and ESRS. Available at www.getsunhat.com/blog/navigating-interplay-of-gri-esrs.

Starks, L.T. (2023) Presidential Address: Sustainable Finance and ESG Issues – Value versus Values. *The Journal of Finance*, *78*(4), 1837–1872.

TCFD (2017) Recommendations of the Task Force on Climate-related Financial Disclosures. Available at assets.bbhub.io/company/sites/60/2021/10/FINAL-2017-TCFD-Report.pdf.

Thammaraksa, C., Gebara, C.H., Hauschild, M.Z., Pontoppidan, C.A. and Laurent, A. (2024) Business reporting of Sustainable Development Goals: Global Trends and Implications. *Business Strategy and the Environment*, 33(6), 5445–5462.

Thomson Reuters (2024) How Companies Can Codify Biodiversity and Nature into Their Sustainability Practices and Reporting. Available at www.thomsonreuters.com/en-us/posts/esg/codifying-biodiversity-sustainability-practices/.

Tilt, C.A., Qian, W., Kuruppu, S. and Dissanayake, D. (2021) The State of Business Sustainability Reporting in Sub-Saharan Africa: An Agenda for Policy and Practice. *Sustainability Accounting, Management and Policy Journal*, *12*(2), 267–296.

TNFD (2023a) TNFD Guidance on the Identification and Assessment of Nature-related Issues: The LEAP Approach, V 1.1, p. 4. Available at tnfd.global/wp-content/uploads/2023/08/Guidance_on_the_identification_and_assessment_of_nature-related_Issues_The_TNFD_LEAP_approach_V1.1_October2023.pdf?v=169840311.

TNFD (2023b) Recommendations of the Taskforce on Nature-related Financial Disclosures. Available at tnfd.global/wp-content/uploads/2023/08/Recommendations_of_the_Taskforce_on_Nature-related_Financial_Disclosures_September_2023.pdf?v=1695118661.

TNFD (2024) Interoperability Mapping between the GRI Standards and the TNFD Disclosure Recommendations and Metrics. Available at tnfd.global/publication/interoperability-mapping-between-the-gri-standards-and-the-tnfd-recommended-disclosures-and-metrics/.

Transition Plan Taskforce (2024) Progress Achieved and the Path Ahead: The Final Report of the Transition Plan Taskforce. Available at transitiontaskforce.net/wp-content/uploads/2024/10/Final-Report-Progress-Achieved-and-the-Path-Ahead-TPT.pdf.

Tryg (n.d.) Our Work with the Sustainable Development Goals. Available at tryg.com/en/cr/sustainable-development-goals.

UN (2000) Resolution Adopted by the General Assembly: United Nations Millenium Declaration. A/RES/55/2. Available at www.un.org/en/development/desa/population/migration/generalassembly/docs/globalcompact/A_RES_55_2.pdf.

UN (2015) *Transforming Our World: The 2030 Agenda for Sustainable Development*, 21 October 2015, A/RES/70/1.

UNCTAD (2022) *Guidance on Core Indicators for Sustainability and SDG Impact Reporting*. Available at unctad.org/system/files/official-document/diae2022d1_en.pdf.

UNCTAD (2021) Case Studies: Practical Implementation of Core Indicators for Sustainable Development Reporting, Volume 2. Available at sdgs.un.org/sites/default/files/2021-07/UNCTAD%20-%20Practical%20Implementation%20Case%20Studies.pdf.

UNEP (2019) Principles for Responsible Banking. Available at www.unepfi.org/banking/bankingprinciples/.

UNEP (2022) Historic Day in the Campaign to Beat Plastic Pollution: Nations Commit to Develop a Legally Binding Agreement. Available at www.unep.org/news-and-stories/press-release/historic-day-campaign-beat-plastic-pollution-nations-commit-develop.

UNEP (2024) UNEP FI – PRB / ESRS Interoperability Package. Available at www.unepfi.org/impact/unep-fi-impact-analysis-tools/portfolio-tool/.

UNESCO (2019) World Water Assessment Programme. Available at www.unesco.org/en/wwap/wwdr/2019.

Unilever (2023) Annual Report and Accounts 2023. Available at www.unilever.com/files/92ui5egz/production/b09c3510ee7cec58440d5f044f02bdefe85aa186.pdf.

United Utilities (2023) Sustainability Report 2023. Available at www.unitedutilities.com/globalassets/documents/pdf/sustainability-report-2023.pdf.

Verhoef, P.C., Broekhuizen, T., Bart, Y., Bhattacharya, A., Qi Dong, J., Fabian, N. and Haenlein, M. (2021) Digital Transformation: A Multidisciplinary Reflection and Research Agenda. *Journal of Business Research*, *122*, 889–901.

Vörösmarty, C.J., McIntyre, P.B., Gessner, M.O., Dudgeon, D., Prusevich, A., Green, P., Glidden, S. … and Davies, P.M.

(2010) Global Threats to Human Water Security and River Biodiversity. *Nature*, *467*(7315), 555–561.

Wiersema, A. (2022) Biodiversity Law in Europe: A Patchwork System? *European Journal of Law*, *39*(3), 345–368.

World Bank (2016) The Cost of Meeting the 2030 Sustainable Development Goal Targets on Drinking Water, Sanitation, and Hygiene. Available at documents.worldbank.org/en/publication/documents-reports/documentdetail/847191468000296045/the-costs-of-meeting-the-2030-sustainable-development-goal-targets-on-drinking-water-sanitation-and-hygiene-summary-report.

World Bank (2018) Incorporating Environmental, Social, and Governance (ESG) Factors into Fixed Income Investment. Available at www.worldbank.org/en/news/feature/2018/04/19/incorporating-environment-social-and-governance-esg-factors-into-fixed-income-investment.

World Bank (2022) Sovereign Climate and Nature Reporting. Available at www.documents1. worldbank.org/curated/en/099615001312229019/pdf/P170336065a94c04d0a6d00f3a2a6414cef.pdf.

World Bank (2023) Developing International Public Sector Sustainability Reporting Standards Project. Available at documents1.worldbank.org/curated/en/099121223160029667/pdf/P18157608abc150c00af060b2c1fd3cf586.pdf.

World Economic Forum (2020) Measuring Stakeholder Capitalism. Available at www3.weforum.org/docs/WEF_IBC_Measuring_Stakeholder_Capitalism_Report_2020.pdf.

World Economic Forum (2024) These Are the Top 3 Climate Risks We Face: And What to Do About Them. Available at www.weforum.org/agenda/2024/01/climate-risks-are-finally-front-and-centre-of-the-global-consciousness/.

World Health Organization (2024) Ambient (Outdoor) Air Pollution. Available at www.who.int/news-room/fact-sheets/detail/ambient-(outdoor)-air-quality-and-health.

WWF (2022) What is Biodiversity? Available at www.worldwildlife.org/pages/what-is-biodiversity.

WWF (2024) Recommendations for a Consistent EU Regulatory Framework on Corporate Sustainability Targets and Transition Plans. Available at wwfeu.awsassets.panda.org/downloads/recommendations_for_a_consistent_eu_regulatory_framework_on_corporate_sustainability__1.pdf.

Yusoff, H., Lehman, G. and Mohd Nasir, N. (2006) Environmental Engagements through the Lens of Disclosure Practices: A Malaysian Story. *Asian Review of Accounting*, *14*(1/2), 122–148.

Glossary

Accelerated Filer (AFs) A reporting organization with significantly shorter deadlines within which to file periodic reports. The organization must have publicly owned stock of a value over $75 million USD but under $700 million USD to distinguish it from a large accelerated filer.

Accountability An organization's ability to be held responsible for its actions.

AccountAbility AA1000 Assurance Standard (AA1000AS) An assurance framework for sustainability management, performance and reporting.

Action plan Structured group of actions necessary to achieve a specific policy objective or target, including allocation of resources.

Agenda 2030 Member states of the United Nations adopted the 2030 Agenda for Sustainable Development, containing 17 Sustainable Development Goals and 169 targets, in 2015. In resolution 70/1, the General Assembly stated that the Goals and targets would be followed up and reviewed using a set of global indicators focused on measurable outcomes.

Air pollutants Particle pollutants are emissions that are often harmful to humans or environments. Examples include sulphur dioxide, nitrogen oxide and carbon monoxide.

Alliance for Water Stewardship (AWS) A Scottish non-profit organisation who's objective is to increase water global water security.

Audit requirements The mandatory evaluations and assessments of a company's financial and sustainability reports by independent auditors.

Base year The reference date or period to track backward-looking information over time. It is used to monitor progress against each target.

Biodiversity conservation The act of conserving biodiversity via different means, such as land management and combating invasive species.

Biodiversity reporting The disclosure of information regarding a company's impacts on and contributions to biodiversity.

Biomass-fuelled CHP plants Combined heat and power (CHP) plants burn biomass to generate electricity and heat.

Capacity building The strengthening of knowledge, process and resources needed by a community or organization to survive in and adapt to a changing environment.

Capital expenditure (CapEx) The expenditure an organization uses for physical assets, be it to obtain or maintain them.

Carbon capture and storage (CCS) A method of reducing carbon dioxide (CO_2) emissions by capturing the CO_2 generated by an organization's activities and storing it underground.

Clean Industrial Deal The Clean Industrial Deal outlines actions to turn decarbonization into a driver of growth for European industries, including lowering energy prices, creating jobs and the right conditions for companies to grow.

Climate Disclosure Standards Board (CDSB) On 31st January 2022, the Climate Disclosure Standards Board (CDSB) was consolidated into the IFRS Foundation to support the work of the newly established International Sustainability Standards Board (ISSB).

CDP A global non-profit that runs the world's only independent environmental disclosure system for companies, capital markets, cities, states and regions to manage their environmental impacts.

Circular economy An economic system aimed at minimizing waste and making the most of resources by reusing, repairing, refurbishing, and recycling existing materials and products.

Climate-related financial disclosures Information provided by companies regarding their exposure to climate-related risks and opportunities.

Committee of European Auditing Oversight Bodies (CEAOB) A framework that, by facilitating supervisory convergence, the CEAOB contributes to the effective and consistent application of the new EU audit legislation throughout the EU.

Comparability Consistency in sustainability information over time and across entities to enable comparisons.

Conference of the Parties to the Convention on Biological Diversity Meetings with members of the Conference of the Parties (COP) to discuss the Convention on Biological Diversity. Not to be confused with *United Nations Climate Change Conference (COP21)*.

Continuing professional development (CPD) A professional worker's ability to learn new skills or enhance current abilities while still working.

Convention on Biological Diversity (CBD) An international convention promoting biodiversity, sustainable resource management and equity in resource allocation, signed at the 1992 Earth Summit.

Corporate governance The system by which companies are directed and controlled, including practices and procedures for ensuring accountability, fairness, and transparency.

Corporate social responsibility (CSR) A company's commitment to manage the social, environmental, and economic effects of its operations responsibly and in line with public expectations.

Corporate Sustainability Reporting Directive (CSRD) Directive (EU) 2022/2464. A directive aimed at standardizing the reporting of sustainability information by companies in the EU.

Corporate Sustainability Due Diligence Directive (CSDDD) A directive promoting sustainable and responsible corporate practices within an organization and within that organization's value chains.

Council of the European Union A meeting of the EU member states' ministers to discuss EU law, budget and policy.

Desertification The end result of a long-term decline in soil quality, where land becomes desert.

CSRD digital tagging requirements The tagging of CSRD statements in a machine-readable manner so that they can be categorized. Companies can use XBRL software to tag the data in their sustainability disclosure reports to relevant CSRD disclosures.

Directive 2008/98/EC (Waste Framework Directive) A directive that defines and outlines key concepts in waste management.

Disclosure requirements Specific information that companies are required to disclose according to ESRS.

Double materiality The criteria which determines whether information is pertinent to a sustainability report, and as such should be included in it.

Due diligence Processes that an organization carries out to identify, assess, prevent, mitigate and remediate the material actual and potential adverse impacts connected with its operations.

Dynamic Global Vegetation Model (DGVM) A computer programme capable of mapping potential changes in vegetation and the resulting land quality in response to climate change.

Ecological illiteracy An inability to understand how ecosystems are organized to support and sustain life.

Ecosystem restoration Any act that helps an ecosystem recover from degradation, including the protection of ecosystems not at risk of degradation.

Ecosystems An active system constituting of organisms and the environment they work in.

Entity-specific disclosures Disclosures developed by an individual organization to address material impacts, risks, and opportunities unique to its specific facts and circumstances.

Environmental impact assessments Evaluations of the environmental consequences of a proposed project or action, conducted before the project is carried out.

Environmental, social and governance (ESG) factors Criteria used to evaluate a company's operations and performance in terms of sustainability and ethical impact.

ESRS digital taxonomy The tagging of ESRS statements in a machine-readable manner so that they can be categorized. Companies can use XBRL software to tag the data in their sustainability disclosure reports to relevant ESRS Standards.

ESRS–ISSB Standards Interoperability Guidance A set of guidelines published by IFRS Foundation and EFRAG to guide organizations on how to apply ISSB Standards and ESRS simultaneously.

EU Accounting Directive A consolidation of existing legislation related to accounting and financial reporting.

EU Biodiversity Strategy for 2030 A long-term plan to protect nature and reverse damage already done to biodiversity, with the goal to have Europe's biodiversity on a recovery path by 2030.

EU Omnibus Proposed legislation with the overall goal to reduce reporting burdens, particularly for smaller and medium-sized organizations and increase efficiency in sustainability reporting.

European Green Bond Standard (EUGBS) A voluntary standard that promotes transparency for issuers and investors of green, low-carbon bonds.

EU Sustainable Finance Package A set of measures that strengthen the EU Sustainable Finance framework and ensures it is supporting financial organizations effectively.

EU Taxonomy A classification system for environmentally sustainable economic activities.

EU Whistleblowing Directive Legal protection for anyone reporting breaches of EU law, usually within a workplace.

European Bank for Reconstruction and Development (EBRD) A investment bank, owned by 74 countries, the EU and the European Investment Bank, that promotes environmentally sustainable development projects.

European Commission The executive body of the European Union. It proposes and implements new laws and manages the EU budget.

European Convention on Human Rights An international convention that protects the rights and political freedoms of people in Europe.

European Financial Reporting Advisory Group (EFRAG) An organization that provides technical advice to the European Commission on the implementation of IFRS and sustainability reporting standards.

European Green Deal A set of policies regarding the goal of ensuring the EU is climate neutral by 2050.

European Parliament A legislative body of the EU composed of elected members from all EU member states.

European Securities and Markets Authority (ESMA) The regulator and supervisor of the EU financial market.

European Single Electronic Format (ESEF) A format for electronic reporting. All organizations trading via EU regulated markets are obligated to format their annual financial reports in accordance with ESEF to promote accessibility and comparability.

European Social Charter A treaty guaranteeing the social and economic rights of individuals, relating to, among others, employment, education, and welfare.

European Sustainability Reporting Standards (ESRS) Reporting standards adopted by the European Commission requiring organizations to disclose information about climate change, biodiversity and human rights.

European Systemic Risk Board (ESRB) A body that oversees the EU financial system and aims to prevent and mitigate systemic risk within it.

European Union (EU) A supernational union of 27 member states in and around the continent of Europe.

Faithful representation Information that is complete, neutral, and accurate, faithfully depicting the reality it describes.

Financial materiality If sustainability information is financially material, it generates financial risks or opportunities for the organization and may therefore influence future cash flows.

Governance The method by which shareholders' interest determine the direction of an organization.

Greenhouse gas (GHG) Greenhouse gases trap heat in the earth's atmosphere and contribute to global warming. Earth's GHGs are primarily water vapour, carbon dioxide, ozone, methane and nitrous oxide, all of which can be byproducts of industrial and other human activity.

Greenhouse Gas Protocol (GHGP) A globally-used framework for measuring and reporting greenhouse gas (GHG) emissions, which works to standardize the disclosure process. It is the most widely used set of GHG accounting standards.

Greenwashing Misleading marketing practices that uses imagery, unsubstantiated claims or falsified data to convince the public and larger stakeholders that an organization's products and operations are environmentally friendly, when in reality they may not be.

Global Reporting Initiative (GRI) A non-profit organization which develops sustainability reporting standards. GRI standards are voluntary.

GRI digital taxonomy The tagging of GRI statements in a machine-readable manner so that they can be categorized. Companies can use XBRL software to tag the data in their sustainability disclosure reports to relevant GRI Standards.

IFRS Foundation An independent non-profit organization that sets global standards for financial reporting. Issuers of the IFRS Standards.

IFRS® Sustainability Disclosure Standards Standards released by the ISSB, namely IFRS S1 and IFRS S2, issued in 2023.

IFRS S1 *General Requirement for Disclosure of Sustainability-related Financial Information* The standard requiring organizations to disclose information about their sustainability-related risks and opportunities.

IFRS S2 *Climate-related Disclosures* The standard requiring organizations to disclose information about their climate-related risks and opportunities.

Impact materiality If sustainability information is material from an impact perspective, it relates to the risks or opportunities an organization may face with relation to people or the environment.

Initial professional development (IPD) Workplace development that takes place before becoming professionally registered (for example as EngTech, IEng, etc.), when future professionals train to apply their knowledge, skills, competence and professional judgement.

Inline XBRL (iXBRL) A way of formatting data so it can be read by humans and machines alike.

Institute of Singapore Chartered Accountants (ISCA) The national accountancy body of Singapore.

Insurance-based Investment Products (IBIPs) A contract of insurance with a maturity or surrender value that is exposed to market fluctuations, either directly or indirectly.

Integrated report An integrated report presents information about an organization's governance, performance and prospects in the context of the organization's external environment. It summarizes the organization's short, medium and long term value creation.

Intergovernmental Panel on Climate Change (IPCC) A United Nations body dedicated to evaluating climate change science.

International Accounting Standards Board (IASB) A group of independent accounting experts responsible for authoring IFRS Accounting Standards published by the IFRS Foundation.

International Bill of Human Rights The collection of the Universal Declaration of Human Rights, the International Covenant on Civil and Political Rights, and the International Covenant on Economic, Social and Cultural rights.

International Covenant on Civil and Political Rights An international treaty committing all adopters to securing and respecting the civil and political rights of all individuals.

International Covenant on Economic, Social and Cultural Rights An international treaty committing all adopters to securing and granting the economic, social and cultural rights to all individuals.

International Education Standards (IESs) A set of principles that ensure the US accountancy profession is robust and capable of meeting demands, issued by IFAC.

International Federation of Accountants (IFAC) A US-based federation that unites member organizations and works to globalize the accountancy profession. They contribute to the development and implementation of international accountancy standards.

International Financial Reporting Standards (IFRS Accounting Standards) A set of accounting guidelines designed to ensure the financial statements of public companies are consistent, transparent and comparable. IFRS Accounting Standards are issued by the International Accounting Standards Board (IASB).

International Integrated Reporting Council (IIRC) A global coalition that develops a framework for reporting on value creation by organizations. The IIRC's goal is to make integrated reporting a standard practice in both the public and private sectors. The IIRC has has now transitioned into the IFRS Foundation's Integrated Reporting and Connectivity Council.

International Labour Organization (ILO) A UN agency that sets labour standards and develops policies and programmes dedicated to equitable and safe work for all.

International Labour Organization's Declaration of Fundamental Principles and Rights at Work Any government or organization signed up to this declaration is committed to uphold basic human values that are essential to social and economic wellbeing, such as the right to collective bargaining, the abolition of child and forced labour and the right to a safe working environment.

International Monetary Fund (IMF) An international financial institution formed in 1944, with goals of international monetary cooperation and financial sustainability, sustainable economic growth and poverty alleviation. They act as the lender of last resort to national governments.

International Organization of Supreme Audit Institutions (INTOSAI) A non-governmental member organization that consults for the ECOSOC of the United Nations and sets standards for public sector auditing.

International Public Sector Accounting Standards (IPSAS) Accounting standards and financial statement preparation guidance for public sector organizations, issued by the IPSAS Board.

International Standard of Sustainability Assurance (ISSA) 5000 *General Requirements for Sustainability Assurance Engagements* An International Standard on Sustainability Assurance issued by the IAASB, aimed at increasing the trust stakeholders have in sustainability information.

International Standard on Assurance Engagements (ISAE) 3000 A standard that outlines the principles and procedures for performing assurance engagements on subject matters other than traditional audits or reviews of historical financial information, allowing for assurance on areas like sustainability disclosures or non-financial reporting.

International Sustainability Standards Board (ISSB) A subsidiary of the IFRS Foundation which develops sustainability disclosure standards that can be used globally.

International Union for Conservation of Nature (IUCN) A member organization that is a authority on the global environment and its safeguarding requirements.

Invasive species A species that, in a non-native environment, causes ecological damage and has an adverse effect on the habitat and species native to it.

ISAE 3410 *Assurance Engagements on Greenhouse Gas Statements* An International Standard on Assurance Engagements issued by the IAASB, aimed at increasing consistency in greenhouse gas disclosure reports.

Kunming-Montreal Global Biodiversity Framework A supporting framework to the UN Sustainable Development Goals, adopted in 2022. The framework's key elements include 4 goals for 2050 and 23 for 2030. Refer also to *Sustainable Development Goals (SDGs)*.

Land degradation The decrease in productivity and health of land as the result of damaging human or natural activity.

Large Accelerated Filer (LAFs) A reporting organization with significantly shorter deadlines within which to file periodic reports. The organization must have publicly owned stock of a value over $700 million to distinguish it from an accelerated filer.

Limited assurance A level of assurance in which enough evidence is collected to support the practitioner's conclusion, but less evidence is required than with reasonable assurance. Refer also to *Reasonable assurance*.

Materiality assessment The process of assessing the extent to which a required disclosure can provide insight that is decision-useful for stakeholders.

Natura 2000 sites Areas across Europe that are protected under the Birds and the Habitats Directives. Areas are deemed to be protected based on the value of or threat faced by its species and habitats.

Natural resources Resources which have natural origins and which are not heavily modified before being used.

Nature-positive outcomes The universal goal to achieve full biodiversity recovery in 2050, via halting and reversing nature loss by 2030 compared to a 2020 baseline.

Net revenue Revenue minus selling expenses.

Net-Zero Banking Alliance (NZBA) A group of leading banks committed to aligning their activities with the goal of net-zero greenhouse gas emissions by 2050, convened by the UN.

Net-zero targets Targets made to reach the goal of reducing greenhouse gas emissions to no more than can be absorbed and sustainably stored by nature or by human-created carbon capture processes.

Non-Financial Reporting Directive (NFRD) Directive 2014/95/EU. The predecessor to the CSRD, which required large public-interest companies to disclose information on how they managed ESG challenges.

OECD Guidelines for Multinational Enterprises An annex of the OECD Declaration on International Investment and Multinational Enterprises that is not legally binding, providing guidelines for responsible business conduct in multinational organizations.

Operating Expenses (OpEx) The expenses a business incurs during its day-to-day operations.

Oracle Cloud EPM An American-based enterprise performance management system hosted on the cloud.

Paris Agreement The United Nations Framework Convention on Climate Change (more commonly known as the 'Paris Agreement') is a legally binding treaty on climate change requiring economic and social transformation, with clear targets and strategies for limiting the global temperature increase to less than 1.5°C above pre-industrial levels. 196 Parties adopted the Paris Agreement when it was first presented in 2015.

Performance metrics Key indicators used to measure and track a company's performance in relation to its sustainability impacts, risks, and opportunities.

Planetary boundaries Boundaries within which humanity can operate safely without compromising the functionality of the Earth. In September 2023, scientists quantified, for the first time, all nine planetary boundaries that regulate the stability and resilience of the Earth system.

Policies Operational decisions with defined objectives, specific coverage of activities, and accountable oversight, adopted to manage material sustainability matters.

Post-2020 Global Biodiversity Framework A strategy put forward in 2022 by Parties to the UN Convention on Biological Diversity for safeguarding biodiversity, after none of the 20 Aichi Biodiversity Targets set in 2010 were achieved at a global level.

Power-to-X (P2X) Schemes that turn surplus energy from renewable sources into different power sources in a manner that significantly reduces CO2 emissions. Examples include power-to-hydrogen, power-to-heat and power-to-fuel.

Principles for Responsible Banking (PRB) A set of guidelines that helps banks align their business practices with the United Nations' Sustainable Development Goals and the Paris Climate Agreement.

Principles for Responsible Investment (PRI) Six principles that provide paths for the inclusion of ESG into everyday investment practices.

Professional Accountancy Education Europe (PAEE) A group of 12 participating institutes with the objective of standardising and enhancing professional accountancy education across Europe.

Public sector organizations (PSOs) Government-owned organizations that provide services to the public such as housing, education and road maintenance.

Qualitative characteristics of sustainability information Non-quantitative aspects of information that ensure it is useful. These qualitative characteristics relevance, materiality and faithful representation.

Research and Development (R&D) Activities that involve the development of new products or services. Also known as Experiment and Design.

Reasonable assurance One level of assurance in which assurance engagement risk is acceptably low, but not non-existent. Refer also to *limited assurance*.

Regulation on Deforestation-free Products Legislation that mandates any products in the EU market or any organization exporting from it must not contribute to forest degradation or originate from recently deforested land.

Relevance Sustainability information that has substantive influence on the assessments and decisions of users.

Reporting boundaries The boundaries for sustainability reporting, which includes the undertaking's own operations and its upstream and downstream value chain.

Resilience analysis The practice of ensuring an organization will be able to adapt to and withstand expected and unexpected changes coming from risk, threat or opportunities.

Resource allocation Decisions taken to support actions and action plans with an organization's financial, human, or technological resources.

Risk management The identification, assessment, and prioritization of risks followed by coordinated efforts to minimize, monitor, and control the probability or impact of unfortunate events.

SB 253, Climate Corporate Data Accountability Act A law mandating Scope 1, 2 and 3 emissions disclosure obligations to businesses operating in California, US, with revenues greater than $1 billion. The law will come into effect in 2026.

SB 261, Greenhouses gases: Climate-related financial risk A law mandating climate-related risk disclosure obligations to businesses operating in California, US, with revenues greater than $500 million. The law will come into effect in 2026.

Science Based Targets initiative (SBTi) An collaboration between three non-profit sustainability organizations and the UN Global Compact, with aims to aid companies setting emission reduction targets to limit global temperature rise to below 1.5°C.

Scope 1 emissions Direct greenhouse gas emissions from sources that are owned or controlled by the company.

Scope 2 emissions Indirect greenhouse gas emissions from the generation of purchased electricity, steam, heating, and cooling consumed by the reporting company.

Scope 3 emissions All other indirect greenhouse gas emissions that occur in the value chain of the reporting company, including both upstream and downstream emissions.

SDG indicators 231 unique indicators that are used to implement the 17 Sustainable Development Goals of the UN and monitor progress being made towards full implementation, allowing for transparency and accountability of stakeholders. SDG indicators are refined annually. Refer to *Sustainable Development Goals (SDGs).*

Sector-agnostic standards Standards that define disclosures relevant across all sectors.

Sector-specific standards Standards that define disclosures relevant to specific sectors.

Securities and Exchange Commission (SEC) A US rulemaking agency that prevents and protects investors from misconduct and encourages a fair and efficient security market.

Small and medium-sized enterprises (SMEs) An organization with revenue or a number of employees under a certain threshold that varies from country to country. In the EU, small enterprises have fewer than 50 employees while medium enterprises have fewer than 250 employees.

Soil sealing The reduction or complete loss of a soil ecosystem resulting from urban development, during which an impervious material (for example, cement) covers or replaces topsoil.

Stakeholder engagement The process by which an organization involves people who may be affected by its decisions or can influence the implementation of its decisions.

Stakeholders Individuals or groups that can affect or be affected by an organization's decisions and actions. This includes affected stakeholders and users of sustainability reports.

Substances of concern A chemical that is harmful to human health or the environment, or suspected to be harmful. Refer also to *Substances of Very High Concern.*

Substances of very high concern A chemical that if mishandled will or may have irreversible effects on human health or the environment. Refer also to *Substances of Concern.*

Supreme Audit Institutions (SAIs) Independent national organizations that conduct audits of government activities.

Sustainable finance The consideration of ESG factors when making investment decisions in the financial sector. Refer to *Environmental, social and governance (ESG) factors.*

Sustainability Accounting Standards Board (SASB) Part of the IFRS Foundation since 2022, SASB aids organizations in the disclosure of sustainability information to stakeholders, mainly investors.

Sustainability information Data on environmental, social, and governance (ESG) issues that companies must report.

Sustainability matters Topics related to environmental, social, and governance (ESG) factors that are significant to the company's sustainability performance.

Sustainability performance indicators Metrics used to assess and track a company's sustainability performance over time.

Sustainability reporting The process of disclosing information on a company's sustainability-related impacts, risks, and opportunities, in accordance with applicable standards.

Sustainability risks Potential negative impacts on a company's financial performance or reputation due to its environmental, social, or governance practices.

Sustainable Development Goals (SDGs) A set of 17 global goals established by the United Nations to address various social, economic, and environmental challenges.

Sustainable Finance Disclosure Regulation (SFDR) Regulation requiring financial market participants to disclose how they integrate ESG factors into their investment decision-making processes.

Targets Goals to be achieved at a sub-topic level in relation to impacts, risks, or opportunities, with specific time frames, a base year, and key performance indicators used to assess progress.

Task Force on Climate-related Financial Disclosures (TCFD) A task force which developed guidance for which information an organization should disclose when discussing climate-related risks. The TCFD completed its task and disbanded in 2023.

Taskforce on Nature-related Financial Disclosures (TNFD) A task force which has published recommendations and guidance to help businesses and financial institutions assess, report, and address their dependencies, impacts, risks, and opportunities related to nature.

The German Corporate Governance Code The code regulating the corporate governance responsibilities of German listed companies.

The Responsible Care® Global Charter A charter from the International Council of Chemical Associations that sets an industry-standard commitment to the safe and sustainable handling of chemicals throughout their life cycle.

Transition plans Specific types of action plans that address public policy objectives and/or entity-specific actions associated with key strategic decisions, major changes in business models, or particularly important objectives or resource allocations.

Transitional provisions Regulatory processes put into place in the interim period between when an amendment or enactment of the statute is announced and when it comes into force.

Tripartite Declaration of Principles Concerning Multinational Enterprises and Social Policy A document detailing the employment, training, conditions of work and life and industrial relations conditions that an enterprise, government, employer or workers' organization is required to uphold.

UK Transition Plan Taskforce (TPT) This framework guides companies to disclose sustainability-related transition plans in a robust and credible manner.

UN Convention on Biological Diversity A global agreement protecting all areas of biological diversity.

UN Declaration on the Rights of Indigenous Peoples A framework that protects the rights of Indigenous peoples worldwide.

UN Guiding Principles on Business and Human Rights A framework of 31 principles aimed at governments and organizations, encouraging them to identify, prevent, mitigate and remedy human rights abuses, whether real or potential.

UN System of Environmental Economic Accounting (UN SEEA) A framework that combines economic and environmental data to impress the two-way relationship between them.

UN Trade and Development (UNCTAD) An international promotor of global trade opportunities for developing countries.

United Nations Climate Change Conference (COP21) The Conference of Parties of those parts of the Kyoto Protocol (CMP). COP21 was held in Paris in 2015. Not to be confused with *Conference of the Parties to the Convention on Biological Diversity*.

United Nations Environment Programme Finance Initiative (UNEP FI) A network of banks, insurers and investors catalysing sustainable development, hosted by the UN.

United Nations Global Compact (UNGC) The largest corporate sustainability initiative in the world, calling for companies to align their strategies with principles of universal rights.

Universal Declaration of Human Rights (UDHR) A document put forward in the 1948 UN General Assembly that holds all peoples and nations to a common set of universally protected rights.

US Climate Disclosure Act An Act requiring US public companies to report on and disclose climate-related metrics.

Value chain The full range of activities involved in the creation of a product or service, including upstream (supply chain) and downstream (distribution and customers) activities.

World Bank An international financial organization that grants governmental grants to low- and middle-income countries to aid with economic development.

World Economic Forum An international organization that provides an impartial platform for communication between governments, businesses and society to tackle world's biggest issues.

Zero pollution action plan for air, water and soil An initiative stating the goal of net zero pollution in water, air and soil by 2050.

Index